EXPLORING COLOSSIANS

RHETORIC OF RELIGIOUS ANTIQUITY

Vernon K. Robbins, General Editor
Duane F. Watson, General Editor
Bart B. Bruehler, Associate Editor
David B. Gowler, Associate Editor
Roy R. Jeal
Harry O. Maier
Michael Trainor

Number 5

EXPLORING COLOSSIANS

Living the New Reality

Roy R. Jeal

Atlanta

Copyright © 2024 by SBL Press

Publication of this volume was made possible by the generous support of the Pierce Program in Religion of Oxford College of Emory University.

Cover design is an adaptation by Bernard Madden of Rick A. Robbins, "His LifeLine" (42" x 50" acrylic on canvas, 2002).

All rights reserved. No part of this work may be reproduced or transmitted in any form or by any means, electronic or mechanical, including photocopying and recording, or by means of any information storage or retrieval system, except as may be expressly permitted by the 1976 Copyright Act or in writing from the publisher. Requests for permission should be addressed in writing to the Rights and Permissions Office, SBL Press, 825 Houston Mill Road, Atlanta, GA 30329 USA.

Library of Congress Control Number: 2024948526

For Jackie

Contents

Editorial Foreword xi
Preface xvii
Abbreviations xxi
Glossary xxvii

Introduction 1
    Sociorhetorical Interpretation   2
    Creativity and Development   14
    The Empty, Deceitful Philosophy   18
    Alternative Cultural Texture   19
    The Text   25
    Authorship   26
    Date   28
    Rhetorical Structure   29

The Opening (1:1–23)

Scene One: Introductory Rhetoric (1:1–23) 35
    Step One: Paul's Prophetic-Priestly Greeting (1:1–2)   35
    Step Two: Paul's Priestly-Prophetic Prayers for People
        in Wisdom Space (1:3–8)   55
    Introduction to Steps Three, Four, and Five   73
    Step Three: Priestly Prayers (1:9–12)   74
    Step Four: Father God's Apocalyptic Actions: Transferal
        to the New Reality (1:13–14)   80
    Step Five: The Precreational Image of God: Over All
        Things (1:15–20)   86
    Step Six: Alienation, Reconciliation, and Faithful Living
        (1:21–23)   112

The Middle (1:24–4:6)

Scene Two: Paul's Genuine Character and Genuine
    Concerns (1:24–2:5)...125
    Step One: Suffering for the *Ekklēsia* (1:24–29)   125
    Step Two: Struggling for Faithfulness (2:1–5)   138

Scene Three: Don't Be Deceived. Live the New Reality (2:6–4:6) 147
    Step One: Walk On Confidently (2:6–7)   147
    Step Two: Beware of Being Captured—You Are Already
        Filled (2:8–10)   149
    Step Three: God in Christ Has Done Everything You
        Need (2:11–15)   160
    Step Four: Do Not Let Someone Judge You (2:16–17)   177
    Step Five: Do Not Be Cheated by the Self-Important
        Complainant (2:18–19)   187
    Step Six: You Died with Christ; Do Not Submit to Useless
        Rules (2:20–23)   194
    Step Seven: You Were Raised with Christ; Seek the Above
        Things (3:1–4)   203
    Step Eight: New Life in the New Reality (3:5–17)   214
    Step Nine: Household Wisdom (3:18–4:1)   234
    Step Ten: Walking Forward, Looking Outward (4:2–6)   257

The Closing (4:7–18)

Scene Four: Personalities Rhetoric (4:7–18)..267
    Step One: Tychicus and Onesimus Reporting (4:7–9)   267
    Step Two: Greetings (4:10–17)   270
    Step Three: Personal Greeting (4:18)   274

Rhetorical Force as Emergent Discourse..277
    Ideology of the Gospel   279
    Ideology of Hope   279
    Ideology of the Son-Christ   280
    Ideology of the New Reality in the Son's Kingdom   281
    Ideology of Fullness   281
    Ideology of Circumcision   282
    Ideology of Orderly Living   282

Ideology of Family and Household 282
Ideology of the Care of Souls 283

Bibliography 285
Ancient Sources Index..301
Modern Authors Index...315

Editorial Foreword

The Rhetoric of Religious Antiquity Series

The Rhetoric of Religious Antiquity (RRA) series uses insights from sociolinguistics, semiotics, rhetoric, ethnography, literary studies, social sciences, cognitive science, and ideological studies in programmatic ways that enact sociorhetorical interpretation (SRI) as an interpretive analytic. This means that SRI is a multidimensional approach to texts guided by a multidimensional hermeneutic. Rather than being a specific method for interpreting texts, an interpretive analytic evaluates and reorients its strategies as it engages in multifaceted dialogue with the texts and other phenomena that come within its purview. It invites methods and methodological results into the environment of its activities, but those methods and results are always under scrutiny. Using concepts and strategies of methods as an interactive interpretive analytic, sociorhetorical interpretation juxtaposes and interrelates phenomena from multiple disciplines and modes of interpretation by drawing and redrawing boundaries of analysis and interpretation.

The corpus of works for the Rhetoric of Religious Antiquity series is writings in the environment of the first four centuries of the emergence of Christianity. The primary corpus is the New Testament, but full-length commentaries may be produced on writings with some significant relationship to the New Testament, such as Wisdom of Solomon, Sibylline Oracles, Didache, Epistle of Barnabas, Protevangelium of James, or Infancy Gospel of Thomas.

The Approach of SREC Commentaries

Sociorhetorical Exploration Commentaries (SREC) enact the interactive interpretive analytic of SRI by exploring, analyzing, and interpreting multiple textures of texts. Interpreters begin sociorhetorical commentary with a description of the blending of rhetorical belief systems that occurs through the sequence of pictures the discourse evokes, which the authors call rhetography. This beginning point is motivated by insights both from conceptual blending theory and from rhetorical interpretation of early Christian discourse. Underlying this beginning point is a presupposition that spoken or written discourse begins its persuasive work by creating a sequence of pictures in the mind. As the commentators proceed, they interpret the rhetography in wisdom, prophetic, apocalyptic, precreation, miracle, and priestly belief systems in emergent Christian discourse to present an initial interpretation of the blending of belief systems that was occurring during the first Christian century.

After the beginning focus on the picturing of belief and action in texts being interpreted, commentators analyze the texts from the perspective of their inner texture, intertexture, social and cultural textures, ideological texture, and sacred texture. This section is called textual commentary. The strategies of analysis and interpretation are guided by a presupposition that humans create patterns of images and reasonings in the inner texture of their elaborations by recruiting great ranges of "background meaning" and building them into rich systems of belief and action through processes of "pattern completion" that create "emergent structures."

The final step in the commentary is the presentation of the rhetorical force of the text as emerging discourse in the Mediterranean world. An overall goal of the commentary, therefore, is to analyze and interpret how emerging Christian belief systems blended graphic imagery and reasoned argumentation into newly configured Mediterranean discourse. Emerging out of contexts within first-century Mediterranean Judaism, early Christians lived in the Roman Empire in the context of Greek philosophy, a wide range of ritual practices, and multiple modes of social, cultural, and ideological perspectives. The sociorhetorical commentary in these volumes explores and exhibits the emergent modes of discourse in the highly diverse environment of religious belief and practice especially during the first-century CE Mediterranean world.

What Stands in Common among SREC Volumes?

Every author of an SREC volume uses nomenclature present in *The Tapestry of Early Christian Discourse: Rhetoric, Society and Ideology* (1996) and *Exploring the Texture of Texts: A Guide to Socio-rhetorical Interpretation*

(1996).¹ This means that each author includes a section titled "Textural Commentary" and within this section refers to basic textures of a text described in the two 1996 publications (inner texture, intertexture, social-cultural texture, ideological texture, sacred texture), and multiple subtextures within the basic textures, such as opening-middle-closing, repetitive, and progressive texture within inner texture.

In addition, each author works with six emergent Christian rhetorolects of the first century CE, and with conceptual blending/integration among these rhetorolects. A rhetorolect is a mode of discourse "identifiable on the basis of a distinctive configuration of themes, topics, reasonings, and argumentations" that develops in cultures.² The six basic rhetorolects that have been identified since 1996 are wisdom, prophetic, apocalyptic, precreation, miracle, and priestly.³ The initial publication that guided the RRA group in interpretation of conceptual blending/integration was *The Way We Think*, by Gilles Fauconnier and Mark Turner.⁴ Since then, a series

---

1. Vernon K. Robbins, *The Tapestry of Early Christian Discourse: Rhetoric, Society and Ideology* (London: Routledge, 1996); Robbins, *Exploring the Texture of Texts: A Guide to Socio-rhetorical Interpretation* (Valley Forge, PA: Trinity Press International, 1996), 7–39. See also David B. Gowler, L. Gregory Bloomquist, and Duane F. Watson, eds., *Fabrics of Discourse: Essays in Honor of Vernon K. Robbins* (Harrisburg, PA: Trinity Press International, 2003).

2. Vernon K. Robbins, "Socio-rhetorical Interpretation," in *The Blackwell Companion to the New Testament*, ed. David E. Aune (Oxford: Blackwell, 2010), 197.

3. Vernon K. Robbins, "The Dialectical Nature of Early Christian Discourse," *Scriptura* 59 (1996): 353–62; Robbins, "Argumentative Textures in Socio-rhetorical Interpretation," in *Rhetorical Argumentation in Biblical Texts: Essays from the Lund 2000 Conference*, ed. Anders Eriksson, Thomas H. Olbricht, and Walter Übelacker, ESEC 8 (Harrisburg, PA: Trinity Press International, 2002), 27–65; Robbins, *The Invention of Christian Discourse*, vol. 1, RRA 1 (Dorset, UK: Deo, 2009); Robbins, "Precreation Discourse and the Nicene Creed: Christianity Finds Its Voice in the Roman Empire," *R&T* 18 (2012): 1–17; David A. deSilva, "A Sociorhetorical Interpretation of 14:6–13: A Call to Act Justly toward the Just and Judging God," *BBR* 9 (1999): 65–117; deSilva, "The Invention and Argumentative Function of Priestly Discourse in the Epistle to the Hebrews," *BBR* 16 (2006): 295–323; Roy R. Jeal, "Starting before the Beginning: Precreation Discourse in Colossians," *R&T* 18 (2011): 287–310; Duane F. Watson, ed., *Miracle Discourse in the New Testament* (Atlanta: Society of Biblical Literature, 2012); Vernon K. Robbins and Jonathan M. Potter, eds., *Jesus and Mary Reimagined in Early Christianity*, WGRWSup 6 (Atlanta: SBL Press, 2015).

4. Gilles Fauconnier and Mark Turner, *The Way We Think: Conceptual Blending and the Mind's Hidden Complexities* (New York: Basic Books, 2002).

of additional publications by members of the RRA group has played an important role.[5]

Since authors understand SRI as an interpretive analytic rather than as a method, they have the freedom to select and foreground certain aspects of the texts more than, or even rather than, others. But every author has agreed to write an SREC volume within the following format: after an introductory chapter to the volume, which includes an explanation of the particular way the author will apply SRI as an interpretive analytic, each volume presents commentary on the text in a sequence of rhetography, English translation display, textural commentary, and rhetorical force as emergent discourse.[6]

The rhetography section presupposes knowledge of the essay titled "Rhetography: A New Way of Seeing the Familiar Text" and regularly is informed by other essays and books as well.[7] The rhetorical force section presupposes ongoing discussion and debate among New Testament scholars concerning the rhetorical role of a particular writing in emerging Christianity in the Mediterranean world. This means there are two "primary" foci in the rhetorical force section: (1) rhetorical force in emerging Christianity itself and (2) rhetorical force in emergent social, cultural, ide-

---

5. Vernon K. Robbins, "Conceptual Blending and Early Christian Imagination," in *Explaining Christian Origins and Early Judaism: Contributions from Cognitive and Social Science*, ed. Petri Luomanen, Ilkka Pyysiäinen, and Risto Uro, BibInt 89 (Leiden: Brill, 2007), 161–95; Robbins, *Invention of Christian Discourse*; Robert von Thaden Jr., *Sex, Christ, and Embodied Cognition: Paul's Wisdom for Corinth*, ESEC 16 (Dorset, UK: Deo, 2012); Thaden, "Pauline Rhetorical Invention: Seeing 1 Corinthians 6:12–7:7 through Conceptual Integration Theory. A Cognitive Turn," in *Cognitive Linguistic Explorations in Biblical Studies*, ed. Bonnie Howe and Joel B. Green (Berlin: de Gruyter, 2014), 101–21.

6. See Robbins, "Socio-rhetorical Interpretation," 192–219, esp. 203–8; Robbins, "Socio-rhetorical Criticism," in *The Oxford Encyclopedia of Biblical Interpretation*, ed. Steven L. McKenzie (Oxford: Oxford University Press, 2013), 311–18.

7. Vernon K. Robbins, "Rhetography: A New Way of Seeing the Familiar Text," in *Words Well Spoken: George Kennedy's Rhetoric of the New Testament*, ed. C. Clifton Black and Duane F. Watson, SRR 8 (Waco, TX: Baylor University Press, 2008), 81–106; Robbins, *Invention of Christian Discourse*; David A. deSilva, "Seeing Things John's Way: Rhetography and Conceptual Blending in Revelation 14:6–13," *BBR* 18 (2008): 271–98; Roy R. Jeal, "Blending Two Arts: Rhetorical Words, Rhetorical Pictures and Social Formation in the Letter to Philemon," *Sino-Christian Studies* 5 (June 2008): 9–38.

ological, and religious discourse and conceptuality in the broader Mediterranean world at the time of the writing (and perhaps later).

What Are Some of the Variations among SREC Volumes?

Freedom for Each Author

Each author is given a range of freedom within the overall sequential framework of rhetography, English translation display, textural commentary, and rhetorical force as emergent discourse. Some authors think it works well to write textural commentary in the sequence in which the textures were presented in *The Tapestry of Early Christian Discourse* and *Exploring the Texture of Texts*: inner texture, intertexture, social-cultural texture, ideological texture, sacred texture. Other authors think it is too constraining to write textural commentary in a sequence like this. Therefore, authors are allowed to write textural commentary in whatever "order" of textures and subtextures they consider most workable for the text on which they are commenting. To indicate to the reader what texture the author is interpreting, bold letters introduce the major five textures (or combinations thereof), and italics introduce subtextures, like *repetitive texture* within **inner texture**.

This SREC Volume on Colossians

Within the established sequence for writing SREC commentaries, Roy R. Jeal offers a comprehensive sociorhetorical analysis that recognizes that Colossians presents developed and profound ideas and rhetoric about the new reality of Christ believers who have been transferred into the light of the son-Christ's kingdom. He provides a thoroughgoing presentation and analysis of the rhetography, the imagery cast on readers' and listeners' imagination by the letter, envisioning the progression of scenes and steps in the portrayal as it moves along. The rhetography reveals the mental and rhetorical spaces and rhetorolects (the developed modes of discourse) that carry audiences along in their understanding. This is followed by English translation that follows the Greek text of each step closely, aiming to be dynamic and understandable without sounding informal. The textural analysis observes the textures described in *Exploring the Textures of Texts*, emphasizing those that shape ideas and reasoning for audience understanding. Argumentative texture, intertexture, and ideological texture stand out prominently. Precreation, apocalyptic, prophetic, priestly, and wisdom rhetorolects convey the themes, topoi, and arguments that shape and drive the language. Textural analysis is followed by sections on the rhetorical force as emergent discourse of each step. The commentary ends with a comprehensive discussion of rhetorical force that displays the creativity of the language of Colossians in evoking ideologies that encourage the development of an alternative culture to the frequently disordered living of the ancient Mediterranean.

Jeal's commentary demonstrates that what emerges in Colossians is rhetoric that encourages believers to trust fully in the actions of God in Christ. There are new ideologies in a new culture of light that has its philosophical and theological foundation in God's domain prior to the creation of all things. Christ believers are no longer dominated by the darkness and insecurity of life. Those things have been made irrelevant by Christ. The believers have been made completely full in Christ and should not yield to complaints or to pressures to conform to the social, cultural, and religious expectations and traditions of people around them. They are called to live orderly lives where they are clothed with love, recognizing "Christ all and in all."

Preface

Colossians wears its concern for Christ believers on its sleeve. It speaks directly into the body-*ekklēsia* with words meant to encourage and words meant to warn. It portrays Paul as suffering for the sake of the Jesus followers in the Lycus Valley, agonizing for them, wanting to fill them with knowledge and strength. In its developed thinking, theology, and rhetoric, the letter emphasizes the gospel that extends from the cosmic-precreational domain of God and his son, the son in whom all the fullness of God houses itself and through whom there is genuine reconciliation and peace. Christ followers have been transferred to the new reality of life in the Son-Christ's light-filled kingdom. They have been made full in Christ, who is himself full of deity. All powers of all kinds, whether seen or unseen, have been made powerless. Believers must not allow themselves to be captured by misleading philosophy, human tradition, and the elements of the world, things that are not according to what they know about Christ. Now in the new reality Christ is all and in all. They are to put on behaviors that do good for others, wearing the overgarment of love.

This commentary provides a sociorhetorical interpretation of Colossians. The words of the letter interact with each other to produce *textures* that interweave in complex images, sounds, rhythms, arguments, movements, ideologies, and philosophical-theological understandings. SRI does not produce a flat, linear interpretation. By taking into account the intricate textures in the letter, it provides a dynamic portrayal of what the letter says and how it says it. It interprets and aims to articulate carefully what the letter *does*. It demonstrates that Colossians is a gospel-centered text designed and presented to move its audiences to know that, despite all the uncertain pressures that people face in the jurisdiction of darkness, there is light, goodness, and security in the new reality that the letter envisions. Things are different now in the son's kingdom. Colossians persuades its audiences to be confident of who they are now and of what they have as the *ekklēsia*-body-household of people who trust in Christ Jesus. The old life in the flesh has been cut away—circumcised—and with it every imagined power and authority made irrelevant. Fullness is provided, given, in Christ. Having been raised with Christ, they are to seek the above things, to anticipate glory.

Colossians draws us into the life—the lived story—of an early *ekklēsia*. Yet entering the story presents many difficulties. I have had a recurring thought while reading, learning, comprehending, and interpreting the story of the letter and its rhetoric: *there is so much we do not know*. The letter itself does not provide complete information about the circumstances that evoked its composition. We do not know all we would like about the pressures faced by the Christ believers in Colossae and the nearby Lycus cities of Laodicea and Hierapolis. The myriad of scholarly reconstructions of historical circumstances is daunting and provokes more uncertainty and continuing debate than confident knowledge. Describing and debating the details of the views is informative, but the disputes do not resolve the questions. The attempts to come to a specific, single conclusion about disputed points are unsuccessful. Definitive answers to some issues will likely never be available, and broadened views rather than a single, definitive interpretation are necessary. What is clear is that there is always more to learn. Every generation of readers and listeners will discover and learn from Colossians. What this commentary does is employ the sociorhetorical analytic that considers multiple textures aimed at understanding the rhetorical force of the letter as it emerged in its ancient Mediterranean contexts. It does not do everything. Certainly in the process the energetic letter has affected my own ideologies and the spaces I inhabit. I am ideologically committed to scholarship and to studying biblical texts for their own sake and to investigating what biblical texts *do* to people, *how* they evoke thoughts and beliefs in human minds, and *how* they move people to faith, faithfulness, and behavior. Colossians proclaims confidence in fullness in Christ, not the uncertainty and fear of the failure of not getting things right. Living with Colossians for a long time has moved me to think deeply about the scope and depth of the philosophical-theological vision it presents. It makes sense to me as a Christ believer. The authors of Colossians did not know everything, but they developed their grasp of the gospel by careful thinking, and they wanted their audiences to learn, grow, and mature. The disputes about questions such as authorship should not be permitted to relegate the letter to the periphery of New Testament studies. Everyone should have a look at Colossians. It still speaks to people.

PREFACE

Heartfelt thanks to Vernon K. Robbins and Duane F. Watson, general editors of the Rhetoric of Religious Antiquity series, for their support and, after a long time, receiving it for publication. Vernon's creativity in conceiving and developing SRI has led many to deep understanding of the texts and their meanings and rhetorical force. Vernon is the embodiment of a scholar who leads with ideas, with analysis, and with support for others. I am grateful for the generous support of the Pierce Program in Religion of Oxford College of Emory University, which assisted with the publication of this volume. The congenial and eager colleagues of the Rhetoric of Religious Antiquity Research Group, at in-person and online meetings and in many conversations, have listened and offered wonderful encouragement and helpful criticism. I thank John Stafford, Claude Cox, James Currie, Harold Dick, Murray Evans, Lee Isaacs, Aimee Patterson, and Will Rew for their always generous and encouraging friendship. Many friends have supported me with their sincere interest, offering questions, comments, criticism, and encouragement. I am always wonderfully supported and encouraged by my family. I am so grateful to them.

Roy R. Jeal
October 2023

Abbreviations

Primary Sources

1 Clem.	1 Clement
1 En.	1 Enoch
2 En.	2 Enoch
1QM	War Scroll
1QpHab	Pesher Habakkuk
1QS	Rule of the Community
11Q5	Psalm Scroll
11Q19	Temple Scroll
Abr.	Philo, *De Abrahamo*
Aen.	Virgil, *Aeneid*
Aet.	Philo, *De aeternitate mundi*
A.J.	Josephus, *Antiquitates judaicae*
Alex. fort.	Plutarch, *De Alexandri magni fortuna aut virtute*
Apoc. Zeph.	Apocalypse of Zephaniah
Apol.	Plato, *Apologia*
Att.	Cicero, *Epistulae ad Atticum*
B	Codex Vaticanus
Ben.	Seneca, *De beneficiis*
B.J.	Josephus, *Bellum judaicum*
Cal.	Suetonius, *Gaius Caligula*
Carm.	Horace, *Carmina*
C. Ap.	Josephus, *Contra Apionem*
Cher.	Philo, *De cherubim*
Conf.	Philo, *De confusione linguarum*
Corp. herm.	Corpus hermeticum
Contempl.	Philo, *De vita contemplativa*
De an.	Aristotle, *De anima*
Decal.	Philo, *De decalogo*

Det.	Philo, *Quod deterius potiori insidari soleat*
Dial.	Justin, *Dialogus cum Tryphone*
Did.	Didache
Diatr.	Epictetus, *Diatribi*
Eloc.	Demetrius, *De elocutione* (*Peri hermēneias*)
Ep.	Seneca, *Epistulae morales*; Horace, *Epistulae*
Epitaph.	Demosthenes, *Epitaphius*
Flor.	Stobaeus, *Florilegium*
Fug.	Philo, *De fuga et inventione*
Garr.	Plutarch, *De garrulitate*
Geogr.	Strabo, *Geographica*
Gig.	Philo, *De gigantibus*
Her.	Philo, *Quis rerum divinarum heres sit*
Hist.	Herodotus, *Historiae*; Polybius, *Historiae*
Hist. Rom.	Cassius Dio, *Historia Romana*
Il.	Homer, *Ilias*
Inst.	Quintilian, *Institutio oratoria*
Is. Os.	Plutarch, *De Iside et Osiride*
Jub.	Jubilees
Leg.	Philo, *Legum allegoriae*
Legat.	Philo, *Legatio ad Gaium*
Let. Aris.	Letter of Aristeas
Lucil.	Seneca, *Ad Lucilium*
LXX	Septuagint
Lys.	Plutarch, *Lysander*
Marc.	Porphyry, *Ad Marcellum*
Mut.	Philo, *De mutatione nominum*
Nigr.	Lucian, *Nigrinus*
Ol.	Pindar, *Olympionikai*
p[46]	Papyrus Chester Beatty II, University of Michigan Library
Pol.	Aristotle, *Politica*
Post.	Philo, *De posteritate Caini*
Prob.	Philo, *Quod omnis probus liber sit*
Pss. Sol.	Psalms of Solomon
Rhet.	Aristotle, *Rhetorica*
Rhet. Her.	Rhetorica ad Herennium
Sacr.	Philo, *De sacrificiis Abelis et Caini*
Sat.	Juvenal, *Satirae*
Somn.	Philo, *De somniis*

Spec.	Philo, *De specialibus legibus*
Subl.	Longinus, *De sublimitate*
T. Ab.	Testament of Abraham
T. Ash.	Testament of Asher
T. Dan	Testament of Dan
T. Job	Testament of Job
T. Levi	Testament of Levi
Tim.	Plato, *Timaeus*
Vit. phil.	Diogenes Laertius, *Vitae philosophorum*

Secondary Sources

AB	Anchor Bible
BBR	*Bulletin for Biblical Research*
BDAG	Danker, Frederick W., Walter Bauer, William F. Arndt, and F. Wilbur Gingrich. *Greek-English Lexicon of the New Testament and Other Early Christian Literature*. 3rd ed. Chicago: University of Chicago Press, 2000.
BDF	Blass, Friedrich, Albert Debrunner, and Robert W. Funk. *A Greek Grammar of the New Testament and Other Early Christian Literature*. Chicago: University of Chicago Press, 1961.
BECNT	Baker Exegetical Commentary in the New Testament
BHGNT	Baylor Handbook on the Greek New Testament
BibInt	Biblical Interpretation
BMSSEC	Baylor-Mohr Siebeck Studies in Early Christianity
BNTC	Black's New Testament Commentaries
BR	*Biblical Research*
BTCB	Brazos Theological Commentary on the Bible
CBET	Contributions to Biblical Exegesis and Theology
EBS	Essentials of Biblical Studies
ECAM	Early Christianity in Asia Minor
ECL	Early Christianity and Its Literature
ESEC	Emory Studies in Early Christianity
ESV	English Standard Version
FN	*Filologia Neotestamentaria*
FRLANT	Forschungen zur Religion und Literatur des Alten und Neuen Testaments
Gk.	Greek

HB	Hebrew Bible
Heb.	Hebrew
ICC	International Critical Commentary
IVBS	International Voices in Biblical Studies
JRS	*Journal of Roman Studies*
JSNT	*Journal for the Study of the New Testament*
JSNTSup	Journal for the Study of the New Testament Supplement Series
KJV	King James Version
Lat.	Latin
LCL	Loeb Classical Library
LEC	Library of Early Christianity
LNTS	Library of New Testament Studies
LSJ	Liddell, Henry George, Robert Scott, and Henry Stuart Jones. *A Greek-English Lexicon*. 9th ed. with rev. supplement. Oxford: Clarendon, 1996
MM	Moulton, James H., and George Milligan. *The Vocabulary of the Greek Testament*. London, 1930. Repr. Peabody, MA: Hendrickson, 1997.
NA^{28}	*Novum Testamentum Graece*, Nestle-Aland, 28th ed.
NASB	New American Standard Bible
NIV	New International Version
Neot	*Neotestamentica*
NT	New Testament
NTL	New Testament Library
NIB	*New Interpreters Bible*. Edited by Leander E. Keck. 12 vols. Nashville: Abingdon, 1994–2004.
NICNT	New International Commentary on the New Testament
NIGTC	New International Greek Testament Commentary
NRSV	New Revised Standard Version
NRSVue	New Revised Standard Version Updated Edition
NTG	New Testament Guides
NTS	*New Testament Studies*
P.Amh.	*The Amherst Papyri, Being an Account of the Greek Papyri in the Collection of the Right Hon. Lord Amherst of Hackney, F.S.A. at Didlington Hall, Norfolk*. 2 vols. Edited by B. P. Grenfell and A. S. Hunt. London, 1900–1901.

PGM	*Papyri Graecae Magicae: Die griechischen Zauberpapyri.* Edited by Karl Preisendanz. 2nd ed. Stuttgart: Teubner, 1973–1974.
PNTC	Pillar New Testament Commentaries
P.Oxy.Hels.	*Fifty Oxyrhynchus Papyri.* Edited by H. Zilliacus, J. Frösén, P. Hohti, J. Kaimio, and M. Kaimio. Helsinki, 1979.
P&R	*Philosophy and Rhetoric*
P.Ryl.	Hunt, Arthur S., et al., eds. *Catalogue of the Greek and Latin Papyri in the John Rylands Library, Manchester.* 4 vols. Manchester: Manchester University Press, 1911–1952.
R&T	*Religion & Theology*
RBS	Resources for Biblical Study
RRA	Rhetoric of Religious Antiquity
RSV	Revised Standard Version
SBLGNT	The Greek New Testament: SBL Edition
SBLSBS	Society of Biblical Literature Sources for Biblical Study
SNTSMS	Society for New Testament Studies Monograph Series
SP	Sacra Pagina
SREC	Sociorhetorical Exploration Commentaries
SRI	sociorhetorical interpretation
SRR	Studies in Rhetoric & Religion
ST	*Studia Theologica*
STJD	Studies on the Texts of the Desert of Judah
TCSGNT	T&T Clark Study Guides to the New Testament
TDNT	*Theological Dictionary of the New Testament.* Edited by Gerhard Kittel and Gerhard Friedrich. Translated by Geoffrey W. Bromiley. 10 vols. Grand Rapids: Eerdmans, 1964–1976.
TENTS	Texts and Editions for New Testament Study
TLNT	*Theological Lexicon of the New Testament.* Ceslas Spicq. Translated and edited by James D. Ernest. 3 vols. Peabody, MA: Hendrickson, 1994.
TNTC	Tyndale New Testament Commentaries
UBS[2]	*The Greek New Testament*, United Bible Societies, 2nd ed.
UBS[3]	*The Greek New Testament*, United Bible Societies, 3rd rev. ed.
UBS[4]	*The Greek New Testament*, United Bible Societies, 4th rev. ed.

UBS⁵	*The Greek New Testament*, United Bible Societies, 5th rev. ed.
v(v).	verse(s)
WC	*Written Communication*
WGRW	Writings from the Greco-Roman World
WGRWSup	Writings from the Greco-Roman World Supplement Series
WUNT	Wissenschaftliche Untersuchungen zum Neuen Testament
ZAW	*Zeitschrift für die alttestamentliche Wissenschaft*

Glossary[1]

Apocalyptic rhetorolect. Discourse that envisions or displays the actions of God or his Son that bring about blessing or benefit or, for other situations, judgment. God and his Son perform actions of rescue, salvation, forgiveness of sins, and reconciliation, or actions that bring about exile and death. Apocalyptic redemption envisions the cosmos as the space where well-being and holiness are provided by God's grace. The analogue is the deified emperor who uses power to conquer in order to produce peace in the emperor's realm. The actions are often described in metaphorical, symbolic ways.

Argumentative texture. The reasoning that occurs inside a text. Rhetorical argument may be logical, asserting or prompting syllogistic reasoning, or qualitative, where the sequence of images, descriptions, and values encourages the reader to accept the portrayal as true and real. Argumentation moves people to thought, belief, understanding, and action.

Conceptual blending. The formation of new and emergent cognitive structures when topoi from particular and clear input frames (or mental spaces) are brought together and elicit understandings of new concepts and conditions not previously understood.

Ideological texture. How people consciously or unconsciously see and understand the spatial and mental worlds in which they live. It involves beliefs, values, assumptions, philosophies, points of view, expectations, notions of right and wrong, behaviors, justifications of positions whether

---

1. See the comprehensive glossary in Vernon K. Robbins, *The Invention of Christian Discourse* (Dorset, UK: Deo, 2009), 1:xxi–xxx; and in Robbins, Robert H. von Thaden Jr., and Bart B. Bruehler, *Foundations for Sociorhetorical Exploration: A Rhetoric of Religious Antiquity Reader*, RRA 4 (Atlanta: SBL Press, 2016), xv–xxv.

well-argued or not, doctrines, systems, politics, and power structures that affect people and things in the cultures in which they live. The particular alliances and conflicts nurtured and evoked by the language of a text, the language of interpretations of a text, and the way a text itself and interpreters of the text position themselves in relation to other individuals and groups. Ideological texture both describes and creates these understandings.

Inner texture. The various ways a text employs language to communicate. This includes linguistic patterns, voices, movements, argumentations, and structural elements of a text, the specific ways it persuades its audiences, and the ways its language evokes feelings, emotions, or senses that are located in various parts of the body.

Intertexture. The representation of, reference to, and use of phenomena in the world outside the text being interpreted. This world includes other texts, other cultures, social roles, institutions, codes, and relationships, and historical events or places.

Narrational texture. The voice (often not identified with a specific character) through which words in texts speak. The narrator may begin and continue simply with assertion that describes, asserts, or greets. Narration may present argumentation or introduce people who act, which creates storytelling or narrative. The narrator is the real or imagined person speaking.

Opening-middle-closing texture. The basic rhetorical structure of the beginning, the body, and the conclusion of a section of discourse. In a text, it indicates where the basic, functional sections are located and how they operate rhetorically. Opening-middle-closing texture provides a sense of wholeness or completeness to a text.

Precreation rhetorolect. Discourse that imagines and speaks of the unseen domain of God and his Son prior to the creation of the heavens and the earth. Precreation interprets the unseen realm of God assumed to exist apart from the created order. The precreational realm is the true home of all things. All things exist under the jurisdiction of God and his Son. The analogue to precreation rhetorolect is the deified emperor and his household and Son, who oversee the empire and its people.

Priestly rhetorolect. Discourse that speaks of religious actions including ritual actions performed to acquire or be given benefits from God. This rhetorolect describes and envisions intercessory actions such as prayer, sacrifice, thanksgiving, blessings, worship, financial and material offerings, and service. The benefits of the actions can be forgiveness, redemption, health, and peace. Priests perform these actions, but so do others such as Jesus Christ, Paul the apostle, and others.

Progressive texture. Progressions and sequences of grammar and ideas in a text. Progressions indicate how the rhetoric moves ahead linguistically, thematically, spatially, and topically.

Prophetic rhetorolect. Discourse that, like the word of the Hebrew Bible prophets, presupposes that God calls prophets to be proclaimers who challenge people, particularly kings and leaders, to repent and establish faith and justice in their domains and in their lives. Prophetic discourse confronts people who might be resistant. The goal of the discourse is to create orderliness and righteousness among people. Prophetic rhetorolect corresponds to prophetic space, the domain of proclaimers and preachers who call people to faithfulness.

Repetitive texture. Repetition of words, phrases, and topoi that help identify social, cultural, and ideological networks of meanings and meaning effects in the rhetoric in a text.

Rhetography. The progressive, sensory-aesthetic, and argumentative textures of a text that prompt graphic images or pictures in the minds of listeners and readers that imply certain truths and realities.

Rhetorical force as emergent discourse. The emerging discourse of a social, cultural, ideological, and/or religious movement such as early Christianity as it moved audiences by eliciting belief, behavior, and community formation.

Rhetorolect. An elision of "rhetorical dialect" that refers to the emergent modes of discourse created by early Christ-believers, who shaped and reshaped language so that they could articulate their new faith understandings about Jesus Christ and the implications of that faith for life in their communities (the *ekklēsia*) and in Mediterranean societies. Modes of discourse are identifiable on the basis of distinctive configurations of themes, images, topics, reasonings, and argumentations. Six major rhetorolects are prominent in early Christian discourse: wisdom, prophetic, apocalyptic, precreation, priestly, and miracle discourse. Rhetorolects correspond to the spaces in which the actions of God and humans take place.

Sacred texture. The manner in which a text communicates insights into the relationship between humanity, the cosmos, and the divine. It addresses redemption, commitment, worship, devotion, community, ethics, holy living, spirituality, and spiritual formation.

Sensory-aesthetic texture. The features in a text that indicate, reflect, or evoke things discerned through visual, oral, aural, olfactory, tactile, gustatory, textual, prosaic, poetic, intellectual, and other sensory and aesthetic human characteristics.

Social and cultural texture. The social and cultural nature and location of the language used and the social and cultural world evoked and created by a text. It can include subtextures such as alternative culture.

SRI (sociorhetorical interpretation). A range of heuristic analytics that analyzes and interprets texts using features of rhetorical, social, and cognitive reasoning to help commentators learn how the texts under examination function to influence thinking and behavior. The *socio-* refers to the rich resources of modern social, cultural, and cognitive sciences. The *rhetorical* refers to the way language in a text is a means of communication among people. A major goal of SRI is to nurture an environment of full-bodied interpretation that encourages a genuine interest in people who live in contexts with values, norms, and goals different from our own.

Texture. Emerging from a metaphor of figuration as weaving, the concept of texture in relation to a text derives from Latin *texere* ("to weave") that produces an arrangement of threads in the warp and woof of a fabric. SRI extends the metaphor of texture to the metaphor of tapestry, approaching a text as a thick network of meanings and meaning effects that an interpreter can explore by moving through the text from different perspectives.

Topos, topoi (pl.), topics. A place to which one may go mentally to find arguments. The topics by which argumentation is made. Thus, topoi are landmarks in the mental geography of thought that themselves evoke networks of meanings in their social, cultural, or ideological use.

Wisdom rhetorolect. Discourse that interprets the visible world by blending human experiences of geophysical, social, cultural, and institutional human experiences with beliefs about God especially through parental and familial nurturing and caring modes of understanding. Wisdom is about doing good in the world and living faithfully, fruitfully, and ethically. Its special rhetorical effect is to conceptualize the function of spaces, places, and people through practices characteristic of households and other teaching-learning environments.

Introduction

The Letter to the Colossians presents a grand vision of messianic reality that extends from the realm of God and his Son before the creation of the cosmos to the time, space, culture, religion, Roman imperial domination, and social pressures faced by the holy and faithful Christ believers of Colossae and the Lycus Valley. The developed vision of the new reality of the holy ones has its source and philosophical and theological foundation in the cosmic-precreational domain of Father God and his Son. This vision emerges from the reality of Christ Jesus, in whom people such as Paul, Timothy, their coworkers, and many others trusted and whom they proclaimed. The vision portrays the certainty that Jesus was raised from death, that he was the preexistent Son of God, the Messiah-Christ, and that his death and resurrection brought about reconciliation and peace for all things in the created realm of the heavens and the earth, including humans.

The *generative cause* of the letter is found ultimately in this gospel reality and in concerns about how and how well believers understood it and how they should live out the new reality in Christ. Gospel convictions and concerns for the life, faith, and faithfulness of the believers underlie the content of the letter. Believers faced pressures locally in Colossae and probably in the Lycus towns of Laodicea and Hierapolis to conform to "empty, deceitful philosophy, human tradition, and the elements of the world" rather than to Christ (Col 2:8). These pressures were the immediate motivation energizing the letter's articulation of the developed understanding of how Father God through his Son Christ Jesus made the Lycus believers and all humans full (2:10), how the flesh has been stripped away (2:11), thereby making the pressures irrelevant. Believers have been rescued out of the darkness of the disordered world in which they live and transferred into the new reality of light in the beloved Son's kingdom, where there is, already present, redemption and the forgiveness of sins. No other kingdom or humanly produced actions—whether political, spiritual, or religious—could or can yet do this. Christ followers must not give in to the deceit that would persuade them to attempt to make themselves right by their personal religious, social, and political efforts. No. They are already full. Christ is all and in all (3:11).

Sociorhetorical Interpretation

SRI is a comprehensive heuristic analytic—a range of analytics—that employs a multiple-accounts evaluation to analyze and reanalyze texts using features of rhetorical, social, anthropological, and cognitive reasoning to learn how the texts function to convey ideas and information in order to influence learning, thinking and behavior.[1] SRI is a full-bodied analytic that aims to discover phenomena in the texts as they emerge in their multiform and multivalent social, anthropological, and rhetorical contexts and as they bring about theological cognition. It is not an adversarial approach that aims to move understanding ahead by comparison and contrast with other interpretations. It is meant to ask about, describe, and interpret what texts *do* to people, their audiences, given their contexts.[2] SRI employs the analytics to discover the rhetoric of topoi, pictures, textures, and emergent structures that the texts set in recipients' minds and by which the audiences are meant to be socially and religiously formed and reformed. The goal of the analytics is to learn not only about what happened in the past or how texts were structured and argued in the past, but to see how they aimed to change things, what they changed, and indeed how they change us.[3]

SRI identifies and examines the multiform and multivalent geometry of the texts of the New Testament and Mediterranean antiquity. Texts are

---

[1]. I draw here on the description in Roy R. Jeal, *Exploring Philemon: Freedom, Brotherhood, and Partnership in the New Society*, RRA 2 (Atlanta: SBL Press, 2015), 2–15, and the literature indicated there. For a recent useful and clear description of SRI, see Ruth Christa Mathieson, *Matthew's Parable of the Royal Wedding Feast: A Sociorhetorical Interpretation*, ESEC 26 (Atlanta: SBL Press, 2023), 30–38. See also B. J. Oropeza, *Exploring Second Corinthians: Death and Life, Hardship and Rivalry*, RRA 3 (Atlanta: SBL Press, 2016), 35–41. For a full introduction to SRI, see Vernon K. Robbins, Robert H. von Thaden Jr., and Bart B. Bruehler, eds., *Foundations for Sociorhetorical Interpretation: A Rhetoric of Religious Antiquity Reader*, RRA 4 (Atlanta: SBL Press, 2016).

[2]. Contexts, plural, because there are always multiple contexts and ideas to consider.

[3]. See L. Gregory Bloomquist, "The Pesky Threads of Robbins's Rhetorical Tapestry," in *Genealogies of New Testament Rhetorical Criticism*, ed. Troy W. Martin (Minneapolis: Fortress, 2014), 218–20.

imagined to be analogous to a tapestry,⁴ a thickly woven textile that presents pictures, stories, argumentation, sensory, and aesthetic details. The tapestries interweave threads from other texts, material culture, social and cultural agency, and many other realms. They employ and create ideologies, and they relate to the sacred and spiritual planes. In doing so they present multidimensional fabrics and pictures that fill spaces of various kinds and that convey and elicit meanings. The interweaving of threads forms textures that are not flat, two-dimensional broadcloth fabrics but are both coarsely and finely textured images with depth and shapes of many kinds. This geometry⁵ brings the shapes together yet recognizes that they interweave in multiple ways and in multiple directions, that they turn and can be turned, and that every turning reveals something not noticed before.

SRI does an important thing for understanding and for writing about biblical texts: rather than trying to judge them from, as it were, the outside—whether to show that what they say is correct, true, historically accurate, inspired, inspiring, authoritative, the word of God, on the one hand, or wrong, false, historically fabricated, misleading, misguided, simply mistaken, on the other—it lets them stand in judgment over their interpreters. It avoids being bound by the static sources, situations, and structures of discourse, being concerned more with the *interplay* of them in the production and evocation of ideas, thoughts, and behaviors. The point is that SRI attends to what the texts say and do, observing the rhetography (the images cast on the imagination), the **inner textures** and **intertextures**, the ideologies, and the sacredness of the texts apart from external methodological or moral constraints. SRI does not aim to make a point for its own or for some third party's sake. It aims to learn and understand.⁶ The text should be heard in its own self-presentation. Because it is a heuristic analytic, it can be performed multiple times.⁷ There is no final, definitive analysis or interpretation. Discovery remains a continuing process. It encourages one

---

4. See the programmatic work of Vernon K. Robbins, *The Tapestry of Early Christian Discourse: Rhetoric, Society, and Ideology* (London: Routledge, 1996).

5. On the concept of geometry, see Margaret Visser, *The Geometry of Love: Space, Time, Mystery, and Meaning in an Ordinary Church* (Toronto: Harper Perennial, 2000).

6. On this see Christopher Bryan, "A Digression: 'Great Literature'?," in Bryan, *Listening to the Bible: The Art of Faithful Biblical Interpretation* (Oxford: Oxford University Press, 2014), 56–65.

7. Duane F. Watson, "Retrospect and Prospect of Sociorhetorical Interpretation," in *Welcoming the Nations: International Sociorhetorical Explorations*, ed. Vernon K. Robbins and Roy R. Jeal, IVBS 13 (Atlanta: SBL Press, 2020), 11.

to do all one can but allows for and encourages more to be discovered by others. SRI aims to *show* (in visuality, visual exegesis, rhetography) and to *describe* (textural analysis) and to explain the *power* (rhetorical force) of biblical and religious discourse as it emerged and was employed in the ancient Mediterranean.

While SRI takes the classical rhetorical tradition indicated in the ancient handbooks seriously, it recognizes that ancient Mediterranean, early Christian, and biblical rhetorics are broader than the handbooks indicate. The three genera of classical rhetoric (judicial, deliberative, epideictic), for example, do not adequately address the range of situations and discourse indicated in the New Testament. Rather than addressing the law courts, political assemblies, or civil ceremonies, New Testament discourse addresses situations centered in "households, political kingdoms, imperial armies, imperial households, temples, and individual bodies of people."[8] Early Christ believers did what groups and communities of all kinds and in all places do: they shaped and reshaped their understandings of the faith and developed their own modes of discourse that expressed and clarified their beliefs, their worldviews, and what had been revealed to them. The developed ideas and reshaped language and discourse were meant for Christ-believing audiences who could recognize it in light of their belief. New Testament documents such as Colossians are living things whose developed ideas, theologies, and language require interpreters to be imaginative, looking for the development in the discourse, getting as close as they can by explanation of its meaning in their own words while recognizing that analysis and interpretation must be done again in every generation. SRI helps overcome a negative hermeneutic of suspicion with a hermeneutic of openness and hope. It aims to examine the letter in a living, breathing world where there are human, ethical, and everlasting concerns, not only (or merely) concerns for facts and reconstructed situations.

Rhetorolects: Distinctive Modes of Discourse

The shaped and reshaped understandings and language that developed among early Christ believers led to the creation of emergent discourse, by

---

8. See Vernon K. Robbins, *The Invention of Christian Discourse* (Blandford Forum, UK: Deo, 2009), 1:1–3. This point is noted by others regarding New Testament texts, e.g., Neil Elliott, *The Arrogance of Nations: Reading Romans in the Shadow of Empire* (Minneapolis: Fortress, 2010), 20.

which they articulated their understandings of faith in Jesus Christ and its implications for life in their communities and societies. This discourse is recognizable in its distinctive rhetorical dialects or modes of speaking and writing.[9] SRI calls these modes of discourse rhetorolects (*rhetórolect*, an elision of "rhetorical dialect"). Each rhetorolect is a mode of discourse "identifiable on the basis of a distinctive configuration of themes, topics, reasonings, and argumentations" that develops in cultures.[10] Early believers employed at least six identifiable rhetorolects: wisdom, prophetic, apocalyptic, precreation, miracle, priestly.[11] The rhetorolects both describe and create particular and specialized understandings.[12] They correspond to the spaces and places in which actions of God and humans occur.[13] They can characterize a speaker, writer, or kind of action performed.[14] They frequently blend together to intensify their force.[15] This commentary points out the employment of precreation, prophetic, priestly, apocalyptic, and wisdom rhetorolects in Colossians and demonstrates how they evoke intelligent, productive, and ethical knowledge and behavior among believers in their *ekklēsia*, household, social, and political locations and situations. Rhetorolects do more than define literary or rhetorical genres. They reveal much about *how* discourse functions rhetorically and argumentatively in the relevant contexts. They are therefore more than stylistics (λέξις), though stylistics can be taken into consideration. Rhetorolects

---

9. See Vernon K. Robbins, "The Dialectical Nature of Early Christian Discourse," *Scriptura* 59 (1996): 353–62; Robbins, "Socio-rhetorical Interpretation," in *The Blackwell Companion to the New Testament*, ed. David E. Aune (Oxford: Blackwell, 2010), 192–219; Robbins, *Invention of Christian Discourse*, 7–9.

10. Robbins, "Socio-rhetorical Interpretation," 197.

11. For a full description and discussion see Robbins, *Invention of Christian Discourse*, 7–9, 90–120; Vernon K. Robbins, "Conceptual Blending and Early Christian Imagination," in Robbins, von Thaden, and Bruehler, *Foundations for Sociorhetorical Interpretation*, 329–64. An analogy that provides a helpful illustration is the ancient Greek concept of modes of music. See Thomas Cahill, *Sailing the Wine-Dark Sea: Why the Greeks Matter* (New York: Doubleday, 2003), 87.

12. What Robbins calls "the invention of Christian discourse."

13. See especially the table in Robbins, *Invention of Christian Discourse*, 109, for a clear description of rhetorolects and their respective spaces; see also Mathieson, *Matthew's Parable*, 36–38.

14. For example, prophetic rhetorolect can characterize a prophet or preacher-proclaimer (κῆρυξ); miracle can characterize a worker of wonders or a healed person.

15. See especially Robbins, "Conceptual Blending."

allow speakers and writers to articulate their understandings of the faith. They are about how discourse works and what it does.

Precreation

Precreation rhetorolect speaks of the realm of God prior to the creation of the heavens and the earth. The precreational time-space precedes and transcends the created orders where humans live.[16] Father God and his Son are imagined though not envisioned in the unseen domain where they are active in the production of order and goodness. Precreation discourse blends the realms of divine emperors and their households—which are unseen by ordinary people—with the unseen realm of Father God and his Son.[17] It interprets created reality by presenting God and his Son in the precreational, unseen realm as the true sources of all things. This means, of course, that Father God and the Son are prior to and superior to all human, spiritual, and cosmic powers and authorities, who are created beings, none of them inherently sovereign or autonomous or independent of the domain of the Father and the Son. This is particularly important because Colossians presents precreational discourse and realities as the philosophical-theological foundation of its argumentation.

Precreation is not presumed to be eternal in the sense of being atemporal and nonspatial. It assumes that creation has to do with setting disordered things in order, making things good, as Gen 1 indicates. Colossians does not address how the previous "formless void and darkness" came about (Gen 1:1 NRSV).[18] It does state that "all things" were created "through" the Son and "for him" (Col 1:16). Colossians claims that redemption, forgiveness, reconciliation, and peace are provided through and in the precreational Son of God. God in the Son has brought about the goodness that humans are given. Precreation was and is an "age" (Gk. noun

---

16. At an earlier stage SRI used the term *cosmic* to describe precreational rhetorolect. More recently there has been discussion about naming it "cosmic-precreation." There has also been consideration of "deep cosmic time." For our purposes here, *precreation* is straightforward and helpful for interpreting Colossians. For theological discussion of deep cosmic time, see John F. Haught, *The New Cosmic Story: Inside Our Awakening Universe* (New Haven: Yale University Press, 2017).

17. See the definition in the glossary; see also Robbins, *Invention of Christian Discourse*, 111; Robbins, "Conceptual Blending," 339–40.

18. "Complete chaos," NRSVue; "unseen and unformed," "darkness," LXX (ἀόρατος καὶ ἀκατασκεύαστος, καὶ σκότος).

αἰών, adjective αἰώνιος; Heb. עוֹלָם), an eon, a long duration, time lasting for an age, not a timeless, eternal realm imagined to exist prior to the creation of the cosmos.[19] Precreation rhetorolect is discourse that speaks of things in the domain of God and his Son, unseen by humans, preceding the creation of the cosmos. It is not meant to describe the beginnings of things as such but to indicate that the Son of God comes from the domain of God and is creator and sustainer of all things.[20] In Colossians it is about who the Son is and what the Son has done in his own precreational domain, that the good gifts of redemption, forgiveness, reconciliation, and peace come from the realm of the image of the unseen God, who precedes and transcends creation. The space of precreation is the realm and dominion of God and the Son, as such the source, the true home or household of all things. As the home of genuine power, rule, authority, and creativity, it is the source and true home of wisdom.

Prophetic

Prophetic rhetorolect presupposes that God calls prophets as proclaimers to humans through speech and actions. Prophets speak authoritatively for God. The discourse draws on the Hebrew Bible, where prophets proclaimed messages of God's will to humans.[21] The prophets challenged people, particularly kings and leaders, to repent and establish faithfulness and justice in their jurisdictions and in their own lives. Prophets and their messages were confrontational, often resisted and rejected, and prophets were sometimes persecuted or even killed. "The goal of prophetic rhetorolect is to create a governed realm on earth where God's

---

19. On αἰών see Hermann Sasse, "αἰών," *TDNT* 1:197–209. On עוֹלָם, see the classic study by Ernst Jenni, "Das Wort *'ōlām* im Alten Testament," *ZAW* 64 (1952): 197–248; 65 (1953): 1–35. See also Heleen M. Keizer, "Life Time Entirety: A Study of ΑΙΩΝ in Greek Literature and Philosophy in the Septuagint and Philo" (thesis, Universiteit van Amsterdam, 2010). αἰών occurs in Colossians only at 1:26.

20. As John F. Haught points out, "Christian theology, however, does not have to worry about whether the universe had a beginning in time because the doctrine of creation is not about temporal beginnings anyway. It is about the dependency of the universe on a gracious source of being other than itself. If questions about origins are pursued in depth, they eventually lead back to the theological question of why anything exists at all. That is the real question." See Haught, *God after Einstein: What's Really Going On in the Universe* (New Haven: Yale University Press, 2022), 48.

21. See Robbins, *Invention of Christian Discourse*, 219–60.

righteousness is enacted among all of God's people in that realm with the aid of God's specially transmitted word in the form of prophetic activity and speech."[22] Prophetic discourse corresponds to prophetic space, the lived domains of proclaimers and preachers who call for continual faithfulness in the lives of believers. In Colossians Paul is envisioned in a prophetic role as "an apostle of Christ Jesus by God's will" who has things to say to the Colossians that will strengthen their faith and encourage their behavior, challenging them to resist the pressure to conform to deceitful, empty, and unhelpful beliefs and behaviors.[23]

Priestly

Priests perform intercessory and ritual tasks. They approach God on behalf of others. Priestly activity aims to obtain benefits for priests themselves and for those for whom they intercede. Priestly rhetorolect envisions ancient Mediterranean religious actions, including ritual actions, performed to acquire or be given benefits from God. The actions include sacrifices, prayers, thanksgivings, blessings, worship and expressions of praise, hymns and songs, offerings of money and goods such as food. The benefits hoped for and anticipated are things such as health, relief from pressures, forgiveness, redemption, peace, and holiness. The greatest offering is one's own life of service and holy living. In the New Testament perspective, priestly actions are performed not only by persons formally designated as priests but by people such as Paul the apostle and all believers (see 1 Pet 2:5, 9). The greatest (high) priest is Christ himself, who gave his life sacrificially (see Heb 2:17–10:21, 13:10–12). Priestly rhetorolect employs this Mediterranean discourse for the benefit of Christ believers.[24] In Colossians Paul is envisioned employing priestly language in priestly space in the greeting of grace and peace (1:2), in thanksgivings (1:3), in prayers (1:3–5, 9–12), in his suffering on behalf of the *ekklēsia* (1:24, 2:1–2), and in Christ's sacrificial actions (2:11–15).

---

22. Robbins, "Conceptual Blending," 339.
23. See "prophetic rhetorolect" in the glossary; see also Robbins, "Conceptual Blending," 336, 339.
24. See "priestly rhetorolect" in the glossary; see also Robbins, "Conceptual Blending," 340–41.

Apocalyptic

Apocalyptic rhetorolect envisions God's actions that have brought about good, righteousness, redemption, forgiveness, peace, and the destruction and removal of evil in the cosmos. The apocalyptic actions of God have created fullness and well-being for humans and the entire cosmos in the presence of God.[25] The actions are often described in metaphorical, symbolic, imagery-filled ways. In other words, apocalyptic does what the meaning of the term indicates: it is revelatory. Apocalyptic envisions the good, righteous, blessed place and environment that God's actions in Christ have brought into existence. "Apocalyptic redemption ... means the presence of all of God's holy beings in a realm where God's holiness and righteousness are completely and eternally present."[26] God is portrayed as a heavenly emperor who acts in dramatic ways for the benefit of humans and the cosmos. In Colossians God's apocalyptic actions are observed in 2:9–15, where believers are described as having "been made full" in Christ, "who is the head of every power and authority." The Son has been raised (1:18), and humans, who have been "circumcised with a nonhandmade circumcision," have been buried and raised with him, made alive and forgiven (2:11–13). Powers and authorities have been disgraced and triumphed by Christ (2:15). God has made things right in the Son-Christ, who comes from the precreational domain.

Wisdom

The rhetorical goal of Colossians is wisdom living practiced by the Christ believers. Wisdom is about doing good in the world and about living faithfully, fruitfully, and ethically.[27] Wisdom discourse describes and encourages the intelligent and productive lives the believers were called to live in their ancient Mediterranean social, cultural, and religious environment.

---

25. Apocalyptic action is not necessarily eschatological, though eschatological events can be apocalyptic.
26. Robbins, von Thaden, and Bruehler, *Foundations for Sociorhetorical Interpretation*, glossary, xv; see also Robbins, *Invention of Christian Discourse*, 110–11; Robbins, "Conceptual Blending," 339.
27. See Jeal, *Exploring Philemon*, 6–8.

This rhetorolect and its corresponding space-time realm interprets and addresses the visible world by blending human bodily experiences of geophysical, social, cultural, and institutional experiences with beliefs about God and the sacred, particularly through parental and familial, nurturing, and caring modes of understanding. Wisdom encourages good and productive behavior. Its *rhetorical effect* is to elicit conceptualization of the function of spaces, places, and people through practices in households and teaching-learning environments. Wisdom is about living the new Christ-believing, ecclesial reality in ancient Mediterranean social, cultural, and religious contexts. Humans perceive that in their bodies they can produce goodness and righteousness through the medium of God's wisdom. Wisdom rhetoric emphasizes "fruitfulness" (productivity and reproductivity) in the domains of God's creation.[28]

Colossians overall has a wisdom intention. Prayers request that the believers be "filled with the knowledge of God's will in all wisdom and spiritual understanding" (1:9–12). Christ is proclaimed, "admonishing every person and teaching every person in all wisdom, so that we might present every person (as) mature in Christ" (1:28). The maturity implies wise thinking and wise behavior. The believers faced pressures that aimed to draw them away from wisdom to conform to local and imperial social and religious expectations. The letter calls them to conform to the gospel understanding of Christ, to the fullness they have in Christ, and to good and productive living in Christ.

Rhetography

> He *saw* everything he related. It passed before him, as he spoke, so vividly that, in the intensity of his earnestness, he presented what he described to me with greater distinction than I can express. I can hardly believe, writing now long afterwards, but that I was actually present in those scenes; they are impressed upon me with such an astonishing air of fidelity.
>
> —Charles Dickens, *David Copperfield*

---

28. Adapted from Robbins, von Thaden, and Bruehler, *Foundations for Sociorhetorical Interpretation*, xxiv–xxv; see also 336. For a thoroughgoing description of wisdom, see Robert H. von Thaden Jr., *Sex, Christ, and Embodied Cognition*, ESEC 16 (Atlanta: SBL Press, 2017), 76–108.

> I gradually integrated the New Drama and the Old in my mind and spirit as well as I ever will; not through reasoning about faith and science but *by creating pictures.*
> —Herman Wouk, *The Language God Talks*

> "Flesh-knowledge." "It's not enough for your mind to believe something, your body must believe it too."
> —Anne Michaels, *The Winter Vault*

> The question is not what you look at, but what you see.
> —Henry David Thoreau, *Journal*

Rhetography (an elision of *rhetoric* and *graphic*) describes and interprets what is seen in the imagination when people read or listen to texts.[29] The term refers to the interrelationships and functions of the visual and persuasive features in texts. Commentaries in the Rhetorics of Religious Antiquity series begin analysis with rhetography. The words, grammar, and sounds of Colossians are understood when read, spoken aloud, and heard. For most people the words of texts cast images on the imagination. They visualize the scenes, places, people, and situations; they hear the voices and sounds and feel emotions conveyed by the texts. This graphic rhetoric draws readers and listeners quite naturally into the ideas and meanings. Rhetography is a first step in interpretation. Aristotle recommends that speakers employ metaphors that "set things before the eyes" (*Rhet.* 3.11.1), stating, "I mean that things are set before the eyes by words that signify *actuality*" (ἐνέργεια, *Rhet.* 3.11.2 [Freese]; see also Quintilian, *Inst.* 6.2.24–36). It is important to make things clear, indeed visible with words, what Aristotle calls *phantasia* (φαντασία), a show, an impression, an appearance in the imagination (*Rhet.* 3.1.6; see Aristotle, *De an.* 428a–431b).[30] *Phantasia* brings what is not seen in visual reality to the human mind in the visual

---

29. See the description of rhetography in Roy R. Jeal, "Visual Interpretation: Blending Rhetorical Arts in Colossians 2:6–3:4," in *The Art of Visual Exegesis: Rhetoric, Texts, Images*, ed. Vernon K. Robbins, Walter S. Melion, and Roy R. Jeal, ESEC 19 (Atlanta: SBL Press, 2017), 55–87; see also Jeal, *Exploring Philemon*, 8–10. For the seminal description, see Vernon K. Robbins, "Rhetography: A New Way of Seeing the Familiar Text," in Robbins, von Thaden, and Bruehler, *Foundations for Sociorhetorical Interpretation*, 367–92.

30. See Ned O'Gorman, "Aristotle's *Phantasia* in the *Rhetoric*: *Lexis*, Appearance, and the Epideictic Function of Discourse," *P&R* 38 (2005): 16–40.

imagination. The point is that texts communicate by what they picture. The visuality draws audiences in, moving them toward understanding. Rhetography along with rhetorolects demonstrates that texts are simultaneously graphic and dialectical.

Textural Commentary

The commentary goes on to provide analysis of the textures of Colossians. Textural commentary describes and interprets the textures to understand how they function together to *do* things to people. The analysis is exploratory, not definitive or final, always aiming to broaden and deepen understanding of the power of the text.[31]

Inner textures are features of the language employed in the text. Analysis involves identifying and examining words, patterns, voices, movements, argumentation, and the structural artistry of the language.

Opening-middle-closing texture is the basic rhetorical structure of the letter. All texts (and generally coherent units of texts) have these parts or variations of them. The terms correspond to beginning (or introduction), body, and ending (or conclusion). *Opening-middle-closing texture* provides a sense of wholeness or completeness to a text.

Repetitive texture refers to repetitions of words, grammaticalizations, and topoi that produce patterns that help identify major themes in the rhetoric and social relations in a text.

Progressive textures are the sequences of grammar and ideas in a text. They indicate where the rhetoric moves ahead linguistically, thematically, spatially, and/or topically.

Narrational texture is observed in the storytelling or narrative presented by the (implied) narrator or speaker. It listens to the voice(s) that conveys the ideas of the discourse. The narration is the story as it is being told in a text.

Argumentative texture is about reasoning that occurs inside a text. The rhetorical argument may be logical or qualitative. This texturing moves people to thought, understanding, belief, and action.

Sensory-aesthetic texture occurs in the features that indicate, reflect, or evoke things discerned through visual, oral, aural, olfactory, tactile,

---

31. The descriptions here are adapted from Jeal, *Exploring Philemon*, 12–13. On textures see Vernon K. Robbins, *Exploring the Textures of Texts: A Guide to Socio-rhetorical Interpretation* (New York: Bloomsbury Academic, 2012).

gustatory, textual, prosaic, poetic, and other intellectual and bodily sensibilities. This texturing produces a recognizable feel in a text.

Intertextures are the connections and interactions between the text being studied and phenomena outside it. This involves intertextuality, connections with other texts, but also relationships with any observable external phenomena.

Social and cultural texture refers to the "social and cultural nature and location" of the language used, and the "social and cultural world" evoked and created by a text.[32] It employs social topoi and categories that denote social and cultural situations addressed and created in the rhetorical discourse.

Ideological texture has to do with how people see and understand the spatial and mental worlds in which they live. It involves the beliefs, values, assumptions, philosophies, points of view, expectations, notions of right and wrong, behaviors, justifications of positions (whether well-argued or not), doctrines, systems, politics, and power structures that affect people and things in the cultures in which they live.

Sacred texture is the texture of relationships among humans, the created order, and God, between and among humans, the cosmos, and the divine. This is the texture that addresses redemption, commitment, worship, devotion, community, ethics, holy living, spirituality, and spiritual formation.

Rhetorical Force as Emergent Discourse

The commentary concludes with analysis of the rhetorical force of the text as emergent discourse in the ancient Mediterranean world. This analysis recognizes that Colossians, like all New Testament and early Christian discourse, is emergent because it presents the developing thinking, theology, and faith of some early Jesus-followers, set down in writing, transmitted, and preserved as they came to it and went along in their lives. Early believers, proclaimers, and authors did not arrive fully formed, speaking and writing with fully developed beliefs, doctrines, and theological knowledge. They understood, interpreted, and wrote about Jesus Christ, the new faith, the new society, and their implications as they came to understand more about them and as they encountered circumstances that called for thoughtful interpretation and application to the actual conditions faced

---

32. Robbins, *Exploring the Textures of Texts*, 71–94.

in the new reality. This emergent discourse was shaped with powerful and dramatic *rhetorical force* in order to move audiences—real people in real locations and circumstances—employing the dynamics of the visual, textural, philosophical, and theological to elicit belief, behavior, and formation among people individually and collectively as the *ekklēsia*. This rhetorical force evoked, encouraged, and strengthened faith, and indicated, reminded of, and sometimes corrected behavior appropriate to the faith. In other words, the rhetorical force of the emergent discourse was meant to shape lives, to make people better, productive, and ethical persons who comprise the body of Christ. In this process new modes of discourse were created and developed while drawing on existing modes, and so were new and strategic communications that affected their audiences. The rhetorical force of the Letter to the Colossians powerfully influenced people. It influences us still.

Creativity and Development

Colossians presents with strikingly developed ideological and theological rhetoric aimed at moving its audiences to the mature understanding that "Christ is all and in all" (Col 3:11). The development describes the deep "spiritual wisdom and understanding" (1:9) of the "mystery hidden from the ages and generations … now been brought to light … which is Christ in you the hope of glory" (1:26–27). The development reflects creativity and deep consideration of what early Jesus-followers considered, learned, and wrote down in letters such as Colossians.

Creativity initiates ideas and the development of ideas. Conversely, ideas and their development arouse creativity. Creativity and the development of ideas blend together and emerge in rhetorical discourse that conveys emerging information. Creativity is the employment of imaginative or original ideas.[33] It is inventiveness. Many, notably psychologist James C. Kaufman, define creativity as new and appropriate ideas. Kaufman states that "creativity must represent something different, new, or innovative" and what is created "must be appropriate to the task at hand."[34] By "appropriate"

---

33. As in *Oxford Dictionary of English*, s.v. "creativity," creativity in classical rhetoric is an aspect of *inventio*.

34. James C. Kaufman, *Creativity 101*, 2nd ed. (New York: Springer, 2016), 5; see also Kaufman and Robert J. Sternberg, eds., *The Nature of Human Creativity* (Cambridge: Cambridge University Press, 2018).

it is meant that whatever is new must be useful. It must have some value; it has to work.³⁵

There are cognitive and experiential aspects to creativity: "Research shows that creative thinking involves making new connections between different regions of the brain, which is accomplished by cultivating divergent skills and deliberately exposing oneself to new experiences and learning."³⁶ A key notion for defining and understanding creativity is *imagination*.³⁷ Creativity is the ability to imagine followed by the movement from imagining to constructing new rhetorical discourse that is analogous to and/or explains what is imagined. Imagination works with mental representations, mental pictures, or mental visualizations (which SRI describes as rhetography), with impressions and ideas in the mind, that can be shaped and blended into the realia of artistic works and into words and discourse (λόγος) and documents that did not exist or exist in the same way(s) previously.³⁸ It is about seeing things that others do not (yet) see.³⁹ The result of creativity is therefore always new and unfamiliar. The unfamiliarity is not meant to confuse or inhibit but to enhance understanding. The unfamiliarity may cause surprise and requires analysis and learning.⁴⁰ The product of creativity in discourse is like what the *progymnasmata* call ekphrasis (ἔκφρασις), descriptive language that "brings [new] things before the eyes."⁴¹ Creative ability and its employment are, in SRI terms, wisdom. The creation of new ideas and new things is the good work of productivity.⁴²

Psychologists and cognitive theorists have offered various definitions and descriptions of creativity. Graham Wallas offered an early twentieth-century description of stages of creativity: preparation (focusing

---

35. So new ideas that are useless or ridiculous are not considered to be creative.
36. "Creativity," *Psychology Today*, https://tinyurl.com/SBL71061.
37. I thank my friend Dr. Aimee Patterson for ideas I rely on here.
38. Image, imagine, imagination all have origin in the Latin *imago*, "image, likeness."
39. The theological analogue is inspiration. People are, sometimes at least, inspired or inspirited with ideas and understandings that come from outside themselves, from the Holy Spirit. Grasping such things is often called insight or illumination.
40. The surprises are often noted. See Donald H. Juel, *A Master of Surprise: Mark Interpreted* (Minneapolis: Fortress, 1994).
41. As in the *progymnasmata* by Theon, Hermogenes, Aphthonius, and Nicolaus, all in George A. Kennedy, *Progymnasmata: Greek Textbooks of Prose Composition and Rhetoric*, WGRW 10 (Atlanta: Society of Biblical Literature, 2003).
42. Wisdom is about productivity, never destruction.

the mind), incubation (internalization in the unconscious mind), intimation (sensing a solution), illumination (conscious creative idea), and verification (conscious verification and elaboration).[43] Gilles Fauconnier and Mark Turner in *The Way We Think*, a work frequently referenced by practitioners of SRI, describe "the ways in which human beings use conceptual integration to *create* rich and diverse conceptual worlds."[44] Humans have the ability to blend notions from multiple conceptual places (domains, input spaces) to create new conceptions in the mind that can be presented in spoken and written language. These new conceptions are "elaborate emergent structures" that creatively build worlds that humans can understand.[45] Mental visual representations can be blended and presented creatively with words that persuade readers and listeners to visualize the representations and blends in their own minds. Daniel Kahnemann in *Thinking Fast and Slow*, drawing on the work of psychologist Sarnoff Mednick, addresses "creativity as associative memory that works exceptionally well."[46] Kahnemann points out that multiple computations continuously occur in human brains. When people encounter things they know (e.g., words, ideas, pictorial representations), they can intuitively and creatively associate them with new (unstated or previously unrecognized) notions. They do this typically when their minds are at ease and they are in happy moods.[47]

It should be expected that early believers would have developed their faith and understandings of Christ and the new reality in the *ekklēsia* in many ways. Situations that they encountered demanded careful, imaginative thinking about how to respond. Colossians presents a number of

---

43. Graham Wallas, *The Art of Thought* (repr., Tunbridge Wells, UK: Solis, 2014). Wallas thought that intimation was a moment or substage immediately preceding and associated with illumination.

44. Gilles Fauconnier and Mark Turner, *The Way We Think: Conceptual Blending and the Mind's Hidden Complexities* (New York: Basic Books, 2002), 309 (emphasis added).

45. Fauconnier and Turner, *Way We Think*, 301–2. The emergent structures relate to what SRI calls "rhetorical force as emergent discourse."

46. Daniel Kahnemann, *Thinking Fast and Slow* (New York: Farrar, Strauss & Giroux, 2011), 67.

47. According to the great rocker Bruce Springsteen, "Creativity is an act of magic rising up from your subconscious." Quoted in David Brooks, "Bruce Springsteen and the Art of Aging Well," *Atlantic*, 23 October 2020, https://tinyurl.com/SBL7106a.

developments beyond earlier Pauline letters.[48] The following are particularly notable:

- Colossians 1:12–20. These verses contain the only reference to "the kingdom of the Son" in the Pauline corpus. In this kingdom is redemption and forgiveness. These good things, like all created things, have their source in the precreational Son-image of God, firstborn out of the dead, first in all things, reconciler of all created things on earth and in the heavens, who existed with God before creation.
- Colossians 1:24–29, 2:2. In these verses the "mystery hidden from the ages and generations," "the mystery of God—of Christ," "Christ in, you the hope of glory" is described as now present. This seems to have developed and expanded from the ideas in Rom 16:25–26 and perhaps 1 Cor 2:1. It is developed further in Eph 1:9, 3:1–10.
- Colossians 2:9–15. The "fullness of deity" houses in Christ bodily, and believers "have been made full in him." This is followed by the creative, apocalyptic, and graphic rhetoric depicting the actions of God in Christ bringing about the redemptive benefits believers enjoy. This rhetoric points out that things are different now because of the work of God in Christ that extends from the precreational domain.
- Colossians 3:18–4:1. The rhetoric about wives, husbands, children, fathers, slaves, and masters develops household relationships and management in striking ways. Many scholars interpret it as regressive rather than progressive development. The verses certainly call for orderly household living.

The entire cosmos is understood relative to the precreational Son, who has brought about change apocalyptically. This is new, insightful rhetorical discourse in the eastern provinces of Asia Minor. Certainly it was meant to move the believers ahead in deepened faith, knowledge, and good behavior. The developments suggest to many that Colossians dates from some

---

48. See Robert McL. Wilson, *Colossians and Philemon*, ICC (London: Bloomsbury T&T Clark, 2005), 27–30; Paul Foster, *Colossians*, BNTC (London: Bloomsbury T&T Clark, 2016), 81–85.

time after Paul had died and that Paul himself was not involved in the composition of the letter.

The Empty, Deceitful Philosophy

The recipients of the letter are warned to beware of being captured by someone "through philosophy and empty deceit, according to human tradition, according to the elements of the world, and not according to Christ" (2:8).[49] The description makes the person and the philosophy seem dangerous, nefarious. This language has instigated the massive and ongoing search to identify "the Colossian philosophy," sometimes referred to as "the Colossian heresy." What was the philosophy? Can it be definitively identified? Was it a single, specific philosophy and human tradition? Was it localized in Colossae and the Lycus Valley? Who or what are the elements of the cosmos? Who was promoting the philosophy? Who was the complainant judging believers about certain religious observances and insisting on others (2:16, 18)?

Scholarly investigation about the philosophy has proliferated, with dozens of possibilities suggested, yet it remains opaque, and no firm conclusions or even consensus has been achieved. Despite the massive work, relatively little can be determined about the precise nature of the philosophy except that it remains "an insoluble riddle."[50] Scholars continue the attempt to reconstruct the situation with broad possibilities to which they become committed but with sparse and incomplete evidence. The fact is that Colossians does not specify or even imply a definition of the philosophy in a full, clear way. The most that can be said with certainty is that the philosophy was insidious and misleading, that its twofold source was "human tradition" and the "elements of the cosmos," neither of which are defined in the letter, and that it is "not according to Christ."[51] This tells readers and listeners that it does not come from the precreational domain of Father God and his Son. It came from the chaos and disorder of humans

---

49. Beware of "someone," spoken of in the singular. Perhaps a number of persons were involved.

50. According to Clinton Arnold, who has written much on the topic. See Arnold, "Initiation, Vision, and Spiritual Power: The Hellenistic Dimension of the Problem at Colossae," in *The First Urban Churches 5: Colossae, Hierapolis, and Laodicea*, ed. James R. Harrison and L. L. Welborn, WGRWSup 16 (Atlanta: SBL Press, 2019), 173.

51. Nor did it come from the good Epaphras, 1:17.

apart from Christ. It was inferior to what comes from the Son and the precreational domain. It came from fallible and imperfect humans who live in the jurisdiction of darkness, thinking they and others—the Christ believers—must engage in religious, dietary, and ascetic practices in order to be socially and religiously acceptable. The complainant aimed to imbue a sense of obligation on the believers to do the purportedly right and necessary things. Colossians makes the developed theological claim that "all the fullness of deity" houses in Christ and that believers have been made full in Christ. The holy and faithful Jesus-followers are already full. It does not help to attempt to fill what is already full.

The answer to the philosophy is, "No, we are already full." This is more important than identifying the philosophy itself. The deceitful philosophy was destructive. It detracted from the full and complete work of Christ described in 2:11–15. The philosophy could not provide the redemption, forgiveness, reconciliation, and peace of the gospel. Succumbing to it might gain some social acceptance, at least from the complainant, but it would be of no other benefit, as Col 2:20–23 states.

Full sociorhetorical analysis of the philosophy is provided in the commentary sections on 2:8–23.

Alternative Cultural Texture

Colossians presents and promotes—it rhetoricizes—an alternative culture where believers are committed to a definition of life that contrasts with, indeed that refuses, the pressure to conform to particularly religious aspects of the imperial culture of the ancient Mediterranean.[52] An alternative culture "rejects explicit and mutable characteristics of the dominant or subculture rhetoric to which it belongs."[53] It envisions situations better than what are otherwise experienced. Authors of the letter assumed that the growing (1:6) Lycus Valley Jesus-followers understood the alternative culture about which they were being informed (reminded) and that they would benefit from the deeply rhetorical-theological information. The pressure was on in the Lycus, like it was throughout the empire, pushing people in the conquered provinces to assimilate to a homogeneous,

---

52. On alternative culture (or counterculture) rhetoric, see Robbins, *Tapestry of Early Christian Discourse*, 167–74 (especially 169–70); Robbins, *Exploring the Textures of Texts*, 86.

53. Robbins, *Exploring the Textures of Texts*, 87.

Roman view of life and the world that was designed to support emperor and empire as the great world saving and sustaining power.[54] Caesar was the great divine king-savior (βασιλεύς-σωτήρ) who, it was imagined, provided goodness and security in governance, economic, political, military, and social domains for all people in the vast geography of the empire. This salvation (σωτηρία) was visible in the exclusivist Pax Romana of order, prosperity (particularly for those already wealthy), hegemony, and expansionism. There was a relative level of peace (*pax*), but it was an imposed peace, brought about and maintained by imperial hegemony. The real situation relied on imperial political and military power, material increase for the wealthy (primarily landowners) and varying levels of poverty for others, taxation, social disparity and repression, pervasive slavery, the threat of brutality, and, to a significant extent, religious observance. The imperial system was obviously hierarchical, with the emperor at the top and slaves at the bottom of a social scale. The vast majority of the population, perhaps as much as 97 percent, lived in varying levels of poverty. Certainly good was done for people, for example, the provision of imported grain/food (the *cura annonae*, from Egypt and elsewhere) for the population of Rome. But the power of the empire was always present, and submission to the Roman ethos was expected. Rebellion was met by force. For New Testament studies, this force is most notable in the Jewish rebellion of 66–73 CE with the destruction of Jerusalem, including the temple, in 70 CE. This was followed by the Bar Kokhba revolt of 132–36 CE, which was similarly put down brutally. Rome was interested in conformity, in maintaining a status quo, not diversity, even if religious and social diversity were generally tolerated.

The Lycus was "a rich agricultural area."[55] Produce included grain, fruits and vegetables, olives, grapes and wine, livestock, wool, and textiles. Local manufacturing included garments, leather, and imitation purple

---

54. On Roman conformity, see Alan H. Cadwallader, "Greeks in Colossae: Shifting Allegiances in the Letter to the Colossians and Its Context," in *Attitudes to Gentiles in Ancient Judaism and Early Christianity*, ed. David C. Sim and James S. McLaren, LNTS (London: Bloomsbury T&T Clark, 2013), 224–41. Roman conformity included economic, religious, family/household, symbolic, architectural, military, judicial, and other aspects of life. See Harry O. Maier, *Picturing Paul in Empire: Imperial Image, Text and Persuasion in Colossians, Ephesians and the Pastoral Epistles* (New York: T&T Clark, 2013), 93–94.

55. Ulrich Huttner, *Early Christianity in the Lycus Valley*, trans. David Green, ECAM 1 (Leiden: Brill, 2013), 18.

dye.⁵⁶ The region in these ways functioned as part of the larger Roman market economy that shaped cultural understanding of the dominating imperial system.⁵⁷ The Pax Romana provided for a relatively stable and secure market system. The huge imperial market was "localized in provinces and towns," that is, places such as Colossae.⁵⁸ It was important for people to conform to this established way of thinking about how things worked. The point here is that the imperial system was powerful and the divine emperor was recognized as a great god like Jupiter.⁵⁹ Economic sustainability, indeed ordinary life in local communities, was understood to have a direct connection, a dependency, on the imperial socioeconomic-religious system.

The particular locus of economic activity was the household. The household (οἶκος; Lat. *domus*) "was 'the most important ancient economic institution in which economic behavior was embedded.' A house was a residence for a large group of people (parents, children, and slaves) and also a manufacturing or production unit within the other business and agricultural institutions, *collegia*, and associations of the Lycus Valley."⁶⁰ Households were productive spaces. The household was also the locus of what in Colossians is called "the body, the *ekklēsia*" (1:18, 24). The house of Nympha is explicitly noted as an assembly location (4:15). The body is, repeatedly, the body of Christ (1:22, 24; 2:17, 19; 3:15–16; see also 2:11–14), and the believers have been reconciled *in* the body of Christ's flesh (1:22). The repetitive texturing of "house" (or "dwelling") οἰκ- words in Colossians reveals a strong imagery: κατοικῆσαι, "because in him all the fullness was pleased to house" (1:19); οἰκονομίαν, "according to the household management of God" (1:25); ἐποικοδομούμενοι, "having been rooted and built up in him" (2:7); κατοικεῖ, "in him houses all the fullness of the deity bodily" (2:9); ἐνοικείτω, "let the word of Christ house itself in you richly"

---

56. See Huttner, *Early Christianity*, 18–30.
57. On this see Michael Trainor, "Rome's Market Economy in the Lycus Valley: Soundings from Laodicea and Colossae," in Harrison and Welborn, *First Urban Churches 5*, 293.
58. Trainor, "Rome's Market Economy," 295.
59. On this see the textural commentary on Col 1:15–20.
60. Trainor, "Rome's Market Economy," 300, with quotation from Ekkehard W. Stegemann and Wolfgang Stegemann, *The Jesus Movement: A Social History of Its First Century* (Minneapolis: Fortress, 1999), 18. For more detail see Harry O. Maier, "The Household and Its Members," in *New Testament Christianity in the Roman World* (New York: Oxford University Press, 2019), 134–73.

(3:16); and οἶκον, "Nympha and those in the *ekklēsia* in her house" (4:15).⁶¹ So the notion of house and household is pervasive in the cultural context and in the actual wording of Colossians. It is enhanced by the striking and extensive family language, where God is "Father God" (1:2, 3, 12; 3:17), where the believers are brothers (1:1, 2; 4:7, 9, 15), and where family members and their relationships are envisioned (the household management wisdom or *Haustafel*, 3:18–4:1).

What is envisioned overall is a household filiated culture that is simultaneously envisioned as the unified body of Christ *ekklēsia* that grows the growth from God as it is held together by its "joints and ligaments" (2:19).⁶² This filiated culture explicitly includes children and slaves (3:20–4:1) and would also involve extended family and in many cases other persons. What emerges is the body-*ekklēsia*-household alternative culture that Colossians presupposes and commends to the audiences of the letter. The body-*ekklēsia*-household is characterized by love (1:4, 7, 8, 13; 2:2; 3:12, 14, 19; 4:7, 9, 14), faith (1:2, 4, 7, 23; 2:6; 4:7, 9), fruitfulness and growth (1:6, 10), by seeking for and thinking about "the above things" (τὰ ἄνω, 3:1–2), heading for the "glory" (3:4) and "Christ all and in all" (ἀλλὰ [τὰ] πάντα καὶ ἐν πᾶσιν Χριστός, 3:11). The body-*ekklēsia*-household is encouraged to do good and live well in its contexts (3:5–4:6). In stark contrast to the dominating Roman material-religious culture fixated on the emperor, the imperial system, and a range of social and religious expectations that the Jesus followers faced,⁶³ the body-*ekklēsia*-household-glory alternative culture was about life transferred to the new reality of the kingdom of Father God's Son Christ Jesus. He is the genuine image of the unseen Father God, creator of all things, and therefore not of the oppressive empire controlling Roman Asia. In this alternative culture it is Christ who is the hope of glory, not the material and mortal Caesar of Rome.

Jesus followers in Colossae and the Lycus region faced complaints regarding their religious observances (see 2:4, 8, 16–23). According to the complainant, there was a lack of conformity to religious behaviors

---

61. κατοικῆσαι is typically translated as "to dwell." οἰκονομίαν is typically translated as "administration." It refers to household management of an "economy." ἐποικοδομούμενοι, built up, as on the foundation of a house. ἐνοικέω, "to dwell or house in a place/location."

62. On being filiated, see Ephraim Radner, *A Time to Keep: Theology, Mortality, and the Shape of Human Life* (Waco, TX: Baylor University Press, 2016), 61–63. From Latin *filius* ("son, child"), *filia* ("daughter"); see also *familia* ("family, household").

63. See the commentary on Col 2:16–23.

expected in the Roman–Phrygian–Lycus Valley polytheistic context.[64] Yet to succumb to the complaints would be to live in the shadow (σκιά, 2:17), the darkness (σκότος, 1:13), out of which the believers had been rescued and transferred (literally "metastasized," μετέστησεν εἰς τὴν βασιλείαν τοῦ υἱοῦ τῆς ἀγάπης αὐτοῦ, 1:13). To succumb would be to give in to Roman conformity and the religious pressures conformity demanded. The alternative culture proclaims that Christ Jesus alone provides reconciliation, redemption, the forgiveness of sins. The dominating cultural philosophy and its imperial, polytheistic pressures and politics are theologically and practically irrelevant because the precreational Son of God (1:15–20) has provided everything needed in his death and resurrection (2:9–15). The believers must not be deceived. Their commitment is to the precreational philosophy-theology, not to a philosophy of the Roman-Phrygian context.

The alternative culture of Colossians is, to be sure, a kingdom culture (βασιλεία, 1:13), but not the kind of human and polytheistic kingdom/empire culture usually imagined in the region. In the new body-*ekklēsia*-household reality of the Son's kingdom there are filiated, productive relationships where people "fit in" (ὑποτάσσω) as members of the loving, faithful, and productive household.[65] This is to live in the "thirdspace," that is, "the ways in which inhabitants of the valley [and the authors of Colossians] used religious imagination and ideological strategies to live and delimit the living of space."[66] The household code is not presented as a set of inviolable

---

64. The complainant is described in the singular as "someone" even if there might have been multiple complainants. On the polytheistic context, see the textural commentary on Col 2:16–23. According to Mary Beard, "Roman religion was not only polytheistic but treated foreign gods much as it treated foreign peoples: by incorporation.... But the basic rule was that as the Roman Empire expanded, so did its pantheon of deities." See Beard, *SPQR: A History of Ancient Rome* (New York: Liveright, 2015), 59.

65. On the word ὑποτάσσω as "fitting in," see Troy W. Martin, "Translating ὑποτάσσεσθαι in First Peter as *Fitting in*, Not as *Submission*," BR 67 (2022): 59–80; Martin, *Apostolic Confirmation and Legitimation in an Early Christian Faith Document: A Commentary on the First Epistle of the Apostle Peter*, NIGTC (Grand Rapids: Eerdmans, forthcoming), on 1 Pet 2:13–3:7. For a full SRI analysis, see the commentary below on Col 3:18–4:1. Household members could include husbands/males, wives/females, children, parents, slaves, owners, and various other persons not mentioned. See also Eph 5:21, ὑποτασσόμενοι ἀλλήλοις.

66. Harry O. Maier, "Salience, Multiple Affiliation, and Christ Belief in the Lycus Valley: A Conversation with Ulrich Huttner's *Early Christianity in the Lycus Valley*," in Harrison and Welborn, *First Urban Churches 5*, 167.

marriage, family, and slavery kyriarchal rules, as some claim, even if it is a "hybrid" development that "mimics" Jewish and Roman forms.[67] It is not mere assimilation to power.[68] It reflects the characterization of the new reality of the body-*ekklēsia*-household culture. The household code exudes love, careful and thoughtful family relations, unity, and fairness and equality to those of the lowest social category, namely, slaves ("Lords/Masters, provide the just thing and equality [τὸ δίκαιον καὶ τὴν ἰσότητα] to slaves, knowing that you also have a Lord in heaven," 4:1).

The household code, rather than demanding subservience and unfair patriarchy, may well have been providing safety for oppressed people. Roman power structures supported a predatory sexual culture. Men could have nonconsensual sexual relations with persons other than their wives provided that they were persons of a lower social class. This meant that people, certainly often slaves, could be abused. Many women were driven to prostitution. Even slaves—including child slaves of friends of a man—could be sexually used and abused.[69] The body-*ekklēsia*-household culture and location was a haven from these oppressive realities. Members of this body were to experience the new reality of the kingdom, where they were not threatened and abused and could live in a household-family situation understood to be culturally normal in the roles of its various members while also being a space where there was acceptance, care, and safety. It was a reasonable, indeed a good way to live in a disordered cosmos. This household was the cosmic body-*ekklēsia* that transcended the things of the

---

67. On hybridity see especially Harry O. Maier, "Paul, Imperial Situation, and Visualization in the Epistle to the Colossians," in Robbins, Melion, and Jeal, *Art of Visual Exegesis*, 193–94; see also Maier, "Reading Colossians in the Ruins: Roman Imperial Iconography, Moral Transformation, and the Construction of Christian Identity in the Lycus Valley," in *Colossae in Space and Time: Linking to an Ancient City*, ed. Alan H. Cadwallader and Michael Trainor (Göttingen: Vandenhoeck & Ruprecht, 2011), 226–29.

68. Alan Cadwallader quite properly asks, "How many within the audience actually saw themselves fitting the paradigm ... just like Paul (1 Cor 7:7)?" "One must be wary of assuming that relationships correlate transparently to households ... but they can be suggestive." See Cadwallader, "One Grave, Two Women, One Man: Complicating Family Life at Colossae," in *Stones, Bones, and the Sacred: Essays on Material Culture and Ancient Religion in Honor of Dennis E. Smith*, ed. Alan H. Cadwallader, ECL 21 (Atlanta: SBL Press, 2016), 181–83.

69. On this see Douglas A. Campbell, *Pauline Dogmatics: The Triumph of God's Love* (Grand Rapids: Eerdmans, 2020), 613.

earth. While often in modern Western understandings seen to be imperfect, this new reality was headed for manifestation in glory (3:1–4).[70]

The alternative culture rhetoric presented in Colossians envisions and promotes a body-*ekklēsia*-household-glory bonded community of Christ believers who recognize what Father God has done for them and the world in the Son-Christ and that they are therefore free from the jurisdiction of darkness and from all powers and authorities of the cosmos (τὰ στοιχεῖα τοῦ κόσμου). In the new reality of the Son's kingdom, they are a developing culture to themselves.[71]

The Text

The commentary follows the well-attested NA[28] and UBS[5] editions of the Greek New Testament. The versions of the Letter to the Colossians in these editions are nearly identical, having only some punctuation and formatting differences. Variants are noted in footnotes to the translation sections in the commentary. Colossians has 1,582 words in Greek, 1,580 when the words δι' αὐτοῦ are omitted from the final line of 1:20, 1,579 when τὰ is omitted from 3:11, 1,578 when τῇ is omitted from 3:16, and 1,577 when Ἰησοῦ is omitted from 4:12.[72] The count could increase by one word if Ἀμήν should be included at the end of 4:18.[73]

The translation of Colossians is placed following the interpretation of rhetography for each section. Translation follows the Greek text closely,

---

70. Perhaps this also ameliorates the view that the *Haustafel* contradicts notions of equality observed in other Pauline letters, notably Gal 3:28.

71. "Culture is a slingshot moved by the force of its own past." Barbara Kingsolver, *The Poisonwood Bible* (New York: Harper Perennial, 1998), 528.

72. See Roy R. Jeal, *Colossians-Philemon: A Beginning-Intermediate Greek Reader* (Wilmore, KY: GlossaHouse, 2015); Constantine R. Campbell, *Colossians and Philemon: A Handbook on the Greek Text*, BHGNT (Waco, TX: Baylor University Press, 2013). For history of textual reception see Jerry L. Sumney, *Colossians: A Commentary*, NTL (Louisville: Westminster John Knox, 2008), 12; Foster, *Colossians*, 112–20; Markus Barth and Helmut Blanke, *Colossians: A New Translation with Introduction and Commentary*, trans. Astrid B. Beck, AB 34B (New York: Doubleday, 1994), 48–56; Wilson, *Colossians and Philemon*, passim.

73. The KJV adds "Written from Rome to the Colossians by Tychicus and Onesimus" to the end of the letter. The Geneva Bible adds "Written from Rome to the Colossians, and sent by Tychicus and Onesimus." Similar additions can be found in other fifteenth- and sixteenth-century versions.

aiming to be accurate, dynamic, and understandable in modern English without sounding informal.

Authorship

Colossians is a disputed letter. A majority of biblical scholars believe it was not written by Paul and comes from a time several years after his death.[74] The question of authorship receives a lot of attention, perhaps more than it deserves. Opinions vary widely: Was it Paul or a later author? It is often one of the first points raised when scholars talk about the letter.[75] There is pressure and often a compulsion to state one's view. Yet authorship is not the most important interpretive issue. The content and rhetorical force (the anticipated and actual effects) of the letter are vastly more important.

The modern conception of an individual person sitting at a desk or table and writing a letter by hand must not be projected back and imposed on the preparation of Hellenistic and New Testament letters of the first century CE.[76] The writing process normally involved several persons. Taken at face value, Timothy is described as cosender of the letter (1:1), and others are implied to have been close enough to know the letter was being prepared and offer their greetings (4:10–14). We do not know the conditions under which Colossians was composed, but there are insights gained from what is generally known about how letters and other documents were produced.[77] Writing was a collaborative process where one person, the imagined author, spoke aloud, and another wrote down what was spoken. Others would typically be engaged with acquiring, manufacturing, and preparing writing materials such as stylus, wax tablets, ink, and papyrus.[78] Paul and others typically spoke letters aloud, and a scribe wrote

---

74. Though a smaller majority than those who consider that, for example, Ephesians and 1 Timothy were not written by or did not come from Paul.

75. My own experience is that very often when I have mentioned to people that I am preparing a commentary on Colossians, the first question asked is, "What do you think about authorship?"

76. Some of what follows is adapted from my *Exploring Philemon*, 16–18.

77. See Margaret Ellen Lee and Bernard Brandon Scott, *Sound Mapping the New Testament* (Salem, OR: Polebridge, 2009), 11–57.

78. See the video descriptions by Daniel B. Wallace, "Scribal Methods and Materials," Center for the Study of New Testament Manuscripts, https://itunes.apple.com/us/itunes-u/scribal-methods-materials/id446658178.

the words on wax tablets (*cerae*), later transcribing them onto papyrus.[79] It is likely that Colossians was composed in this way. What was written on wax tablets could be corrected, amended, and revised as dictation went along, or when it was transcribed on papyrus. The scribe doing the actual writing could soon be forgotten, though Tertius inserted his own greeting as "writer" in Rom 16:22. Apart from the physical actions involved in gathering materials, writing, and transcribing, the process depended on sound spoken and sound heard.[80] A letter was dictated and written with oral presentation in mind, so was rhetorical by its nature.[81] It could be corrected, altered, and edited when transcribed to papyrus. A scribe or speaker could add notations or a name.

It follows that Paul did not *write* letters. This stark declaration may at first sound odd, yet it makes the point that Paul and other letter writers did not work alone.[82] He spoke them aloud. But did he himself speak Colossians aloud? Did he add his handwritten name in the closing line (4:18)? Certainly the implied narrational voice is Paul's, with Timothy nearby. Certainly there is development in Colossians and a range of differences obvious when compared with the undisputed letters. It is true that Colossians does not mention justification by faith or the Holy Spirit. The household language of Col 3:18–4:1 is problematic when set alongside Gal 3:28 and Paul's views about slavery indicated in the Letter to Philemon. Is the Onesimus named in Col 4:9 the same Onesimus who is central to the argument in the letter to Philemon? Could the names of real persons in 4:7–17 have been drawn from other letters and inserted without their knowledge? Well, yes, they could have. It remains a question as to why these differences matter. Could Paul *not* have developed his ideas and language in these ways? A more useful question than asking whether Paul was the author is to ask whether he was still alive and present when the letter was prepared and sent to Colossae. Were he and Timothy the only speak-

---

79. Lee and Scott, *Sound Mapping*, 16–18, with examples. See "Ancient Writing Materials: Wax Tablets," University of Michigan Library, https://tinyurl.com/SBL7106b.

80. At the other end of the process recipients, most of whom would have been illiterate, heard the letter read aloud rather than reading it on their own. Sound was a crucial feature of the communication process.

81. Lee and Scott, *Sound Mapping*, 24–28. They are texts prepared for utterance. See the helpful comments of Christopher Bryan, "The Drama of the Word," in *Listening to the Bible*, 114–26.

82. See Jeal, *Exploring Philemon*, 16–18; see also Scot McKnight, *The Letter to the Colossians*, NICNT (Grand Rapids: Eerdmans, 2018), 8, 18.

ers? Other contributors cannot be ruled out. Discussion among coworkers cannot be ruled out. Might he have approved what had been stated, discussed, and written down and said, "Send"? How long would it have taken for ideas and theological understanding to develop? Decades? Perhaps not long. People can develop creative ideas very quickly. Would it help to know? Yes, certainly. The issues have been discussed at length by many interpreters and are not rehearsed here.[83] We are left with what is true about much in the work of interpreting Colossians: *there is so much we do not know*. Opinions are welcome, but it is not possible to be definitive. The issue of authorship frequently becomes more of a distraction than something useful.

So the authorship of Colossians remains a disputed matter. Many interpreters seem unable to refrain from voicing their opinions and conclusions, but clarity remains elusive. Does one need to make a choice? We do not have definitive answers to the issues. It is much more important to do the exegesis, the analysis, than claim any certainty about authorship. Robert McL. Wilson offers what seems to be a wise statement: "Such tentative and hesitant conclusions will not, of course, satisfy those who must at all costs have a definite and clear-cut answer to every question, but there are times when it is important to recognize the limitations of our knowledge. We do not always have the evidence upon which to base a firm judgment."[84]

In this SRI commentary I have used the name *Paul* in the sections on rhetography because the actual Paul is the person envisioned when the letter is read or heard. In the textural commentary I have used terms such as "virtual Paul," "implied Paul," and the plural "authors" to take into account what readers and listeners imagine when they encounter the text regardless of who composed the letter. SRI helps along the way as we seek to learn about what the text does more than being concerned to resolve the critical issue of authorship.

Date

Saying anything confidently about when Colossians was written, sent, and received has an obvious and direct relationship to the items just described

---

83. See the commentaries, particularly the extended discussions in Wilson, *Colossians and Philemon*, 9–35; Foster, *Colossians*, 61–81; McKnight, *Colossians*, 5–18.
84. Wilson, *Colossians and Philemon*, 35.

about authorship. If Paul was the speaker whose words and ideas were written on papyrus and sent to Colossae, he was likely imprisoned, as Col 4:3 ("on account of which I have been imprisoned") and 4:18 ("remember my chains") suggest. The location of this imprisonment is not known and is debated by scholars as being in Caesarea Maritima, Rome, or Ephesus.[85] Certainly Paul was imprisoned in Caesarea Maritima and Rome and also in other places for unspecified periods of time.[86] There has been speculation about a second imprisonment in Rome sometime after 64 CE. Though there is no record of imprisonment in Ephesus, many scholars think it likely. If Colossians was spoken, written, and sent after Paul died, then possible dates could extend into the early second century.[87] Recent studies by Douglas Campbell and Jonathan Bernier argue for dating of Colossians (and Ephesians and Philemon) as early as mid-50 CE (Campbell) and 57–59 CE (Bernier). Campbell and Bernier present plausible but not decisive and completely convincing arguments and conclusions.[88]

How much does dating the letter matter? The answer is *it depends*. Much to some, little to others. Taking a firm position does not resolve the uncertainty or the dispute. Argument for a broad range of dates from 50 to 80 CE is plausible.

Rhetorical Structure

The commentary interprets Colossians in a careful, structured way, employing the SRI analytic that follows the progressive textures that move the rhetoric, argumentation, and development of ideas ahead. Overall, the commentary follows the foundational structure of *opening-middle-closing texture*, recognizing that understandable texts have a beginning, a middle (or body), and a closing that both furnish and shape coherence.[89]

---

85. See Jeal, *Exploring Philemon*, 28–31.

86. Very briefly in Philippi, less than one day, according to Acts 16:19–40.

87. For a survey of scholarship and the possibilities see the table in Foster, *Colossians*, 73–78.

88. Douglas A. Campbell, *Framing Paul: An Epistolary Biography* (Grand Rapids: Eerdmans, 2014), 260–309, 412–14; Jonathan Bernier, *Rethinking the Dates of the New Testament: The Evidence for Early Composition* (Grand Rapids: Baker Academic, 2022), 163–71. Campbell (274–76) suggests Apamea as the location of imprisonment and writing.

89. On *opening-middle-closing texture* see Robbins, *Tapestry of Early Christian Discourse*, 50–53; Robbins, *Exploring the Textures of Texts*, 19–21.

The rhetography, translation, textural commentary, and rhetorical force as emergent discourse sections follow the progressions of scenes and steps as they emerge. The rhetography and rhetorical force sections by themselves provide a sociorhetorical interpretation of Colossians. Reading the sections on textural commentary provides detailed description and interpretation of the interwoven threads that form the fabric of the text.

The Opening (1:1–23)
    Scene One: Introductory Rhetoric (1:1–23)
        Step One: Paul's Prophetic-Priestly Greeting (1:1–2)
        Step Two: Paul's Priestly-Prophetic Prayers for People in Wisdom Space (1:3–8)
        Step Three: Priestly Prayers (1:9–12)
        Step Four: Father God's Apocalyptic Actions: Transferal to the New Reality (1:13–14)
        Step Five: The Cosmic-Precreational Image of God: Over All Things (1:15–20)
        Step Six: Alienation, Reconciliation, and Faithful Living (1:21–23)

The Middle (1:24–4:6)
    Scene Two: Paul's Genuine Character and Genuine Concerns (1:24–2:5)
        Step One: Suffering for the *Ekklēsia* (1:24–29)
        Step Two: Struggling for Faithfulness (2:1–5)
    Scene Three: Don't Be Deceived. Live the New Reality (2:6–4:6)
        Step One: Walk On Confidently (2:6–7)
        Step Two: Beware of Being Captured—You are Already Filled (2:8–10)
        Step Three: God in Christ Has Done Everything You Need (2:11–15)
        Step Four: Do Not Let Someone Judge You (2:16–17)
        Step Five: Do Not Be Cheated by the Self-Important Complainant (2:18–19)
        Step Six: You Died with Christ; Do Not Submit to Useless Rules (2:20–23)
        Step Seven: You Were Raised with Christ; Seek the Above Things (3:1–4)
        Step Eight: New Life in the New Reality (3:5–17)
        Step Nine: Household Wisdom (3:18–4:1)

Step Ten: Walking Forward, Looking Outward (4:2–6)

The Closing (4:7–18)
  Scene Four: Personalities Rhetoric (4:7–18)
    Step One: Tychicus and Onesimus Reporting (4:7–9)
    Step Two: Greetings (4:10–17)
    Step Three: Personal Greeting (4:18)

The Opening (1:1–23)

Scene One: Introductory Rhetoric (1:1–23)

Step One: Paul's Prophetic-Priestly Greeting (1:1–2)

Rhetography

Colossians begins by casting visual images of persons and activities on the imaginations of audiences of the letter. Paul appears first, a human male and apostle (1:1), one sent to be a proclaimer. Paul is sent by the next person who appears, Christ Jesus. As the letter begins, listeners imagine Paul not only as a follower and proclaimer of Christ Jesus, but also a representative who speaks authoritatively for Christ. They visualize Paul as one empowered to speak and write words on behalf of Christ. They may imagine him speaking aloud to an amanuensis who writes down what he is saying on a wax tablet, although the text does not itself define this for them to imagine.[1]

The image of Paul himself, the empowered apostolic speaker and writer, is enhanced by a more abstract visualization of the next named person, God,[2] through whose will Paul exists and functions as an apostle. Timothy the brother appears next, visually present with Paul as a coworker and cosender of the letter.[3] Timothy is a flat character in the narrative, not appearing again in the opening picture but filling a useful function. Presenting Timothy as brother creates the image of a close, affectionate, familial relationship between him and Paul and perhaps an image of kinship between him and the audience. These brothers exist in

---

1. Audiences draw this imagery from what they know about the social conventions (social **intertexture**) of letter writing.
2. Abstract because the unseen God (1:15) cannot be seen or recalled visually.
3. Although it is not explicit, Timothy can be imagined to have collaborated in substantial ways to the letter, as amanuensis, source and author of ideas, and some actual wording. See the introduction.

a distinctly prophetic space.[4] Paul and Timothy are authoritative proclaimers, hence prophets, who speak by God's will. In this space, Paul's is explicitly prophetic apostolic, sent out by Christ Jesus to engage in specific prophetic tasks.

The audience members appear next as holy (ἁγίοις) and faithful brothers and sisters in Christ in Colossae.[5] Listeners picture human residents of the city of Colossae who, like Paul, have a connection with the already visualized Christ and who in that relationship are holy and faithful people.[6] These residents are visualized spatially both "in Christ" and in Colossae.[7] The picture depicts very good persons who collectively live deeply religious lives. Listeners-viewers do not imagine anything negative about their character or manner of life. As brothers and sisters like Timothy,[8] they are people who actively care for one another and for Paul and Timothy. Listeners also visualize the city, Colossae, as the geographical and political location (space) in which these people live their good and faithful lives.[9] The opening language of Colossians moves audiences to visualize a community of faithful people. All of them appear as believers in God and in Jesus Christ. Their beliefs are fundamental to the communication. The words assume the existence of an audience in Colossae, and they evoke a picture of people whose religious and moral affections hold them in a common bond with one another.

---

4. The discourse of the letter thus also begins in a prophetic rhetorolect (mode) or religious texture.

5. τοῖς ἐν Κολοσσαῖς ἁγίοις καὶ πιστοῖς ἀδελφοῖς, 1:2. That is, consecrated, sanctified people, not morally perfect. The word ἁγίοις is an adjective and, since it is joined by καί to "faithful brothers" and governed by the same article, is translated accordingly here, not as the noun "saints," as is commonly done. The word ἀδελφοί, "brothers," is understood socially to include sisters. An inclusive community is envisioned.

6. The first intended recipients of the letter would, of course, have pictured themselves as Christ believers resident in Colossae. Other readers and listeners such as us will imagine residents of Colossae or perhaps other people in other places, times, or situations.

7. The phrase "in Christ" refers to the new "sphere of existence" of the holy and faithful brothers and sisters where Christ Jesus is Lord (see Wilson, *Colossians and Philemon*, 73).

8. A repetitive texture that blends people in different spaces as brothers and sisters.

9. Colossae was a medium-sized city on the Lycus River in Phrygia, Asia Minor, a few kilometers from Laodicea and Hierapolis. The first audience of the letter extends explicitly to believers in Laodicea and implicitly to those in Hierapolis (4:13, 15–16).

The greeting "Grace to you and peace from God our Father" (1:2)[10] envisions Paul and Timothy thinking warmly of the brothers and sisters who are recipients of the message. The image of the various parties as brothers and sisters is complemented by the picture of God as both deity and father, presumably to indicate this dual nature of God related to all the characters: Paul, Timothy, others named in the letter, the audience in Colossae, and all other audiences of Colossians. The wishes for "grace and peace from God our Father" draw all of them into a vision that imagines (and desires) beneficent conditions that are provided by fatherly God.

The rhetography of this first step of Colossians blends prophetic, wisdom, and priestly discourse textures and spaces with one another. Prophetic and wisdom textures blend together in multiple ways. The prophetic, proclamatory space of Paul himself—who is visualized in human bodily form working with Timothy, who is also visualized bodily—blends with the prophetic space where God wills good things and with the wisdom space where humans actually live together in relationships.[11] The wisdom texture depicts the holiness, faithfulness, and kinship that are observable among the Colossians while blending with the prophetic texture to show God as their Father and Paul and Timothy as brothers who speak to them. This blending indicates that the filiated relationships are the result of God's will, through which Paul the apostle and Timothy the brother speak. Prophetic and wisdom discourse textures blend, in addition, with priestly discourse texture as Paul and Timothy engage in the priestly task of pronouncing a blessing of grace and peace from God on the people in Christ in Colossae. The pictures, in their various spaces, are kinetic; they indicate movement, the actions of the persons envisaged. The portrayal evokes theological and christological understandings that are seen in an ecclesial space where Paul, Timothy, and the Colossians share in fellowship.

The picture or rhetograph already itself makes an argument. It evokes a visualization of Christ-Messiah Jesus, that is, as Jesus identified as the

---

10. The genitive phrase ἀπὸ θεοῦ πατρὸς ἡμῶν places "God" and "Father" together as a single description that could be translated as the hyphenated "our God-Father." But to render it as "God-Father" could convey misleading ideas to modern readers. Some manuscripts add "and of Lord Jesus Christ" or "and of Jesus Christ our Lord."

11. On Paul and the prophetic tradition, see Christopher R. Seitz, *Colossians*, BTCB (Grand Rapids: Brazos, 2014), 57–59. The prophetic, proclamatory space of God corresponds to and blends with the precreational realm of God. See below on Col 1:15–20.

anointed superior figure by messianic designation, not as a resident of Colossae or as a Roman functionary. This presentation implicitly argues for Christ Jesus in higher rank, status, and power than others the audience members can imagine. Paul is presented as an emissary of this Christ, by God's will. The audience members live under the same authority. All this argues already for a particularized religious, social, and political situation that guides the rest of the letter.[12]

Translation

> **1:1** Paul, an apostle of Christ Jesus by God's will, and Timothy, the brother, **1:2** to the holy and faithful brothers and sisters in Christ[13] in Colossae, Grace and peace to you from our Father God.[14]

Textural Commentary

Opening-middle-closing texture.[15] The opening texture of the introductory rhetoric is clearly formed by the epistolary prescript of 1:1–2. This opening sets up a rhetorical, communicative context from the outset of the letter where Paul possesses an authoritative, prophetic voice, and "the holy and faithful brothers [and sisters] in Christ in Colossae" are the receivers of the message from the prophetic voice. They receive a blessing-greeting already from the beginning. This opening sets the rhetorical expectation that good and probably helpful discourse will follow.

Inner textures generate understanding about how texts work internally to communicate their pictures and messages.

Repetitive texture indicates rhetorical patterns, movements, and contents.[16] Repetitions of words, phrases, and grammatical constructions form patterns of ideas that arouse expectations in audience members' minds. The expectations may be subtle, frequently unrecognized, but are rhetori-

---

12. Which situation has Jewish intertextures that would be intertexturally-contextually important to someone such as Paul.

13. Some manuscripts read ἐν Χριστῷ Ἰησοῦ, "in Christ Jesus."

14. Some manuscripts add καὶ κυρίου Ἰησοῦ Χριστοῦ, "and Lord Jesus Christ," or καὶ Ἰησοῦ Χριστοῦ τοῦ κυρίου ἡμῶν, "and Jesus Christ our Lord."

15. The introductory rhetoric has its own *opening* (1:1–2)-*middle* (1:3–23)-*closing* (1:24–2:5) *textures*, which are analyzed as the commentary progresses.

16. Robbins, *Exploring the Textures of Texts*, 8.

SCENE ONE: INTRODUCTORY RHETORIC

cally influential.[17] There are a surprising number of functional repetitions of words and ideas in the introductory rhetoric that begin already in this first step and recur in the letter. Paul's name (Παῦλος) stands out from the beginning, and repetition of it in 1:23 forms an *inclusio* that frames the introductory ideas in the voice of a specified speaker.[18] The repetition of first-person "I" verbs through to 2:5 continues this emphasis. The denotation of Paul as "apostle of Christ Jesus" and the image of believers situated "in Christ" (ἐν Χριστῷ) forms an early repetition of Christ words that become dramatically significant as the letter progresses. Χριστοῦ, Χριστοῦ Ἰησοῦ, or Ἰησοῦ Χριστοῦ occur five times in the introductory rhetoric and eleven times in Colossians. The phrase ἐν Χριστῷ (or ἐν Χριστῷ Ἰησοῦ) occurs three times (1:2, 4, 28), setting things up for the many pronouns and phrases that refer to Christ subsequently: "beloved Son"; "in whom"; "he is"; "he"; "through him"; "his flesh"; "in front of him."[19] These repetitions indicate and emphasize the authors' distinct Christ Jesus (christological) orientation that shapes the entire rhetorical presentation.[20] This step begins repetitions of kinship, where occurrences of "brother(s)" and "holy ones" indicate an awareness of people who are connected in close relationship. Timothy is "the brother"; the Colossian addressees are "holy and faithful brothers in Christ."[21] The term "holy ones" is repeated in 1:4, 12, 22. These kinship repetitions are picked up and matched by "you" pronouns throughout the letter. Tychicus and the Laodicean believers are also called "brother(s)" (4:7, 15). The kinship repetitions demonstrate that the relationship among the faithful persons portrayed has a sanctified and familial nature. The designation "God" occurs first in 1:1 but is repeated in 1:3, 6, 10, 15, situating God as the prime mover in the overall action and

---

17. Repetitions or reduplications amplify ideas and evoke emotional responses in listeners' minds. See Rhet. Her. 4.28.38.

18. The name "Paul" recurs in the closing greeting in 4:18.

19. The dative phrase σὺν Χριστῷ or equivalent occurs later four times (2:20; 3:1, 3, 24). Forms of Χριστός occur twenty-five times in Colossians. Pronominal phrases such as "in him," "in whom," and "in the Lord" occur multiple times. See the list in Charles H. Talbert, *Ephesians and Colossians*, Paideia (Grand Rapids: Baker Academic, 2007), 180.

20. The name "Jesus" always appears together with "Christ" in Colossians except at 3:17. Even there, however, the wording "the Lord Jesus" is a natural progression from "the word of Christ" in 3:16.

21. The Greek ἀδελφοί, "brothers," is inclusive. See n. 5 above.

ideas described.²² God is tied closely to the repeated word *Father*, indicating kinship of a higher level because God is "*our* God" and "*our* Father" (θεοῦ πατρὸς ἡμῶν, 1:2), and the father of "*our* Lord Jesus Christ" (1:3; see 1:12, 3:17). Understanding God as Father elaborates the understanding of God as the prime mover. This first step also introduces the repeated notion that God has a will, in 1:9 and later in 4:12. This repetition grounds the discourse and the prayers for the audiences in the idea of God's will. Paul acts as an apostle by the will of God, and the audiences are meant to mature, knowing God's will (1:9). The repetition binds apostle and audiences prophetically to God's will and sets in mind a vision of a relationship with God for productive, wisdom living. Additionally interesting in this light is the signal given by the repetition of the word *grace*, which is directed toward the audiences (1:2) and has its natural source in God (1:6). A final word of grace closes the letter, forming a rather grand *inclusio* of grace at 4:18 (ἡ χάρις μεθ' ὑμῶν).

What emerges is that repetitive textures begin or are signaled in the first introductory step and have implications for the rhetoric of the entire sequence and the entire letter. They aim, already at this early stage of the discourse, at the wisdom goals of Colossians. They begin to set a grand framework of ideas to which receptivity is strongly encouraged. Readers and listeners are already stimulated to nod their heads in agreement, perhaps with glimpses of things to come in the letter, yet without knowing where the ideas will lead as the rhetoric moves along.

Narrational texture evokes interpretation of the voice(s) of the person(s) implied to be presenting the discourse and begins to indicate the flow of narrative storyline in which the rhetography, texturing, and blendings are set.²³ The implied and envisioned (or virtual) narrator throughout the entire letter is Paul. While first-person plural verbs tie Timothy and probably other coworkers to Paul as participants in scene one (1:1–23), Paul's explicitly first-person singular and dominating voice

---

22. θεός is repeated 21 times in Colossians.

23. "The voices through which the words in texts speak" (Robbins, *Exploring the Textures of Texts*, 15). *Narrational texture* depends on the narrator, the voice or person with a voice, not on audience(s). *Narrational texture* indicates what a narrator puts into the message(s) being conveyed, overarching and omniscient/omnipresent understandings that guide and explain. It is characterized by the flow of ideas that are being stated aloud, as it were, and by explanation of what is going on or what is being visualized.

(e.g., ἐγὼ Παῦλος, 1:23; εἰμι, 2:5) is heard throughout the letter. Even when pronouns and the subject of verbs that refer to the voice change to plurals (εὐχαριστοῦμεν, ἡμῶν, ἡμεῖς, ἠκούσαμεν) to include at least Timothy in the flow of thought, it is still clear that implied Paul is the narrator of the letter (as in 1:23–25, 29; 2:1–5).

As narration begins, virtual Paul introduces himself, identifies himself by offering his distinct credential as "an apostle of Christ Jesus by the will of God," and places himself and Timothy in speaking and therefore in authoritative prophetic space as the persons directing the situation coming into view and the language describing it. The narration places "the holy and faithful brothers in Christ in Colossae" in the role of receivers of the narration and as the persons being informed by it. They are the implied listeners who engage with the narrator's message and are expected to accept and act wisely on Paul's prophetic advice. By offering the specialized greeting "grace and peace," the narrator welcomes the audience into the rhetoric and mediates benefits to them from God. The greeting serves as an invitation to engage with whatever is presented as the narration goes along and draws listeners into it. Paul's authoritative narration as apostle by God's will is matched, later in the introductory sequence and in light of what he has narrated to the holy ones, by the self-designation "servant" (διάκονος, 1:25) of the hope of the gospel. But here in step one the narrator introduces himself and Timothy, though Timothy's voice is not heard. This first step in narrational texture makes Paul's implied voice clearly heard and signals that the text is a letter communication. This texturing establishes the apostolic, authoritative sense of the entire letter.

The first *progressive texture* is the sequence and progression of words and phrases that emerge out of repetition.[24] Progression is the forward movement from-to. The progression here indicates movement *from* Paul an apostle of Christ Jesus *to* the holy and faithful brothers and sisters in Christ in Colossae, from one person to a group of persons. The move occurs in the priestly greeting statement "grace and peace to you from our Father God." The progression arouses the expectation of intriguing and beneficial communication since both Paul (as apostle) and the Colossians (as holy and faithful brothers and sisters) are imagined as people implicitly expected to be wise and productive. As brothers like Timothy,

---

24. Robbins, *Exploring the Textures of Texts*, 9–10.

the Colossians are expected to be concerned for others. The progression evokes the social anticipation of more information to follow.

Analysis of *sensory-aesthetic texture* involves looking at "the range of senses the text evokes or embodies (thought, emotion, sight, sound, touch, smell, taste, balance, temperature, pain, location) and the manner in which the text evokes or embodies them (reason, intuition, imagination, humor, disgust, etc.)."[25] Sensory-aesthetic texturing has to do with features that indicate or reflect things that are discerned through visual, oral, aural, olfactory, tactile, gustatory, textual, prosaic, poetic, intellectual, and emotional sensibilities.[26] Sensory, human, and living features play a powerful role in the communication of faith understandings.[27] Wording in texts exhibits a feel and an appearance that make it recognizable and that establishes expectations regarding its rhetorical form and function. Appeal is made to the bodily sensory-aesthetic responses such as sounds, to the sensory-aesthetic qualities of being, personality, intellect, and affections, and to sensory-aesthetic prophetic, priestly, and wisdom activity and spaces.[28] Texts can appeal to the eyes when they are written in pleasing styles, and words are recognized visually by shape as much as by linguistic form.

In the first rhetorical step there are already several clear sensory-aesthetic qualities. As the rhetography indicates, sensibilities of persons, places, and activities are placed in the imagination. The sensory actions and qualities of being, personality, affections, and intellect belong to the "zone of emotion-fused thought" and are observed and felt in the texturing of the

---

25. Robbins, *Exploring the Textures of Texts*, 29–30. "Attentiveness to sensory-aesthetic texture may reveal dimensions that provide tone and perhaps even color to the discourse." Many things may be understood as hard, soft, loud, quiet, dramatic, harsh, angry, belligerent, etc.

26. In addition to the traditionally recognized five senses (sight, sound, smell, touch, taste), there are many other human senses such as proprioception, thermoception, balance, pain, hunger, and thirst. Some features will be sensory and aesthetic to some and less so to others. A person's perceptions relate to taste and sense of physicality, color, beauty, culturation, and education. But there are some sensory-aesthetic universals that are perceived by most people.

27. On sensory-aesthetic connections with the sublime, see Roy R. Jeal, ed., *Exploring Sublime Rhetoric in Biblical Literature*, ESEC 28 (Atlanta: SBL Press, 2024).

28. Sounds, according to Bruce Malina's taxonomy, belong to the "zone of self-expressive speech" (see Robbins, *Exploring the Textures of Texts*, 30–31). The sensory-aesthetic prophetic, priestly, and wisdom activity and spaces belong to the zone of purposeful action.

rhetoric.²⁹ The descriptions of Paul and Timothy, of speaking and writing, and of holy and faithful people who have a (fictive) kinship relationship indicate physical and mental qualities. God has a will, hence a conscious desire for Paul to be an apostle. Implied Paul indicates affection and warmth in his greeting wish of "grace and peace."³⁰ God is "God our Father," understood as provider of the benefits of grace and peace. Speaking (by Paul) and hearing (by the Colossians) are primary sensory-aesthetic textures at play. The text itself, though, offers the sensory-aesthetic texture of ear and sound in melodic, rhythmic patterning. Prose texts exhibit patterns and rhythms in ways different from poetry, but patterns are there in a natural rhetoric. These patterns form melopoeia, the orchestration of sound in language that attracts attention, enhances the flow of language, and helps to convey meaning.³¹ There is patterning even in New Testament letter prescripts:

Παῦλος ἀπόστολος Χριστοῦ Ἰησοῦ
διὰ θελήματος θεοῦ
καὶ Τιμόθεος ὁ ἀδελφὸς
τοῖς ἐν Κολοσσαῖς ἁγίοις καὶ πιστοῖς ἀδελφοῖς ἐν Χριστῷ
χάρις ὑμῖν καὶ εἰρήνη
ἀπὸ θεοῦ πατρὸς ἡμῶν.

This verbless opening begins with two nominative nouns (Παῦλος ἀπόστολος), followed by two genitive nouns (Χριστοῦ Ἰησοῦ), followed in turn by two more genitives (διὰ θελήματος θεοῦ). This use of *homoeoptoton*³² provides an attractive sensory sound. The following nominatives (Τιμόθεος ὁ ἀδελφὸς) balance the two initial nominative nouns with pleasing sound. The chain of dative plurals (τοῖς ἐν Κολοσσαῖς ἁγίοις καὶ πιστοῖς ἀδελφοῖς) combined with the dative singular ἐν Χριστῷ gives further effective *homoeoptoton*. The greeting χάρις ὑμῖν καὶ εἰρήνη ἀπὸ θεοῦ πατρὸς ἡμῶν is a bal-

---

29. Robbins, *Exploring the Textures of Texts*, 30–31.

30. Although Hellenistic letters characteristically had a greeting statement, Colossians' christianized "grace and peace" greeting is sincere, reflecting genuine affection.

31. On melopoeia or "sound orchestration," see Ezra Pound, *How to Read* (New York: Haskell House, 1971). For analysis, see Roy R. Jeal, "Melody, Imagery and Memory in the Moral Persuasion of Paul," in *Rhetoric, Ethic, and Moral Persuasion in Biblical Discourse*, ed. Thomas H. Olbricht and Anders Eriksson, ESEC 11 (New York: T&T Clark, 2005), 160–78.

32. Where words appear in the same case and with the same terminations, producing a rhythmic, ear-pleasing effect (Rhet. Her. 4.20.28).

anced statement of two parts with eight syllables each. Verbless statements are aesthetically attractive precisely because they are clearly understood in the absence of verbs. They speak to the immediacy of a moment.[33] These sensory-aesthetic features present a rhetorical tone from the first words of Colossians that indicate the congenial disposition of the implied speaker and aim to evoke the receptive disposition of the audience. The authoritative (prophetic) speaker-writer-narrator cheerfully recognizes the holy and faithful people and intercedes for them with wishes for their well-being in Christ.

While Col 1:1–2 provides what looks straightforwardly like a standard New Testament letter greeting, examination of the texturing indicates that warmth, emotion, goodwill, and good wishes are conveyed by nouns, adjectives, and prepositions. Paul and Timothy in expressive speech have set out prophetic and priestly sensibilities aimed at producing sensory effects among the audience members.

As the rhetoric emerges, the prophetic role of Paul surfaces and with it the first, quite straightforward *argumentative texturing*:

> **Case:** Paul is an apostle of Christ Jesus.
> **Rationale:** Because it is God's will.
> **Implicit Result:** The recipients of the message are expected to receive the message.

The argument amounts to a persuasive social imperative: receive the message(s) in the letter. This is, of course, what holy and faithful brothers and sisters would be presumed to do with a message from apostolic, prophetic Paul. The reasoning is supported by the greeting of grace and peace, which indicates Paul's good feelings toward the recipients and his priestly reliance on God to provide the grace and peace. The implication is that God will indeed provide grace and peace for the recipients. A friendly, amenable situation is elicited.

"**Intertexture** is a text's representation of, reference to, and use of phenomena in the 'world' outside the text being interpreted."[34] Analysis

---

33. Ezra Pound believed that avoiding verbs intensified metaphors. See his poem "In a Station of the Metro," in *Personae: The Collected Poems of Ezra Pound* (New York: New Directions, 1926), 111; see also Northrop Frye's comment in *Anatomy of Criticism* (Princeton: Princeton University Press, 1957), 123.

34. Robbins, *Exploring the Textures of Texts*, 40.

SCENE ONE: INTRODUCTORY RHETORIC   45

involves determining the nature and effect of this texturing. **Intertexture** is not always observed in a quotation but may be any point of contact with language or concepts or other phenomena outside a text. **Intertexture** may involve cultural, social, and historical knowledge and phenomena that are explicit or implicit in a text.[35] Texts configure phenomena outside themselves to create relationships among ideas. The New Testament letters, Colossians in particular, draw on known language and ideas in order to speak about Christ Jesus.[36] This is an important feature in the production of emergent rhetorical discourse. It draws on language and ideas from the cultural milieux that are in the air—or at least in an author's-speaker's air[37]—in order to convey information that would be understood and promote wisdom living. **Intertexture** might involve a quotation or direct word connection with another text but can take other forms. Words can be recited, recontextualized, reconfigured, amplified, and elaborated.[38]

Colossians does not recite or quote directly from the Old Testament/Hebrew Bible/LXX. There are, however, many intertextures with the world of texts and other phenomena outside the letter.[39] The obvious intertextures with this first step in Colossians are the usages in other letters in the Pauline corpus, in the New Testament, and in ancient Hellenistic letters generally. The Pauline and New Testament letters typically, if not always, begin with similar statements (see Rom 1:1, 7; 1 Cor 1:1–2; 2 Cor 1:1–2; Gal 1:1–3; Eph 1:1; Phil 1:1–2; 1 Thess 1:1; Phlm 1–3; 1 Pet 1:1–2; Jude 1–2). Colossians names Timothy as cosender with Paul, an unusual practice in Hellenistic letters[40] though not uncommon in the Pauline letters (see 2 Cor 1:1; Phil 1:1; 1 Thess 1:1; 2 Thess 1:1; Phlm 1). Identifying Paul as "apostle … by the will of God" is a frequent feature of the letters (1 Cor 1:1, 2 Cor 1:1, Eph 1:1, 2 Tim 1:1) and sets a rhetorical tone of legitimation

---

35. Robbins, *Exploring the Textures of Texts*, 58–68.
36. Drawing primarily on the memory of language and ideas.
37. For example, the standard epistolary form that Paul employs and adapts to communicate his apostolic concern for people and churches.
38. See Robbins, *Exploring the Textures of Texts*, 40–58. See also Christopher A. Beetham, *Echoes of Scripture in the Letter of Paul to the Colossians* (Leiden: Brill, 2010), 15–35. Beetham describes quotations, allusions, and echoes as modes of intertextuality.
39. See Roy R. Jeal, "Sociorhetorical Intertexture," in *Exploring Intertextuality*, ed. B. J. Oropeza and Steve Moyise (Eugene, OR: Cascade, 2016), 151–64.
40. Andrew T. Lincoln, "Colossians," *NIB* 11:587, citing E. Randolph Richards, *The Secretary in the Letters of Paul*, WUNT 2/42 (Tübingen: Mohr-Siebeck, 1991).

for Paul's work and for the letter.⁴¹ Timothy is included as "the brother" (see 2 Cor 1:1; Phlm 1). Being an "apostle of Christ Jesus" connects Paul and his apostolic work to Christ and the entire tradition of which the audience members are now part, and with the messianic traditions that preceded them (e.g., Pss 22, 69, Isa 53). Calling the audience members "holy ones" draws on Jewish usage for description of the people of God (e.g., Num 16:5; LXX Ps 15:3; Dan 7:18; Wis 18:9; 1QM III, 5), here reshaped to include gentiles faithful to Christ Jesus in Colossae (see Acts 9:13, Rom 1:7, 1 Cor 1:2). While Colossians is the only Pauline letter to refer to its recipients as "holy and faithful brothers," the family/kinship imagery it suggests along with God as Father shares texturing employed elsewhere in the rhetoric of New Testament letter introductions (e.g., Rom 1:7; 1 Cor 1:3; 2 Cor 1:2; Gal 1:1, 3, 4; Eph 1:2; Phil 1:2; 2 Thess 1:2; 1 Tim 1:2; 2 Tim 1:2; Titus 1:4; Phlm 3; 1 Pet 1:2; 2 John 3). The idea of God as Father was known in Hebrew texts (e.g., Deut 32:6; Isa 63:16; Wis 2:16; Pss. Sol. 13.9) and in Hellenistic traditions where Zeus is described as father (e.g., Homer, *Il.* 1.503, 533). Here it is clearly the God of Israel who is in mind and as Col 1:3 makes clear. The family and particularly the father intertextures were entirely sensible in ancient Mediterranean cultures where family members and fathers were to be honored and where God was to be honored by families (see Sir 3:10; Philo, *Spec.* 1.316). The typical χαῖρε or χαίρειν "Greeting!" statement is reshaped and recontextualized with "grace and peace from God our Father," apparently drawing on both gospel (grace) and Jewish (shalom) notions. The wish for peace draws intertexturally on the idea of wholeness, health, and contentment, of flourishing rather than the notion of the absence of conflict in physical or psychological senses. The "in Christ" phrase is widespread in the Pauline letters, texturing the rhetoric with a locative, incorporated, and relational feel and visuality.⁴²

Compared to the broader intertextual context of Hellenistic letters, Colossians (and other Pauline letters) reshapes and recontextualizes the rhetoric of the prescript to suit social and rhetorical exigencies. The intertextures of this first step take on traditional Hellenistic letter and early Christian cultural and social understandings and reshape them in a particularly Christian epistolary rhetoric. Ideas and forms from several spaces are blended together to create a Christian intertextural rhetoric

---

41. See James D. G. Dunn, *The Epistles to the Colossians and to Philemon*, NIGTC (Grand Rapids: Eerdmans, 1996), 46.

42. Perhaps also an instrumental or agency rhetoric, as in 1 Cor 1:4.

SCENE ONE: INTRODUCTORY RHETORIC 47

particularly discernible by Christ-believing audiences who recognize the discourse.[43] The intertextures are not only epistolary and scribal; they are cultural and social, where the concepts of apostle (as an authority figure), of being holy people and faithful brothers existing in Christ, of grace and peace, and of God as their Father are understood by persons who live in a Christian context and therefore grasp the rhetorical intertextures in specific ways.[44] What this intertexturing shows is that Colossians is set in and employs rhetoric understood by Christ believers. The rhetoric shapes the letter to influence an informed and agreeable audience.

Social and cultural texture. It is important to consider the holy and faithful Christ believers in Colossae from the perspective of the spaces in which they lived and the ideas and ideologies of the social and cultural milieux of the Asian provinces that were brought to mind when they heard the words and nuances of the letter. Social and cultural forces related to living in the empire had critically important implications for the gospel and for their trust in Christ Jesus.[45]

Social and cultural spaces: The dominant culture consciousness. The believers in Colossae lived in multiple spaces or cultural environments simultaneously. Among these spaces, they are most immediately observed in the dual sociocultural space of a moderately important city in the Lycus Valley and an early Christ-movement *ekklēsia*. These spaces naturally carry with them social, behavioral, and religious expectations of both the city-region and believers' faith and community. As residents of Colossae, they have social, cultural, political, and religious connections with other Phrygian and Asian locations such as the explicitly noted nearby cities Laodicea and Hierapolis (2:1; 4:13, 15, 16), and with regional locations such as Aphrodisias, Apamea, and others.[46] As members of the *ekklēsia*,

---

43. See Dunn, *Epistles to the Colossians and to Philemon*, 51.

44. On social and cultural intertextures, see Robbins, *Exploring the Textures of Texts*, 58–68. On Paul as an authority figure, see Margaret Y. MacDonald, *Colossians and Ephesians*, SP 17 (Collegeville, MN: Liturgical Press, 2000), 33–36.

45. The notion of mental (and physical) spaces and their importance is here drawn primarily from Gilles Fauconnier and Mark Turner and their understanding of conceptual blending (*Way We Think*).

46. See the regional sociocultural and geographical information in Huttner, *Early Christianity in the Lycus Valley*; Alan H. Cadwallader and Michael Trainor, eds., *Colossae in Space and Time: Linking to an Ancient City* (Göttingen: Vandenhoeck & Ruprecht, 2011); Alan H. Cadwallader, *Fragments of Colossae: Sifting through the Traces* (Hindmarsh, Australia: ATF, 2015). On Aphrodisias, see Harry O. Maier, "Paul,

they are a community characterized by particular beliefs that have their own social, cultural, political and religious connections and expectations that in turn have implications for life in the city.[47] It is evident that these spaces stand in tension with one another at a number of critical points.

Always present with the holy and faithful *ekklēsia* in Colossae was the consciousness of the dominating presence and cultural influences of the eastern provinces (Asia Minor) and the larger Roman world. The dominant culture in a location (or region) sets the identity markers that indicate the attitudes, values, and norms functioning in the location. These markers become so well known that they are presupposed and implicitly understood by people living with them. Social structures develop to support and impose the dominant culture and its identity so that people are *seen* to be in conformity or nonconformity to the culture and its demands.[48] There are often subcultures that imitate and reflect the dominant culture and claim to observe the features of the dominant culture more closely than others. Members of subcultures imagine that they understand and practice the cultural demands correctly and that they should point out both their own understandings and the shortcomings of others. While many cultural features were influential, one remarkable and major dominant cultural phenomenon with its own rhetoric for people living in Colossae and the region and for New Testament interpretation was religious consciousness.

Many studies have made it clear that the Roman empire and the Pax Romana were maintained not only by massive, diverse, and often brutal military, political, and economic powers.[49] Religion, in varied forms and with multiple deities, was dramatically prominent and powerfully influential as a sociocultural and pragmatic phenomenon. Religion pervaded

---

Imperial Situation, and Visualization in the Epistle to the Colossians," in *The Art of Visual Exegesis: Rhetoric, Texts, Images*, ed. Vernon K. Robbins, Walter S. Melion, and Roy R. Jeal, ESEC 19 (Atlanta: SBL Press, 2017), 188–91.

47. On early Christian community identity and outside relationships, see Huttner, *Early Christianity*, 5–7.

48. On dominant culture, see Robbins, *Exploring the Textures of Texts*, 86–88.

49. Life in the Roman Mediterranean was difficult for the vast majority or persons. The wealthy believed they possessed power over the poor by natural right. Peace was imposed by power. According to Mary Beard, the historian Tacitus (ca. 56–120 CE) referred to Romans as "the robbers of the world, insatiable for domination and profit" and said of Roman efforts at domination that "they create desolation and call it peace" (*SPQR*, 511). See Epictetus, who suggested that Caesar could give peace from war but not from fever, shipwreck, or sorrow (*Diatr.* 3.13.9–11).

the social fabric of the ancient Mediterranean. Roman power was imagined to exist and be supported by having the gods on the Roman side. Having the gods on one's side was acquired and maintained by ritual observances: "Their pious devotion guaranteed their success."[50] Failure was considered to be due to having made religious errors.[51] "Religion ... underwrote Roman power."[52] In other words, conquest and prosperity were understood to be due to practicing good works in the form of rituals that were designed and believed to keep the gods happy.[53] Religion had little concern for personal morality, sin, or character formation.[54] In the Roman provinces of Asia Minor, certainly in Phrygia, the province in which Colossae was located, and indeed in Colossae itself, many religions and deities were influential in these ways, including ritual worship of Cybele (the Great Mother goddess), Artemis, Tyche, Apollo, and Zeus, the ruler of all gods and patron god of Laodicea.[55] While there was a Jewish

---

50. Beard, *SPQR*, 102.

51. Bruce W. Longenecker, *In Stone and Story: Early Christians in the Roman World* (Grand Rapids: Baker Academic, 2020), 52: "What really mattered was success—success at every level of existence: personal, neighborhood, civic, regional, national, and international forms of success. Worshiping the deities was part of the formula for success at all these levels. Consequently, if misfortune struck at any level, it was natural to assume that devotion to the deities had gone wrong in some way." This was encultured in Mediterranean societies. As Longenecker points out, "For the vast majority of his [Paul's] contemporaries, temples were critical components in the smooth running of society" (39).

52. On all this see Beard, *SPQR*, 101–3.

53. So, as Beard points out, religion was not concerned with salvation or morality in the ways Christians or the New Testament perceived them (*SPQR*, 103).

54. Longenecker, *In Stone and Story*, 52: "For many people, honoring the deities and making offerings to them may have had little to do with rectifying moral failings in their own character—either making restitution for their past failings or preventing their future failings. Honoring the deities was often an exercise in pragmatic self-advancement; people offered reverence to the deities in order to enhance their prospects."

55. On Tyche, see the related name Tychicus in Col 4:7. On Apollo, see Huttner, *Early Christianity*, 44–48. On Zeus, see Huttner, *Early Christianity*, 42–66. See especially Alan H. Cadwallader, "The Gods in City and Country," in *Fragments of Colossae*, 45–73. This chapter includes much inscriptional and numismatic evidence. Cadwallader suggests that Zeus might have been patron god of Colossae (67). On Cybele, see "Cult in Phrygia (Asia Minor)," Theoi Greek Mythology, https://tinyurl.com/SBL7106c. On Tyche, see "Cult in Lydia (Asia Minor)," Theoi Greek Mythology, https://tinyurl.com/SBL7106d.

population in Hierapolis, Laodicea, and the Maeander River Valley that, like Jews elsewhere in the empire, had legal privilege to practice their own traditions and rituals such as Sabbath observance, there is no completely clear evidence of Jews resident in Colossae.[56]

One of the developments of ritualistic worship that sought to please the gods and meet recognizable social expectations was devotion to the imperial cult of emperor worship.[57] The autocratic emperor was the figurehead and guardian of the empire, the symbol of authority who was imagined to take on divine features in order to maintain power and general peace.[58] Christopher Mackay points out,

---

56. Huttner argues for a significant Jewish population in the Lycus including Hierapolis and Laodicea, but his reconstructions do not offer clear evidence for Jewish residents in the city of Colossae (*Early Christianity*, 67–79). Alan H. Cadwallader states, "There is simply no evidence for Jews at Colossae between [= from] the first and [= to the] twelfth century." See Cadwallader, "On the Question of Comparative Method in Historical Research: Colossae and Chonai in Larger Frame," in Harrison and Welborn, *First Urban Churches 5*, 131–32. Cadwallader suggests that the Jewish-sounding terms may be more "rhetorical than historical." See the commentary on Col 2:16–17 below.

57. The connection of the imperial cult to New Testament studies has been something of a growth industry in recent years. Many scholars have written on the topic, including Richard A. Horsley, *Paul and Empire: Religion and Power in Roman Imperial Society* (Harrisburg, PA: Trinity Press International, 1997); Horsley, ed., *In the Shadow of Empire: Reclaiming the Bible as a History of Faithful Resistance* (Louisville; Westminster John Knox, 2008); Jeffrey Brodd and Jonathan L. Reed, eds., *Rome and Religion: A Cross-Disciplinary Dialogue on the Imperial Cult*, WGRWSup 5 (Atlanta: Society of Biblical Literature, 2011); Warren Carter, *The Roman Empire and the New Testament: An Essential Guide* (Nashville: Abingdon, 2006); John L. White, *The Apostle of God: Paul and the Promise of Abraham* (Peabody, MA: Hendrickson, 1999), 110–35; Brigitte Kahl, *Galatians Re-imagined: Reading with the Eyes of the Vanquished* (Minneapolis: Fortress, 2010); Bruce W. Winter, *Divine Honours for the Caesars: The First Christian Responses* (Grand Rapids: Eerdmans, 2015); Maier, *Picturing Paul in Empire*; N. T. Wright, *Paul and the Faithfulness of God* (Minneapolis: Fortress, 2013), 1271–1319; Adam Winn, ed., *An Introduction to Empire in the New Testament* (Atlanta: SBL Press, 2016). On Colossians in particular, see Brian J. Walsh and Sylvia Keesmaat, *Colossians Remixed: Subverting the Empire* (Downers Grove, IL: InterVarsity Press, 2004). The general force of these publications is about the perceived resistance of the New Testament and early Christianity to Roman power and to emperor worship. There is significant debate about the topic.

58. See Longenecker, *In Stone and Story*, 43: "As long as devotion was directed toward the emperor in one fashion or another, people were thought to be exercising their proper duty to the overarching system that had been set in place and legitimated by the deities of Rome. Artifacts and texts from the ancient world repeatedly

> While the imperial government of the Principate [27 BCE to 235 CE] did not intrude directly into most people's daily lives, the concept of the emperor was nonetheless a widespread symbol of authority. The subjects and citizens of the Empire gave expression to their loyalty through a common institution that makes little sense to those whose religious sensibilities are based on the single god of the Judeo-Christian tradition.... In the Greco-Roman conception the "divine" was considered to be anything that had supernatural abilities. This basic premise then gave rise to the habit of granting divine honors to kings.... If you imagine the divine to possess powers that impress those normal humans, then it is not entirely unreasonable to include kings in such a category, since they have the ability to carry out acts that no mere mortal could conceive.... Caesar the dictator ... adopted some of the quasi-divine trappings of the Hellenistic kings in his abortive attempt to regularize his autocracy.[59]

Because Rome was the power center, many people, particularly the elite and others who desired social advancement, wished to associate themselves with that power. A major way of doing so was to engage in ritual worship of Roman deities. From the declaration of imperial divinity following the death of the first emperor, Augustus, onward, the imperial cult spread quickly. The figure and the image of the divine emperor served, as much as other foci of ritual and worship, to unite and sustain the diverse, multicultural, multilingual empire.[60] Cult practices were pervasive as an everyday feature of life in the Asian provinces with the presence of temples, shrines, priests, and regular ceremonies.[61]

While the worship of many Roman deities was widespread, including worship of the primary god Jupiter (= Zeus in the Greek pantheon), the identity of the gods was fluid across language and cultural barriers, so much so that Plutarch and Seneca, as two examples, considered that the various names of gods and the varying cultic activities used in various locations all referred to the same god (Plutarch, *Is. Os.* 67 [377f–378a];

---

testify that the modern differentiation of 'religion' and 'state' within separate spheres of life fails to do justice to the intricate connections between governance and the deities (including the emperor) that characterized the central nexus of power within the Roman world."

59. Christopher S. Mackay, *Ancient Rome: A Military and Political History* (Cambridge: Cambridge University Press, 2004), 258.

60. On this see James B. Rives, *Religion in the Roman Empire* (Oxford: Blackwell, 2007), 141, 148.

61. See Rives, *Religion in the Roman Empire*, 27, 151.

Seneca, *Ben.* 4.7–8).[62] James Rives points out that strategies developed to bring the diversity of deities together into a unity in the single and "concrete embodiment" of the emperor.[63] To sacrifice to a man was to treat him as a god (Plutarch, *Lys.* 18); thus the emperor could be reasonably understood as a god. The emperor was the beneficent power far away in Rome who provided peace, unity, and good things for the diverse peoples living in an extended empire: "The emperor was the only person in the empire who could bestow benefits on everyone without himself receiving benefits from everyone."[64] The imperial cult became fundamental to the operation of the empire:

> Moral legitimation of the emperor's rule was a central plank in the public presentation of imperial ideology. Concern for others and lack of self-interest were particularly prominent in such legitimation. Seneca writes, "God says: 'Let these men be kings because their forefathers have not been, because they have regarded justice and unselfishness as their highest authority, because, instead of sacrificing the state to themselves, they have sacrificed themselves to the state'" (*Ben.* 4.32.2).[65]

The notion of the unifying presence of the emperor, along with his own family (his household), was present everywhere, certainly in the Asian provinces. It was visible, even palpable, in temples, altars, coinage, and statuary in which the emperor often appeared as the enthroned Jupiter.[66]

The holy and faithful recipients of Colossians could scarcely have missed the not-so-subtle language in the letter that evokes knowledge of the divine emperor. They lived in the religious-cultural realm of the empire. But, as analysis goes along, it becomes clear that the perspective and rhetoric the letter presents is not about overt opposition or direct

---

62. For these references see Rives, *Religion in the Roman Empire*, 142–48. Rives states that this was a kind of theoretical monotheism (148).

63. Rives, *Religion in the Roman Empire*, 148–49.

64. Rives, *Religion in the Roman Empire*, 148–49.

65. Peter Oakes, "God's Sovereignty over Roman Authorities: A Theme in Philippians," in *Rome in the Bible and the Early Church*, ed. Oakes (Grand Rapids: Baker Academic, 2002), 136.

66. See especially Harry O. Maier, "Barbarians, Scythians and Imperial Iconography in the Epistle to the Colossians," in *Picturing the New Testament*, ed. Annette Weissenrieder, Friederike Wendt, and Petra von Gemünden, WUNT 2/193 (Tübingen: Mohr, 2005), 385–406; see also Rives, *Religion in the Roman Empire*, 148–56.

resistance to the ritualistic religions of the time, nor to the empire or the imperial cult. The concern, rather, is to emphasize that ritualistic and ascetic observances, experiences, and behaviors intended to keep the gods and God amenable and responsive to human needs are, at least religiously speaking, *irrelevant* for Christ believers. This can be imagined as revolutionary for the recipients of the letter. Relationship with God and Christ Jesus was not maintained by culturally understood pious devotion and ritual works. It is the gift of God.

Ideological texture is found in the rhetorical goal that texts aim to achieve among their audiences. This is the goal of creating a conscious world where audiences are affected by the text and are moved or persuaded to think and behave in accord with the symbolic world created by the texturing. The locus of this ideology is in the social, cultural, and religious location of the authors.[67] Analysis aims to come to an understanding of the ideology of the authors, of the ideology shared between authors and audiences, and the ideology evoked by the text and how it brings about change among audience members.[68]

We should not be surprised to see that the opening greeting in 1:1–2 is shaped rhetorically to move its audiences toward a point of view or frame of mind. Its rhetoric urges audiences to listen as Paul speaks, within God's will, from prophetic space. They are moved to openness to the prophetic speaker and the prophetic message. They will be likely to accept the priestly good wishes and the sense of kinship conveyed. They will recognize and be persuaded to begin thinking from a Christ-centered point of view. They will recognize themselves as "the holy and faithful brothers in Christ in Colossae" who already inhabit an ideological space that blends with Paul's space to form an implicit third space and ideology where listening and being shaped toward wisdom thinking and behavior is formed.[69] This first step in the rhetoric of Colossians challenges people to stay in the

---

67. See Robbins, *Exploring the Textures of Texts*, 111.

68. On **ideological texture**, see Roy R. Jeal, "Clothes Make the (Wo)Man," in *Foundations for Sociorhetorical Exploration: A Rhetoric of Religious Antiquity Reader*, ed. Vernon K. Robbins, Robert H. von Thaden, and Bart B. Bruehler, RRA 4 (Atlanta: SBL Press, 2016), 393–414; and L. Gregory Bloomquist, "Paul's Inclusive Language: The Ideological Texture of Romans 1," in *Fabrics of Discourse: Essays in Honor of Vernon K. Robbins*, ed. David B. Gowler, L. Gregory Bloomquist, and Duane F. Watson (Harrisburg, PA: Trinity Press International, 2003), 165–93.

69. In pastoral terms, this is spiritual formation.

space they have entered (see 1:6–7). They will begin developing a sense of identification with the wisdom the author wants to communicate.[70] The language of this step is their language because it is easily identified as corresponding to their beliefs, wishes, and ideology. Ideologically, this step begins to create a conscious world among the Colossian faithful that they recognize and inhabit. They are "in Christ" and live wisely as holy and faithful brothers and sisters. They receive grace and peace from "our God and Father." Living in this ideological space is clearly the right thing to do.

The presence of **sacred texture** figures prominently in the opening statement. The presence and will of God is perceived by virtual Paul, and in his priestly role he conveys the grace and peace of the Father God on the audience members.[71] Father God is one who blesses people. The realm of author and audience is clearly a sacred space where the author can be an apostle of Christ Jesus and the listeners are visualized functioning as holy and faithful people. Placed in the imagination from the outset of the letter is a deep sense of living a holy life in a holy space. This sacred space itself calls out to the audience to continue participating in holy and faithful living.

Rhetorical Force as Emergent Discourse

This first step in Colossians, the epistolary prescript, is, from a sociorhetorical point of view, surprisingly powerful emergent discourse. Obviously, it was recently written and recently received from the standpoint of the holy and faithful brothers and sisters in Colossae. It emerges as Hellenistic letter form reshaped as Christian epistolary rhetoric. This discourse engages its listeners with images, argumentation, and ideology that has their continuing and increasing holy and faithful behavior in mind. Kinship relationships involving Paul, Timothy, Christ Jesus, God, and the recipients of the discourse implicitly invite listeners toward continued listening and participation in productive faithfulness. The "in Christ" terminology enhances

---

70. On the rhetorical notion of identification, see Roy R. Jeal, *Integrating Theology and Ethics in Ephesians: The Ethos of Communication* (Lewiston, NY: Mellen, 2000), 67–70; Kenneth A. Burke, *A Rhetoric of Motives* (Berkeley: University of California Press, 1969), passim; and L. H. Mouat, "An Approach to Rhetorical Criticism," in *The Rhetorical Idiom*, ed. D. C. Bryant (New York: Russel & Russel, 1966), 161–77.

71. "The role of the priest is to act on behalf of others." John W. Rogerson, *Perspectives on the Passion* (Sheffield: Beauchief Abbey, 2014), 68.

the relational feel. Such congenial tone and coloring of language produces a receptive disposition toward what follows in the letter. The prophetic first space and priestly second space of Paul begin already to generate a blended wisdom third space where the faithful in Colossae live. This discourse is the emergent and understandable language of the Colossians because it corresponds to their emergent Christ-believing ideology. At this early stage in the letter, the idea is already forming that living in wisdom third space is the right thing to do. The first rhetorical step in Colossians has power, a sense of direction, a strong impact, and an implied result.

Step Two: Paul's Priestly-Prophetic Prayers for People in Wisdom Space (1:3–8)

Rhetography

The second step portrays Paul and Timothy describing their prayers of thanks to Father God for the holy ones in Colossae. Paul and Timothy appear as honest, sincere men who are genuinely thankful for the believers. The picture expands (*ekphrasis*) with the presentation of Paul and Timothy in regular prayers ("always") of thanksgiving, emphasizing their priestly actions for people.[72] God in this verse is now visualized as "the Father God of our Lord Jesus Christ," creating a particular vision of God's identity and God's relationship to Jesus Christ.[73] Visioning Jesus as Lord and Christ shows him as master and Father God's anointed, hence in a much more exalted position than the visible Colossian humans, for whom God is "our" Father God. In all of this, audiences visualize Paul and Timothy as persons who pray; indeed, they mentally observe Paul and Timothy praying for them. The rhetograph produces images of the friendship, the sense of kinship, and the benevolent activity Paul and Timothy practice for the believers.[74] Paul and Timothy are also listeners who have heard about the faith and love the Colossians have for all their fellow holy ones (1:4).

---

72. The repeated thanksgivings and prayers (πάντοτε ... προσευχόμενοι) may point to Paul's Jewish and regular habit of daily prayer.

73. There are many theological, biblical, and rhetorical connections and implications of the concept of father. Father can be understood as originator, creator, progenitor, or as one who cares for people as a parent.

74. A *captatio benevolentiae* that has the effect of eliciting a positive emotional response toward Paul and Timothy, thus pathos, an **inner texture**.

Paul and Timothy are therefore seen as persons who closely observe how people "in Christ Jesus" relate to others.

While listeners picture Paul and Timothy engaging in the priestly activities of prayer, thanksgiving, and listening for reports about the holy ones, they also envision themselves entering the picture as people of character who possess and practice faith and love. Their faith and love are founded in the hope stored up for them in the heavens (plural, ἐν τοῖς οὐρανοῖς), a notion evoking visualization of a location, a created space (see 1:16, 20), where good things are being kept for them (1:5). Hope is visualized objectively as a *thing* stored up, not subjectively as the thoughts or actions of *hoping*. This hope is a presently existing thing, not the anticipation of something that will come to exist in the future. This present hope is eventually seen in direct connection with Christ, "the hope of glory" (1:27; see 3:11), who is "above ... seated at God's right hand" (3:1). The stored-up hope thus eventually becomes envisaged as a person, Christ himself.[75] The believers' knowledge of this stored-up hope is imagined as having been heard by them at an earlier time, indicated in the appositional statement "the word of the truth of the gospel" that comes to them (1:6a).[76] The listeners are people who know the word of truth, the gospel, which speaks of stored-up hope. By this point the picture has expanded to include the Colossians themselves as knowledgeable listeners so that all of the visible participants in the letter (Paul, Timothy, the audiences) have been brought into view. Listeners to the letter by now have a mental image of the speakers and of themselves that gives a clear idea of the logistical situation, that is, where each stands relative to each other and to the letter. The gospel message that has been proclaimed, heard, and believed appears under the grand and congenial word of *truth*. This is very upbeat imagery, encouraging, because in a few words it brings about a comprehensive vision of a happy, pleasing situation.[77] All of the persons visualized form a community of faithful listeners.

This rhetography appears out of the blended priestly discourse where prophetic, wisdom, and apocalyptic discourse textures explain and support the priestly activity. The speakers address the recipients from the

---

75. Barth and Blanke, *Colossians*, 170–72.

76. Where "the gospel" stands in apposition to "the word of truth." The present participle παρόντος suggests that the gospel continues to come to them.

77. This moves the rhetography to rhetology, i.e., how the imagery functions to make a point.

space of priestly intercession, thanking God for the faithful people living in the space of the community in Colossae. Priestly texture blends with prophetic because Father God, who is imagined in blended prophetic-priestly space, is addressed in the thanksgiving, and because the Colossians had heard and been influenced by the confronting prophetic word of the truth of the gospel. The priestly language of thanksgiving in prayer blends with and is supported by wisdom language because the Colossians' lives of faith and love in the world elicit the thanksgiving.

As it continues, this step broadens and strengthens the scene from the implicit locations of Paul, Timothy, and the "holy ones" to the Mediterranean world by means of a καθώς, "just as," clause ("just as also in all the world it is bearing fruit and growing," 1:6).[78] The believers will project knowledge of their hope and understanding of the word of the truth of the gospel in their location in the Lycus Valley (1:5), to a much larger geographical realm where the gospel is bearing fruit and growing.[79] This picturing of the productivity and maturation of Christ believers in the world they know evokes mental images of a κόσμος and a πόλις parallel but superior in fruitfulness, faith, love, and hope compared to the imagined productivity and peace of imperial hegemony.[80] The agricultural images of fruitfulness and growth are placed in the mind to convey the encouraging and promising notion that people like the Colossians have come to know the same gospel. A second καθώς statement, "just as it also is in you, from the day you heard and knew the grace of God in truth" (1:6), turns the view back to the Colossians, to the time when they heard the message. God's grace has been bearing fruit and growing in them since that day. The message they recall hearing was true gospel, not some deceptive or manip-

---

78. The Greek of Col 1:6–8 is rather awkward and can be syntactically confusing. Are the three uses of καθώς, a comparative conjunction, to be understood to begin three elaborative statements (the view taken here), or should καθώς be connected directly with the preceding language? See discussion below.

79. On projection, see Todd V. Oakley, "The Human Rhetorical Potential," WC 16 (1999): 98.

80. The superiority of "the truth of the gospel" is emphasized in the parallel language of 1:23, "the hope of the gospel which you heard, the one proclaimed in all creation under heaven." See Harry O. Maier, "*Histoire Croisée*, Entangled Bodies, Boundaries, and Socio-political Geography in the Letter to the Colossians," in *Borders: Terminologies, Ideologies, and Performance*, ed. Annette Weissenrieder, WUNT (Tübingen: Mohr Siebeck, 2016), 87.

ulative teaching.⁸¹ A third καθώς statement ("just as you learned from Epaphras our beloved fellow slave, who is a faithful servant of Christ on your behalf," 1:7) narrows the view from the Colossians to the individual person Epaphras, who is recalled and visualized in multiple roles as the person from whom they learned about the grace of God. He is a beloved fellow-slave (σύνδουλος) of Paul and Timothy and a faithful servant (διάκονος) of Christ (who is again brought into focus) on behalf of the Colossians, who know him personally. Visualizing Paul, Timothy, and Epaphras as slaves is socially striking. Slaves were at the lowest social level in the ancient Mediterranean, but here, seen as slaves of Christ and the gospel, they are simultaneously elevated to being preachers of true good news. These preachers speak true gospel in contrast to those of more respectable social status who do not proclaim genuine good news.⁸² Epaphras plays an additional role as the person who has clearly declared to Paul and Timothy that the believers display love in (the) Spirit (1:8). The images observed envision, sequentially, Paul and Timothy, the maturing Colossian audience members, believers who are similarly maturing in other locations in the world, the Colossians once again, and finally Epaphras, from whom the Colossians have learned much.⁸³

Here the wisdom space inhabited by the Colossian believers, the productive space in which they have heard and understood the grace of God and in which they experience growth, blends with the priestly work of Epaphras. This blend portrays the person and the time connected with the Colossians' contact with the gospel. Both of these social spaces blend with the location of Paul and Timothy, to whom Epaphras has communicated that the Colossians are loving people. Consequently, the rhetography emerges out of blended wisdom space, where priestly discourse reveals how the gospel has affected the Colossians and how it has connections with and implications for other persons. The lives of the persons in view so far in the letter are by now quite clear visually in the interweavings of spaces and modes of discourse. Readers of the letter have a vision of the people who are involved in the communication.

---

81. A hint of the deception that appears in 2:4, 8. "In truth" (ἐν ἀληθείᾳ) can be understood adjectivally as "true grace of God," adverbially as "truly understood grace," or in both senses.

82. See below on **intertexture**.

83. On Epaphras, see Michael Trainor, *Epaphras: Paul's Educator at Colossae* (Collegeville, MN: Liturgical Press, 2008).

Translation

1:3 We give thanks to the Father God[84] of our Lord Jesus Christ for you[85] always when we are praying, **1:4** having heard of your faith in Christ Jesus and the love which you have for all the holy ones **1:5** because of the hope stored for you in the heavens, about which you heard previously in the word of the truth of the gospel **1:6** that is present in you, just as also in all the world[86] it is bearing fruit and growing, just as it also is in you, from the day you heard and knew the grace of God in truth, **1:7** just as[87] you learned from Epaphras, our beloved fellow slave, who is a faithful servant of Christ on your[88] behalf, **1:8** who also made clear to us your love in [the] spirit.

Textural Commentary

The **repetitive texturing** of the words *Christ* (1:3–4, 7), *Jesus* (1:3–4), *God* (1:3, 6), *Father* (1:3), *holy* (*ones*) (1:4),[89] *love* (1:4, 8), and *all* (πάν- words, 1:3–4, 6) that appear in this step and continue through the letter tie the characters and their characteristics together in the flow of progressions. The repetition of words of hearing (ἀκούσαντες, 1:4; προηκούσατε, 1:5; ἠκούσατε, 1:6) explains the basis of Paul's regular prayers of thanks to God for the Colossians and makes clear that the holy ones are people who have heard the gospel and about whom Paul and others in turn have also heard. The sequence of ideas draws attention to *hope, heaven, word,* and *gospel* (1:5), words and ideas that are repeated later. These repetitions signal understandings that are foundational to the movement of the letter. Three καθώς constructions (1:6–7) provide comparative considerations that expand the scope of the prayers and thanksgiving to the world of the day, the imperial regions of the Mediterranean basin, and explain some of the history behind the reception of the gospel, the hope it generates,

---

84. Some manuscripts read θεῷ καὶ πατρί, "God and Father."
85. Some manuscripts read ὑπὲρ ὑμῶν rather than περὶ ὑμῶν.
86. Some manuscripts read τῷ κόσμῳ καί, "in all the world also it is bearing."
87. Some manuscripts read καθὼς καί, "just as also you learned."
88. Some manuscripts read ὑπὲρ ἡμῶν, "our behalf," possibly due to attraction to the preceding and following first-person plural pronouns.
89. In both adjectival and substantival usages.

and the faithfulness of the audience members. Dramatically impressive is the image of bearing fruit and growing, which appears in this step and is repeated in the next (1:6, 10).[90] This repetition emphasizes the wisdom location of the recipients of the letter, who are already maturing in their faith, and the goal and progression of further growth the prayers are meant to evoke. This texturing is enhanced by the repetitive employment of the cognate verb and noun for "growth" (αὔξει τὴν αὔξησιν; "grow the growth") later in 2:19, where appropriate maturing comes about through being connected with the head of the body, Christ, not through personal achievement. What the repetitive texturing in this step begins to reveal are wisdom notions integral to the point of the letter: the life the holy ones are experiencing in Christ is a good thing, and it will get better. It is something to be taken seriously.

The *progression* here occurs in the movement from the focus on Paul and Timothy to the faithful audience members in Colossae. Paul and Timothy have heard about and been impressed by their faith and love. What has been heard by Paul and Timothy has its roots in what the Colossian believers themselves heard previously about the hope stored for them in the heavens, of which they had heard in the proclamation of the gospel. The progression relies on the *repetitive texture* of words of hearing. The rhetorical force of the progression is in how it indicates that the action of giving thanks and the intention of the letter are for the benefit of the holy ones. The progression draws attention to *hope* and to *gospel*, words and ideas that will be used significantly later.

Internally, movement ahead is indicated by the three καθώς statements discussed above. They function as progressive sequencing that moves thought away from the notion of thanksgiving by focusing on the gospel and its effects. The gospel the believers were taught by Epaphras is producing fruit and growth in the cosmos and among the audience members. Two relative clauses describe the faithfulness of Epaphras, who informed Paul and Timothy of their love (vv. 7–8). The *progressive texture*

---

90. The particle καρποφορούμενον is in middle voice, perhaps emphasizing that the gospel *itself* is bearing fruit. The conjoined participle αὐξανόμενον is passive, possibly indicating that the gospel is not itself growing but being caused to grow, a kind of divine passive. Surely the authors used the forms intentionally. Nevertheless, the translation "bearing fruit and growing" captures the meaning and rhetorical force of the wording. See also 1:10, where καρποφοροῦντες is active and αὐξανόμενοι is passive.

of this step, then, is woven together by a sequence that begins with Paul and Timothy praying and offering thanks, shifts to God, who receives the prayers, moves on to envision the faithful listeners who had received and believed the gospel, expands dramatically to envision faithfulness spreading in all the world, shifts back again to the audience members who had been productive and maturing for some time, and shifts to picture, at some earlier time,[91] the faithful and much-loved Epaphras, with the audience members learning from him. The *progressive texture* of this step serves to indicate that the listeners have been deeply affected by the gospel. This notion is taken up in the next step in the way in which it progresses toward prayers for more growth.

Rhetoric of grammar. The Greek syntax of 1:6–8 is awkward and difficult to translate. It is important to ask whether grammar or rhetoric (or both) should be the determining factor for understanding the wording. The awkwardness of meaning lies in the apparent repetitiveness, hence tautology, of the language. The gospel had come to the audience members in Colossae, as 1:5b–6a makes clear. The gospel was similarly having its effect in the world, and it was also—and here is the apparent redundancy—having its continuing effect on the Colossian audience ("just as also with you"). Grammatically, the words καθὼς καὶ ἐν παντὶ τῷ κόσμῳ ἐστὶν can be understood to modify the following phrase, καρποφορούμενον καὶ αὐξανόμενον, or the preceding τοῦ παρόντος εἰς ὑμᾶς. In translation, placing commas at differing points indicates the alternatives for syntax.[92] Similarly, the words καθὼς καὶ ἐν ὑμῖν can modify the following ἀφ' ἧς ἡμέρας ἠκούσατε καὶ ἐπέγνωτε τὴν χάριν τοῦ θεοῦ ἐν ἀληθείᾳ or the preceding καρποφορούμενον καὶ αὐξανόμενον. When the first two καθώς statements are read to modify their preceding phrases, the progression flows as follows:[93]

> which you heard previously in the word of the truth of the gospel that comes to you just as it is [coming] in all the world, bearing fruit and growing just as [it does] also in you, from the day you heard and understood the grace of God in truth, just as you learned from Epaphras our beloved fellow slave.

---

91. A kind of rhetorical flashback.
92. See the discussion in Barth and Blanke, *Colossians*, 157.
93. On this choice see Sumney, *Colossians*, 31–32.

When καθώς is attached to the following phrases, the sentence progresses like this:[94]

> which you heard previously in the word of the truth of the gospel that comes to you, just as it is bearing fruit and growing in all the world, just as [it does] also in you from the day you heard and understood the grace of God in truth, just as you learned from Epaphras our beloved fellow slave.

In both cases καθώς functions normally as a comparative conjunction. Clearly the intention is to make comparisons (i.e., to show similarities) between the Colossian believers and others in the world in order to demonstrate the power of the gospel to affect people's lives.

The first reading reduces the redundancy and makes the καθώς statement to be a declaration about the spread of the gospel. It does make, however, for rather awkward Greek, placing a comma after ἐστιν, separating the verb from the following participles. This would be the only place in Colossians where ἐστιν occurs as the last word in a clause.[95] This reading has the advantage of avoiding the notion that the "bearing fruit and growing" has only occurred anywhere in the world since the Colossians heard and understood the gospel, though it may be unlikely that readers or listeners would take this meaning. While it is an angle on the grammar, it makes the flow stiff, less freeform, less stream of consciousness, thus less in accord with the relatively relaxed rhetoric of the letter to this point.

The second reading retains some grammatical awkwardness and contains the apparent tautology but is more rhetorically felicitous. The participle phrase "bearing fruit and growing" is a rhetorical elaboration likely given spontaneously and naturally, developing out of the vision of the power of the gospel coming into the speaker's mind. The spontaneity permits the visualization of the intensive and more inward "fruit bearing" and the more external "growing"[96] and allows for a less formal but still meaningful and easily understood style. Keeping the verb ἐστιν together with

---

94. On this choice see, e.g., Douglas J. Moo, *The Letters to the Colossians and to Philemon*, PNTC (Grand Rapids: Eerdmans, 2008), 87–88.

95. Cf. J. B. Lightfoot, *Saint Paul's Epistles to the Colossians and Philemon* (London: Macmillan, 1879), 135. He claims that the verb goes with the participles to indicate continuity of present action.

96. See Lightfoot, *Colossians*, 135.

the participles καρποφορούμενον καὶ αὐξανόμενον as part of the first καθὼς statement forms a periphrastic present construction that rhetoricizes and emphasizes not only the arrival but also the power of the gospel. That the emphasis is on the image of "you" (καθὼς καὶ ἐν ὑμῖν)—that is, on recognizable people in Colossae and other people "in all the world" maturing in faith, love, and hope, rather than on a declaration about the spread of the gospel in the world—accords more congenially with the rhetoric of the entire step, where the maturation of the audience members in Colossae has been a major point.

Analysis of *progressive texture* is particularly helpful because it indicates that the Colossian audience is portrayed strongly but also appears in the larger world context among all who are bearing fruit and growing, and then again more locally, despite the sense of redundancy. The sequence in this way doubles back on itself and in so doing emphasizes the place and faithful activity of the audience members strongly. It is the audience members, after all, who are the focus of interest. The repetitive progression is elaborated by the recurrence of "bearing fruit and growing" in 1:10, where the view is narrowly focused on the Colossians. This rhetoric, while part of the authors' somewhat uneven syntax, is easygoing and flows understandably in its progressive movement, and it is to be preferred.

Readers and listeners continue to be moved by *sensory-aesthetic textures*. This step speaks of beautiful and pleasing things that call the holy ones (and others, such as ourselves) to hear the text and to be drawn toward understanding it and displaying the faithful social formation it describes. The thanks offered to God, the things that have evoked the thanksgiving, and the words of the text itself have sensory-aesthetic features that make rhetorical contact with the sensibilities of ear, eye, and mouth (and other bodily senses), and with the emotions. Since the text is composed of words, the senses and sensory functions of hearing and speaking are particularly prominent, with hearing bringing about spoken responses. The audience members have heard the gospel (1:5–6), having learned from Epaphras (1:7), who spoke to them. What they heard has brought about faith, love, and hope. Virtual Paul in turn has heard about these qualitative sensory responses and is moved to give thanks and pray for the audience members. This demonstrates that words spoken and heard have sensory-aesthetic effects on authors and audiences. Saying these things now in the letter places the memory of the events of speaking and hearing during past days in mind and sets the image of Paul and Timothy offering thanks and prayers in the imagination.⁹⁷ This rhetoric is bound to have a profound effect in the way it shapes receptivity toward Paul this early in the letter. The senses will be warmed to Paul's prophetic and priestly modes of discourse and consequently amenable to the rhetoric of the entire letter.

The abstract sensibilities of faith, love, hope, productivity, growth, Epaphras's personal qualities, and his observed characteristics of being a beloved fellow slave and a servant produce strong emotional and sensory-aesthetic effects. The mental sensibility of knowing (1:6) brings knowledge and the memory of knowledge into the foreground. A sense of the future may come to the minds of some with the reference to the hope stored up for people (1:5), though the direct meaning is about the present. These things do not require argumentative proof to make striking points because recognition and memory of them already have rhetorical power.

The length of the Greek sentence of this step (102 words) balances well with the following sequence (1:9–14, 106 words) and with the rhythmic language of 1:15–20 (112 words).⁹⁸ The natural evenness created, certainly not intentionally by the author, makes for a sensorily and aesthetically pleasing flow that helps bind the progression of ideas together. In this step the priestly Paul looks back to the days when the Colossians heard the proclamation of the gospel and were influenced by it to become faithful, loving, hopeful people. The following step, which like 1:3 begins with first-person plural statements, focuses on Paul's wishes for the present and future wisdom living of the Colossians in the kingdom of God's Son. The final step in the balanced sequence shifts to a sensory-aesthetic, poetic description of God's Son and his reconciling work.

Internally, step two uses speech, sound, hearing, sight, growth, faith, love, hope, spaces (heavens, world), word, truth, and time to convey its meaning. While the more obvious poetic language does not occur until 1:15–20, there are patterns here that endow the step with melodic power. The initial first-person plural εὐχαριστοῦμεν opens the step with the sensory-aesthetic, priestly, and gratifying image of words being addressed to the Father God. Then the sounds of the words "of our Lord Jesus Christ" are balanced with "your faith in Christ Jesus." The description of the audience members' faith (τὴν πίστιν ὑμῶν ἐν Χριστῷ Ἰησοῦ) is audibly balanced (homoeoteleuton) in length and structure with the description of their love

---

97. See Pound's notion of *logopoeia* in *How to Read*, 25–26; and for analysis Jeal, "Melody, Imagery, and Memory," 162, 175–77.

98. See Moo, *Letters to the Colossians and to Philemon*, 107–8.

(τὴν ἀγάπην ἣν ἔχετε εἰς πάντας τοὺς ἁγίους) and "the hope stored in the heavens" (διὰ τὴν ἐλπίδα τὴν ἀποκειμένην ὑμῖν ἐν τοῖς οὐρανοῖς), all of which are descriptions in the accusative case. The sensory emphasis placed on the bodily "you," that is, on the faithful and loving audience members, in all three clauses is continued by the words explaining that the gospel is "present in [εἰς] you," that it is productive and growing "in you," and that all this stems from what "you learned" from Epaphras.[99] The three compound clauses of the sentence offer a balanced and aesthetically pleasing flow:

Εὐχαριστοῦμεν τῷ θεῷ πατρὶ τοῦ κυρίου ἡμῶν Ἰησοῦ Χριστοῦ πάντοτε περὶ ὑμῶν προσευχόμενοι,
ἀκούσαντες τὴν πίστιν ὑμῶν ἐν Χριστῷ Ἰησοῦ καὶ τὴν ἀγάπην ἣν ἔχετε εἰς πάντας τοὺς ἁγίους
διὰ τὴν ἐλπίδα τὴν ἀποκειμένην ὑμῖν ἐν τοῖς οὐρανοῖς, ἣν προηκούσατε ἐν τῷ λόγῳ τῆς ἀληθείας τοῦ εὐαγγελίου τοῦ παρόντος εἰς ὑμᾶς.

This is followed by the three καθώς clauses (see above on *progressive texture*), which form a sound sequence:

καθὼς καὶ ἐν παντὶ τῷ κόσμῳ ἐστὶν καρποφορούμενον καὶ αὐξανόμενον
καθὼς καὶ ἐν ὑμῖν, ἀφ' ἧς ἡμέρας ἠκούσατε καὶ ἐπέγνωτε τὴν χάριν τοῦ θεοῦ ἐν ἀληθείᾳ·
καθὼς ἐμάθετε ἀπὸ Ἐπαφρᾶ τοῦ ἀγαπητοῦ συνδούλου ἡμῶν.

The repeated καθώς establishes a sound pattern that keeps attention focused on what the preaching of the word of truth, the gospel, brings about in the lives of people. The sound patterning is an artistic usage of words that aims to drive home the point that the kind of direct learning encountered ("you learned," ἐμάθετε) results in "bearing fruit and growing" among people in the world. The beautiful things they learned from Epaphras are the very things that have dramatic effects in the world and among the letter recipients. The dyads "bearing fruit and growing" and "you heard and you came to know" emphasize what was learned. The final two balanced clauses, "who is a faithful servant of Christ on your behalf" and "who also has made known to us your love in [the] Spirit" (eight and

---

99. On the poetic nature of the description of Epaphras, see Trainor, *Epaphras*, 63–64.

nine words, respectively, in Greek), provide an aesthetic capstone to the three καθώς statements. The relationships among all these people are mutually edifying. The word gets around.

All this creates the warm expectation of more pleasant sensory things and thereby elicits the attention of the audience. There is a sensory-aesthetic picture of very fine people, including Paul and Timothy, at prayer. Emotions are evoked that establish an accepting environment for eyes and ears that encounter the message of the letter.

Argumentative texture. The argumentation in this step is quite complex because it moves consecutively in two related directions. First, supporting argumentation for virtual Paul's prayers is provided, but this argument flows into a second texture supporting the arrival and continuing presence of the gospel among the recipients. These arguments are interwoven into a single idea that presents the recipients as faithful and loving believers.

The argument supporting the thanksgivings and prayers for the recipients is clear enough. The rationale for this praying is found in what Paul and Timothy have heard about them, presumably from Epaphras, who has clearly conveyed information about the Colossians (1:8). This texture can be described as follows:

> **Case:** Paul and Timothy offer thanks and unceasing prayers for the recipients.
> **Argument:** They offer the prayers, certainly with genuine gratitude, because they have heard about the faith and love the recipients have for all the holy ones. They are grateful to know that these people have come to a level of maturity indicated in their faith and love. This moves them to pray.
> **Progressive Rationale:** The recipients have this faith and love because of the hope stored up for them in the heavens, which hope they heard about in the gospel that had arrived among them. This rationale is only indirectly concerned with the reason for the prayers. It is more concerned with why the recipients are faithful and loving. But even indirectly it supports the thanksgiving and prayers because it presents the recipients as good people for whom others are likely be thankful. Support for the case, then, comes from the blending of information from two spaces, the wisdom space of the faithful and loving recipients and the space of things stored in the heavens. The blending produces a third space

of faithful, loving people looking to the hope in the heavens and who know the truth-gospel.

A shift in the argumentative texture occurs at 1:6b with the introduction of the series of καθώς statements. Here the argument flows from the subordinate clause "that is present in you" (1:6a), which addresses the arrival and continuing presence of the word of the truth of the gospel among the recipients.[100] The argument alters from its focus on reasoning supporting Paul's thanksgiving and prayers to reasoning about the gospel's effect in the world and among the recipients, and how the effect among them stems from the work of Epaphras, from whom now in turn Paul and Timothy have heard about the faithful people. This broadened view might have been elicited by virtual Paul's mentioning that the recipients have love for all the holy ones, presumably wherever in the world those persons may be. The argument can be laid out in this way:

> **Case:** The gospel has come to and remains with the recipients of the letter. Similarly, it has come to others in the world and is bearing fruit and growing among those others just like it does among the Colossians since the time they heard and understood the message from Epaphras.
> **Argument:** The argument turns on the repetitive employment of the comparative conjunction "just as" (or "just like"). The gospel has come to the Colossians "just like" it has come to others in the Mediterranean region, "just like" the Colossians learned about this grace of God from Epaphras. Argumentative support for the power of the gospel is found in the productivity and growth it brings about in all the world. What the Colossian believers learned from Epaphras is being learned in many locations. By implication, people in many places are becoming faithful and loving like the Colossians (see 1:23).
> **Result:** The gospel has been and continues to be productive. It is impressively effective in the extent and power of its productivity.

---

100. The verb πάρειμι used in the phrase τοῦ παρόντος εἰς ὑμᾶς indicates not only arrival or coming but things that have arrived and remain. The present tense supports the notion of continuation.

The effect of the gospel on the Colossians in particular, in terms of the love that has developed among them, has been reported to Paul and Timothy by Epaphras. The argumentation indicates that the word of the truth of the gospel—which, the repeated ἀκού- words demonstrate, is passed on with dramatic rhetorical power through speaking and hearing—is having a widespread effect. This relatively complex texturing blends ideas from three spaces together: the space of the world/cosmos, where the truth grows; the local space of the recipients, where growth also occurs; and the space of Epaphras and the recipients, where learning about the truth took place earlier. Together these spaces produce an implied space—which readers of the text believe is very real—where the good things for which Paul is thankful and for which he prays continue on appropriately. Wonderful!

The obvious **intertextual** weaving is with the similar and typical thanksgiving statements in other Pauline letters. The thanksgiving language is an expected feature in ancient Hellenistic letters and is here a modified priestly, intercessory prayer report that is socially pleasing and attractive (**social intertexture**) in a letter claiming to be from Paul (see Rom 1:8-10; Phil 1:3-4; 1 Thess 1:2-3; Phlm 4-5; Eph 1:15-16; 2 Thess 1:4).[101] The description of thanks in prayer being offered "to the Father God of our Lord Jesus Christ" occurs with only slight grammatical variations in 2 Cor 1:3; 11:31; Eph 1:3, 17; 1 Pet 1:3 (see also Rom 15:6).[102] This usage indicates the widespread, developed understanding of people who had come to believe Jesus Christ to be their Lord, whose Father is God, that this God is not only the God and Father of Israel (Isa 63:16; 64:7; Jer 3:4, 19; 31:9; Mal 2:10) but the God of all people who call on him as Father (Rom 8:15, Gal 4:6). This intertexture hints already at the connections suggested later in 1:15-20 and 2:6-17, where Jesus Christ as the particular Lord who is preeminent over all others is emphasized. The word *always* (πάντοτε) is frequently used in descriptions of Paul's prayers for his letter recipients (Rom 1:10; 1 Cor 1:4; Phil 1:4; 1 Thess 1:2; 2 Thess 1:3; Phlm 4). The cheerful language aims at assuring the recipients of the senders' goodwill for them and at gaining their continuing goodwill yet reflects sincere concern for people and perhaps indicates the social and cultural

---

101. Some English versions have a sentence break between 1:6a and 6b (e.g., NRSV, NIV), while others follow the Greek original more closely without a sentence break (e.g., RSV, NASB, ESV, KJV).

102. See also the Jewish statement of thanks in 2 Macc 1:10-13.

intertextures of the Jewish habit of praying three times per day (see LXX Dan 6:9, 11–12; Acts 3:1; Did. 8.3).

Cultural intertexture is evident in the description of the triadic faith, love, and hope of the addressees. That is, they themselves form a personified intertexture with the developing Christian culture of faith, love, and hope, three qualities often set together in early Christian thinking and practice (see Rom 5:1–5, 1 Cor 13:13, Gal 5:5–6, 1 Thess 1:3, 5:8, Eph 1:15). While "the hope stored up in the heavens" might at first glance be thought to refer the eschatological hope for the life of fullness and completeness with Christ (see 2 Tim 4:8, 1 Pet 1:4; also 2 Cor 5:1, Phil 3:20), the wording here is not about the eschaton but about *stored* hope present in the heavens. In Colossians "the heavens and the earth" are created realms of the present (1:16, 20) rather than some future postconsummation realm.[103] This spatial rather than temporal conceptuality of hope contrasts with what is observed in other Pauline introductions. While future expectation is typically indicated relative to the time of Christ's return (1 Cor 1:8; 2 Cor 1:14; Phil 1:6, 19; 1 Thess 1:10; 2 Thess 1:6–10), the hope in Col 1:5 describes a reality of the present. This was an aspect of the gospel that had been proclaimed in Colossae as being truth (1:5–6). There is no concern here about the future but only of hope as a *thing* existing in the present. The "word of the truth of the gospel" draws on the notion of God's word of truth in the Torah (Ps 119:43, 160) and Christ believers' contextual understanding that the gospel proclaimed to them is truth. This suggests that the **cultural intertexture** of this step connects with the prophetic and priestly spaces that Paul and Timothy are visualized to inhabit.

The metaphors envisioning fruitfulness and growth (1:6) are well-known images seen elsewhere. "Bearing fruit and growing in all the world" echoes and reconfigures the language and tradition that begins with Gen 1:28, where the humans created in God's image were directed to "grow and multiply and fill the earth."[104] Productivity illustrated by fruit production is common, as many texts indicate (Matt 7:16–20; 13:23; Mark 4:20, 28; Luke 8:15; Rom 7:4–5; conversely Hab 3:17, Wis 10:7). Maturation indicated by growing plants is similarly familiar (Mark 4:8, 1 Cor 3:6–8, 2 Cor 9:10, 10:15, Eph 4:15–16, 1 Pet 2:2). The double metaphor of bearing fruit and grow-

---

103. "Heavens," plural. The location of God is described by the singular noun phrase ἐν οὐρανῷ (Col 4:1; see 1:23).

104. And continues in the Noah and Abraham stories. On this see Beetham, *Echoes of Scripture*, 44–55. "Bearing fruit and growing" is a hendiadys here and in 1:10.

ing is used again almost immediately in Col 1:10 (see 2:19). This is popular imagery that was (and is still) obvious to readers. The gospel itself here has a clear wisdom function rhetorically suggestive of new-creation theology. It has produced holy ones in Colossae who exemplify what fruitfulness should look like.[105] We can also wonder whether, at this early point in the letter, there are implicit intertextural allusions to Roman imperial power structures and imagery that might be recognized by Lycus Valley residents. Truth is seen and understood in the gospel, and the gospel is fruitful and growing in the world. Empires—Rome at the time of the composition of Colossians— were imagined to be the sources of truth, security, and abundance despite the fact that they were oppressive, exploitive, and brutal. The phraseology here would have prompted these contextual notions. The gospel and the hope stored up in the heavens are the things that present truth and were the realities present in the lives of the holy ones in Colossae rather than the deceptive and false claims of empire. This portrays the imperial power, dominant as it may have seemed, as irrelevant because the faith/trust in mind here is in the gospel, not in political. economic, and military power.[106]

Calling the coworker Epaphras a fellow slave is unusual in the Pauline corpus, found only in Colossians (here and in 4:7), though the notion of being a slave in the service of the gospel is prominent intertexturally, particularly in 1 Cor 9:19–23 and especially in Gal 5:13 (see also Rom 1:1, Gal 1:10, Phil 1:1). Although slaves were at the lowest social level in the ancient Mediterranean, in fact effectively considered to be nonpersons,[107] when all Christ believers are imagined as slaves, the intertextural connotations of being a fellow slave could sound attractive. Epaphras has moved up to a respected place as a fellow slave with Paul (see 4:12; Phlm 23). The term is thus an honorific.[108] Being a servant (Col 4:7) is a common designation (1 Cor 3:5, 2 Cor 3:5–6, 6:4, 11:23, Phil 1:1). *Slave* and *servant* describe aspects of the nature and the commitment involved in gospel work (see Mark 10:44–45). The reference to Epaphras and previous learning from him looks much like an approach employed by moral philosophers who

---

105. A major wisdom point of the entire letter is that the Colossians should continue in fruitful wisdom behavior.

106. On this see Walsh and Keesmaat, *Colossians Remixed*, 71–76. As Colossians goes along, faith/trust is also in the household management (οἰκονομία, 1:25) of God.

107. On this see Jeal, *Exploring Philemon*, 138–52.

108. Cf. Dunn, *Epistles to the Colossians and to Philemon*, 64–65; MacDonald, *Colossians and Ephesians*, 39.

recommended that people remember their teachers (Lucian, *Nigr.* 6–7; Seneca, *Ep.* 11.8–10), what they had been taught (Porphyry, *Marc.* 3.46–51), and the changes brought about in their lives (Epictetus, *Diatr.* 3.22.13; Seneca, *Ep.* 6.1).[109]

The **ideological texture** of the rhetoric in this step aims to evoke a wisdom ideology among the holy ones that views their continuing lives as believers. They are presented with a vision of their lives in the Lord Jesus Christ. They are ideologically and consciously connected with the gospel. In their love in the Spirit, they stand in solidarity with Epaphras, who has reported about them. All this expands ideologically on the conscious wisdom space to which the letter alluded already in 1:1–2. The priestly and prophetic discourse in this step aims toward creating consciousness of the wisdom space where life continues in Colossae and the Lycus Valley. Hope is secure in the heavens, an ideologically transcendent and implicitly good space to which the gospel points. Life is to be lived within this frame of reference.

The sacred space of prayers of thanksgiving forms a clear **sacred texture** in the rhetoric. Father God is addressed with words of thanks for the recipients of the letter. The sense of holy living indicated in the previous step continues here with people who are "in Christ" and recognize Father God as the Father of Jesus Christ, who is their Lord. Genuine faith in Christ, love for all the holy ones, and the hope stored in the heavens are truly alive, not mere social constructs. There is a sacred solidarity in the gospel between the Colossians and Epaphras. They have a common connection to the gospel and have been deeply affected by it. All the described participants have a profound religious consciousness. This texture stands at the core of the rhetorical force of this step. The sacred connections provide motive and energy for the continuation of the letter. The wisdom space of the believers in Christ Jesus is a sacred space where consciousness of and contact with God in Christ dominates. The sacred texture and space already begins to convey the idea that no other supposed sacred spaces are relevant.

Rhetorical Force as Emergent Discourse

This step emerges as rhetoricization of known modes of speaking and topoi into distinctly Christian shapes. The common Hellenistic letter

---

109. For these references see Talbert, *Ephesians and Colossians*, 175–76.

thanksgiving and prayer report is formed into a priestly statement of prayers of thanks and concern for people possibly unknown personally to the declared author (see 2:1). The prayers produce a distinct worship context and at the same time generate a wisdom environment of the actual experience of life of the holy ones and others in the purview of the letter. Paul's rhetoric about Epaphras and what was learned (i.e., heard) from him explains the origin of the wisdom experiences of the Colossians. All this is precisely what emergent Christian discourse should *do*, that is, it should function rhetorically to convey ideas to listeners and readers. It sets up a rhetorical immediacy where people become aware of who they are, what they believe, and how they live, and therefore of how they should behave in wisdom space as life continues.[110] This rhetoric, then, sets the stage for what follows in the next steps (1:9–13, 14–20). The rhetoric invites listeners and readers into the spaces described: they imagine themselves as the holy people of the rhetograph. They know that they are the people who heard the proclamation made by Epaphras and recognize the hope stored in the heavens. This rhetoric already elicits a fearless service wisdom among them, just like that of Paul and Epaphras, who are coslaves of Christ and of themselves. They need not put their trust and hope in any other forces, whether religious, social, economic, political, or military. They possess and are encouraged to continue, be productive, and mature in their faith in Christ. Because they identify with it, the rhetorical force of the language makes them amenable to the larger discussion that continues as the letter goes along. This discourse creates a safe and sacred space in listeners' minds where they, Father God, the Lord Jesus Christ, Paul, Timothy, Epaphras, and others live out "love in the Spirit" (1:8). Perhaps residents of Colossae would already recognize certain social and political implications of this rhetoric? Faith, love, and hope are not focused in or dependent on the benefits of Rome, empire, and the Pax Romana or on other powers and religious practices. The powers to trust are Father God and Lord Jesus Christ. The true word that is spreading in the world is the good news about Christ. The love being produced in the holy ones came from what they learned from Epaphras, not from anywhere or anyone else.

---

110. That is, it *blends* notions from multiple spaces.

SCENE ONE: INTRODUCTORY RHETORIC   73

Introduction to Steps Three, Four, and Five

Colossians 1:9–20 is a long, complex sentence where multiple clauses are joined together by conjunctions, an infinitive, prepositions, relative pronouns, and poetic formulations.[111] The sentence is composed of three steps or progressions (*progressive textures*) evident in subtle shifts of rhetoric. The typical Greek New Testament editions display the sentence in differing ways. The NA[28], UBS[4], and UBS[5] editions insert a sentence break following the word μακροθυμίαν near the end of 1:11 and begin a new sentence with μετὰ χαρᾶς connected to the word εὐχαριστοῦντες in verse 12. The NA[28] begins a new paragraph with Μετὰ χαρᾶς εὐχαριστοῦντες. The older UBS[2] and UBS[3] editions make no sentence and paragraph break but insert a comma following μακροθυμίαν, thereby connecting μετὰ χαρᾶς with the following εὐχαριστοῦντες.[112] The SBLGNT makes no sentence break in the entire section, simply inserting a comma at the end of verse 11 that ties μετὰ χαρᾶς to the preceding clause.[113] Reading the prepositional phrase μετὰ χαρᾶς with either the preceding or following clause is thought by some to be a matter of interpretive judgment, but from a rhetorical point of view connecting it with εὐχαριστοῦντες is the sound reading in the way it follows the use of prepositional phrases in the sentence and particularly in the sequencing of actions envisioned in verses 9–12.[114] Thanksgiving should be offered with joy.[115] The NA[28] displays 1:15–20 in poetic form, while the UBS and SBLGNT editions present the verses entirely in prose form.[116]

Step three (1:9–12) moves ahead with the words "Because of this also we" (Διὰ τοῦτο καὶ ἡμεῖς), indicating that the statements of the previous step provide reason why virtual Paul and Timothy pray continually for the

---

111. John C. O'Neill, much too extremely, claims, "To translate all this as one sentence is impossible, and no modern translator would even consider making the attempt." See O'Neill, "The Source of the Christology in Colossians," *NTS* 26 (1980): 89. Interpreters of the rhetoric of the sentence should not analyze it so negatively.

112. The UBS[2] edition inserts a period and sentence break at the end of 1:17. Later editions have a comma and no sentence break.

113. The SBLGNT in fact continues the long sentence through to the end of 1:23.

114. See Sumney, *Colossians*, 51.

115. The action envisioned is thanksgiving *with* joy, i.e., joy accompanying thanksgivings, not the adjectival "joyful thanksgiving" (NRSV), "giving joyful thanks" (NIV), or adverbial "joyously giving thanks" (NASB).

116. See Sumney, *Colossians*, 60 n. 80.

recipients (1:9). The opening first-person sequence "we ... we heard ... we do not cease" emphasizes that the continuing priestly discourse describing prayerful activity is a response to what Epaphras reported to them. The continuous prayers envision the productivity, growth, and strengthening of the believers with the anticipation that they will offer thanksgivings to the Father.[117] The Father has taken the apocalyptic action of qualifying the believers for a share of the allotment that has brought them (= ὑμᾶς, "you") into the light (1:12). Step four emerges in a relative clause at 1:13 with expanded images of the apocalyptic actions of God, who has rescued and transferred them (= ἡμᾶς, "us") into the kingdom of the Son. The progression from second-person to first-person plurals is a natural rhetoric that turns to the larger and inclusive "us" who now inhabit the new reality of the kingdom of the Son, in whom there is redemption and forgiveness of sins.

Step five arises powerfully and dominantly at 1:15 to focus directly on the precreational identity and activity of Father God's Son, who by the end of the sentence at verse 20 is portrayed as the one through whom reconciliation and peace have been accomplished comprehensively for "all things" (τὰ πάντα) of the created realm of the earth and the heavens. The *progressive textures* move the visuality and ideas forward from the localized "you" to the more inclusive "we" to the fully comprehensive "all things."

Step Three: Priestly Prayers 1:9–12

Rhetography

This step brings Paul, Timothy, and other coworkers again into focus in the visual foreground, where they are engaged in the priestly task of unceasing intercessory prayer for the holy ones (1:9). The unceasing prayer is visualized occurring, as in the previous step (1:3), during their regular practice of prayer. The news received from Epaphras has motivated them to pray earnestly, requesting and now visualizing in advance life ongoing in productive wisdom space where the holy ones live as mature believers who have been filled with the knowledge of God's will in all wisdom and spiritual understanding, who are thereby seen to be walking worthily of the Lord in every pleasing thing, being fruitful and increasing in their

---

117. "Thanksgivings," εὐχαριστοῦντες, plural.

knowledge of God, and are strong, having been strengthened according to the power of God's glory (1:9b–11a).[118] This maturity is visible proleptically in the anticipated practice of endurance and patience (1:11b). It is also observed as the holy ones give thanks with overt joy to Father God, who has qualified them for a share[119] of the inheritance with the (other) holy ones in a striking flood of light that illuminates the scene (1:11c–12).

Translation

1:9 Because of this also we, from the day we heard, have not stopped praying and asking for you, that you may be filled with the knowledge of his will in all spiritual wisdom and understanding, **1:10** to walk[120] worthily of the Lord in every pleasing thing, in every good work bearing fruit and growing in the knowledge[121] of God, **1:11** in every strength being strengthened according to the power of his glory in every endurance and patience, with joy **1:12** giving thanks to the father who qualified[122] you[123] for the share of the allotment of the holy ones in the light,

Textural Commentary

The description of continuous praying by Paul, Timothy, and their coworkers (reasonably inferred to include at least some of those persons mentioned in 4:7–14) forms a persuasive *repetitive texture* with the prayers of thanksgiving mentioned in verses 3–8, now with intercessory prayers for the ongoing development of the faithful holy ones. The prayers have in sight the filling and strengthening of the believers that enables them to walk in ever maturing ways. The striking internal repetition in the doubling of noun and verb forms of the word for "strength" (or "power") in

---

118. περιπατῆσαι ("walking") can indicate either or both purpose and anticipated result of the prayers. On the voice of the participles καρποφοροῦντες and αὐξανόμενοι, see above, note 90. πληρωθῆτε, "filled," and δυναμούμενοι, "strengthened," are divine passives.
119. "Share, portion, lot."
120. Some manuscripts add ὑμᾶς, "you."
121. Some manuscripts include the variant preposition "in," ἐν τῇ ἐπιγνώσει.
122. NA[28] indicates the variant καλέσαντι καὶ ἱκανώσαντι, "called and qualified."
123. Some manuscripts read ἡμᾶς, likely by attraction to ἡμᾶς in 1:13.

1:11 (ἐν πάσῃ δυνάμει δυναμούμενοι) emphasized by the following synonym κράτος evokes notions of wonder of the great power of God, who enables and reinforces believers with the spiritual wisdom, understanding, perseverance, and patience they will employ in their worthy walking.[124] Repetitions of forms of πᾶς, four times in 1:9–11, emphasize the wisdom-behavioral nature of what the prayers request. This underscores the major point that it is God and God's power and action that have accomplished all the believers need.

The verb *hear* in 1:9 repeats the idea of hearing seen already in 1:4 and 1:9, hence also the learning experienced by the believers from the speaking of Epaphras (1:7). The filling of the audience members is raised in this step (1:9) and is repeated as a leading idea later in the rhetoric of the letter, notably in 2:10, where Christ, in whom the fullness of deity dwells (1:19, 2:9), is the one in whom believers have been made full, and in 4:12, where they are envisioned in a mature and full (πεπληροφορημένοι, a πληρ- compound word) wisdom condition.[125] The prayers request that the holy ones be made full of knowledge, whether the knowledge of God's will (1:9) or of God himself (1:10). Knowledge is emphasized by the subsequent repetitions in 2:2 and 3:10. Living in wisdom space is in this step for the first time described as walking, an image repeated in 2:6, 4:5, and, in reference to former life, in 3:7. The walking also anticipates the ways of living described in 3:1–4:6. The repetitions indicate the key notion that all that believers need comes from God and Christ, not from themselves or from their own actions or religious works. Indeed, what they have from God and Christ works to produce good works in them (1:10).

The *sensory-aesthetic texturing* of Paul's and Timothy's sense of hearing continues in the memories of what they have heard about the letter recipients, and it continues to motivate their prayers. The hearing motivates the prayers for movement toward maturity in wisdom space, where the holy ones engage in the actions and sensations of walking worthily (living suitably, properly) of the Lord in pleasing ways (1:10). Metaphorical mental and bodily actions are in sight here. While Paul and Timothy ("we") are engaged in the intellectual and bodily actions of constant prayer, the recipients ("you") of the benefits of the prayers are expected to be "filled," walking in every pleasing manner, bearing fruit and grow-

---

124. See the similar doubling of noun and verb forms for "power" (ἐνέργεια, ἐνεργέω) in 1:29.

125. See also the use of πληρ- root words in 1:25, 2:2.

ing in every good work, strengthened in all power, and giving thanks to the Father, who has enabled them to share the inheritance of the holy ones. Producing fruit and growing evoke senses of color, ripeness, maturity, taste, touch, nourishment, the satisfaction of a full belly. The word pairs in verses 9–10, "praying and asking," "in all spiritual wisdom and understanding," "bearing fruit and growing," and "in all endurance and patience," are dyads or hendiadyses that function audibly to emphasize ideas. The strongly emphasized wording "in all strength being strengthened" evokes thoughts of a muscular faithfulness that makes for endurance and patience that cannot be defeated.

Reasoning (*argumentative texture*) in support of the prayers is an argument of result, a continuation of prayers argued by the explicitly deductive first words of the sentence, Διὰ τοῦτο, "because of this." Because Paul and his coworkers had heard, received, and been deeply impressed by the report from Epaphras about the faithful, loving believers, they had been continually praying and making requests for the Colossians. To the prayers of thanksgiving described in verses 3–8 have been added intercessory prayers with specified goals: (1) that you may be filled with the knowledge of his will in all spiritual wisdom and understanding, (2) to walk worthily of the Lord in every pleasing thing, (3) in every good work bearing fruit and growing in the knowledge of God, and (4) in every strength being strengthened according to the power of his glory in every endurance and patience.

The prayers request and anticipate maturity of mind and behavior. The maturity itself anticipates thanksgivings offered to the Father (1:11–12).[126] The goals have a long-term view toward endurance and patience. Underlying these ideas is recognition of the apocalyptic action of the Father, who himself has "qualified" (ἱκανώσαντι, aorist participle)[127] people to "share" (εἰς τὴν μερίδα, "to have a portion, to share") in the inheritance of the holy ones in the light (1:12). God has performed the operative, apocalyptic action that brings about the goodness of life in the light.

---

126. In the flow of the long sentence it is clear that the holy ones, "you," are the subject of the participle εὐχαριστοῦντες (see Dunn, *Epistles to the Colossians and to Philemon*, 75).

127. Codex Vaticanus has καλέσαντι, "called," an apparent conflation, rather than the correct ἱκανώσαντι. See Bruce M. Metzger and Bart D. Ehrman, *The Text of the New Testament: Its Transmission, Corruption, and Restoration*, 4th ed. (Oxford: Oxford University Press, 2005), 265.

The direct literary **intertextures** with this step are the similar reports of priestly actions and prayers for the recipients of other Pauline and New Testament letters (Rom 1:9–10, 1 Cor 1:4, Eph 1:15–16, Phil 1:4, 1 Thess 1:2, 2 Thess 1:3, 2 Tim 1:3), though only here in 1:9 is the wording "we have not stopped praying and asking for you." Ephesians 1:15–16 employs very similar construction and wording in the first-person singular. The rhetoric of ceaseless prayer may not have been familiar to the first recipients of the letter, but it was culturally comprehensible. An **intertexture** certainly in the air among people living in the eastern provinces is the notion of wisdom and understanding. Aristotle, in *Nichomachean Ethics* 1.13, speaks of three chief virtues: wisdom, understanding, and prudence (or thoughtfulness or purpose, φρόνησις, which is not employed in Colossians).[128] Greek speakers of the Lycus Valley would have recognized the ideas. The combination of wisdom and understanding as things given by God or the Spirit of God appears in a number of places in the LXX (Exod 31:3; 1 Chr 22:12; 2 Chr 1:10–12; Isa 11:2; Prov 1:7; 2:2–3, 6; 9:10; 24:3; Job 12:13; 28:20). LXX Deut 4:6 states that observance of the Torah in the land by Israel demonstrates wisdom and understanding to the gentiles. So there is a clear intertextural tradition of the idea and usage of the language that could be known by the authors and understood by Lycus Christ believers.[129] What distinguishes the dyad is that it is *"spiritual wisdom and understanding,"* that is, like the filling of knowledge which comes from God, it is given by the Holy Spirit, is not self-generated, and does not come from other religious sources.

Walking (1:10) is a common Jewish and biblical intertextural idiom for living life (see, e.g., Prov 2:12–20; 1QS III, 17–26; V, 8–11; Phil 1:27; Eph 4:1; 1 Thess 2:12). Its rhetorical meaning is clear and not dependent on specific texts. "Bearing fruit and growing," however, have intertextures in the Genesis creation account (Gen 1:22, 28). Created organisms are meant to be productive and reproductive. In biblical context this is wisdom par excellence, the creational task of living things. Correctly understood, every good work from the time of creation onward is aimed at productivity. The intertextural idea does not permit destructive activi-

---

128. Moo, *Letters to the Colossians and to Philemon*, 94.

129. It is unlikely that first audience members would have recognized these biblical references and their implications. What is likely is that they would recognize the sociocultural ambience where the ideas were understood. On the other hand, the authors seem to be familiar with the tradition of the actual language.

ty.¹³⁰ Destructive and deceitful powers are to be endured and avoided, certainly not obeyed (see Col 2:4, 8–9). God's children are created to walk in wise lives of productivity. The language of being "qualified" by the Father for "the share of the allotment" (μερίς, "share"; κλῆρος, "allotment"; lit. "into [εἰς] the allotment") has intertextural connections with LXX passages describing possession of the promised land (Deut 10:9, Josh 19:9) and indeed the people of Israel themselves (Deut 32:9).¹³¹

Rhetorical Force as Emergent Discourse

The believers in Colossae learn from the rhetoric of this step that the authors of the letter seek, through their prayers, fullness of knowledge, spiritual wisdom and understanding, good behavior, productivity, growth in the knowledge of God, and strength for perseverance and patience. The language not only reports about the prayers and concerns; it creates the expectation that the good things requested will be provided by God. The words have the psychological effect of creating amenability to the letter and affection for its senders. The recipients will be moved to accept and practice what the letter calls for as it goes along. The rhetoric prompts a view toward their future as Christ believers living in the Lycus Valley. It evokes a vision of continuing productivity and growth, of faithful, knowledgeable, spiritual existence. The view toward thanksgiving with joy creates the mental vision, expectation, and atmosphere that makes it likely to occur. They will be thankful that they have already been qualified to share in God's provision of goodness. Audiences are likely to experience the head-nodding effect that moves them to think or say "Yes, we will be thankful. We have much for which to be thankful. God has done great things for us." The rhetography and interweaving of textures creates agreement and actual behavior. The narration of images and expectations evokes understanding that maturation is important and possible, supported by the memory that listeners and readers have already been brought a long way.

---

130. Implements of destructive war are refashioned into implements of productive agriculture according to Isa 2:4.
131. See Talbert, *Ephesians and Colossians*, 186. Contra Talbert, Col 1:12 has no eschatological reference. The wording of 1:12–13 indicates that believers have already been qualified for and transferred into the new reality of the Son's kingdom. On intertextures with Exodus, see G. K. Beale, *Colossians and Philemon*, BECNT (Grand Rapids: Baker Academic, 2019), 62–65, 68–71.

Step Four: Father God's Apocalyptic Actions: Transferal to the New Reality (1:13–14)

Rhetography

The visualization of God's action of qualifying the holy ones for a share of the allotment (1:12) brings about a shift in a relative clause (ὃς ἐρρύσατο ἡμᾶς, 1:13) that fleshes out more fully the apocalyptic actions by the Father, who has "rescued us" (no longer the "you" of verses 10–12), that is, all persons in sight: Paul, Timothy, coworkers, the believers in Colossae, and other Lycus audiences of the letter (4:13–16). Humans are completely passive in the rescue. Father God himself is the rescuer (ἐρρύσατο, aorist middle). With the rescuing Father, audiences also see "the Son of his love," the Lord Jesus Christ, who possesses his own kingdom and is thus viewed as Son-king. Listeners and readers see the Father as the rescuer who has transferred (literally, has performed a metastasis, μετέστησεν; aorist active from the verb μεθίστημι) the humans out of the jurisdiction or control space of darkness into the space of his Son's kingdom, the new and light-filled (1:12) domain in which they are now observed.

This transfer from one space to another is amplified and colored with the explanation that the relocation from darkness to light is also a relocation to a new space "in" the Son, "in whom we have redemption," in turn described by the appositional "forgiveness of sins" (1:14). The picturing keeps the human characters (the "us") of the rhetograph in view while at the same time visualizing the apocalyptic actions of the divine Father on their behalf. The humans are seen now as redeemed, forgiven, and located in the light-filled, kingdom space,[132] which is simultaneously visualized as "in" the Son. Exactly what things look like visually in this kingdom is not explicated, though it is anticipated that people there will behave wisely and maturely, offering thanksgiving with joy. What exactly it will look like to be "in" the Son is similarly not explicated except that it will be light, not dark.[133] It is clear, though, that being in the Son and in his kingdom is a very good thing. Readers and listeners will develop their own mental images through associations or blends of what they already know about darkness, light, kingdoms, redemption,

---

132. Although the former space of darkness is still clear in memory.
133. As noted earlier, Wilson describes "in Christ" as the new "sphere of existence" (*Colossians and Philemon*, 73).

and the forgiveness of sins. But for people living in Colossae, the Lycus Valley, in Phrygia, the usual meaning of kingdom was unmistakable: the empire of Rome. They have been transferred into a different empire. This raises the inevitable questions: What does this mean? Since the believers now dwell in, walk in, the kingdom of Father God's Son, what are they to think of dominating Rome? The vision does not extend far enough, not yet, to answer the questions.

In this step virtual Paul, Timothy, and coworkers remain in priestly space where they continue to pray for the holy ones. The Father is imagined in blended priestly-apocalyptic space in the role of rescuer and transporter of humans, providing redemption and forgiveness in his Son. The priestly-apocalyptic activity enhances vision of a wisdom space where holy ones behave maturely, producing the fruit of wisdom (1:10). God's actions have resituated believers in a new reality that benefits them dramatically. While the humans formerly lived in the space and jurisdiction of darkness, they now live in the light-filled kingdom space of redemption and mature, righteous living. Paul and Timothy pray continuously, here particularly for the Colossian believers, so that the knowledge of what God has done will bear even more fruit in the future. The strengthening performed by the Father comes out of apocalyptic space, from which God's power and righteousness *metastasizes* humans into light. This is the space of the Father's glory, the realm from where the allotment for the holy ones comes (1:11) and where the authority of darkness is forced to yield to the kingdom of the loved Son.

This step in the rhetography, then, employs blended priestly rhetorolect where priestly views about Paul, Timothy, and the Father are blended with wisdom discourse describing the understanding and behavior the priestly activity requests, and with apocalyptic that pictures the power and action that transfers humans into a better existence where fruitful behavior is practiced. Priestly discourse texture describes the foundational activity; apocalyptic describes actions, power, and salvific benefits; and wisdom describes the product enabled by priestly and apocalyptic action. Readers/listeners will imagine the maturity and fruitful behavior they will perform in their own lives. That is, the rhetography that emerges from the blended discourses indicates the likelihood that the mature behavior will actually occur.[134]

---

134. Thus the rhetography makes the rhetology.

Translation

1:13 who rescued us out of the jurisdiction of darkness and transferred us into the kingdom of the Son of his love, **1:14** in whom we have redemption,[135] the forgiveness of sins,

Textural Commentary

This *progression* is formed by descriptions of the actions of the Father "who rescued us ... and transferred us" (1:13), to the vastly better, apocalyptically produced new existence in the Son-Christ. As noted earlier, the verbs and pronouns shift from first-person plurals referring to Paul and his coworkers (1:9), to second-person plurals referring to the audience (1:10–12), to first-person plurals that refer to all together (1:13–14). In other words, the progression moves thought from consideration of the Colossians apart from virtual Paul and the coworkers to consideration of all of them together. The progression is foundational (with the following step, 1:15–20) to the rhetorical force of the entire letter: things are different now. Life is no longer lived in the restrictive darkness of ordinary Phrygian and imperial life. The social, cultural, religious, and political pressures, though still very real, become gradually understood as irrelevant for Christ believers, who live in the light of the kingdom of the Father's Son. More learning occurs—like they learned things from Epaphras (v. 7)—as the holy ones listen to the letter. As becomes clear as the rhetoric of the letter advances further, life in the economy (οἰκονομία, household management, 1:25) of God changes the pressure points in a community that focuses on "the above things" rather than the things of the earth (see 3:1–2). The growth and maturation that the prayers request is understood in light of the apocalyptic actions of the Father in rescuing and transferring "us" to the new and secure reality of fullness in Christ (see 2:9–10).

The metaphors of darkness and light form a poignant *sensory-aesthetic texture* and imagery together with the emotional notion of rescue. Formerly, people existed in the dark realm, where the senses of sight, direction, and balance were impaired. The dark realm is restrictive, so strongly limiting that those in it need rescue from it. People cannot see where there

---

135. Some manuscripts add διὰ τοῦ αἵματος αὐτοῦ, "through his blood," drawn from Eph 1:7.

is no light. Plants do not bear fruit and grow in the dark. God rescued "us" (1:13) from this desensitizing and directionless space and placed us in the Son's kingdom, a space of light (1:12) and clear vision toward the maturity that the prayers request. The kingdom-light space evokes sensory and aesthetic images of a beneficent king, liberation, clear vision, and happy, productive experiences of goodness. Darkness, by implication also a kingdom (hence the translation of ἐξουσία as "jurisdiction"), is a disordered, confusing, and unproductive space. Rescue and transfer (metastasis) are felt movements done to "us." All this has a view toward bodily senses and actions of mature living in a liberated space.[136] Added to the sense and beauty of liberation are the already possessed redemption and forgiveness of sins (v. 14). These terms are here near synonyms indicating release from oppressive, dark forces.

Along with the affective sensory texturing of the restrictive jurisdiction of darkness and the new reality of the Son's kingdom is a subtle and implicit (so far) **social and cultural texture**. The dark jurisdiction, in stark contrast to the Son's kingdom in light—which is presented as the realm of genuine redemption and forgiveness—will have evoked thoughts of life in the other very present kingdom, the empire of Rome. Residents of Colossae were aware of where they lived and of the social, cultural, and political visibility and pressures of empire. They were aware of kingdom-empire authorities and the social, political, and religious expectations of conformity. The ancient Mediterranean East faced the pressures of political-spiritual powers and cosmic spiritual powers. The stressful social-political-religious darkness of life in Colossae is still implicit but would have become unmistakable when listening to the rhetoric of the next step (1:15–20) and the rhetoric of Col 2–3. The holy ones have been rescued and transferred from the darkness of Roman, Phrygian, and religious subjection to perceived cosmic, political, and social authorities (ἐξουσίαι). Darkness is no longer the dominant spatial and moral reality. They live now in safety in the kingdom of light and God's οἰκονομία (1:25). This is a foundational notion for those who are in Christ.

The reasoning of this step (*argumentative texture*) is the argument of result brought about by God. Things are different now for "us." Light is dramatically, sensorily, and metaphorically different from and better than darkness. Being rescued and transferred by the apocalyptic actions

---

136. A space of uninhibited proprioception.

of the Son's Father is to exist in a new reality where the old darkness is no longer relevant. The argumentative rhetoric presses these notions on the mind. The reasoning occurs in the graphic description itself rather than being argued more explicitly. What is clear in the argument is that it was God who acted to bring about the new reality. The letter recipients could not have acquired rescue, transferal, and forgiveness on their own. These actions of God are likely to have persuaded the believers to the thanksgiving with joy anticipated in 1:12.

The topos of light in contrast to darkness has common **intertextures** in literature and human discourses. In biblical texts light represents good, orderliness, righteousness, and visibility, while darkness stands for disorder, evil, and constraint (e.g., Gen 1:3–4, Isa 9:2, 42:16, Lam 3:1–3, John 3:19–21, 2 Cor 4:6, 6:14, Eph 5:8–11, 6:12, 1 Thess 5:4–10, 1 John 1:5, Rev 16:10, 21:23–24, 22:5). Light-darkness imagery is prominent in the New Testament. The visual and near palpable power of this intertexture is unmistakable. Cultures and religions everywhere understand the idea and the contrast. Closely connected with light is kingdom. Kingdom is a profound and deeply woven intertexture in the Hebrew Bible/Old Testament, particularly in the texture of expectation of the coming time. Kingdom is integral to the proclamation of Jesus indicated in the Synoptic Gospels (beginning already with Mark 1:14–15). It appears infrequently in the Pauline letters but is there often enough to indicate the notion that being placed in God's and Christ's exclusive kingdom is a central notion (1 Cor 4:20; 15:24, 50; 1 Thess 2:12; 2 Tim 4:18). While typically envisioned as a realm of the future in the letters, βασιλεία is visualized, like Col 1:13, as a realm of the present, notably in Rom 14:7 and 1 Cor 4:20. This kingdom is the proper wisdom space for believers. The exclusive intertextual kingdom tradition makes its case strongly against any other kingdoms—for the Colossian holy ones, obviously the Mediterranean kingdom-empire of Caesar—which by implication must be kingdoms of darkness, not light. Transferal out of darkness into a space of liberation in the Son's kingdom employs the intertextural threads of the exodus out of the kingdom of Egypt and the return from exile out of the empire of Babylon.[137] These more political textures, possibly unknown to the believers in the Lycus but certainly known to the authors, begin to set the stage for the transfer out of the Roman and cosmic darkness that

---

137. See Beale, *Colossians and Philemon*, 72–74.

emerges more clearly later in the letter. In other words, the intertextures in these verses are rhetorically suggestive regarding cosmic-spiritual and political-spiritual powers that Colossians makes irrelevant. Redemption and forgiveness of sins have tightly woven intertextures, notably in prophetic expectation (e.g., Jer 31:31–34), in introducing the gospel (Mark 1:4), in the work of Jesus as described in Acts (Acts 5:31), and in Paul (Rom 3:24; Eph 1:7, 14; 4:30).

The intertextures of this step emphasize the understanding that all good things, all wisdom behaviors, and redemption and forgiveness of sins (hence the removal of guilt and its penalties) are connected with Jesus Christ, who is Father God's Son. Paul and Timothy are described as constantly praying that the letter recipients be filled with such knowledge. By implication, no other sources may be presumed to have the same power or ability to provide the same benefits. It is God who in Christ redeems and forgives.

The **ideological texture** and goal continues from the previous verses. A conscious ideological and politicized, wisdom point of view continues to be elicited. The priestly discourse combined with apocalyptic discourse produces the wisdom discourse texture and ideological space to which the audience is expected to be amenable. The rhetoric moves people to think that their rescued existence is important. Redemption and the forgiveness of sins are God-provided benefits they have in the kingdom of God's beloved Son alone. This ideology informs their walking, their behavior of life, where they are productive and growing, being thankful persons who are apocalyptically powered and share the lightened inheritance with all other holy ones. Only the new reality in the Son's kingdom is now relevant. The ideology of rescue and transferal is impressed on recipients' minds as the correct way of envisioning reality: this is what has been done and this is where "we" are.

As with the ideological texturing, **sacred texture** flows from the previous step. All of the characters—those praying, those listening—are in sacred space, where they are holy ones conscious of their locations. They are, after all, situated in the kingdom of God's Son. They are not in a dark space under disordered powers where there is no redemption and where the disorder dominates life so much that people cannot perform well enough to overcome it. It is God's apocalyptic action that has made them fit for life in the light. Help has come from the outside, from God, making things good in their lives. This sacredness makes its own holy appeal, persuading readers to know it more deeply and stay in it.

Rhetorical Force as Emergent Discourse

What is strikingly emergent and forceful about this language in its Mediterranean context is its portrayal of God as the Father of the Lord Jesus Christ, as the apocalyptic rescuer who has transferred "us" out of the dark empire where "we" groped along without clear sensory direction, in confusion, unproductive, unredeemed, and guilty, into the Son's light-filled kingdom, where everything is clear, where there is redemption and forgiveness. This is the realm of order, productivity, and good living. The Son of God is the beneficent king in the space of happy and productive good, and redemption and forgiveness of sins are located "in" him. The force of this rhetoric is aimed at establishing and confirming the knowledge that this is the new and sure reality for the believers. Clearly it is not offered or provided in such an effective and full manner by any humans or human systems. It must be the case that the empire and space of perceived existence—of life in the Lycus Valley, the larger Asian context, and the larger still Roman imperial context—is not the wisdom space the letter has in sight. It is not the domain in which creationally fruitful life is properly lived. The Son's kingdom is the proper wisdom space of rescue and transferal into light. This discourse is leading listeners and readers toward fullness of power behind it. There is more to come.

Step Five: The Precreational Image of God: Over All Things (1:15–20)

The sentence *progresses* from the inclusive first-person view of "we" as rescued and transferred persons in the Son's kingdom "in whom we have redemption and the forgiveness of sins" to a dramatically developed, comprehensive precreational vision of Father God's Son, who created, sustains, is preeminent over, and has reconciled all things (τὰ πάντα) to himself, the things on the earth and the things in the heavens.

Rhetography

This step presents a dramatic alteration of the visual scene. The sentence that began at verse 9 continues, but the rhetoric and the rhetography expand here, poetically, a little subtly, and in an unexpected direction, by a developed theological and philosophical vision of reality that starts before the beginning of the creation of the heavens and the earth in the precreational realm of Father

God and his Son.[138] This means that some features and ideas are understood not by what is seen in the visual imagination but precisely by what is not seen. Appearing with the unseen are visualized portrayals of the Son's apocalyptic actions that bring reconciliation and peace to the earth and the heavens. The comprehensive rhetographic vision aims to move the holy ones into a central contextual environment of discourse, understanding and praxis.

> In sociorhetorical terms, the rhetography of a text invites interpreters and readers to picture a contextual environment for the discourse in their minds. This environment provides meanings that persuade a hearer or reader to think in particular ways about the world, about the people who live in it, and about the specific ways to live responsibly in it.[139]

In these verses the believers are persuaded to picture the contextual environment where the Son-Christ is understood to be the image of God, creator and sustainer of the cosmos, the preeminent one in whom houses all the fullness of God, and the one who has reconciled all things of the created orders. This environment is to be imagined as the reality in which they live and which guides their lives. In other words, where they now live in the Son's kingdom, the divine Son "in whom" is redemption and forgiveness (1:14)—the divine Son himself and no other—is visualized as the provider of the goodness described and is so from precreation time-space. This understanding of the Son-Christ is the foundational and dominating philosophy of the letter. It expands understanding of "the Father God of our Lord Jesus Christ" (1:3) to include the father's and the Son's existence and activity in the precreational realm.

While the characters and action in the rhetograph have been observed until now in present time, the conceptions that are presented in 1:15–18a take viewers away from the present to the precreational domain of God. This unseen realm cannot be visualized because it precedes and transcends the spaces and abilities to which humans have access.[140] It is, rather,

---

138. See the discussion of precreation rhetorolect in the introduction. See also Roy R. Jeal, "Starting before the Beginning: Precreation Discourse in Colossians," R&T 18 (2011): 1–24.

139. Vernon K. Robbins, *Sea Voyages and Beyond: Emerging Strategies in Sociorhetorical Interpretation*, ESEC 14 (Atlanta: SBL Press, 2014), 89.

140. The word ἀόρατος, "unseen," in 1:15–16 refers to the human inability to see God or into the precreational realm, not to invisibility as a characteristic of either deity or the realm itself.

to conceive of the theological-philosophical, thought-filled yet sensorily imperceptible idea of Father God and his Son apart from the created order of the heavens and the earth. The Son of the Father is remembered, perhaps still in view mentally, as the man Jesus (1:3), but in this step he is not seen. Here the Son is the "image of the unseen God" (εἰκών τοῦ θεοῦ τοῦ ἀοράτου, 1:15). This existence is presented by bright, visibly, and audibly poetic features that explain things using a precreational texture.[141] What is certain is that the Son is like the Father. God is unseen, and the unseen precreational Son, as God's image, represents the identity of God in the imaginations of the holy ones who live in the created realm (1:16). The phrase "image of the unseen God" evokes the visual memory of humans who were created in the image of God (Gen 1:26–27).[142] In the following parallel (but not appositional) statement, the unseen Son-image is "firstborn of all creation" (πρωτότοκος πάσης κτίσεως), that is, the preeminent one over creation (i.e., the most important authority over the created order). A more visual perspective emerges in the following dependent clauses, where the Son is imagined as the one in whom creation occurred (ὅτι ἐν αὐτῷ ἐκτίσθη τὰ πάντα), in his "sphere of existence,"[143] presumably also indicating instrumentality in creative action. The creative action is envisioned comprehensively, encompassing "all things in the heavens and on the earth," including all seen and unseen powers (1:16). This will at this point have induced mental images, memories, and recalled experiences of the thrones, lordships, rulers, and authorities recognized by the listeners in their contexts. These powers are visualized as created beings who have been created (ἔκτισται, perfect passive) through and for the Son (δι' αὐτοῦ καὶ εἰς αὐτόν). The precreationally active Son is described as preeminent over anyone and anything else, emphasized in this description of his creative and proprietary roles. In three conjoined (καί) clauses, the Son is "before all things" (1:17), indicating prior preeminent existence, as the one in whom "all things hold together" or have their proper place (1:17),[144] and as "head of the body, the *ekklēsia*" (1:18). These clauses

---

141. See Paul Holloway's use of the term "pre-metamorphic existence" in *Philippians: A Commentary*, Hermeneia (Minneapolis: Fortress, 2017), 115.

142. And, for people who read the Bible, memories of the Logos-Jesus of John 1:1–4.

143. As Wilson notes above (*Colossians and Philemon*, 73).

144. συνίστημι literally means "stand with" or "stand together," hence "hold together, consist, be organized, functioning."

enlarge understanding by indicating that all created things continue in organized ways because they are ordered and operate relative to God's Son. Although unseen, this imagined rhetography moves listeners and readers to have a developed conception of the Son, of themselves as members of the *ekklēsia*, and of the entire space-time creation as functioning in orderly ways with Christ preeminent over it.

The poetic sequence continues in a relative and two dependent clauses that again portray the Son preeminently ("who is … so that … because," 1:18b–19). Here the Son is presented as the "beginning, firstborn out of the dead" (ἀρχή, "origin, first cause"; πρωτότοκος, "preeminent child"), thus appearing as the one who exists above and before all others and as the most important of all persons who have been raised from the dead. The dependent clauses indicate intentionality and purpose: the Son visualized being raised from the dead, *so that* he might himself become first of all, this envisioned *because* all the fullness of Father God was pleased to house itself in him.[145] The Son is now visualized as raised and as the one in whom the fullness resides. The meaning of "the fullness" is not explicated but will be presumed by viewers to be the fullness of God. It enhances the not-quite-visual imagery of the Son as completely preeminent, as one who is above and more important than all things connected with human and creational existence.

This step ends in 1:20, where the eternal Son is described in apocalyptic space and activity as the one through whom "all things," that is, created things, whether on the earth or in the heavens, are reconciled to himself[146] and as performing the apocalyptic and priestly peacemaking action of the shedding of his blood on the cross. The peacemaking action, visible in the imagination of space-time, brings about the visual memory in the minds of audience members of what they have heard and believed about the Son, Christ Jesus, being executed by crucifixion, his blood, and the resulting reconciliation and peace.[147] Reconciliation and peace are not in this portrayal provided or possible by any other means.[148] These are strik-

---

145. Many translations add interpretively "of the father" or "of God," or similar renderings, to explain that Father God was the one pleased or that "the fullness" (τὸ πλήρωμα) is God's fullness, assumed retroactively from 2:9. These words do not occur in the Greek text.

146. He being the creator and sustainer of them all.

147. This alludes to the apocalyptic descriptions of 2:12–15.

148. For example by military, economic, or religious action.

ing images. While Christ-believing audiences know immediately what to envision because it is at the heart of their faith, the visualization of blood, cross, and death is nevertheless graphic, pressing home the images of reconciliation and peace, benefits that are pictured as good, safe, and congenial, even if provided through horrifying suffering. The images portray reconciliation and peace not only for human believers in Colossae but for the entire created realm.

This step continues the visualization of the Son of the Father's love (1:14), employing blended precreation discourse where, to make a striking point, the Son's divine nature, his precreational existence, his creative, proprietary, and sustaining role over the creation, and his role as head of the *ekklēsia* are blended with apocalyptic and priestly discourses to portray the benefits that accrue to the entire creation (τὰ πάντα). In the precreationally existent Son is observed the apocalyptic ("the firstborn out of the dead"; reconciliation) and priestly ("through the blood of his cross") activity that benefits the entire creation. This blended discourse and its imagery points to the *ekklēsia*, in which the holy ones now live. The precreational Son reveals what God is like and has brought about the good and holy situation in which they now live.

The contextual environment created by the rhetograph generates an overarching understanding of the identity, prominence, and actions of the Son for the benefit of the entire creation. What has been done for "you," for "us," and for "all things" was provided by God in the precreational Son, who acted apocalyptically and sacrificially and continues, even if unseen, as creator of every possible power, head of the *ekklēsia*, first in all things, one in whom the Father houses (κατοικῆσαι),[149] reconciler and provider of reconciliation and peace. This developed, comprehensive picture dramatically surpasses the individualized views of "you" and "we" in 1:9–14 by extension to cosmic scope. In sight is the accomplished reconciliation and peace of the heavens and the earth "through the blood of his cross." Things are different now in the creation. There is genuine reconciliation and peace regardless of how things look in day-by-day life. The rhetorical implication is that the holy ones need not fear or hesitate, not be troubled, not be persuaded to conform to pressures they encounter in Colossae, the Lycus region, or in the dominating Roman imperial context because the most powerful and generous Son from the precreational realm of God, the one

---

149. Note the οἰκ-, "house," root of this infinitive.

in whom they trust, has moved apocalyptically to provide the sure hope stored up (1:5), even if it is unseen. This is the new vision of reality. Do not worry, do not be persuaded despite the pressures. All will be well. You can trust in what is unseen. Not only is the Son the image of God; he also has the redeeming, forgiving characteristics of the Father.

Translation

> **1:15** who is [the] image of the unseen God,
> firstborn of all creation,
> **1:16** because in him were created all things
> in the heavens and on the earth
> the seen and the unseen things,
> whether thrones, whether lordships, whether rulers, whether authorities,
> all things have been created through him and for him;
> **1:17** and he is before all things,
> and all things hold together in him,
> **1:18** and he is the head of the body, the *ekklēsia*,
> who is the beginning,
> firstborn out of the dead,
> so that he might become himself first in all things,
> **1:19** because in him all the fullness was pleased to house,
> **1:20** and through him to reconcile all things to himself,
> making peace through the blood of his cross,
> whether things on the earth, whether things in the heavens.

Textural Commentary

While it is implied that Paul has been speaking from the beginning of the letter, there is a more distinct *narrational texture* in the developed poetic, theological, and patterned language and ideas in these verses.[150] The voice of implied Paul emphatically narrates poetic understandings of perceived realities regarding the divine and precreational identity of the Son-Christ that had developed by the time Colossians was prepared and delivered. The narration is typically referred to by scholars as a hymn, though it is not

---

150. On narrational texture see Robbins, *Exploring the Textures of Texts*, 15–19.

a single, clear, and consistent poem or liturgy.[151] It might be a composite recitation of preformed lines used liturgically, or it might be a more ad hoc creation of rhythmic and parallel clauses based on developing theologies.[152] The poetic narration presents what was believed to be logical and true about the Son. At the same time, it employs language that speaks to the social, cultural, political, and religious times in the Lycus region and Roman Asia Minor by making clear for Christ believers where genuine power and authority are located. The foundational realities lie in the divine realm of Father God and his Son extending from the precreational domain. The existence of "all things" presupposes God's precreational realm. The narration in this step, then, is not merely offering a high Christology. It is narration intended to draw attention to the perceived reality: the heavens and the earth have been created and are sustained by God's Son. The narrational goal is to draw people into understanding an exclusivity that does not allow for any other perceptions. The rhetorical expectation is that listeners-readers will be moved to acceptance of the reality.

The crucial sociorhetorical features in this step are *repetitive texture*, *sensory-aesthetic texture*, and especially the **intertextures**. The *repetitive texture* of pronouns (ὅς, αὐτός) enact the rhetorical patterning and flow

---

151. Many interpreters think it likely to have been a preformed independent poetic or hymnic unit adapted to fit into Colossians, particularly since Eduard Norden, *Agnostos Theos: Untersuchgungen zur Formgeschichte Religiöser Rede* (Darmstadt: Wissenschaftliche Buchgesellschaft, 1923), 250–54. The lines are rhythmic, metered, poetic but inconsistently so. The term *hymn* is therefore misleading. Whether the verses reflect a real hymn in some way is simply not known (see Dunn, *Epistles to the Colossians and to Philemon*, 84–86). Many have attempted to define the arrangement, sources, and authorship of the language, with remarkable disagreement among them. Many arguments are highly speculative or forced (see the comments in Moo, *Letters to the Colossians and to Philemon*, 108–15, among many others). For extended bibliography see Wilson, *Colossians and Philemon*, 123 n. 1. Certainly there is a poetic, melopoeic effect. See below on *sensory-aesthetic texture*. For argument favoring a preformed tradition, see Lincoln, "Colossians," 601–5. For the contrary view see Sumney, *Colossians*, 60–62; N. T. Wright, "Poetry and Theology in Colossians 1.15-20," *NTS* 36 (1990): 444–68. See also Matthew E. Gordley, *The Colossians Hymn in Context: An Exegesis in Light of Jewish and Greco-Roman Hymnic and Epistolary Conventions*, WUNT 2/228 (Tübingen: Mohr Siebeck, 2007); Jeal, "Starting before the Beginning," 5–6.

152. On rhetorical discourse introducing poetic language as a feature of the rhetoric, see George A. Kennedy, *Comparative Rhetoric: An Historical and Cross-Cultural Introduction* (Oxford: Oxford University Press, 1998), 71–73.

of ideas that focuses attention on the Son as the subject of the poetry. The Son is described by "who is" (twice), "he is" (twice), "in him" (four times), "through him" (once),[153] "through him and for him" (once), and "he"/"him" (twice). Six nouns name aspects of the Son's identity. Repetition of the word *firstborn* (πρωτότοκος, 1:15, 18) sets the Son clearly above all other sons, including imperial sons. Three occurrences of noun and verb forms of the root κτισ- draw attention to the created order of the heavens and the earth (two occurrences), strongly accentuated in turn by eight repetitions of forms of πᾶς ("all"; "all things") and four drumbeat repetitions of εἴτε ("whether"). The adjective "unseen" (ἀόρατος) in 1:15 and 1:16 demonstrates that the unseen realm of divine and nondivine beings is significant to the precreational conceptuality and to the worldview of the holy ones. This large quantity of repetitions functions to demonstrate the Son's divine preeminence and authority as creator, sustainer, head of the *ekklēsia*, and reconciler of the *entire* cosmos.

A notable grammatical thread occurs in the repetitions of the verb κτίζω in 1:16. Both ἐκτίσθη (aorist passive) and ἔκτισται (perfect passive) are third-person singular forms nevertheless translated as the plurals "all things were created" and "all things have been created." This is because "all things" is the synonym of the singular "all creation" (πάσης κτίσεως) in verse 15. The verb forms envision individual things of creation as a whole.

The poetic nature of this step is overt, even though how it flows as poetry is not clear to all interpreters and it has been subjected to a dismaying number of opposing interpretations regarding its origins, structure, preexistence theology, and broader Christology.[154] Clearly the subject of the poetry is the Son of Father God, into whose kingdom believers have been transferred. As poetry, the verses call us to consider *sensory-aesthetic texture*. Sensory-aesthetic texture "resides prominently in the range of senses the text evokes or embodies … and the manner in which the text

---

153. Not counting the unlikely variant δι' αὐτοῦ in 1:20.
154. See above, n. 151. Some propose varying chiastic structures, e.g., Beale, *Colossians and Philemon*, 99–101; Vincent A. Pizzuto, *A Cosmic Leap of Faith: An Authorial, Structural, and Theological Investigation of the Cosmic Christology in Col. 1:15–20*, CBET (Leuven: Peeters, 2006), 118–205. Chiasm was not a category in the ancient rhetorical handbooks. They do describe *antimetabolē* (Lat. *commutatio*), the cross arrangement of words and cola (see Rhet. Her. 4.28). Chiasmus, typically much shorter than 1:15–20, relies on the *inversion* of word order, not merely the repetitions and parallelisms seen here.

evokes or embodies them."[155] This is precisely what poetry (and poets) aims to do. It is about poetic effect, which goes in turn to understanding the rhetorical force of the text. The poetic rhythm is not completely consistent, yet it flows in a patterned structure. It is somewhat in the way of free-verse poetry that has structure, parallelisms, similar and repeated sounds, balanced clauses (syllables and number of words), and developed philosophical and theological ideas that guide the aesthetic argument. What these verses present are aesthetic features that have sensory effects on listeners and readers.

The poetry is set out in three sections or stanzas, 1:15–16, 17–18a, 18b–20.[156] The first and third sections parallel each other, with the opening relative clause beginning with "who is" (ὅς ἐστιν) and with parallel argumentative (explanatory) clauses beginning with "because in him" (ὅτι ἐν αὐτῷ). The second section is composed of two parallel clauses both beginning with "and he is" (καὶ αὐτός ἐστιν). These parallel-repetitive structures indicate the *progressions* or forward movements of the poetry. It is these rhetorical progressions, not the sources or possible redaction of the poetry, that "evoke or embody" senses that move people to insights and understandings. The insights and understandings in turn mediate amenability to what the entire letter is meant to achieve. Similarly, the sensory-aesthetic power of the poetry *moves* its audiences but does not call them to analyze the semantic and theological meaning of every word and line. It is about sensory effects that make for insights to developed Pauline thinking that have pragmatic, wisdom goals.

Stanza 1 (1:15–16)

ὅς ἐστιν εἰκὼν τοῦ θεοῦ τοῦ ἀοράτου,
   πρωτότοκος πάσης κτίσεως,
ὅτι ἐν αὐτῷ ἐκτίσθη τὰ πάντα
   ἐν τοῖς οὐρανοῖς καὶ ἐπὶ τῆς γῆς,
   τὰ ὁρατὰ καὶ τὰ ἀόρατα,

---

155. Robbins, *Exploring the Textures of Texts*, 29–30.

156. Though some interpreters analyze it as having two stanzas, 1:15–17 and 18–20 (e.g., Barth and Blanke, *Colossians*, 227; Sumney, *Colossians*, 62, Beale, *Colossians and Philemon*, 99), and others with four or more (e.g., Wright, "Poetry and Theology"). See also N. T. Wright, *Colossians and Philemon*, TNTC (Grand Rapids: Eerdmans, 1986), 64–66.

εἴτε θρόνοι εἴτε κυριότητες εἴτε ἀρχαὶ εἴτε ἐξουσίαι·
τὰ πάντα δι' αὐτοῦ καὶ εἰς αὐτὸν ἔκτισται·

Balance is evident in the number of syllables, with the first and seventh lines having thirteen syllables each; the second, third, fourth, and fifth lines nine, eleven, ten, and ten syllables respectively; and the interposed sixth line striking its own repetitive εἴτε rhythm with twenty-one syllables. The poetry draws attention to the precreational dimensions of the Son's existence. The Son, into whose kingdom believers have been transferred, is the εἰκών, the "image," that is, the precreational existence or presence of the unseen God.[157] That God is unseen would not be doubted or questioned by the holy ones. The Son, whom they know to be "Lord Jesus Christ" (1:3), manifests the presence of the unseen God to them from cosmic existence. The following "firstborn of all creation" emphasizes and explains the preeminent place and role of the Son over all created things, hence possessing precreational existence as the image of God. This is the developed philosophical-theological understanding about the identity of the Son-Christ. The rest of the stanza presents clear argumentation (*argumentative texture*) for the precreational dimension: "*because* [ὅτι] in him were created all things, the seen and the unseen" in the created orders of the heavens and the earth. It is all-encompassing and inclusive. Everything that has or imagines that it has control in the disordered world in which people live—"whether thrones, whether lordships, whether rulers, whether authorities"—has been "created through him and for him." Nothing is left out or overlooked. This rhetoric carries the Christ believers along. They have no reason to dispute or disagree with the rhythms and meanings of what they hear. Heads nod in embodied agreement. The poetic movement accords with what they already know or sense, even if the philosophical ideas are new. Poetry and their sense of truth make it convincing. The terms employed—"image," "firstborn," "created," "unseen," "heavens," "all things," "for him"—strike the mind as true and believable. They evoke awe, recognition, and agreement, impressing the senses with the precreational Son's being and actions.[158]

---

157. On the wisdom of connections of εἰκών, see below on **intertexture**.

158. None of this or of the following stanzas anticipates the christological debates of later centuries. The poetic point is not doctrinal but indicates the intent of foundational understanding of reality (see Talbert, *Ephesians and Colossians*, 193–95).

Stanza 2 (1:17–18a)

καὶ αὐτός ἐστιν πρὸ πάντων
 καὶ τὰ πάντα ἐν αὐτῷ συνέστηκεν,
καὶ αὐτός ἐστιν ἡ κεφαλὴ τοῦ σώματος τῆς ἐκκλησίας·

This stanza has two parallel lines, both beginning with the copulative καὶ αὐτός ἐστιν, "and he is," and an internal line also beginning with "and" (καί). The lines present broadly similar but not identical ideas that emphasize the prominence, power, authority, and continuing activity of the precreational Son of Father God.[159] The poetic flow of sound in the "and he is ... and he is" parallelism maintains focus on the Son. The sense of recognition and awe of the Son relative to created things and to the community of believers is expanded by stating that the Son has priority positionally, temporally (πρὸ πάντων), and over the body-*ekklēsia* (ἡ κεφαλὴ τοῦ σώματος τῆς ἐκκλησίας).[160] The intermediate "and all things hold together in him" evokes the additional, perhaps obvious understanding that "all things" were not only created by the Son; they are also sustained by him. The Son continues to be at work as everything holds together in him, not in any created systems or beings.[161] Believers in the Son-image of God have a personal, sensory connection with these ideas. The Son of Father God, in whom "we" trust and in whose kingdom we have been placed, is foremost over *everything*. He sustains every good thing that is observed in the cosmos. The holy ones are made to feel that he is head of *our ekklēsia*, our local body of fellow believers. In the created space in which humans live, it is the Son of God who can be trusted. The poetry evokes individual and collective embodied agreement. It inspires confidence and deepened faith.[162]

Stanza 3 (1:18b–20)

ὅς ἐστιν ἀρχή,
 πρωτότοκος ἐκ τῶν νεκρῶν,

---

159. Some interpreters think the verb ἔστιν should be accented to emphasize the Son's precreational existence. It is impossible to be certain either way.

160. Where τῆς ἐκκλησίας stands in apposition to τοῦ σώματος.

161. Thus emphasizing the point that the Son is creator of systems and powers indicated in 1:16.

162. See MacDonald, *Colossians and Ephesians*, 69.

ἵνα γένηται ἐν πᾶσιν αὐτὸς πρωτεύων,
ὅτι ἐν αὐτῷ εὐδόκησεν πᾶν τὸ πλήρωμα κατοικῆσαι
καὶ δι' αὐτοῦ ἀποκαταλλάξαι τὰ πάντα εἰς αὐτόν,
εἰρηνοποιήσας διὰ τοῦ αἵματος τοῦ σταυροῦ αὐτοῦ,
εἴτε τὰ ἐπὶ τῆς γῆς εἴτε τὰ ἐν τοῖς οὐρανοῖς.[163]

This section parallels stanza 1 with the opening "who is" and the argumentative "because in him" structure. They balance nicely with forty-four words in stanza 1 and forty-six in stanza 3. The Son "who is the image" is also the one "who is the beginning." The "firstborn of all creation" is also "firstborn out of the dead." These poetic repetitions intensify listeners' knowledge about the Son and their faith in him. The effect is to remind, assure, and reinforce among the *ekklēsia* members that the Son dominates "all things" from their creation and that he has fully addressed the deep sensory and emotional reality of death. Death is not final. Argumentatively, the Son is the beginning and the firstborn "so that" (ἵνα) he might become and be recognized as "first in all things." The homoeoteleuton of the endings of "dead" (νεκρῶν) and "first" (πρωτεύων) make the melodic point. The "so that" statement also concludes and drives home the "and he is" lines of stanza 2 in the aural completion of the genitive πρὸ πάντων (v. 17a) with the similar-sounding and parallel nominative πρωτεύων (v. 18b). The Son is "before all things" and "first in all things."

As in stanza 1, this section employs "because in him" wording to introduce the precreation dimension: "because in him all the fullness was pleased to house." The fullness is not defined but assumed to be understood in the poetry. The Son is the image of God, creator, sustainer of all things, thereby conveying the insight that the fullness is the fullness of Father God. This becomes explicit in Col 2:9. Listeners to the poetry will recognize in their own lives the truth that this Son is the one in whom God houses, who has reconciled all things whether in the heavens or on the earth—which they view intuitively and experientially as disordered—and is the peacemaker through "the blood of his cross." The metaphor "blood

---

163. The phrase δι' αὐτοῦ occurs at the beginning of this line in some of the best manuscripts but not in many others. It reflects the usage of the phrase in 1:16 and earlier in 1:20. If original, it is meant to reemphasize that the good things have been provided through the Son. From a rhetorical point of view it is a pleonasm that throws the flow of words and syllables out of balance. See the discussion in Foster, *Colossians*, 200–201.

of his cross" is a known and immediately understood sensory-aesthetic image. Blood and crosses go together as crucifixion and death go together. They learned of it from Epaphras (1:7). Blood and cross do not need further explanation. The poetry of stanza 1, "whether thrones, whether lordships, whether rulers, whether authorities," is encompassed by the Son's reconciliation and peace, "whether on the earth or in the heavens." Everything. The listeners understand this. It is embodied in them as people of faith and love.

For first-century Lycus Valley people who have just been told they have been transferred into the new reality of the Son's kingdom, the poetry has a supportive and profoundly sensory force. The preeminent and living Son portrays Father God to them. The very being of the Son draws their minds to imagine the precreation dimensions of reality and to *feel* the goodness of the reconciliation and peace that extends to all things. Though he had died, he is raised out of the dead and lives to hold all things together. Listeners will perceive the "poetic moment" when the ideas are understood and embodied, when they get it.[164] All this evokes awe, respect, and a foundational sense of security. These sensory effects create in them an amenability to what follows in the letter. Whatever seems threatening in the world is becoming irrelevant.

Intertexture. The obvious intertexture with Col 1:15–18a is the creation account of Gen 1. The κτισ- cognate words bring this out immediately,[165] but the entire poetic sequence draws the mind and the sense of visuality to Genesis storytelling. The creation story, however, is reshaped by focusing on the Son as image of God and creator rather than on God and his creative activity. The reshaping is a recontextualization that picks up on the words, ideas, and storyline from Gen 1 without indicating it explicitly.[166] Listeners in the Lycus might be persuaded to recall their own ideas about the creation of "all things" and precreational divine existence. As Christ believers, they now add the knowledge that the Son was present with God prior to creation and was himself engaged in creative action. A similar but not identical intertexture is in the poetic language of Phil 2:5–11, where

---

164. What Ezra Pound calls a "flash of understanding" and "an affective psychological event." See Marianne Korn, *Ezra Pound: Purpose, Form, Meaning* (London: Faber & Faber, 1961), 78.

165. Even though Genesis employs the verb ποιέω, not κτίζω.

166. Robbins, *Exploring the Textures of Texts*, 48.

"Christ Jesus" existed in the "form" (μορφή) of God, took on the "form of a slave," and became a human (2:6–7).[167]

A foundational intertexture is the wisdom storyline found in Prov 3:19–20, 8:22–31, Wis 7:22–8:1, and Sir 1:4–10, 24:1–34. In these texts the feminine wisdom (σοφία, LXX) is personified as a protological existence who was present at creation and participated with God in the creative acts:

> The Lord by wisdom founded the earth;
>   by understanding he established the heavens;
> by his knowledge the deeps broke open,
>   and the clouds drop down the dew. (Prov 3:19–20 NRSV)

> The Lord created me [σοφία] at the beginning of his work,
>   the first of his acts of long ago.
> Ages ago I was set up,
>   at the first, before the beginning of the earth.
> When there were no depths I was brought forth,
>   when there were no springs abounding with water.
> Before the mountains had been shaped,
>   before the hills, I was brought forth—
> when he had not yet made earth and fields,
>   or the world's first bits of soil.
> When he established the heavens, I was there,
>   when he drew a circle on the face of the deep,
> when he made firm the skies above,
>   when he established the fountains of the deep,
> when he assigned to the sea its limit,
>   so that the waters might not transgress his command,
> when he marked out the foundations of the earth,
>   then I was beside him, like a master worker;
> and I was daily his delight,
>   rejoicing before him always,
> rejoicing in his inhabited world
>   and delighting in the human race. (Prov 8:22–31 NRSV)

> for *wisdom*, the fashioner of all things, taught me.
> There is in her a spirit that is intelligent, holy,
> unique, manifold, subtle,

---

167. See the discussion in Holloway, *Philippians*, 114–29. See the possibly contemporary precreational-apocalyptic language of 2 En. 24–25.

mobile, clear, unpolluted,
distinct, invulnerable, loving the good, keen,
irresistible, beneficent, humane,
steadfast, sure, free from anxiety,
all-powerful, overseeing all,
and penetrating through all spirits
that are intelligent, pure, and altogether subtle.
For wisdom is more mobile than any motion;
because of her pureness she pervades and penetrates all things.
For she is a breath of the power of God,
and a pure emanation of the glory of the Almighty;
therefore nothing defiled gains entrance into her.
For she is a reflection of eternal light,
a spotless mirror of the working of God,
and an *image* of his goodness.
Although she is but one, she can do all things,
and while remaining in herself, she renews all things;
in every generation she passes into holy souls
and makes them friends of God, and prophets;
for God loves nothing so much as the person who lives with wisdom.
She is more beautiful than the sun,
and excels every constellation of the stars.
Compared with the light she is found to be superior,
for it is succeeded by the night,
but against wisdom evil does not prevail.
She reaches mightily from one end of the earth to the other,
and she orders all things well. (Wis 7:22–8:1 NRSV)

I [σοφία] came forth from the mouth of the Most High,
    and covered the earth like a mist.
I dwelt in the highest heavens,
    and my throne was in a pillar of cloud.
Alone I compassed the vault of heaven
    and traversed the depths of the abyss.
Over waves of the sea, over all the earth,
    and over every people and nation I have held sway....
Before the ages, in the beginning, he created me,
    and for all the ages I shall not cease to be. (Sir 24:3–6, 9 NRSV)[168]

---

168. See also Philo, "your mother, wisdom, by means of which the universe was completed" (*Det.* 54) and Ps 104:24, "in wisdom you have made them all" (LXX 103:24).

Wisdom is described as having divine and noble characteristics and exists as the "pure emanation of the glory of the Almighty" (ἀπόρροια τῆς τοῦ παντοκράτορος δόξης εἰλικρινής, LXX Wis 7:25),[169] the "image" (εἰκών) of God's goodness, and the "radiance [ἀπαύγασμα; see Heb 1:3] of eternal light" (7:26) who "renews all things," "orders all things well," and "shall not cease to be" (LXX Sir 24:9). Wisdom possesses absolute motion, and "her pureness pervades and penetrates all things" (LXX Wis 7:24). Colossians recontextualizes these ideas to describe God's Son as the divine and noble one who functions as God's agent in the world in whom God's fullness (πλήρωμα) houses, in whom "all things hold together," and who is preeminent over all created things and beings. Wisdom provides a grand resource of ideas for the precreational Son. According to Sirach, wisdom was created prior to the ages and, like God, "will never come to an end" (emphatic double negative "not never," οὐ μὴ ἐκλίπω, 24:9).

Describing the Son as the image of the unseen God recalls Gen 1:26–27, where humankind was created in God's image (see also Gen 5:1, 9:6), and Wis 7:26, where wisdom is the image of God's goodness. The rhetoric does not portray the Son as a man, even if he is the man Christ Jesus, in view since Col 1:3. The divine image of God himself is not explicit in the Genesis story but does appear in Philo's interpretation of Gen 1:27. Philo understood Gen 1:27 to indicate that, because humankind was made in the image of God, it must be the case that the image already existed. This image he also designated as *logos*, the eternal word and creator:

> But the divine *word* [λόγος] which is above these does not come into any visible appearance, inasmuch as it is not like to any of the things that come under the external senses, but is itself an *image* [εἰκών] of God, the most ancient of all the objects of intellect in the whole world, and that which is placed in the closest proximity to the only truly existing God, without any partition or distance being interposed between them: for it is said, "I will speak to you from above the mercy seat, in the midst, between the two Cherubim." So that the word [λόγος] is, as it were, the charioteer of the powers, and he who utters it is the rider, who directs the charioteer how to proceed with a view to the proper guidance of the universe. (*Fug.* 101)[170]

---

169. Or "emanation of the pure glory of the ruler of all." The word *emanation* is from ἀπόρροια, "flow" or "pour out."

170. Translations of Philo follow Philo, *Works of Philo Judaeus, the Contemporary of Josephus*, trans. Charles D. Yonge (London: Bohn, 1854).

For which reason I was induced a little while ago to praise the principles of those who said, "We are all one man's Sons." For even if we are not yet suitable to be called the sons of God, still we may deserve to be called the children of his eternal *image* [τῆς ἀειδοῦς εἰκόνος αὐτοῦ, his incorporeal image], of his most sacred *word*; for the *image* of God is his most ancient *word* [θεοῦ γὰρ εἰκὼν λόγος ὁ πρεσβύτατος]. (*Conf.* 147)

For as those who are not able to look upon the sun itself, look upon the reflected rays of the sun as the sun itself, and upon the halo around the moon as if it were the moon itself; so also do those who are unable to bear the sight of God, look upon his *image* [εἰκόνα], his angel *word* [λόγον], as himself. (*Somn.* 1.239)

In the Pauline letters the description of Christ as "image of God" occurs in 2 Cor 4:4 (ὅς ἐστιν εἰκὼν τοῦ θεοῦ). Males are described as "the image and glory of God" (εἰκὼν καὶ δόξα θεοῦ ὑπάρχων) in 1 Cor 11:7. The term *image* as something of the same likeness, form, nature, or as representative of someone or something else, occurs in various New Testament passages (e.g., Mark 12:16, Matt 22:20, Luke 20:24, Rom 8:29, 1 Cor 15:49, 2 Cor 3:18, Col 3:10, Rev 13:15). The idea of God as unseen is found in the New Testament in Rom 1:20, 23; 1 Tim 1:17; and Heb 11:27 and in other early Christian texts such as 2 Clement 20:5 and Epistle to Diognetus 7:2.[171] In the LXX "unseen" (ἀόρατος) describes the earth at the beginning (ἡ δὲ γῆ ἦν ἀόρατος καὶ ἀκατασκεύαστος, Gen 1:2), God's unseen treasures (Isa 45:3), and God's unseen activity (2 Macc 9:5). In Philo, similarly, God is the unseen being:

When, therefore, the soul that loves God seeks to know what the one living God is according to his essence, it is entertaining upon an obscure

---

171. The εἰκών motif occurs in later gnostic literature: "Matter is one; and this whole Cosmos—the mighty God and *image* of the mightier One, both with Him unified, and the conserver of the Will and Order of the Father—is filled full of Life. Nothing is there in it throughout the whole of Aeon, the Father's [everlasting] re-establishment—nor of the whole, nor of the parts—which does not live. For not a single thing that is dead, has been, or is, or shall be in [this] Cosmos. For the Father willed it should have life as long as it should be. Wherefore it must be a God" (*Corp. herm.* 12.15). With most scholars today, I take the view that Colossians does not have a gnostic redeemer myth in its intertextural background, as claimed by Ernst Käsemann, "A Primitive Christian Baptismal Liturgy," in *Essays on New Testament Themes* (London: SCM, 1964), 154–59.

and dark subject of investigation, from which the greatest benefit that arises to it is to comprehend that God, as to his essence, is utterly incomprehensible to any being, and also to be aware that he is *unseen*. (*Post.* 15)

But the divine being, both *unseen* and incomprehensible, is indeed everywhere, but still, in truth, he is nowhere seen or comprehensible. But when he says, "I am he who stands before Thee," he appears indeed to be displayed and to be comprehended, though before any exhibition or conception he was superior to all created things. (*Conf.* 138, modified)

The concept of the firstborn (πρωτότοκος, 1:15, 19) is frequent in the Hebrew Bible and LXX, where it describes males (including livestock) born first chronologically (e.g., Gen 19:31, 33–34; 27:32), or, metaphorically, one preeminent (whether chronologically or not) over other persons (e.g., Exod 4:22, Ps 89:27). Philo applies the idea to the λόγος:

And even if there be not as yet any one who is worthy to be called a son of God, nevertheless let him labour earnestly to be adorned according to his *first-born word*, the eldest of his angels, as the great archangel of many names; for he is called, the authority, and the name of God, and the Word, and man according to God's image, and he who sees Israel. (*Conf.* 146; see also *Sacr.* 118–119)

The words describing various "powers" ("whether thrones, whether lordships, whether rulers, whether authorities") are drawn from the world of recognizable textual and cultural ideas.[172] The words work together rhetorically as a poetic chain of nominative plurals that, individually and in combination, frequently appear in biblical texts to refer to human (e.g., Luke 12:11, Titus 3:1) and cosmic (Eph 6:12) beings who have or aim to have power over humans or the earth (θρόνοι, Heb 8:1, Rev 2:13, 13:2, 16:10; κυριότητες, Eph 1:21; 2 Pet 2:10; Jude 8; ἀρχαί and ἐξουσίαι, Rom

---

172. See, e.g., Clinton E. Arnold, *The Colossian Syncretism: The Interface between Christianity and Folk Belief at Colossae* (Grand Rapids: Baker, 1996). Contrary to the view of some, because the powers in view can be created human beings and spirit beings and things (e.g., sun and moon), they are not only or even primarily demonic beings over which the Son is preeminent. They include things of the physical universe and powers of empire. Precreation rhetorolect by definition imagines God and his Son relative to the emperor and his Son. The empire of Father God and his Son is preeminent over all other empires.

8:38, Col 2:15, Eph 3:10, 6:12, Titus 3:1).[173] The creation narrative of Gen 1 describes the sun as ruler of the day and the moon as ruler of the night (1:16). According to 1 Sam 13:17–18, three "rulers"[174] of Philistine soldiers set out to fight against the army of Saul and Jonathan. The terms ἀρχαί and ἐξουσίαι commonly appear in Jewish texts in reference to cosmic, unseen beings (1 En. 61.10; 2 En. 20.1; T. Levi 3.8; see Philo, *Gig.* 8–16), while θρόνοι and κυριότητες were recognizable as terminology used by gentiles and Jews in various religious and magical practices.[175]

We should not think that Christ believers in Colossae and the Lycus knew the Hebrew Bible, LXX, other Jewish, and New Testament intertextures or recognized the connections in direct ways. The authors of the letter, on the other hand, pretty clearly knew the intertextures that had helped form the sophisticated development of their theological thinking. They may have known pieces of liturgical-poetic material, or they might have developed their own in the way it appears in 1:15–20, but undoubtedly they knew the intertextures, drew from the language and ideas, and were able to employ them to convey the philosophical-theological poetic description of the identity and work of the Son of God. As noted in the discussion of **social and cultural texture** in the commentary on step one (1:1–2), religion was pervasive, powerful, and diverse in the ancient Mediterranean, certainly so in Asia Minor and the Lycus Valley towns. Residents of Mediterranean towns such as Colossae, Laodicea, and Hierapolis were oriented to the interconnected nature of religion and politics. Religion and politics were not separate, disconnected social and cultural systems.[176] They were tightly interwoven. Characteristic of the religions was ritual observance aimed at gaining or maintaining the favor of the gods.[177] Humans and imperial authorities wished to know what the gods

---

173. The nouns describe things that are personalized to mean human and cosmic beings.

174. Translated as "companies" in most English versions.

175. On this see especially Clinton E. Arnold, *Ephesians: Power and Magic; The Concept of Power in Ephesians in Light of Its Historical Setting*, SNTSMS 63 (Cambridge: Cambridge University Press, 1989); Arnold, *Powers of Darkness: Principalities and Powers in Paul's Letters* (Downers Grove, IL: InterVarsity, 1992); Arnold, *Colossian Syncretism*.

176. See Andrés Cid Zurita, "Similar to Gods: Some Words in the Imperial Cult in the Roman Empire," *Gephyra* 20 (2020): 129.

177. Beard, *SPQR*, 101–3; Cadwallader, *Fragments of Colossae*, 45–69.

willed. They also had a penchant for practices[178] that they were encultured to imagine would please the gods or God, usually in order to get what they wanted or to avoid what they feared. People believed this was important to their well-being, so far as it was possible to acquire well-being in an empire controlled by a tiny minority of wealthy persons.[179]

What emerges in the long sentence (1:9–20, steps three, four, five) is terminology that brought Roman imperial social and cultural ideologies to mind.[180] Where Caesar was the worthy lord who directed the behavior of the empire, Col 1:10 anticipates that believers will "walk worthily of the Lord [κύριος, i.e., Christ Jesus] in every desire to please." Strength comes "according to the power of his glory" (v. 11), and it is God who rescues believers out of the jurisdiction of darkness and transfers them into "the kingdom of the Son of his love" (v. 13). In the Son is redemption and forgiveness (v. 14). It is the Son of God, not the emperor of Rome, whom the holy ones are called to trust. The sentence makes the point, in an oblique way, that true power, authority, kingdom (empire), redemption, peace, and the reconciliation of all things are provided by God through his Son, who is "*the* Lord" (with the article, τοῦ κυρίου), not the emperor in Rome. The new reality comes from God, not from the non-god Caesar. This a dramatic point in the **social and cultural texture** of the letter. God is the one to whom thanksgiving and honor are given. Terms such as these inevitably aroused images of the empire in Lycus Valley minds. People knew their own local and Mediterranean imperial social and cultural spaces. They recognized the dominating social and cultural effects of Roman imperial power and how the Pax Romana was maintained by political, military, economic and religious factors. Images of the emperor in, for example, statuary quickly lose significance in contrast to the Son-image of God.

While some interpreters limit the terms *thrones, lordships, rulers,* and *authorities* to hierarchies of cosmic, spiritual, unseen powers,[181] the

---

178. Or, in more Pauline terminology, "works."

179. According to Carter, the "small elite" that controlled the empire was composed of only 2 to 3 percent of the population (*Roman Empire and the New Testament*, 3).

180. See Harry O. Maier, "Colossians, Ephesians, and Empire," in *An Introduction to Empire in the New Testament*, ed. Adam Winn, RBS 84 (Atlanta: SBL Press, 2016), 186–91.

181. Arnold, *Colossian Syncretism*, 251–70. See also Dunn, who claims that the thrones must be located in heaven, as Dan 7:9, Rev 4:4, along with "dominions," as Eph 1:21 (*Epistles to the Colossians and to Philemon*, 92). Dunn suggests there is "a hierarchy of heavenly powers—'thrones' superior to 'lordships' and so on" in view. But

words *seen* and *unseen* indicate that some of them can be seen. They envision human imperial and political powers.[182] The noun θρόνος occurs many times in the LXX in reference to the seat of kingly political and military power.[183] What becomes evident with the use of these terms is that the precreational image of the Son presented in Col 1 is highly politicized. The rhetoric draws on the cultural intertextures of words and ideas, setting them together to make clear that the Son is protologically, proprietarily, and politically preeminent over all powers.[184] Some of the powers are malevolent, vicious, and brutal, whose realm is darkness (1:13; see 2:8), having fearful concern only for their own disordered interests. The Son as creator is preeminent over against not only unseen *cosmic-spiritual* powers, but also seen (i.e., visually perceptible, known) *political-spiritual* powers, personified in the Mediterranean context by the empire and the emperor, who was portrayed as "the beginning of life and vitality," "savior," and "god-manifest," and was the object of public veneration.[185] The imperial cult became prominent with the veneration accorded to Augustus from the time of his death and subsequently to other emperors:[186]

---

the repeated word εἴτε does not mean "superior to" but does indicate a rhetorical and melopoeic catena that impresses the scope of powers on the mind.

182. See Barth and Blanke, *Colossians*, 201–2. Including imperial and political powers significantly affects the argument being made. Against this view, see Andrew T. Lincoln, "Liberation from the Powers: Supernatural Spirits or Societal Structures," in *The Bible in Human Society: Essays in Honour of John W. Rogerson*, ed. M. Daniel Carroll R., David J. A. Clines, and Philip R. Davies (Sheffield: Sheffield Academic, 1995), 344–45. Lincoln claims that the list of powers refers only to those "unseen" (ἀόρατα).

183. On this see Walter Wink, *Naming the Powers: The Language of Power in the New Testament* (Philadelphia: Fortress, 1984) 11–18; Lincoln, "Liberation from the Powers," 344.

184. For a creative and helpful study of the political implications of these verses, see Walsh and Keesmaat, *Colossians Remixed*, 80–95.

185. For these references see Richard A. Horsley, "The Gospel of the Savior's Birth," in *Christmas Unwrapped: Consumerism, Christ and Culture*, ed. Richard A. Horsley and James Tracy (Harrisburg, PA: Trinity Press International, 2001), 16; Walsh and Keesmaat, *Colossians Remixed*, 90. For a general discussion of deification and worship of Roman emperors, see Simon R. F. Price, *Rituals and Power: The Roman Imperial Cult in Asia Minor* (Cambridge: Cambridge University Press, 1984).

186. See above on **social and cultural texture** in step one. See, among others, Cid Zurita, "Similar to Gods," passim.

SCENE ONE: INTRODUCTORY RHETORIC

Since Emperor Caesar, *son of god*, god *Sebastos* has by his benefactions to all men outdone even the Olympian gods… (Coan decree)[187]

The providence which divinely ordered our lives created with zeal and munificence the most perfect good for our lives by producing Augustus and filling him with virtue for the benefaction of humankind, sending us and those after us a *savior* [σωτήρ] who put an end to war and established all things … and whereas the birthday of the *god* [Augustus] marked for the world the beginning of *good tidings* [εὐαγγέλιον] through his coming… (proposal by the assembly of the province of Asia, 9 BCE)

The birthday of the *divine* Caesar is a matter of greater pleasure or benefit. We could justly hold it to be equivalent to the beginning of all things, and he has restored at least to serviceability, if not to its natural state, every form that had become imperfect and fallen into misfortune.… Therefore it seems proper to me that the birthday of *the most divine Caesar* shall serve as the same New Year's Day for all citizens. (proposal to start the new year on Augustus's birthday)

The Council and the people (of the Ephesians and other Greek) cities which dwell in Asia and the nations acknowledge Gaius Julius, the son of Gaius Caesar as High Priest and Absolute Ruler … *the god visible* who is born of Ares and Aphrodite, the shared *Savior* [σωτήρ] of human life. (decree of the city council of Ephesus regarding Caligula, 38 CE)[188]

Many temples and shrines of the imperial cult were established in Asia Minor and were well-known.[189] Certainly there were levels of resistance to the notion that emperors were gods, yet even Tiberius, who famously discouraged divine respect, in fact allowed his statue in Pergamon to "be worshipped among the gods."[190]

Socially and culturally, the rhetoric of Colossians is not directly resistant or subversive but indicates that, in the emerging society of the holy ones in Christ, the Mediterranean religious concern to please and appease

---

187. *Coan* describes things related to the island of Kos (Cos in Acts 21:1).

188. These inscriptions are recorded in Price, *Rituals and Power*, 54–55.

189. See the catalogue of sites in Price, *Rituals and Power*, 249–74. See also the description of the sebasteion at Aphrodisias in Maier, *Picturing Paul in Empire*, 51–55, 76–92. See also the statements of praise of Tiberius made by Philo, *Legat.* 149–151.

190. On this see Joan E. Taylor, "Pontius Pilate and the Imperial Cult in Roman Judaea," *NTS* 52 (2006): 569; see also Cid Zurita, "Similar to Gods," 127.

the gods in order to get what people want is irrelevant. Caesar and empire are not providers of all humans need. The holy ones in Christ are encouraged to "walk worthily of the Lord," not of Roman and regional lords, and it is Father God himself who qualifies people to share in the great inheritance.[191]

The divine presence in the person of the emperor is evident in a kind of theological literature that developed in authors such as Virgil, Horace, and Livy during the time of Augustus where, while Jupiter is acknowledged as supreme, Caesar is set in second divine space. The following selections from Horace display this:[192]

> What man, what hero, will you raise,
> By what shrill pipe or deeper lyre!
> What god, O Clio, will you praise,
> And teach the Echoes to admire?
>
> Whom should I first record, but Jove [Jupiter],
> Whose sway extends o'er sea and land,
> The king of men and gods above,
> Who holds the seasons in command?
>
> To rival Jove shall none aspire;
> None shall to equal glory rise....
>
> The fates, O Sire of human race,
> Intrust great Caesar to thy care;
> Give him to hold thy second place,
> And reign thy sole viceregent here.
>
> While on our groves thy bolts are hurled,
> And thy loud car shakes heaven above,
> He shall with justice awe the world,
> To none inferior but Jove. (*Carm.* 12, *To Augustus*)

---

191. It may be imagined that few persons in the Roman world ever received much in the way of financial or material inheritances. Most people lived in varying levels of poverty, and few were likely to have had much of value to leave to heirs. Being qualified to receive an inheritance made Christ believers privileged persons.

192. Quotations from Horace follow *The Odes, Epodes, Satires, and Epistles* (London: Warne, 1889).

> But your deserts maturer honours claim,
> And shrines already consecrate your name,
> All prompt to own, ere yet you mount the skies,
> That nothing such has ris'n nor e'er shall rise.
> And yet your people (wisely thus and well)
> On this point agreed, that you excel,
> Whose name they justly rank on earth
> Above all Greek—above all Roman worth. (*Ep.* 2.1, *To Augustus Caesar*)

Even if poetically described in second place, the Gemma Augustea cameo depicts, in material form, Augustus enthroned as Jupiter as he was imagined during the years 10–20 CE, a depiction of emperors that continued subsequently.[193] Augustus even became described as the one whom Rome implored for the removal of sin:

> To whom shall Jove assign to purge away
> The guilty deed? Come, then, bright god of day,
> But gracious veil thy shoulders beamy bright,
> Oh! veil in clouds th' unsufferable light. (Horace, *Carm.* 2, *To Augustus*)

The ritual observances of the cult involved celebrations, processions, sacrifices, obeisance before statues and images, calendrical events such as special anniversaries, ceremony involving the use of incense, speeches, feasts, and athletic games. Among the most notable of these are the calendrical observances of imperial anniversaries, particularly the emperor's birthday, the anniversary of the emperor's accession to the throne, and anniversaries of the emperor's major military victories.[194] These anniversaries were marked by celebrations and sacrifices. The underlying idea was that participants in the observances would engage in ceremonial as if the emperor himself were actually present.[195] People were expected to participate. Classicist Ken Dowden states,

> It was important to have a good track-record of loyal emperor cult in case you ever needed it. But it also mattered to the well-adjusted community that its rituals expressed and demonstrated its place in the world,

---

[193]. See "Gemma Augustea," Wikipedia, https://tinyurl.com/SBL7106e.
[194]. Rives, *Religion in the Roman Empire*, 149.
[195]. On this see Bruce W. Winter, *Seek the Welfare of the City: Christians as Benefactors and Citizens* (Grand Rapids: Eerdmans, 1994), 129–31.

including its dependence on the emperor. In the Greek East in particular, where a meticulous system of festivals finely tuned the concerns of the community, a flourishing emperor cult meant a vital aspect of the well-being of the community was comfortably expressed.[196]

The visible performance of cultic observances indicated that people met social and cultural expectations and supported the unity of the people. Refusal to practice the observances led to social tensions in the communities. It is evident, as time went along, that many Christ believers refused to participate. Mackay observes,

> Generally speaking, sane emperors did not expect to be treated like gods, but it was regular practice to use adjectives like "sacred" and "divine" to describe the emperor and to make a small offering of wine or incense before an image of the reigning emperor as a sign of loyalty. The refusal of Christians to participate in this civic ceremony became an important element in the conflict that was to arise between the new cult and the imperial government.... Certainly no sane person considered the emperor to be a god in the normal sense of the word, and a fair number of Romans—including certain emperors—made fun of the institution. Nonetheless, the persistence of the cult and the fact that the driving force behind the practice was not governmental coercion but the spontaneous impulse of the "worshippers" show that it fulfilled a deeply felt need. In effect the emperor was the personification of the state, and the performance of divine ritual in his honor not only provided a vivid means of expressing one's allegiance to the state but also allowed the subject to feel that he had a personal relationship with that state.[197]

It is clear that Colossians has this Roman imperial culture consciousness in sight. Transferal to the empire of the Son-Christ is transfer to a new culture and new ideology that transcends all Rome offers. The good news (εὐαγγέλιον, 1:23) is about the Son, not Caesar. Because the Colossians lived where they did and were embedded in the dominant cultural consciousness of the eastern provinces, because such things were features of the cultural milieux, it was impossible for them to miss the implications of the letter. They would naturally blend perceptions from the multiple spaces of their existence and understand the nuances of the language. This

---

196. Ken Dowden, *Religion and the Romans* (London: Bristol Classical Press, 1992), 62.
197. Mackay, *Ancient Rome*, 259.

does not mean that only the empire and the Caesar cult are in view in Colossians but that it is a major feature of the letter and an unmistakable and unavoidable sociocultural connection.

Rhetorical Force as Emergent Discourse

For people who now see themselves having been transferred to the new kingdom reality, this poetry has penetrating meaning and force. The poetry impresses their minds with the undergirding philosophy for the faithful and loving lives they now experience and practice in Christ. It evokes awe and confidence in the Son-Christ, of whom they have heard and in whom they have placed their trust. What they believe and where they are located in Christ is not a construct of human or cosmic powers, is not a construct of political, social, or cultural forces, but is securely founded in the identity and actions of the precreational Son of God, who is creator, reconciler, and peacemaker of all things whether on the earth or in the heavens. This rhetoric elicits the recognition and trust that the Son-Christ provides order in the created realm in contrast to the domination, disorder, stress, and suffering under all other perceived powers. It therefore presents an exclusive philosophy-theology extending to "all things" (τὰ πάντα). Christ Jesus is the sole Son of God, the sole creator and sustainer, the sole reconciler, and peace in the created orders is made solely through the blood of his cross. This multidimensional, apocalyptic Son dominates over all things. Nothing is untouched, and everything is different now. This is stark, dramatic rhetoric in ancient Mediterranean contexts. The chaos of life in the ancient Mediterranean and in the much-promoted Pax Romana is contrasted to the order of the Son's kingdom. This is not meant to generate direct anti-Roman, subversive ideologies. The power of Rome is not ignored or directly undermined, only made, theologically speaking, irrelevant.[198] The supposed logic of the political-spiritual and cosmic-spiritual powers is obviated. What the Lycus audiences will understand is the exclusivity of the Son's identity, preeminence, apocalyptic actions, and the results of the actions. It all works because it is true.

The rhetorical force is, of course, headed somewhere as the letter proceeds. As we will see, the ideas are brought to a major goal in 1:21–23,

---

198. This is not to say that the empire was irrelevant to people who lived there. It is to say that the *power* of Rome did not transcend the power of the Son-Christ. The theological extends to the practical.

which envisions the believers being presented as "holy and without blemish and without reproach in front of him" (the Son-Christ). It also anticipates the concerns of Col 2:6–23 that the holy ones not be carried away by empty, deceitful ideas, by the disordered ways of the "elements of the cosmos," and by things that seem logical but in fact have no value. The poetry provides a philosophical framework that gives reasons to hang on to the faith (1:23). What eventually is envisioned is the statement of Col 3:11, "Christ all and in all." As development of Paul's thinking observed in the earlier (undisputed) letters, the poetry suggests a thoughtful deepening of Paul's righteousness/justification understanding based on Hab 2:4 (recited in Rom 1:17 and Gal 3:11). The oracles of Habakkuk (late seventh–early sixth centuries BCE) call for relief from violence and envision God's apocalyptic intervention. In the end, Habakkuk rejoices in Yahweh: "God the Lord is my Strength" (Hab 3:18–19). In the meantime, he encourages watching and waiting in anticipation of "the appointed time" (2:1–3), noting that "the righteous live by their faith" (2:4). The poetry of Col 2:15–20 imagines that God has acted to bring fullness of reconciliation and peace through the violence done to his Son.[199]

Whether the authors borrowed a familiar bit of early Christian liturgy, or adapted something found elsewhere, or wrote a new melodic poem is of little consequence. What is important is how it employs ideas, concepts, and modes of discourse, how it draws on social and cultural frameworks, argues a case, and presents ideologies that convey understanding of a rich mental, intellectual, religious space, where the holy ones can rest confidently.

Step Six: Alienation, Reconciliation, and Faithful Living (1:21–23)

Rhetography

This step focuses the line of sight on the reconciliation God provides for believers through his Son. The Son continues here to be viewed as the reconciler (hence also peacemaker, as 1:20) by means of the death of his own body of flesh in order to present people as holy, faultless, and without reproach before (in front of) himself. This reconciliation was performed despite the fact that the holy people, displayed in a brief flashback to their

---

199. How long would it take to develop this theological thinking? Years? Decades? Perhaps it would not take intelligent, thoughtful persons such as Paul or his coworkers very long.

former existence, were estranged, enemies in mind in evil deeds (1:21). Reconciliation is graphically envisioned "in the body of his flesh through death," reinforcing the image that appeared in the previous step, "the blood of his cross" (1:20). Death of another, in this case, benefits humans. They appear in the presence of the very one who was crucified, shed his own blood, and died for their benefit.[200] They are visualized as having been undeserving people who nevertheless now stand purified.

The picture changes focus from the Son to the Lycus believers themselves in the conditional statement "if indeed you continue in the faith" (1:23). Their continued position in front of him assumes they remain in the faith and unmoved from the hope of the gospel. This altered focus is significant because since verse 12 the rhetograph has centered attention on Father God and the Son-Christ as the active characters who bring about blessings for believers. Now letter recipients are moved to view themselves as people who consciously keep themselves securely in the faith and hope brought about by the gospel.[201] They are of course seen as people who do have a solid faith, and they have not yet shifted away from or weakened in the hope they have obtained from the gospel. The picture, however, suggests that these people are standing in a place from which they could fall, that the possibility of being shaken from their position exists. They have been viewed since the opening lines of the letter (1:2, 6) as faithful people who bear fruit, and they are seen to have been rescued and reconciled, yet they are here reminded to stay where they are.[202] The following relative clause calls the audience to envision the time when they heard the proclamation of the gospel, when it came to them as a prophetic word (1:23). The scene of that proclamation and hearing is expanded with an image of the proclamation of the gospel "in all creation under heaven," giving a sense of the effect of the gospel.[203] Finally, the scene closes with another look at

---

200. See Barth and Blanke, *Colossians*, 222. Some interpreters argue that they are presented before God, not Christ.

201. The audience members are not observed to be actively acquiring a secure and steadfast faith and hope but to be unmoved from faith and hope.

202. This signals what is to come later in the letter, where the audience is warned against belief and behavior that can jeopardize what they have in Christ.

203. This rhetoricized statement should not be taken either literally or as hyperbole. The authors and the recipients would have known that not every person in the creation had heard the gospel message. It is better to understand it as referring to the effect of the gospel on the reconciliation of all things (1:20). Everything has been affected by the death and resurrection of the Son-Christ (see Foster, *Colossians*,

Paul, not here as the apostle viewed in verse 1 but as a servant (διάκονος) of the gospel.

This step sharpens the visual focus on the priestly actions of the precreational, firstborn, preeminent, fullness-inhabited Son, who through his own death has brought about reconciliation for the formerly alienated, hostile persons who engaged in evil activities. Priestly discourse is blended with apocalyptic explanation to bring out the contrast between past and present. The priestly language then blends with wisdom rhetorolect, aiming to encourage them to remain steadfastly connected to the hope brought about by the Son's reconciling death along with a reminder of the prophetic proclamation of the gospel that they, along with other persons, had heard. These blends focus the line of sight directly on the reconciling Son and also on the audience members themselves. Paul is visualized only at the edge of the picture as servant of the gospel.

The entire first scene has cast a comprehensive visual image on the minds of readers and listeners to the letter. The audiences observe a happy setting where Paul and Timothy address faithful, loving members of the community among whom the gospel is producing much fruit. Virtual Paul is observed in continuous prayer for these people, envisioning as he does so their ongoing fruitful lives and their growing knowledge of God. The lines of sight draw eyes upward with the visualization of Jesus Christ, the preeminent, precreational Son of God, who in his own death has brought about the cheerful scene of reconciled people. What is developed is a rhetographic, visual conceptuality that draws minds to a scene where the various players exist in a community where there are good relationships among all. This has been brought about by priestly work of the Son. They must be sure that they remain as participants in the scene that they are being called to visualize. This introductory rhetography sets the visual imagery for what follows in the letter.

Translation

> **1:21** And you were then estranged and enemies in the mind in evil works, **1:22** but now he reconciled[204] (you) in the body of his

---

209–10). Interestingly, the wording does not envision the heavens and the earth as in 1:16, 20, but all creation under heaven, singular.

204. NA[28] and UBS[5] use the strongly attested ἀποκατήλλαξεν but indicate variant readings ἀποκαταλλαγέντες, ἀποκατήλλακται, ἀπήλλαξεν.

flesh through death to present you holy and without blemish and faultless and without reproach in front of him, **1:23** if indeed you remain in the faith, having been established and steadfast and not shifted from the hope of the gospel which you heard, the one proclaimed in all creation under heaven, of which I Paul have become servant.

Textural Commentary

The range of **inner textures** draws audiences along in this sentence. The *progression* ahead is obvious in the connector *and*, joining the ideas to the long preceding sentence, but the continuation is interpreted here as beginning a new sentence. More prominently, the ideas move ahead in the ποτέ/νυνί, "then"/"now," sequencing and in how this step picks up and moves ahead on the reconciliation concept mentioned already in 1:20. The *then/now* packages the progression in a framework where the former situation where "you" were in a very evil condition and mindset contrasts with the present situation where "you" are presented as holy, faultless, and without reproach. The movement to "now" progresses ahead further in the conditional statement "if indeed you remain in the faith." Do not be moved away from what you have heard (see 1:5–6). The gospel, too, has moved ahead into new spaces, being effective everywhere under heaven, which, of course, reminds of the "all creation" and "all things" language of 1:6, 15–17, 20. The entire progression returns to where the introductory rhetoric began, to Paul, the apostle (1:1), now with the self-description "servant" of the proclaimed gospel. As first-person *narrational texture* ("I Paul"), attention shifts back to describing the Lycus audiences, employing the "then" and "now," before and after, rhetoric to emphasize their reconciled, holy, blameless state. The implied narrator makes clear, however, that they have a continuing role. They may not be passive observers. They must remain in the faith, solidly grounded and not shifting from the hope of the gospel. The narrational repetition of *hope* and *gospel* (see 1:5) elicits memories of what was already mentioned, followed by the amplification that the gospel has been proclaimed everywhere. Listeners are being prepared to be led on to continue in their faithfulness as reconciled people and to be ready to listen to more.

Repetition of the verb "reconcile" (ἀποκαταλλάσσω) in 1:22 after its use in 1:20 sets the special focus on the major theme of this step. The holy ones were formerly distant from God, estranged, enemies, doing evil things, but have been reconciled. The reconciliation brought about by means of the blood of the Son's cross noted in 1:20 is repeated and given clarity in differing language and an altered picture in 1:22 with the terms *body*, *flesh*, and *death*. These repetitions function on their own to make the argument of the step. Paul's role relative to the reconciliation and to proclamation is to be "servant" (διάκονος, 1:23), a repeated term placing Paul in the same category and prophetic space as Epaphras (1:7), repeated again in 1:25. The narrational repetition of *hope* and *gospel* (from 1:5) keeps the gospel location of the letter's concerns in sight.

The ποτέ/νυνί, before/after, sequencing is a naturally *sensory-aesthetic texture*. It draws out emotion-fused feelings of memories of the past contrasted with gratitude for the present condition. The reminder of the past brings out the felt recollection of what life then was like: estranged, having hostile minds, practicing evil activities. The past "then" condition was far from an aesthetic existence, being characterized by separation, selfishness, and disorder. Recognition of the present evokes the much more edifying sense of peace and reconciliation, even if the very notion of reconciliation immediately brings out the emotive sense of pain experienced in Christ's body of flesh. The near tactile sense of being presented in front of the visualized suffering but now raised Christ ("firstborn out of the dead," 1:18), as holy, unblemished, and blameless people while surrounded by memories of the past, gives a visual positioning of the new wisdom space, brought about as it is by priestly and apocalyptic activity.[205] Priestly and apocalyptic blending produces the line of sight toward the now inhabited wisdom space. Alienation, hostility, evil works, body of flesh, and death are sensory, unaesthetic, and pathos-filled conditions now removed and contrasted with standing in the presence of God's Son/king/emperor in a pure state. This present condition is directly connected to the sense of hearing (1:23). The Colossian believers—along with many others—heard the gospel message during their former "then" life and by it were persuaded to live in the reality of the "now" aesthetic life. It was hearing that brought about conscious knowledge of the newly oriented existence. The sensory experience is extended to the entire creation, a filling out of the aesthetic of the fruit bearing and growth in all the world presented in 1:6.

---

205. On the significance of the infinitive παραστῆσαι (παρίστημι), see on **intertexture** below.

SCENE ONE: INTRODUCTORY RHETORIC 117

The artistry and rhetoric of the language of this step is visible and audible:

Καὶ ὑμᾶς ποτε ὄντας ἀπηλλοτριωμένους καὶ ἐχθροὺς τῇ διανοίᾳ ἐν τοῖς ἔργοις τοῖς πονηροῖς,
νυνὶ δὲ ἀποκατήλλαξεν ἐν τῷ σώματι τῆς σαρκὸς αὐτοῦ διὰ τοῦ θανάτου παραστῆσαι ὑμᾶς ἁγίους καὶ ἀμώμους καὶ ἀνεγκλήτους κατενώπιον αὐτοῦ,
εἴ γε ἐπιμένετε τῇ πίστει τεθεμελιωμένοι καὶ ἑδραῖοι καὶ μὴ μετακινούμενοι ἀπὸ τῆς ἐλπίδος τοῦ εὐαγγελίου
οὗ ἠκούσατε, τοῦ κηρυχθέντος ἐν πάσῃ κτίσει τῇ ὑπὸ τὸν οὐρανόν, οὗ ἐγενόμην ἐγὼ Παῦλος διάκονος.

These four statements present the rhetoric. They progress in a logical sequence: "and you then…," "but now…," "if indeed you…," and "which you heard…." Second-person verbal forms have the holy ones as subjects, while the action of the Son is third-person: "you being estranged," "he reconciled," "you remain," "you heard," and at the end is the first-person reference to Paul: "I became." The shift from second- to third-person action with νυνὶ δὲ ἀποκατήλλαξεν moves ear and eye to grasp the sensory contrast from the physical (and moral) inability of humans to achieve reconciliation to the very physical reconciling activity of the Son-Christ in his own body.[206] His body is the pain-feeling entity that provides purity for the reconciled. This is felt, emotional contrast. Evil works in human behavior are taken up and overcome in the evil and painful things done to the Son. The leading terms that describe before-and-after situations, ἀπηλλοτριωμένους and ἀποκατήλλαξεν, are aurally harmonious in their similar prefixes, parallelism of vowels and consonants, and number of syllables.[207] Memories of the hearing experienced by the Colossians, presumably an allusion to the sensorily experienced preaching of Epaphras (1:7), makes clear that the reconciliation and presentation before the true king is something that

---

206. Some manuscripts have the less well-attested second-person passive textual variant ἀποκατηλλάγητε. The active voice agrees more felicitously with the "now" condition being described.

207. The perfect passive participle ἀπηλλοτριωμένους indicates that the breach was imposed on people, not something self-produced. Their "evil deeds" were their own (καὶ ἐχθροὺς τῇ διανοίᾳ ἐν τοῖς ἔργοις τοῖς πονηροῖς). This matches the action of the other side because reconciliation (ἀποκατήλλαξεν, third-person singular) has been performed by the Son-Christ.

came to them from the outside. The copulative terms (ἀπηλλοτριωμένους καὶ ἐχθροὺς; ἁγίους καὶ ἀμώμους καὶ ἀνεγκλήτους; τεθεμελιωμένοι καὶ ἑδραῖοι) form descriptive, euphonic (by genitive and dative endings, homeoteleuton, alliteration) and appealing images empowering the rhetoric. The believers hear the threefold sound that they have been solidly founded (τεθεμελιωμένοι, built on a foundation), firmly seated (ἑδραῖοι), and are not being moved away (μὴ μετακινούμενοι) from their hope.

The *argumentative texturing* extends from the preceding poetry-philosophy portraying the Son as the one through whom all things are reconciled. Not only have all things been reconciled, but in a more directly personal way God in him has reconciled "you," members of the *ekklēsia*, through his physical death. It is an uncomplicated and reasonable argument to grasp: given all that you have in the Son, remain in the faith (1:23). The point is made in the nicely textured then/now argumentative form that makes the point clearly: *then* you were estranged enemies, *now* you are reconciled.[208] The spaces people inhabit have been reversed.[209] Everything is different now in the new reality. Remaining in the new kingdom reality is the right thing to do.

The conditional statement "if you remain in the faith" is probably not meant to suggest doubt about people's continuing reconciliation or the potential loss of it but envisions the reality of living in the present, where there are threatening things that require knowledge, perseverance, and patience (1:9–11).[210] The gospel truth believers have learned (1:5–7) must not be forgotten. Threats are already being faced by the Lycus *ekklēsiai* (2:6–23). The philosophical-theological foundation and argumentation of 1:9–23 anticipates discussion of them.

An internal argument claims that the reconciliation brought about by Christ, in his body through his death, was done "to present you holy and faultless and blameless in front of him" (1:22). The infinitive παραστῆσαι can be understood to have either causative[211] or resultative force, but either way it argumentatively states that the condition and space the Colossian holy ones inhabit "in front of" Christ is privileged and pure.

---

208. The expression "but now" is, according to Dunn, a paulinism indicating divine reversal; see Rom 3:21; 6:22; 7:6; 11:30; 1 Cor 15:20; Phlm 11 (*Epistles to the Colossians and to Philemon*, 107).

209. See the language of "far" and "near" in Eph 2:12–22, especially 2:13, 17.

210. See Lincoln, "Colossians," 606.

211. Its typical function in the present; LSJ, 1340.

Case: Through the Son you who were formerly estranged from God are now reconciled.
Purpose/Result: You are now holy, blameless, and without reproach in Christ's presence.

This argumentation emphasizes the sanctified and guilt-free wisdom space inhabited by Christ believers. It enhances the desirability of accepting the larger argument of the step encouraging ongoing faithfulness.

The then/now argumentation has many points of **intertextural** contact.[212] Before-and-after descriptions are always powerful because they evoke understanding of change. The direct New Testament intertexture is with Eph 2:1–10, 11–22, where the same harmonious-sounding, oppositional before-and-after words ἀπαλλοτριόω (Eph 2:12, 4:18) and ἀποκαταλλάσσω (Eph 2:16) are explicit, as they are in Col 1:21–22.[213] The words were in the air and understandable to people in Asia Minor. Familiarity with the language made the rhetoric effective. The stark texture of estrangement occurs in LXX Ps 57:4; 68:9; Jer 27:8; Ezek 14:5, 7; Hos 9:10; Sir 11:34, indicating alienation from God or from people. In Eph 2:12, gentiles are alienated, disconnected from Israel by virtue of being gentiles. The nearer **intertexture** to Col 1:21 is Eph 4:18, where ἀπαλλοτριόω is closely connected with the mind (διάνοια) and with behavior.[214] That those who were estranged were also hostile in their minds emphasizes the stark, bare rhetorical intertexture of the estrangement by illuminating its adversarial nature. It receives further stark elaboration by being observable "in evil works," which has many particularly Jewish oral-scribal points of contact (e.g., T. Dan 6.8; T. Ash. 6.5; Pss. Sol. 17.13). Romans 5:10 employs the same language where former enemies have been reconciled by God through the

---

212. It may well have been a frequent feature of early Christian sermons (see Lincoln, "Colossians," 606). On the then/now motif in Eph 2, see Jeal, *Integrating Theology and Ethics*, 130–63. See also Ernst Tachau, *"Einst" und "Jetzt" im Neuen Testament. Beobachtungen zu einem urchristlichen Predigt-Schema in der neutestamentlichen Briefliteratur und zu seiner Vorgeschichte*, FRLANT 105 (Göttingen: Vandenhoeck & Ruprecht, 1972).

213. Ephesians most likely draws on Colossians, or the authors draw on their memories of using the same terms and ideas.

214. The word διάνοια is more inclusive than the intellectual mind in intertextural usage. In the LXX it is frequently used to translate the word לֵב, meaning "heart, will, mind" (Exod 36:1, Lev 19:7, Deut 29:17, Josh 14:8, Isa 35:4; see Barth and Blanke, *Colossians*, 219).

death of his Son and "much more will be saved in his life."[215] The apocalyptic intertexture of reconciliation is frequent in the Pauline letters (Rom 5:10–11, 11:15, 1 Cor 7:11, 2 Cor 5:18–20). Here in Col 1:20–21 reconciliation is connected to peace. In Roman imperial context, people, such as those in Colossae, understood that peace was imagined to be the product of empire. This tradition had a long history indicated in many texts (Plutarch, *Alex. fort.* 6 [329c]; Virgil, *Aen.* 6.851–853; *Res gestae Divi Augusti* 13, 26).[216] Peace, however, was perceived to come about not in reconciliation but by the conquering of nations and subjugation of people. Similarly, New Testament intertextures state that the powers and the disobedient who aim to be powerful in the world face subjugation (1 Cor 15:24–28, Phil 3:21, Col 2:15, 3:6). But according to 2 Cor 5:18–19, God reconciled "us" to himself and was reconciling "the world to himself." Reconciliation is cosmic activity that transcends local, regional, religious, and imperial efforts to address the alienation people and nations experience. Genuine reconciliation is brought about only in the body of the Son's flesh through his death. It would be difficult for Lycus residents to miss the implication that it is not the empire or the emperor or cosmic powers that reconcile the diverse peoples across the Mediterranean and larger Roman world but is Father God in his Son-Christ who does this in the Son's own body and flesh. This is a rhetorically powerful implication that textual, social, and historical intertextures help clarify.

These intertextures are elaborated by the purpose statement "to present you holy and faultless and blameless in front of him." Here the aorist infinitive παραστῆσαι induces stark intertextural images because, while having a fairly broad semantic range, the word frequently functions for the presentation of sacrifice on an altar (as Rom 12:1) or an accused person before a judge (see Col 1:28). There are many examples of usage from ancient Greek times (Pindar, *Ol.* 6.41f, fifth century BCE) to later Greek and Roman writers (Polybius, *Hist.* 3.72.9, 16.25.7, second century BCE; Virgil, *Aen.* 12.171, late first century BCE; Cicero, *Att.* 10.16.6, first century BCE; Josephus, *A.J.* 4.113, first century CE), and in many first-century CE and later papyri that describe persons being presented before various kinds of judicial proceedings (e.g., P.Ryl. 2.94 [14–37 CE]; P.Oxy.Hels.

---

215. Being reconciled and being saved are closely connected in Rom 5:10.
216. These references from Talbert, *Ephesians and Colossians*, 196. *Res gestae Divi Augusti* is "The Deeds of the Divine Augustus," the funerary inscription of Augustus.

259 [23 CE]; P.Amh. 2.66 [124 CE]).[217] Polybius used the verb παρίστημι to describe the presence of priests and priestesses and of sacrifices brought to an altar: "the priests and priestesses lined the street on both sides: all the temples were then thrown open; victims were placed ready at all the altars; and the king was requested to present [παραστήσαντες] sacrifice" (*Hist.* 16.25.7). Josephus, recounting the story of Balaam and Balak, describes sacrificial offerings using the infinitive παραστῆσαι: "Now when he saw them, he desired the king to build him seven altars, and to present [παραστῆσαι] as many bulls and rams; to which desire the king did presently conform" (*A.J.* 4.113).

In the LXX παριστάνω occurs frequently to describe human, angelic, demonic, or cosmic beings presenting themselves or being presented before God (e.g., LXX Num 16:9; Deut 10:8; Job 1:6; 2:1; Dan 7:10, 13; Zech 6:5; Tob 12:15; many others). In the New Testament the raised Jesus is described in Acts 1:3 as presenting himself alive to people, and παριστάνω appears in Acts 23:33 to describe Paul being presented before Felix. New Testament usage typically refers to the presentation of people in literal or metaphorical bodily form (Rom 6:13, 16, 19; 12:1; 14:10; 2 Cor 11:2; Eph 5:27; 2 Tim 2:15). The intertextures indicate cultural connections among religious, judicial, ceremonial, and behavioral activities and meanings. When people were presented before a king, they were expected to be irreproachable in character and appearance. According to the LXX Torah **intertexture**, animals presented for sacrifice were to be unblemished (ἄμωμος, e.g., Exod 29:1; Lev 1:3, 10; Num 6:14; Ps 14:2). Reconciled humans are correspondingly presented as holy, faultless, and irreproachable in the **sacred** space before of the Son-Christ, the king and priest of his kingdom. They do not appear as blamable persons presented before a magistrate. They are not presented as sacrifices but as the beneficiaries of the Son's sacrifice. The implication is that only the reconciliation provided by the Son can provide this holy condition.

Rhetorical Force as Emergent Discourse

The force of this sentence is in its then-now argument about the good reconciliation brought about in the body of the precreational Son, by his

---

217. For references, see Bo Reicke and Georg Bertram, "παριστήμι, παριστάνω," *TDNT* 5:837–41; BDAG, 627–28; MM, 494. In Latin παρίστημι/παριστάνω is translated *admoveo*.

death. Things are not like they were before. The stress of estrangement, of hostile imaginings, of evil practices is gone.[218] Now there is reconciliation and holiness in the presence of the Son. It comes not from the dark jurisdiction of thrones, rulers, powers, and authorities but from the precreational realm of God and his Son. This is knowledge that is too important to be lost. The believers must remain in it, must not be shaken from the hope of the gospel. This step reinforces the rhetoric of the entire first scene. The developed philosophical focus on the Son-Christ is sharpened by emphasizing that the reconciliation was brought about in his own "body of flesh through death." Listening to this rhetoric moves people further along in their recognition of the goodness of the gospel. The rhetoric moves them to visualize themselves living the wisdom life being encouraged. The rhetoric creates a mindset amenable to faithfulness.

Reconciled people are no longer what they used to be, and the change has not been brought about by their own efforts. Rather than making themselves acceptable for presentation before an emperor, they have been made presentable and actually presented by the Son-Christ himself. This is the gospel that Paul the servant proclaimed.

---

218. Some of the evil commonly practiced is delineated in 3:5–11.

The Middle (1:24–4:6)

Scene Two: Paul's Genuine Character and Genuine Concerns (1:24–2:5)

This scene is crucial for understanding the entire letter because its rhetoric leads toward major concerns described further on. Moving ahead from the first-person "I Paul" in 1:23 are two first-person steps (1:24–29 and 2:1–5) that portray images of virtual Paul's stressful experiences for the sake of the holy ones. The rhetoric generates convincing visions of Paul's commitment to the gospel and his willingness to suffer for the sake of the *ekklēsia*. In the first step Paul describes the things he does as proclaimer, while in the second explains how he works to strengthen the believers so that they will not be carried away by deceitful arguments. His genuine concern for the continuing faithfulness of "every person" (πάντα ἄνθρωπον, 1:28) demonstrates his honest character. Although Paul is described as not physically nearby, he assures his presence in the spirit, concerned that seemingly plausible arguments could lead believers away from the mystery that has been brought to light in Christ.

Step One: Suffering for the *Ekklēsia* (1:24–29)

Rhetography

Following the first-person "I Paul" in 1:23 the new visual and audible scene, this sentence focuses on virtual Paul, who is heard in direct speech, narrating things about himself as servant in the context of gospel proclamation. Paul's coworkers and the audiences of the letter remain in view peripherally. While the first scene closed with Paul speaking from the edges as servant of the gospel, he now steps into the foreground, still as a servant and laborer (vv. 25, 29), though now specifically for the benefit of the *ekklēsia*, the body of Christ (1:24–25).¹ Paul continues in challenging, prophetic space and with a prophetic voice, but graphically as one who works hard to the point of serious suffering (πάθημα, v. 24) and agonizing struggle (ἀγωνίζομαι, v. 29) in order to make known the word of God about Christ. Paul's first-person exclamation "Now I rejoice" marks the movement ahead and adds enthusiastic yet disturbing coloring to the vision. Here Paul, who is seen bodily, in his "flesh," functions simultaneously in prophetic and priestly roles. He engages in proclamation and in actions that parallel the priestly work of Christ: he offers sacrificial suffering and is himself a physical, bodily person who suffers. The holy ones visualize Paul doing these things for them, willingly in the service of the *ekklēsia*. Surprisingly, Paul is observed rejoicing in the sufferings because it benefits others, not himself. At the same time, Christ is seen in his own afflictions (θλῖψις),² and Paul states that he himself in turn fills up or completes the things lacking (τὰ ὑστερήματα, deficiencies) in his own flesh the kinds of things Christ suffered (ἐν τοῖς παθήμασιν).³ Paul has given his entire life over for the sake of the gospel and the *ekklēsia*. His suffering is a testimony that the gospel was being proclaimed and was effective in the world. He does not object to suffering, envisioning what Christ endured, but rejoices in it for the good it does for the body-*ekklēsia*. The rhetograph, then, envisions the suffering of Christ and the suffering of Paul. Three bodies are presented to the mind: Christ's, Paul's, and the *ekklēsia* as the body of Christ. Christ's and Paul's suffering come from forces not visible in the rhetograph.

As a servant of the *ekklēsia* "according to the management [οἰκονομία, household management] from God," Paul is portrayed as being given the

---

1. Paul is not presented as an institutionalized power figure. He is διάκονος, not βασιλεύς. He seeks to be persuasive, not as one demanding obedience.

2. "Oppression, pressure." Used only here in the New Testament to refer to the sufferings of Christ.

3. I translate the Greek compound clause as "Now I rejoice in the sufferings on your behalf and I fill up the things lacking in my flesh of Christ's afflictions on behalf of his body, which is the *ekklēsia*." This translation indicates that Paul had deficiencies, not that Christ was lacking in atoning suffering. Paul did not engage in reconciling activity. Only Christ's actions redeem and reconcile, as 1:20–22 has already made clear. Many interpretations attempt to resolve concerns with this verse in varying ways. See the surveys in Barth and Blanke, *Colossians*, 289–95; Sumney, *Colossians*, 99–101; Foster, *Colossians*, 216–19. See the translation by David Bentley Hart, *The New Testament: A Translation* (New Haven: Yale University Press, 2017), 398–99; see also Talbert, *Ephesians and Colossians*, 200–202; Wilson, *Colossians and Philemon*, 171.

task "to fulfill the word of God" for the holy ones (εἰς ὑμᾶς, "for you"), which in the context of the sentence envisions making the mystery of Christ known in proclamation. Paul and his coworkers (the pronoun and verbs shift to first-person plurals, v. 28) are seen fulfilling the word by suffering and by proclaiming it in order "to present every person mature in Christ." The goal of maturity is emphasized by the trebling of terminology ("every person … every person … every person")[4] and where the approach to and content of the instructions and teachings portray Paul and his coworkers as wise persons who present wise and mature persons.[5] Both actions of filling, the suffering and the proclamation seen simultaneously, are gospel tasks aimed toward the benefit of the Christ community. The beneficiaries are visualized simultaneously as having Christ in them (v. 27) and as being in Christ (v. 28). The double imagery conveys the interconnectedness, the interweaving of rhetographic textures that enhance the picture.[6]

Paul's joy is observed graphically in the prophetic tasks of filling. His mode of narration shifts to apocalyptic discourse as he specifies the content of the word of God he presents by naming it as the mystery hidden from ages and generations "but now brought to light [ἐφανερώθη] to his (God's) holy ones" (v. 26).[7] The hidden mystery could not be seen, but the wording does cast a vision on the mind of something not known or understood by all previous ages and generations. This is reminiscent of but different from the pictures of 1:12–14, 21, where the humans listening to Paul's narration lived in darkness as estranged enemies. What was hidden is now seen clearly in the new reality of the Son's kingdom, where all are reconciled and display purity. Now brought to light, in complex imagery, is Christ himself *in* the humans who visualize the ideas being presented (ὅ ἐστιν Χριστὸς ἐν ὑμῖν, 1:27). Believers once again have their

---

4. Greek νουθετοῦντες πάντα ἄνθρωπον καὶ διδάσκοντες πάντα ἄνθρωπον … ἵνα παραστήσωμεν πάντα ἄνθρωπον.

5. It is not immediately clear whether ἐν πάσῃ σοφίᾳ refers to the method or the content of the proclamation. Are the preachers wise in every way, or do they hope that the content of their proclamation will generate wisdom among their audience members? Possibly the latter is more likely, given the following purpose statement.

6. Which comes to completion in 3:11.

7. The phrase "but now brought to light" (νῦν δὲ ἐφανερώθη) employs the verb φανερόω, "bring to light, manifest, cause to shine." Interestingly, the verb ἀποκαλύπτω ("reveal") and noun ἀποκάλυψις ("revelation") do not occur in Colossians. See on Col 3:1–4 below. Apocalyptic discourse or rhetorolect refers to the actions of God, not to the method of actions.

mental vision directed to Christ.⁸ They see themselves as God's holy ones (1:26; see 1:2) who, along with all others among the gentiles, comprise the larger body. All these people are observed as those to whom God wished to make known the riches of the glory of the mystery (1:27). In all of this the unseen God is imagined as the beneficent provider who *wants* people to know and to visualize the wealth of the glory—a bright, attractive, and happy image—of the formerly hidden mystery, "Christ in you, the hope of glory." The hope of glory is now in them, alive in them, the mystery brought to light.⁹ The imagery enhances the visualizations of 1:15–20. The cosmic-precreational image of God now is the Son-Christ in believers. The Son is preeminent from before creation of all things and now is manifested as Christ.

This portrayal of Christ moves the narrator to return to first-person language that again places him directly in the line of sight: "in whom also I work hard, struggling in accord with his energy working in me in power" (1:29). Paul works hard at the task given to him. He suffers, knows the sacrifices he makes. He does not waver. He remains in the faith (1:23), struggling along, working with and in the energizing power of the gospel. Audiences of Colossians see him there not seeking pity but setting the example, along with the suffering Son-Christ.

This sentence is Paul's way of saying he continues to do the right thing, continues on in apostolic work even though it means suffering. He fulfills his God-given service of the word. His suffering shows him in vibrant solidarity with Christ. This is not self-aggrandizement. It speaks to Paul's perceived ethos, his character as one who can speak authoritatively to Lycus Valley Christ believers. Description of facing afflictions on behalf of people is rhetorically powerful, moving them to be receptive to the voice and to the imagined visible presence of the afflicted speaker.[10]

The imagery blends the suffering Christ in first space, the afflicted Paul in second space, and the body-*ekklēsia* in the third space as beneficiary.

---

8. Christ, whom they have had in sight since 1:1, the image of God.

9. That is, the glory has arrived in Christ. See Isa 40:5, "Then the glory of the LORD shall be revealed" (NRSV), and Hab 2:14, "But the earth will be filled with the knowledge of the glory of the LORD, as the waters cover the sea" (NRSV).

10. On the ethos of Paul in Colossians see Sumney, *Colossians*, 95–96, and Jerry L. Sumney, "The Function of Ethos in Colossians," in *Rhetoric, Ethic, and Moral Persuasion: Essays from the 2002 Heidelberg Conference*, ed. Thomas H. Olbricht and Anders Eriksson, ESEC 11 (New York: T&T Clark, 2005), 301–15.

The blending of pictures and colors makes clear that the *ekklēsia* is foregrounded as the recipient of benefits being obtained from both Christ and Paul. The members of the *ekklēsiai* will see themselves as people ("every person") blessed by the actions see in the spaces where Christ and Paul are at work.

Translation

> **1:24** Now I rejoice in the sufferings[11] on your behalf and I fill up the things lacking in my flesh of Christ's afflictions on behalf of his body, which is the *ekklēsia*, **1:25** of which I became servant according to the management from God given to me for you, to fulfill the word of God, **1:26** the mystery hidden from the ages and the generations but now brought to light to his holy ones **1:27** in whom God wishes to make known what is the wealth [riches] of the glory of this mystery among [in] the nations, which is Christ in you, the hope of glory; **1:28** whom we proclaim, admonishing every person and teaching every person in all wisdom, so that we might present every person (as) mature in Christ;[12] **1:29** in whom also I work hard, struggling in accord with his energy working in me in power.

Textural Commentary

The *narrational texture* that began at 1:23 continues in another long, complex sentence beginning with "Now I rejoice." It is a narrative rhetoric of what virtual Paul does personally and what he experiences as servant of the gospel. The opening "now" (νῦν) is obviously a rhetoricized continuation, not a temporal marker. What Paul does and what he experiences is what he was given to do, precisely to proclaim the great wealth of the glory of the formerly hidden mystery specifically to gentiles. The proclamation is "Christ in you" and for "every person" to be presented as mature, perfect (τέλειος) in Christ. This all for the body-*ekklēsia*, the assembly, envisioned here as gentiles, people of the nations, as were certainly most, perhaps all, of the Lycus Christ believers. The narrator self-describes as being in

---

11. Some manuscripts read τοῖς παθήμασίν μου, "my sufferings."
12. Some manuscripts read Χριστῷ Ἰησοῦ, "Christ Jesus."

joyful solidarity with Christ, suffering and agonizing in his concern for the knowledge and maturation of believers. Rather lofty language about "the mystery hidden for ages and generations" but now made visible and clear (φανερόω) alludes to ideas and realities not explicated. The metanarrative, however, has already been given in 1:15–20. It is the cosmic-precreational reality of the Son of Father God, image of God in whom all the fullness houses, creator and sustainer of all things, raised out of the dead, the one in whom is reconciliation and peace, "Christ in you" and you "in Christ." These, of course, are virtual Paul's convictions. It is what Paul proclaims. It is likely to have been effective.

The self-presentation of virtual of Paul as suffering, hardworking, struggling servant is an *argumentative texture* targeted in a specified trajectory: it is "on your behalf" and "on behalf of his body, which is the *ekklēsia*" (1:24).

> **Case:** Paul suffers and exerts himself with the great energy supplied to him by Christ (1:29). He does this joyfully, not with regret or with any attempt to avoid the struggle and pain.
>
> **Rationale:** The suffering and toil is for the benefit of the Lycus believers, the body-*ekklēsia*, for the people of the nations, indeed for "every person" (1:24, 27–28). While Paul's suffering is imagined to be deficient when compared to Christ's, he is willing to fill it up (ἀνταναπληρόω)[13] in his gospel care for people. He fulfills the word of God, proclaiming the visibility of the long-hidden mystery of Christ, of the hoped-for glory.
>
> **(Anticipated) Result:** The suffering, admonishing,[14] and teaching is done "so that we might present every person mature in Christ" (1:28).[15] The suffering and hard labor is intended to lead to deepened maturity.

The internal argument in this step is about the formerly hidden mystery that has been brought to light. This is argumentation about the great metanarrative of expectation that now has been made visible (1:26–27). The hope of glory has arrived in the person of the Son-Christ.

---

13. A double compound verb, ἀντί + ἀνά + πληρόω, "I fill up."

14. Putting in mind.

15. The shift to the first-person plural "so that we might present" now includes Paul's coworkers.

Case: The hidden mystery, implicitly anticipated but not seen through ages and generations, has been brought to light to the holy ones.
Argument: The mystery now revealed is the Son-Christ himself, becoming known among the nations, the now present hope of glory (1:27; see 2:2). This argument assumes the reality of the metanarrative regarding the cosmic-precreational Son of God-Father.[16]
Result: The "riches of glory" is made known (οἷς ἠθέλησεν ὁ θεὸς γνωρίσαι, 1:27) and proclaimed. Paul suffers and toils, struggles in proclamation of this message.

A striking *repetitive texture* (repetitions here analyzed for the entire scene, 1:24–2:5) is the occurrence of first-person (singular and plural) verbs and participles along with first-person pronouns. Step one begins with χαίρω and step two with θέλω. Twenty-one first-person references stress Paul (and perhaps Timothy or others) as the active parties.[17] The repetition of second-person plural forms is also crucially important because the multiple first-person repetitions indicate actions performed for the sake of the second-person holy ones. Repetitions about being a servant, experiencing sufferings, afflictions, the hard work, and the agonizing continually faced by Paul and those with him (1:24, 25; 2:1; see also 4:18) no doubt draw some sympathy, but its force is to place him in a position of power. This ethos, characterization, says in effect, "Listen to me. I know what I'm talking about." Suffering is painful, but when the suffering is for the benefit of others and for the sake of the preaching of the word of God (1:24, 25, 28; 2:1, 4, 5) attention is focused on the one suffering and what that person says. Paul suffers so that "every person" (three occurrences) will become mature and able to withstand pressures to conform to deceitful and persuasive words. Paul appears as a powerful character, and attention is drawn to his apostolic, prophetic, authoritative proclamation.[18] Repetition of the

---

16. Perhaps implicit in virtual Paul's mind is the blessing anticipated for nations already in Gen 12:3 (ἐνευλογηθήσονται ἐν σοὶ πᾶσαι αἱ φυλαὶ τῆς γῆς). See Gal 3:8. It may be imagined as completion of the Habakkuk theology noted above in the analysis of 1:15–20.

17. "I rejoice; I fill up; my flesh; I became; given to me; we proclaim; admonishing; teaching; we may present; I toil, agonizing; he works in me; I want; I have; my face; we might encourage; this I say; I am absent; I am; rejoicing; seeing."

18. See Sumney, *Colossians*, 100.

word *mystery* (μυστήριον) in 1:26, 27 and 2:2 emphasizes that Paul's work extends from the precreational realm of the Son-Christ and the goodness of the new reality. The mystery is about Christ and the benefits of Christ, not anyone or anything else. This repetition maintains the emphasis on Christ that has come through clearly in the first scene.

The inner textural repetitions function to carry the ideas along. While they describe the experiences of Paul and his coworkers, they emphasize that the experiences and hard work are for the good of the body-*ekklēsia*.

The scene has a moving *sensory-aesthetic texture* that says much about Paul personally, about his bodily, intellectual, and emotional experiences of the work in which he engages. While Paul in bodily form is central to the sensory texture, there is a dual body focus because the recipients of the benefits of Paul's experiences ("you," "Christ's body, which is the *ekklēsia*," "his holy ones") were aware of their own bodies. They were the people to whom the long-hidden mystery had been made clear, who were inhabited by Christ "the hope of glory." These foci evoke sensory-aesthetic responses. Paul's joy indicates the zone of emotion-fused thought[19] that portrays an aspect of his personality, emotion, and intellect. He rejoices when good is done for people, even if the process is personally painful. Paul's joyful sensibility is rhetorically effective because it suggests to believers that they can share the joy in the face of their own suffering. Paul's body, referred to as "my flesh" (ἐν τῇ σαρκί μου, 1:24), is the zone of purposeful action, in which Paul is dedicated and knowingly works at hard labor despite serious suffering.[20] Paul's characterization elicits a sense of pathos and a parallel sense of transferred, sympathetic suffering among listeners. He is their bodily servant whose task is to engage in proclamation for their sake.[21] He is in this way at bodily work in both prophetic and priestly spaces. The descriptive words "sufferings" (πάθημα) and "afflictions" (θλῖψις, literally "pressure") tend to evoke enhanced physical and emotional responses among audience members. Sensitive audience minds will feel the pressure and the joy with Paul and recognize it in their own circumstances.

The assertion that what Paul proclaims was a mystery, something "hidden from the ages and the generations," elicits the aesthetic vision of

---

19. Robbins, *Exploring the Textures of Texts*, 30–31.
20. Robbins, *Exploring the Textures of Texts*, 31. See the usage of "flesh" in 1:22 in reference to Christ (ἐν τῷ σώματι τῆς σαρκὸς αὐτοῦ).
21. Literally "to fill the word of God."

SCENE TWO: PAUL'S GENUINE CHARACTER

mysterious but pleasing things in which people delight. Humans like to hear of mysteries and how the mysteries are resolved. They are now refreshingly informed about the metanarrative of God's economy (οἰκονομία). The rich glory of the mystery is impressed on the mind in the climactic statement "which is Christ in you, the hope of glory."

Paul embodies the impassioned life of the new reality in the Son's kingdom. He gives his body over to it, with all its senses. His goal is the maturity of all the believers. Sensitive minds will feel the pain symbolically with Paul and appreciate it emotionally. The sensory-aesthetic rhetoric aims to elicit this kind of wisdom understanding. Paul struggles along in the energy Christ gives him. He is not engaging in self-promotion or being pretentious. What he has is a sensory-aesthetic knowledge of what his work means in sensory-physical ways and what it can do for people.

At the more internal and subtle level, the language of this step flows with sensory-aesthetic features observable in how they look and sound. It opens with three first-person singular verbs (χαίρω, ἀνταναπληρόω, ἐγενόμην emphasized with ἐγώ). The central section follows, focused on the beneficial results of proclamation for the audience members, particularly on God's desire to reveal the fulfillment of the precreational metanarrative among them. The step closes by again employing first-person verbs, now two plurals (ἡμεῖς καταγγέλλομεν, παραστήσωμεν) and one singular (κοπιῶ) that retain the emphasis on the suffering Paul, who works at proclamation on behalf of the repetitive "every person" (πάντα ἄνθρωπον). Paul as afflicted, toiling, agonizing yet rejoicing sufferer stands prominently at beginning and end, filling up the gaps in his own flesh, forming an *inclusio* to the entire step. Two accusative clauses (τὴν οἰκονομίαν τοῦ θεοῦ τὴν δοθεῖσάν μοι εἰς ὑμᾶς πληρῶσαι τὸν λόγον τοῦ θεοῦ and τὸ μυστήριον τὸ ἀποκεκρυμμένον ἀπὸ τῶν αἰώνων καὶ ἀπὸ τῶν γενεῶν) are evenly balanced (twenty-six and twenty-five syllables respectively). The nominative phrases about glory (τὸ πλοῦτος τῆς δόξης and ἡ ἐλπὶς τῆς δόξης) match each other melodically and appositionally. The features form a sensory-aesthetic force that works with other textures to convey the rhetoric.

Intertexture. While personal suffering of the kind virtual Paul describes here—for the sake of the good of others, for the body-*ekklēsia*—at first glance may seem surprising, perhaps something people would want to avoid, it does have a place in intertextural contexts where such suffering was understood. It was already recognized in the Pauline letters that believers may encounter suffering and pressure that can be understood to be beneficial for maturation and that those who suffer can approach it joyfully (Rom 5:3–5; see Rom 12:12, 2 Cor 6:4–10, 7:4, 8:2, Phil 1:12–18, 3:10, 1 Thess 1:6, Gal 6:17).[22] Such suffering will not separate believers from God's love (Rom 8:35), and the wisdom benefit is that people will be τέλειος, mature, complete. Suffering for the body-*ekklēsia* is an important notion for Paul (2 Cor 1:3–11, 4:7–15).[23]

The concept of noble suffering for the good of others (or for the sake of principle) is well-known in stories from Jewish history, as 4 Maccabees 6 graphically portrays in the scene of the torture and death of Eleazar. Eleazar prays:

> "You know, O God, that though I might have saved myself, I am dying in burning torments for the sake of the law. Be merciful to your people, and let our punishment suffice for them. Make my blood their purification, and take my life in exchange for theirs." After he said this, the holy man died nobly in his tortures; even in the tortures of death he resisted, by virtue of reason, for the sake of the law. (4 Macc 6:27–30 NRSVue; see 4 Macc 7:1–23, 2 Macc 6:18–31)

Fourth Maccabees indicates later that the suffering of Eleazar and others was understood to have atoning efficacy:

> These, then, who have been consecrated for the sake of God, are honored not only with this honor but also by the fact that because of them our enemies did not rule over our nation, the tyrant was punished, and the homeland purified—they having become, as it were, a ransom for the sin of our nation. And through the blood of those pious ones and their death as an atoning sacrifice [καὶ τοῦ ἱλαστηρίου τοῦ θανάτου αὐτῶν], divine Providence preserved Israel that previously had been mistreated. (4 Macc 17:20–22 NRSVue)

The stories of Shadrach, Meshach, and Abednego (Dan 3), of Daniel (in the den of lions, Dan 6), and the Prayer of Azariah describe noble suffering for the sake of principles. People suffered for refusing to submit to

---

22. The joy may be experienced during the suffering or because of it. Sumney, *Colossians*, 98.

23. See L. Ann Jervis, *At the Heart of the Gospel: Suffering in the Earliest Christian Message* (Grand Rapids: Eerdmans, 2007).

idolatry, oppressive powers, and threatening situations (1 Macc 6:43–46, 2 Macc 7:1–42, 14:37–46).[24]

Greco-Roman literature contains many intertextures that demonstrate that the idea of suffering and of noble death was widely discussed and understood (see, e.g., Diogenes Laertius, *Vit. phil.* 9.26–28, 58–59; Plato, *Apol.* 28a–30b; Demosthenes, *Epitaph.* 60).[25] The Stoic Seneca (ca. 4 BCE–65 CE, hence a contemporary of Paul)[26] wrote of many examples of noble deaths, thereby advising against fearing it. He notes Socrates in particular: "Socrates in prison discoursed, and declined to flee when certain persons gave him the opportunity; he remained there, in order to free humankind from the fear of two most grievous things, death and imprisonment" (*Ep.* 24 [Gummere]). In *De providentia* (*Ad Lucilium*) Seneca writes, "'Yet,' you say, 'many sorrows, things dreadful and hard to bear, do befall us.' Yes, because I could not withdraw you from their path, I have armed your minds to withstand them all; endure with fortitude. In this you may outstrip God; he is exempt from enduring evil, while you are superior to it" (*Lucil.* 6.6 [Basore]).

Suffering and even death, particularly when a principle, other persons, or some good cause was in view, was considered a good and noble thing in the ancient Mediterranean. The intertextures circulating through the ancient environment made the idea familiar enough to make the language of Col 1:24–29 comprehensible and impressive. In the Christian context of the *ekklēsia*, this would be clearly grasped since the idea of the suffering of Christ was known and understood. Such suffering is painful but not finally destructive. The rhetorical effect is to place the sufferer in a position of power. Paul gains status as the sufferer—alongside Christ—and thereby increases the level of attentiveness given by believers in Colossae. The suffering is, after all, for their good and for the sake of the gospel. This rhetoric will move them to become increasingly amenable to the wisdom message of the letter.

---

24. For these references see Sumney, *Colossians*, 100–101. See also Philo, *Prob.* 88–91; also the description of the final suffering of Jewish people at Masada (Josephus, *B.J.* 7.389–406).

25. For many references, see Jan Willem van Henten and Friedrich Avemarie, *Martyrdom and Noble Death: Selected Texts from Graeco-Roman Jewish and Christian Antiquity* (London: Routledge, 2002).

26. There is a tradition, undoubtedly false, that Paul and Seneca engaged in correspondence and that Seneca became a Christian. Seneca was a lifelong Stoic.

The intertexture of the image of Paul as servant springs out of the repetitive texture that began in 1:23. Paul functions as a servant in all he does. Epaphras is already described as "servant" in 1:7, and Tychicus is similarly described in 4:7. Paul is by self-description elsewhere counted among the servants of God (1 Cor 3:5, 2 Cor 6:4, 11:23). This intertexturing is closely connected with the description of Paul's God-given management task.[27] Having a commission has in mind, intertexturally, the basic administrative responsibilities usually given to persons of low social status, often slaves, and corresponds to "servant" (social intertexture).[28] The portrayal of Paul as having such a commission is observed in 1 Cor 9:17; Eph 1:10; 3:2, 9. This service corresponds to the grace given to Paul to preach the gospel to gentiles (Rom 12:3, 15:15–16, 1 Cor 3:9–10).

The apocalyptic notion of the mystery (1:26–27; see 2:2, 4:3) is here not the Greco-Roman idea of some undisclosed secret known only by initiates but refers to the gospel that Paul is visualized proclaiming. It is the openly manifested word of God concerning the Son-Christ Jesus. The hidden mystery, though not clear prior to the presence of Son-Christ in the world (and "in you," 1:27), is now clear. Paul offers a similar thought in the doxological statement of Rom 16:25–27:

> Now to the one who is able to strengthen you according to my gospel and the proclamation of Jesus Christ, according to the revelation of the mystery kept in silence for long ages but is now made clear [φανερόω] through the prophetic writings to all the nations, according to the command of the God of ages, to bring about the obedience of faith—to the only wise God, through Jesus Christ, to whom be the glory forever! Amen. (my translation)

The same idea is found in 1 Cor 2:2, Eph 1:9, 3:2–20, 6:19, 1 Tim 3:16. The manifestation of the mystery demonstrates that gentiles and Jews are in Christ joined together in the body, as Col 1:27 indicates—that the riches of the mystery reach to every person, to the nations. The notion of the mystery occurs in LXX Jewish texts such as Tob 12:7, 11, which indicate that, unlike a king's mystery (secret), God's mystery is to be acknowledged and honored ("It is good to conceal the *mystery* of a king, but to acknowledge

---

27. Or, as is often translated, "commission," "stewardship," "administration," "responsibility" or, more literally, "economy" (οἰκονομία).

28. Sumney, *Colossians*, 103. On this quite widely used term, see MM, 442.

and reveal the works of God, and with fitting honor to acknowledge him" [NRSV modified]; see also Wis 2:22; Jdt 2:2; 2 Esd 10:38; 1 En. 103.2; 2 En. 24.3; 1QS III, 23; IV, 18; 1QpHab VII, 5). In Col 1:27 the great riches of the glory of the revelation is that Christ is "in you, the hope of glory." Very similar ideas are found in Rom 8:10, 2 Cor 13:5, and Gal 4:19. While it is not possible to know whether the holy ones in Colossae recognized these intertextures, they stand in the rhetorical environment.

The proclamation in which Paul and his coworkers engage is missionary preaching.[29] The word for proclamation in 1:28, καταγγέλλω, is infrequently used in the Pauline letters (six times) and elsewhere in the New Testament only in Acts.[30] It occur intertexturally in descriptions of official reports and frequently to proclaim sacred festivals, religious messages, and imperial rule.[31] It implies solemn authoritative announcements.[32] While other αγγέλ- compounds are typically employed to proclaim imperial rule, an inscription or *psephisma* at Smyrna uses καταγγέλλω to honor "the Venerable Gaius Caesar Germanicus" (Caligula) when he was named emperor in 37 CE.[33] By stark contrast, Paul and his coworkers[34] proclaim Christ as the hope of glory. The word choice intentionally honors Christ above all others. Lycus audiences would likely make the connection. Caligula famously claimed divinity and regularly made boastful claims about himself:

> After he had assumed various surnames (for he was called "Pious," "Child of the Camp," "Father of the Armies," and "Greatest and Best of the Caesars"), chancing to overhear some kings, who had come to Rome to pay their respects to him, disputing at dinner about the nobility of their descent, he cried: "Let there be one Lord, one King." And he came near assuming a crown at once and changing the semblance of a principate into the form of a monarchy. But on being reminded that he had risen above the elevation both of princes and kings, he began from that time on to lay claim to divine majesty; for after giving orders that such statues

---

29. MacDonald, *Colossians and Ephesians*, 83.
30. Though other compound words indicating proclamation formed on the root αγγέλ- are quite common.
31. See Julius Schniewind, "καταγγέλλω," *TDNT* 1:70–72.
32. MM, 324.
33. See Schniewind, "καταγγέλλω," 70–71. *Psephisma* were proclamations inscribed on tablets commonly placed in front of official buildings.
34. "Whom we proclaim," using the plural καταγγέλλομεν.

of the gods as were especially famous for their sanctity or their artistic merit, including that of Jupiter of Olympia, should be brought from Greece, in order to remove their heads and put his own in their place, he built out a part of the Palace as far as the Forum, and making the temple of Castor and Pollux its vestibule, he often took his place between the divine brethren, and exhibited himself there to be worshiped by those who presented themselves; and some hailed him as Jupiter Latiaris. He also set up a special temple to his own godhead, with priests and with victims of the choicest kind. In this temple was a life-sized statue of the emperor in gold, which was dressed each day in clothing such as he wore himself. (Suetonius, *Cal.* 22 [Rolfe])

According to Cassius Dio, Caligula considered himself to be Jupiter (*Hist. Rom.* 59.26, 59.28).[35] By describing Paul's proclamation of Christ, this step makes the imperial proclamations of imperial divinity quite irrelevant for Christ believers.

Step Two: Struggling for Faithfulness (2:1–5)

Rhetography

Paul continues to stand prominently in this *progression* of the scene, still speaking in the first-person "I." He is, of course, at a distance from his audience, which now expands to include Christ believers in Laodicea and presumably other locations in the Lycus region (see 4:13). They are meant to hear his voice in the words of the letter. Paul draws them along by reinforcing his picture of personal struggle—"I want you to know how much anxiety I have for you" (ἡλίκον ἀγῶνα ἔχω ὑπὲρ ὑμῶν, 2:1).[36] His tone presents him having great stress. The concerns parallel but rephrase what was just heard in the preceding step: encouragement, love, understanding, knowledge of the mystery, wisdom—in short, maturity in the new reality, but now, revealingly and importantly, worry that the holy ones could be deceived by someone presenting plausible but misleading arguments (ἵνα μηδεὶς ὑμᾶς παραλογίζηται ἐν πιθανολογίᾳ).[37] Someone speaking deceptive words can be imagined attempting to infiltrate the assem-

---

35. Early third century CE.
36. Or "how much I *struggle* for you."
37. πιθανολογία occurs only here in the Bible. Its usual meaning as "persuasive speech" here imagines plausible but misleading and dangerous ideas (MM, 512).

bly. This concern recalls the conditional words "if you remain in the faith" in 1:23. More specific warning about deceitful ideas will emerge shortly in 2:8. Paul is struggling from a distance to strengthen the *ekklēsiai* with that energy from Christ that works in him (see 1:29). The beating of the encouraged hearts of the holy ones can be almost felt in the imagery along with their knowledge of "the mystery of God—of Christ in whom are all the treasures of wisdom and knowledge." Once again (as in 1:23), these are things not to be lost; the believers must not succumb to deceptive words. It is Christ in them, the cosmic-precreational Son of Father God, in whom they must maintain their solid trust (τὸ στερέωμα τῆς εἰς Χριστὸν πίστεως ὑμῶν).[38] Though absent from them and likely not recognizable if he were to arrive on the scene (v. 1),[39] Paul nevertheless presents himself as being with them in the spirit (ἀλλὰ τῷ πνεύματι σὺν ὑμῖν εἰμι, 2:5). The imagery and reality of distance, in other words, is not an obstacle to Paul's genuine concern for people.

Virtual Paul presents in these verses as an honest, trustworthy man who has genuine concerns for people and the *ekklēsiai*. He speaks to his letter audiences from blended prophetic and priestly spaces. He speaks from the conviction that "all the hidden treasures of wisdom and knowledge" are in Christ. He confronts and challenges Lycus believers because he envisions the likelihood that they will listen to and be affected by dangerous teachings. He agonizes over the prospect of it and warns of it. Yet he rejoices at their orderliness and steadfastness. The vision moving forward is promising even if it gives the impression that there is much more to say.[40]

---

38. στερέωμα, related to our modern word *stereo*, envisions solid, firm, steadfast belief, people, or things.

39. It is typically presumed that Paul had not been to Colossae or the Lycus, so was not known there in person. This is likely the case, though, strictly speaking, the language of Col 2:1 does not demand that his face had never been seen by everyone (or anyone) in the Lycus *ekklēsiai*.

40. For analysis of how repetitions carry ideas along, see the description of *repetitive texture* in the preceding step, 1:24–29.

Translation

2:1 For I want you to know how much anxiety I have for you[41] and those in Laodicea[42] and as many as have not seen my face in [the] flesh, **2:2** so that their hearts may be encouraged,[43] held together in love and in all wealth[44] of the certainty of [the] understanding, in knowledge of the mystery of God—of Christ— **2:3** in whom are all the hidden treasures of wisdom and knowledge. **2:4** I say this so that no one may deceive you with persuasive speech. **2:5** For even though I am absent in the flesh, I am with you in the spirit, rejoicing and seeing your orderliness and the steadfastness of your faith in Christ.

Textural Commentary

The personalized *narration* continues from the previous step in the leading argumentative words "For I want you to know..." (2:1). Paul continues to address the audience directly in first-person speech about the struggling he described in the previous step. This is a great struggle, and its point is emphasized by repeating that it is "for you," the holy ones in Christ in Colossae, its range broadened with the inclusion of those presumed also to be holy ones in Laodicea and for that matter all who, like the Colossians, do not know Paul personally. The narrative is directional in its orientation away from Paul and toward the audiences of the letter. Paul states that the source of his anxiety is in his concern for the encouragement, understanding, and knowledge of the audiences. The expansion of scope to include believers in Laodicea and elsewhere leads to a change in 2:2 from the second-person plural "for you" (ὑπὲρ ὑμῶν) to the third-person plural "them" (αὐτῶν), but the return to second person (ὑμᾶς, 2:4) indicates that the narrative always has the first audience in Colossae in mind. The narrator wants them all to have sure knowledge regarding the mys-

---

41. Some manuscripts read περὶ ὑμῶν rather than ὑπὲρ ὑμῶν.

42. Some manuscripts add καὶ τῶν ἐν Ἱεραπόλει, "and those in Hierapolis" (see 4:13).

43. The aorist passive nominative participle συμβιβασθέντες does not agree with the nominative subject αἱ καρδίαι but with the implied "you" from 2:1. NA[28] indicates variant readings: συμβιβασθέντων, συμβιβασθῶσιν.

44. Some manuscripts add the article to read "all the riches," πᾶν τὸ πλοῦτος.

tery, a notion repeated from the previous step and with its metanarrative still in mind. The mystery, once again, is the Son-Christ himself, in whom are hidden all the treasures of wisdom and knowledge, a striking, exclusive, and monumental claim, to say the least, but a claim that fits with the narration already presented in 1:15–20. While Paul as narrator makes his first-person statements, it is the precreational, preeminent, raised Christ with whom Paul suffers who is at the center of interest, and the audiences who remain as the object of the narrative. The narration is fundamentally about Christ and what Christ has done for the human recipients of the letter. That the recipients are the object of the narrative is driven home by the final clear statements of the scene: "I am saying this so that no one may deceive you with plausible words, for though I am absent in the flesh, but with you in the spirit, rejoicing and seeing the orderliness and steadfastness of your faith in Christ" (2:4–5).

The force of the narrative is unlikely to have been missed. It describes Paul as deeply concerned for the letter's audiences. He genuinely cares for them. He emphasizes that Christ is the singularly most important person for them. He does not want them to be persuaded by any rhetoric, however plausible, other than his own. This narrative, particularly given forces of the dual space of city-region and *ekklēsia* inhabited by the audiences, intensifies their receptivity and expectation for what the narrator will say next.

The *argumentative texture* continues and expands from the preceding step with "For I want you to know…" (2:1). The argumentative conjunction γάρ demonstrates the continuation. The struggle continues, but with it now comes explication of what has been a major concern from the outset. Suffering, agonizing, and proclaiming the mystery to the body-*ekklēsia*, now described as encouraging the hearts of the Lycus believers (ἵνα παρακληθῶσιν αἱ καρδίαι αὐτῶν), is designed to prevent them from being deceived by persuasive yet false speech. There are recognized and present dangers. There are persons (presented in the singular "so that no one," ἵνα μηδεὶς, v. 4) who virtual Paul knows will attempt to persuade people to adapt their "steadfast faith in Christ" to what seem to be plausible beliefs and actions that are in fact mistaken and misleading. Paul argues for the maturity in Christ envisioned in 1:28. He struggles to encourage the maturity in which his listeners will "be held together in love" (2:2).[45] The goal is developed wisdom

---

45. The passive participle συμβιβασθέντες, from the verb συμβιβάζω, "to bring together, unite," alludes to the reconciliation of 1:20, 22. See Col 2:19.

that will prevent them from being distracted from their steadfast faith. This, of course, is the argumentative setup for the warnings about false teaching about to be given in 2:6–23. What the nature of the deceptive words exactly might be is not yet stated, but the fear is there, and virtual Paul agonizes that the holy ones could submit to it. They must not turn from "knowledge of the mystery of God—of Christ" (ἐπίγνωσιν τοῦ μυστηρίου τοῦ θεοῦ, Χριστοῦ), in other words from the metanarrative of the Son-Christ that extends from the cosmic-precreational ages and is now present in them. The implication of the argument is that believers could be persuaded to move from trust in Christ as reconciler of all things on earth and in the heavens and as peacemaker to the more do-it-yourself approach of appeasement of the powers and authorities that was pervasive in the Mediterranean world. They must not trust in themselves to get things right. They must not trust in the disorderly forces of the cosmos. They must not be diverted from the foundational precreation philosophy described in 1:12–20.

Like the preceding step in this scene, the rhetoric presents Paul as someone who feels his concerns on a deeply emotional, *sensory*, personal level. He functions in the zone of emotion-fused thought where his struggle or "anxiety" (ἀγών) manifests in his eagerness to encourage, hold things together, and in his rejoicing in people's faithfulness. The flow of first-person verbs "I want you to know ... I struggle ... I say this ... I am absent ... I am with you" points to Paul's committed pastoral conscience. This Paul agonizes about believers' understanding of the gospel and their continuing faithfulness.

Both steps in this scene have **social and cultural textures** woven in and around Paul's prophetic and priestly work. Readers and listeners are drawn into Paul's society of service and suffering. This is a dyadic personality[46] rhetorical effect where the Lycus holy ones come to know important things about themselves by interacting with implied Paul's language. The priestly Paul suffers nobly for them; they will view themselves as beneficiaries of Paul's pain. Paul, his coworkers, and others continue their prophetic task of proclamation of the formerly hidden mystery about Christ in them; the believers view themselves as beneficiaries of the preaching. The believers are woven into the social texturing of "in Christ" and "Christ in you." This is the texture of the *ekklēsia*. The glory of the *ekklēsia* is, implicitly,

---

46. Robbins, *Exploring the Textures of Texts*, 77–78. Paul's identity and work provides identity and the possibility of action for the audience members.

not found in the great empire of Rome with its οἰκονομία, with its power to control and to cause suffering for the sake of world domination. The glory is present in Christ. In Paul's sociocultural ideology one properly suffers willingly for Christ, not because of the forceful imposition of imperial power. The cultural ideology and the social proclamation is about Christ, not anyone else. The relevant kingdom is the one into which they have been transferred, not any other. For Paul and the Colossian holy ones, the dominant culture consciousness has shifted and is clearly about the Son-Christ even if that involves pain for Christ's sake and the sake of the body-*ekklēsia*. This *ekklēsia* culture is transformative, but it also stands in tension and paradoxical relationship with the dominant imperial culture.[47]

Socially and culturally, Paul favors suffering, not personal glory. "Christ in you" *is* "the hope of glory" rather than a constructed glory generated by self-promotion, self-importance, or allegiance to power. In Christ are "all the hidden treasures of wisdom and knowledge." The implied **social and cultural texture**, where there are threatening religious and political views about who and what provides glory, maturity, wisdom, community, security, and knowledge, is not pertinent to the new reality. Paul, in blended prophetic and wisdom space, considers other understandings to be irrelevant. Do not be persuaded by them. This places Paul in a social space of honor as proclaimer and sufferer for the sake of others. A new culture is created. The new culture in turn produces new **ideological texturing**. This step moves people toward the enactment of the particularized concerns and presuppositions of the gospel.[48] The developed understanding of the cosmic-precreational Son shapes and reshapes the presuppositions of both senders and recipients of Colossians. The Mediterranean world where they live with all its political, religious, military, social, and cultural structures and expectations is at best secondary to Paul and Christ believers. Its ideologies are far too chaotic. The new (and true) ideology is Christ ideology. It is found "in knowledge of the mystery of God—of Christ—in whom are all the hidden treasures of [the] wisdom and knowledge." This is the worldview of the new reality. Lycus believers are unlikely to have missed the political and religious implications.

---

47. Compare the classic cultural typology of H. Richard Niebuhr in *Christ and Culture* (San Francisco: HarperSanFrancisco, 2001). Niebuhr favored the notion of Christ transforming culture but also addresses Christ in paradox with culture.

48. See Robbins, *Exploring the Textures of Texts*, 95–96.

Some particular **intertextures**, no doubt known to Paul and perhaps to authors and senders of the letter, are exhortations in the Psalms that warn of the dangers of relying on humans and political authorities. Only God can be always trusted:

> For God is the king of all the earth; sing praises with a psalm.
> God is king over the nations; God sits on his holy throne.
> The princes [ἄρχοντες, "rulers"] of the peoples gather as the people of the God of Abraham.
> For the shields of the earth belong to God; he is highly exalted. (LXX Ps 47:7–10)

> It is better to take refuge in the LORD than to put confidence in mortals.
> It is better to take refuge in the LORD than to put confidence in princes [ἄρχοντας]. (LXX Ps 117:8–9)

> Do not put your trust in princes [ἄρχοντας], in mortals, in whom there is no help.
> When their breath departs, they return to the earth; on that very day their plans perish. (LXX Ps 145:3–4)

Rhetorical Force as Emergent Discourse

The rhetoric of this scene is a setup for what follows in Col 2. It draws audiences along. Paul is presented as a noble sufferer, hence a man of character who experiences physical and emotional distress for the benefit of the body of Christ, the *ekklēsia*. He rejoices in his ongoing suffering because he can do good things for Christ believers in the Lycus region despite being located at a distance from them. While attention is drawn to Paul (or virtual Paul), it is not meant to exalt him personally but to demonstrate that he is a sincere servant who proclaims the good and true gospel, the mystery of Father God and his Son that extends from the cosmic-precreational realm and is now clear and visible. He proclaims that the promised glory of the Lord is present in Christ Jesus (Ps 24:7–10, Isa 40:5, Hab 2:14). The rhetoricized description of Paul's actions make him more than an example of service; it gives him the power to speak. Paul is a power person who is respected, who knows what he is talking about and can speak authoritatively about faith (trust) in Christ. The rhetoric evokes the personal sense that Paul cares for *us*. He wants to present *us* as mature, perfect people in Christ. Mediterranean audiences will be moved by this and be amenable to Paul's ongoing words and ideas. The rhetoric makes the argumentative, moral, and emotional case for the growth toward the maturity Paul has in mind for them. They will be conscious of pressures to adopt seemingly plausible but misleading religious views and behaviors that would divert them from the reconciliation and peace in Christ to succumb to what from a gospel point of view are irrelevant powers and authorities.

In Mediterranean context, these verses present Paul supporting the theology presented in the preceding scene, which understands God and his Son as the actual and exclusive divine beings with the Son-image of God being creator and sustainer of all things. This means that social, cultural, religious, and behavioral pressures to take on other theologies should be ignored. The "hidden treasures of wisdom and knowledge" are in Christ, nowhere else.

Scene Three: Don't Be Deceived. Live the New Reality (2:6–4:6)

Step One: Walk On Confidently (2:6–7)

Rhetography

Paul as implied narrator continues to be imagined visually, and his prophetic voice heard, but he is a step removed from his previous prophetic position due to a shift from the first-person focus on himself to the second-person "you," thereby bringing listeners into the foreground. He challenges them to move ahead intentionally from their strong, secure position in Christ. The prophetic discourse encourages wisdom thinking and behavior. Audiences are reminded that they "received Christ Jesus the Lord" or, more literally, they "took on Christ Jesus the Lord" to themselves (παρελάβετε, "you took on").[1] Christ Jesus appears as "the Lord" (τὸν Χριστὸν Ἰησοῦν τὸν κύριον),[2] like a master or monarch as well as Messiah. This image reminds them again that they heard and believed the gospel that they heard from Epaphras (1:5–7) and reiterates that they are in Christ and Christ is in them (as in 1:27–28). Life "in him" (ἐν αὐτῷ, vv. 6–7)[3] is pictured with the mixed metaphors of motion and solid stability, walking while simultaneously being "rooted and built on a foundation and established in the faith." The walking is active motion (active-voice verb περιπατεῖτε), while the solid stability was given to believers (three passive-voice participles:

---

1. The word does not mean "receive" in the sense of "take" or "accept" (see Barth and Blanke, *Colossians*, 300).
2. With the articular nouns specifying singular identity.
3. Talbert takes the first ἐν αὐτῷ as "in dependence on him" and the second instrumentally as "through him" (*Ephesians and Colossians*, 210). Both can be understood as being in Christ's sphere of existence, as noted earlier (see Wilson, *Colossians and Philemon*, 73).

ἐρριζωμένοι, ἐποικοδομούμενοι, βεβαιούμενοι). The horticultural ("having been rooted") and construction ("being built on") images demonstrate stability, and the more commercial image ("being assured") indicates confirmation.[4] These people have these stabilities in Christ. They are not hoped for; they are possessed. They are securely established people who can and should move ahead confidently. They imagine themselves walking along with sure-footed confidence as people who understand the wealth of the mystery now manifested, "Christ in you" (1:27). The way they walk is just like what they were taught, in a look to the past, by Epaphras and perhaps other teachers. Now, as they walk along, they call out in an overflow of thanks (περισσεύοντες ἐν εὐχαριστίᾳ). This is an appealing scene of strong, faithful, no-nonsense people, encouraged by how they are living in Christ. The visual scene makes an implicit argument: how they see themselves mentally is how they should behave in reality.[5]

Translation

> **2:6** As therefore you received Christ Jesus the Lord, walk in him, **2:7** having been rooted and being built on a foundation in him and assured in the faith,[6] just as you were taught, overflowing in thanksgiving.[7]

Textural Commentary

The focus on the lives of holy ones is carried along by the *repetitive texturing* that continues to emphasize their location *in* the Son-Christ: "the Lord Jesus Christ ... in him ... in him." They live in the realm of Christ. This of course is the same Son-Christ who is the image of God, creator, preeminent, raised out of death, the mystery now known and proclaimed. The Son-Christ-Lord is whom the listeners have taken on (παρελάβετε) and is where they are now rooted. Though they are faithful people, they nev-

---

4. The verb for "being built on" is ἐποικοδομέω, as a house built on a foundation. The verb βεβαιόω, "confirm, secure, assure, establish," was frequently used in legal and commercial transactions where a vendor confirmed promises about product sold to a purchaser (MM, 108).

5. See my description of the rhetography of 2:6–7 in Jeal, "Visual Interpretation: Blending Rhetorical Arts," 72–73.

6. NA[28] and UBS[5] indicate variant ἐν τῇ πίστει.

7. NA[28] and UBS[5] indicate variants ἐν αὐτῇ ἐν εὐχαριστίᾳ and ἐν αὐτῷ ἐν εὐχαριστίᾳ.

ertheless hear the exhortation to continue in the faith. The phrase "in the faith" with the article (τῇ πίστει) therefore refers to the truths of the new reality in Christ. The repetition of the descriptive noun "Lord" (κύριος) used earlier in the letter (1:3, 10) emphasizes Jesus's identity as Christ. The *argumentative texture* is clear in the "As therefore you have received ... walk in him" phrasing. Yet there is an implicit argument at work that says in effect, "There is nothing more important than what you have taken on about Christ. You could be deceived by plausible but false teaching (2:4). So keep going. Do not be misled." This implicit argument echoes 1:23 ("if you remain in the faith"). The worry that believers could be persuaded to accept dangerous ideas is at the heart of virtual Paul's concerns. In other words, live your lives according to what you have already learned about the Son-Christ, the Lord. Overflow in thanksgiving for what you have in Christ. This implicitly reiterates the importance of the redemption, forgiveness, reconciliation, and frankly the safety that is exclusively in Christ. This is the basic argumentative imperative of the letter: "Walk in him."[8]

Intertextures provide some contextualization and support for the ideas. The metaphor of walking is so common in the Pauline letters that it scarcely needs mentioning. Holding firmly to the proclamation that was received (παραλαμβάνω) is familiar from 1 Cor 15:1–3 (see also Gal 1:12). Warning against receiving a false gospel stands out in Gal 1:9. The *ekklēsia* of the Thessalonians received from Paul and his coworkers teaching about how they should walk (1 Thess 4:1). The imagery of walking is developed strongly in Eph 2:10; 4:1; 5:2, 8, 15.

Step Two: Beware of Being Captured—You Are Already Filled (2:8–10)

Rhetography

In this step the images in the picture change again, with the listeners shifting their eyes, at virtual Paul's call (βλέπετε), to a person introduced into the scene for the first time.[9] The new person is not recognized by appearance or name. Rather, this person appears in negative, possibly violent

---

8. The concern, then, is not about ethics, as many interpreters claim. It is about continuing on in what was taught and about not being deceived and misled.

9. The grammar is singular, τις ... ἔσται, a person. The singular may well stand for a number of persons, perhaps a group of people working together.

mental imagery as someone who attempts to capture[10] the believers, perhaps proudly by using "philosophy" and "empty deceit," something that operates "according to human tradition" and "according to the elements of the cosmos" but does not operate "according to Christ." The attempted capture is instigated by a person but is accomplished intellectually and emotionally by affecting how the people think and act.[11] This coloring emphasizes the sense of danger.[12] The rhetograph displays a threat against believers intended to intimidate them with a philosophy counter to what they have learned about Christ, solely from human sources. The holy ones become wary of this person and the person's message. The notions of "philosophy and empty deceit," "human tradition," and "the elements of the cosmos"[13] are more abstract conceptualizations, but their implied sensory and intellectual power along with the statement that they are "not according to Christ" indicates that they are adversarial concepts and realities. They add threatening appearance and tone to the portrayal. Each threat envisions human, present-age concerns rather than the new reality of life in the Son's kingdom. What occurs in 2:8 is that the space of the audience members is blended with the space of the persons trying to capture them,

---

10. The term employed, ὁ συλαγωγῶν, from the verb συλαγωγέω, is a *hapax legomenon*. It suggests being seized and carried off as booty (MM, 596; Wilson, *Colossians*, 194). τῆς φιλοσοφίας and κενῆς ἀπάτης form a hendiadys, and the two nouns stand in apposition to each other (the genitive article governs both nouns). The philosophy *is* the "empty deceit." It is possible to construe "empty deceit" adjectivally, giving the reading "empty and deceitful philosophy." The singular "truth of the gospel" mentioned already in 1:5 stands against any other philosophy.

11. On the identity of this person, hence on the nature of the philosophy and the much-debated issue behind the writing of Colossians, see below on **social and cultural texture** and **intertexture**.

12. The imperative βλέπετε has the force of "beware."

13. The interpretive translations of τὰ στοιχεῖα τοῦ κόσμου, "elemental spirits," "elemental spiritual forces," or "elementary principles," where στοιχεῖα is rendered as an adjective, are inaccurate and misleading. The word στοιχεῖα is a plural noun, not an adjective. The interpretations seem to rely on ideas in the later Eph 6:12. The straightforward translation is "the elements of the cosmos." There is no *linguistic* reason to add the notion of spirits here. The identity of the στοιχεῖα is, of course, a matter of ongoing debate. But the proximity of the term to "philosophy and empty deceit" and "human tradition" in the context demonstrates that they are connected with the confusing *present-age* issues that arise for humans: eat/don't eat; drink/don't drink; participate/don't participate; love/hate; obsessions/compulsions; power; etc. See below on **social and cultural texture** and **intertexture**.

producing a third space of caution in the presence of a threat. There are persons who want to make a show of power and authority, who want to persuade the Christ believers that their beliefs and practices are deficient.

Virtual Paul warns strongly about these persons. It is in Christ, indeed in Christ bodily, that all the fullness of deity houses (ὅτι ἐν αὐτῷ κατοικεῖ πᾶν τὸ πλήρωμα τῆς θεότητος σωματικῶς, v. 9).[14] This is an extension of the precreational philosophy of the Son-Christ stated already in 1:15, 19.[15] The rhetoric evokes the mental imagery of the Son-Christ Jesus embodying God physiologically—in his own body. The picture conveys the understanding that it is Christ Jesus alone, preeminent and firstborn out of the dead, who displays deity and presents truth about God to humans and the world. Negatively, it shows that those attempting to capture Christ believers do not have the power, authority, or knowledge they presume to possess. The holy ones have been made full in Christ alone (καὶ ἐστὲ ἐν αὐτῷ πεπληρωμένοι),[16] so no more filling is required. They do not need more religio-philosophical filling. Careful listeners will recognize that the fullness they already have is the mystery that is now visible in the light. The mystery visualized is Christ himself, in whom God houses. Christ who is full makes "you" full, complete. The imperative to beware of those who presume to know about more or better filling becomes stunningly important. Christ is "the head of every power and authority," an exclusive claim. Additional and adversarial claims are empty and deceitful, and as they come the believers are observed avoiding them. Do not be persuaded to fill what is already full.

This rhetograph makes clear that the audience members should have their confidence solely in the precreational Christ—where deity fully resides—and not in humans or in human and earthly teachings.

Translation

> **2:8** Beware so that no one captures you through philosophy and empty deceit, according to human tradition, according to the ele-

---

14. The word *houses* understood as a verb (κατοικεῖ, "houses, dwells, inhabits").
15. See Jeal, "Starting before the Beginning," on this verse.
16. Or "have been filled," πεπληρωμένοι, perfect passive participle. Nouns ending in -μα can have active (i.e., πλήρωμα can mean that which fills) or passive (i.e., that which is filled) senses. On this see Roy R. Jeal, "A Strange Style of Expression, Ephesians 1:23," *FN* 10 (1997): 129–38.

ments of the world, and not according to Christ; **2:9** because in him houses all the fullness of the deity bodily, **2:10** and you have been made full in him who is the head of every power and authority.

Textural Commentary

This rhetoric takes up the *negative texture* mentioned in 2:4 and develops it further. The faithful believers, who had taken on the Lord Jesus Christ to themselves (v. 6), must watch out for someone who wants to capture them with an empty and deceitful philosophy. Prepositions convey the nature of the danger: "*through* [διά] philosophy ... *according to* [κατά] human tradition ... *according to* [κατά] the elements of the world ... *not according to* [οὐ κατά] Christ." The philosophy is insidious and misleading. The κατά phrases offer preliminary characterization of the philosophy, but more about it is not indicated until ideas progress through the following steps (2:11–15, 16–17, 18–19, 20–23). Even then, very little can be determined about what it is. The terms and syntax employed have generated huge debate among scholars about the identity of what gets called "the Colossian philosophy" and, sometimes, "the Colossian heresy" assumed to be at the center of the purpose of the entire letter. The words *philosophy* and *heresy* for many scholars presuppose an established underlying issue that can be properly identified and analyzed.[17] They have made gigantic efforts to come to satisfying historical and theological reconstructions of the philosophy. There are vast differences of interpretation and speculations.[18] The assumption is that the "philosophy," the "human traditions," and the "elements of the world" denote specific, false, and dangerous religious teaching and praxis.[19] The word *philosophy*, employed in verse 8, calls for

---

17. Although some, notably Morna Hooker and more recently Adam Copenhaver, argue that there was no one or no group pressuring the believers either inside or outside the *ekklēsia* in Colossae. See Hooker, "Were There False Teachers in Colossae?," in *Christ and Spirit in the New Testament*, ed. Barnabas Lindars and Stephen Smalley (Cambridge: Cambridge University Press, 1973), 315–31; Copenhaver, *Reconstructing the Historical Background of Paul's Rhetoric in the Letter to the Colossians*, LNTS 585 (London: Bloomsbury T&T Clark, 2018), 33–39, 235–37.

18. As Clinton Arnold points out, "The nature of the problem at Colossae has been an insoluble riddle.... We are no closer to a consensus solution than we were thirty years ago" ("Initiation, Vision, and Spiritual Power," 173).

19. John Barclay describes how many scholars run too quickly to their own points of view: "It is almost universally assumed by scholars that this phrase [τὰ στοιχεῖα

interpretation. The term *heresy* has a more pejorative connotation. From a hermeneutical point of view, both are misleading insofar as they persuade interpreters to imagine that they can and should reconstruct the specific and singular problem that the entire letter was intended to address, even though little clear information about the problem is provided.

The first thing to say is that *there is so much we do not know*. While much research and writing has been produced regarding the historical, philosophical, social, religious, and spatial connections of Colossians, the exact nature, identity, and details of a number of items, particularly the "philosophy and empty deceit" (τῆς φιλοσοφίας καὶ κενῆς ἀπάτης), "the elements of the cosmos" (τὰ στοιχεῖα τοῦ κόσμου), and "the powers and authorities" (τὰς ἀρχὰς καὶ τὰς ἐξουσίας), are not defined or even clearly implied by the text. It can be assumed by the authors that their first audiences understood the meanings and nuances, but even this is not absolute. There are literally dozens of views (and points of view), with much based in speculations, possibilities, presumed parallels, and perhaps some possibilities to which individual scholars are committed.[20] What was the philosophy? Or was there a specific, single philosophy?[21] What human tradition is in view? What or who are τὰ στοιχεῖα τοῦ κόσμου? What is crucial

---

τοῦ κόσμου] takes us straight to the language of 'heresy,' so that one may immediately debate what kind of 'elements' were meant and what sort of fear or veneration they elicited in the 'heresy.'" Assumptions easily become presumptions. See Barclay, *Colossians and Philemon*, NTG (Sheffield: Sheffield Academic, 1997), 51.

20. For a recent survey see Copenhaver, *Reconstructing the Historical Background*, 1–39. See the extensive and referenced survey by Wilson, *Colossians and Philemon*, 35–58, 61–63. See also the survey in Troy W. Martin, *By Philosophy and Empty Deceit: Colossians as Response to a Cynic Critique*, JSNTSup 118 (Sheffield: Sheffield Academic, 1996), 11–17. See the summary of views in McKnight, *Colossians*, 226–28. For critical methodological comments, see Barclay, *Colossians and Philemon*, 39–48, 52–54; Talbert, *Ephesians and Colossians*, 206–9; and especially Jerry L. Sumney, "Paul and His Opponents: The Search," in *Paul Unbound: Other Perspectives on the Apostle*, ed. Mark D. Given, ESEC 25 (Atlanta: SBL Press, 2022), 79–98. See also Thomas H. Olbricht, "The Stoicheia and the Rhetoric of Colossians: Then and Now," in *Rhetoric and Scripture: Collected Essays of Thomas H. Olbricht*, ed. Lauri Thurén, ESEC 23 (Atlanta: SBL Press, 2021), 118–27.

21. The proposals for and analyses of the philosophy include Jewish calendrical and dietary rules, Jewish *merkabah* mysticism, Jewish halakic practices, gnosticism, cosmic (demonic or angelic) beings, Cynic philosophy, syncretistic philosophy, magical practices, ecstatic visions, angel worship, the imperial cult, combinations of some of these, and other traditions.

for any clarity in these questions is to analyze and interpret the ideas in the context as we have it, that is, in the **social and cultural texture** progressions and **intertextures** of Col 2:4–23.[22]

The word "philosophy" (φιλοσοφία) occurs only here in the New Testament. **Intertexturally**, it occurs in the LXX in 4 Maccabees 1:1–2; 5:11–12, 22; 7:9, 21–23 in argumentation urging that philosophy properly practiced as good reasoning that does not succumb to emotion is right and proper.[23] According to these texts, the aim of philosophy is to describe and support the virtuous, productive, wisdom way of life. Philo describes "the proper fruit" of philosophy as productive, virtuous living (*Mut.* 73–75; see also Philo, *Legat.* 156, 245).[24] Josephus similarly uses the term *philosophy* to refer to how people[25] think about how life is to be lived appropriately (*C. Ap.* 2.47, 140–141; *B.J.* 2.119; *A.J.* 18.11). The second-century BCE Letter of Aristeas defines philosophy in the same wisdom way:

> The king said that this man had answered well, and asked another "What is philosophy?" And he explained, "To deliberate well in reference to any question that emerges and never to be carried away by impulses, but to ponder over the injuries that result from the passions, and to act rightly as the circumstances demand, practicing moderation. But we must pray to God to instill into our mind a regard for these things." (Let. Aris. 256 [Charles])

The point is that philosophy was understood to be a very good thing when it employed good reasoning and promoted good living. This understanding of philosophy extends back to the great philosopher Socrates. Socratic philosophic investigation has the understanding and practice of virtue in mind.[26] The philosophy Col 2:8 presents as empty, deceitful, and dangerous does not, in the view of the authors of the letter, employ good reasoning, and it promotes unnecessary and destructive behaviors.

---

22. See Barclay, *Colossians and Philemon*, 49–50.
23. The verb φιλοσοφέω occurs in, e.g., 4 Macc 8:1, and the noun φιλόσοφος in, e.g., LXX Dan 1:20.
24. Colossians uses similar metaphors of productivity: fruit bearing, rooted, growing.
25. Not only Jews but also others such as Egyptians.
26. See Thomas G. West, "Introduction," in *Four Texts on Socrates: Plato's "Euthryphro," "Apology," and "Crito" and Aristophanes' "Clouds,"* trans. Thomas G. West and Grace Starry West (Ithaca, NY: Cornell University Press, 1984), 12, 16.

SCENE THREE: DON'T BE DECEIVED. LIVE THE NEW REALITY   155

The description of the philosophy as "according to human tradition" (κατὰ τὴν παράδοσιν τῶν ἀνθρώπων) or, more literally, "the tradition of humans," makes a clear rhetorical point about the source of the philosophy in the **social texture** of tradition and simultaneously points back to what Colossians presents as the true and full reasoning that the philosophy does not take into account. Being "of humans" sets it in stark contrast as a counterphilosophy to the cosmic-precreational description of the Son-image of God, creator of all things, in whom "we" have (ἔχομεν) redemption and through whom is reconciliation and peace (1:13–20).[27] Father God has rescued "us" (ἡμᾶς, 1:13) out of chaotic darkness and transferred us into his Son's kingdom. The philosophy of 2:8 has a human, not cosmic-precreational source, so it is reasoned to be naturally inferior. It does not extend from the realm of God. It is empty and misleading, promoting the ways of fallible and imperfect humans who on their own live with the pressures of the jurisdiction of darkness, attempting to make themselves and others safe, healthy, and peaceful, practicing rituals and observances in attempts to please the gods by virtue and devotion according to the social, cultural, and religious philosophies and systems they recognized.[28] The implicit irony is that proponents of the philosophy have themselves been deceived and misled.

The word "elements" (στοιχεῖα, plural of στοιχεῖον) in the second κατά phrase, "according to the elements of the world," occurs twice in Colossians, at 2:8 and 2:20. It makes a second rhetorical point about the source of the philosophy. There are **intertextures** in the New Testament at Gal 4:3, 9; Heb 5:12; 2 Pet 3:10, 12. Attempts to define the στοιχεῖα have proliferated in the history of the interpretation of Colossians. Interpreters have often been quick to shape the noun into the adjective *elemental* by adding "spirits," "spiritual forces," "principles" or other interpretive terms to translations.[29] The word was employed widely in the ancient Mediterranean.[30] Euclid's Geometry was named *Elements* (Στοιχεῖα). Aristoxenus used the term to describe the harmonics of music (*Elementa harmonica*, fourth century BCE). Its roots are in the term στοῖχος, referring to a row or a line of things or series of things. From this στοιχεῖα came to mean the

---

27. See the commentary above on 1:15–20.
28. On Mediterranean religious practices, see the commentary on scene one, step one (1:1–2), **social and cultural texture**, and step five (1:15–20) on **intertexture**.
29. See note 13 above.
30. For a survey, see Gerhard Delling, "στοιχεῖον," *TDNT* 7:670–87.

steps of things from one end to another, hence a series or "what belongs to a series."³¹ The στοιχεῖα are thus the parts that constitute the whole of something. It was applied to many things: letters of an alphabet, numbers, the four physical elements, four human temperaments;³² after the New Testament period, it was used to refer to stars and astral bodies. During the first century CE, it generally referred to the four elements earth (ὕλη), water (ὕδωρ), air (ἀήρ), and fire (πῦρ).³³ In other words, στοιχεῖα envision what were imagined to be the basic materials of the cosmos shaped into the created order. Some contemporary Jewish texts employ the same four-element understanding (4 Macc 12:13; Wis 7:17; 19:8; Philo, *Cher.* 127; *Her.* 133–134, 140; *Abr.* 162; *Contempl.* 3; *Decal.* 53; *Aet.* 107–109). All matter was imagined to be constituted of systematic combinations of the four στοιχεῖα (see Plato, *Tim.* 31–33).

Many interpreters connect the στοιχεῖα with "the powers and authorities" (αἱ ἀρχαὶ καὶ ἐξουσίαι, 1:16; 2:10, 15), usually imagined to be malevolent spiritual, cosmic beings who aim to evoke and promote evil in humans and world affairs.³⁴ Yet the word does not inherently envision personal beings and is not employed to do so in first-century CE texts.³⁵ Certainly ancient Mediterranean people believed in personal cosmic-spiritual and political-spiritual powers and authorities but did not use the word στοιχεῖα to describe them.³⁶

---

31. Delling, "στοιχεῖον," 670.

32. Related to Hippocrates's theory of four humors in humans: black bile (earth), yellow bile (fire), blood (air), phlegm (water). Illness was caused when the humors were out of balance. These in turn were related to the four seasons: autumn, winter, spring, summer.

33. A fifth, ether, a substance like air in the atmosphere above the clouds, is sometimes mentioned.

34. As Arnold argues in *Colossian Syncretism*.

35. Sumney, *Colossians*, 131. Sumney points out how quite often "reconstruction dominates exegesis" ("Paul and His Opponents," 89).

36. See, however, the work of Kahl, *Galatians Re-imagined*. Kahl describes the στοιχεῖα as oppositional, binary polarities that envision hierarchical structures. Air and fire (light, superior elements) stood against earth and water (heavy, inferior elements). In Roman imperial thinking, the gods and Rome itself, being superior, were associated with air and fire, while inferior humans and dominated nations with earth and water. The chief Roman god, Jupiter, was frequently associated with the superior realms of air and fire, and the imperial cult imagined the divine emperor as Jupiter. The sociocultural expectation was that people would respect this construct (a human tradition, Col 2:8) and behave accordingly. See also Fredrick J. Long, "Ephesians:

What can be said confidently is that στοιχεῖα had many meanings in many contexts and functioned as a *utility word* that could be applied to many things, here in Colossians to some religious practices of the ancient Mediterranean.[37] Read in the context of the two occurrences of τὰ στοιχεῖα τοῦ κόσμου in Col 2:8, 20, the term στοιχεῖα envisions religious behavioral practices. The pressure and the practices are "human traditions" and of "the world," so do not come from the cosmic-precreation realm of God and his Son. They come from the chaotic, disordered ways of human traditions that pressure people to imagine that they must generate their own fullness in order to be accepted and assisted by God or gods.[38] The warning has in view someone who wants to capture Christ believers in order to impose the unnecessary and unhelpful religious practices—and probably others like them—named in 2:16–19 and 20–23. The pressure will come from someone who wants the holy ones to have a sense of obligation that would move them to submit to a do-it-yourself approach to religion and religious behavior. The practices are attractive because they appear to be very pious (v. 23) and practitioners seem to fit in with sociocultural expectations, but they are, to pick up now on the third κατά phrase of 2:8, "not according to Christ." They are described with the utility term "the elements of the world," which points to the way of the world that believes that religion *demands and depends on doing* the right things in the right ways, that people have to make their own way in the world. The gods of the disordered cosmos are not gracious but demanding. And there are people watching, looking for reasons to "deprive you" (2:18), presenting themselves as those who know what are the correct observances and behaviors, ready to tell you when you have it wrong. "Do not handle, do not taste, do not touch!" (2:23).

This, of course, is not the gospel of rescue and transfer to the new reality that the letter proclaims (1:5, 12–14). It was a thread in the **cultural**

Paul's Political Theology in Greco-Roman Political Context," in *Christian Origins and Greco-Roman Culture: Social and Literary Contexts for the New Testament*, ed. Stanley E. Porter and Andrew W. Pitts, TENTS 9 (Leiden: Brill, 2012), 255–309.

37. A catchall representative term. Meaning varies with context. See Neil Martin, "Returning to the *stoicheia tou kosmou*: Enslavement to the Physical Elements in Galatians 4.3 and 9?," *JSNT* 40 (2018): 434–52; Michael Lapidge, "ἀρχαί and στοιχεῖα: A Problem in Stoic Cosmology," *Phronesis* 18 (1973): 240–78.

38. In other words, that you must do the right things if you want God or gods to give you what you want.

texture of the imperial world. The empire viewed the civil-political state and religion together, not as separate and distinct entities. The cosmic-spiritual and political-spiritual were interpenetrating planes. The ever-expanding polytheistic empire was happy to incorporate more gods into its pantheon of deities, but the relationship to them was contractual and mechanistic.[39] Priests managed the relationships, and the aim was to keep the gods happy, to appease them by the correct behaviors, by sacrifices, by obeisance, by doing what was imagined necessary, in hope of goodwill and benefactions.[40] Conformity to this kind of religious philosophy was expected.[41] Practicing the στοιχεῖα of the world involved this kind of do-it-yourself religion. The **intertextures** in Gal 4:3, 9 describe living according to the στοιχεῖα as "enslavement" (ὑπὸ τὰ στοιχεῖα τοῦ κόσμου ἤμεθα δεδουλωμένοι). The authors of Colossians have come to know that this religious widespread philosophy is empty and deceitful. They envisioned "the grace of God in truth" (1:6), the redemption (liberation) and forgiveness of sins provided in the Son-Christ, neither acquired nor maintained by particular observances.

To succumb to the philosophy, to human tradition, and to the elements of the world would be to appeal to the chaotic, disordered jurisdiction of darkness rather than to Christ and to slip back into the shadow (2:17). Things "not according to Christ" are described as "according to the flesh" in Paul's letters (κατὰ σάρκα, Rom 8:13, 2 Cor 1:17, 5:16, 10:2–3). The world is the realm of domination and oppression. In the world humans are always struggling to get ahead, to make life better. The *argumentative texture* of verses 9–10 is generated from the phrase "not according to Christ" at the end of verse 8, making the case that fullness of living comes from Christ, in whom is the fullness of God.[42] The rhetorical argu-

---

39. As Beard points out, "Roman religion was not only polytheistic but treated foreign gods much as it treated foreign peoples: by incorporation.... But the basic rule was that as the Roman Empire expanded, so did its pantheon of deities" (*SPQR*, 519). "In general, it was a religion of doing, not believing" (103). On Roman religion and politics, see 100–109.

40. "So why was reverence for the deities deeply embedded within Roman culture? Ultimately devotion to the deities derived from the fear that failing to honor them would incur their wrath and from the hope that capturing their favor might enhance a person's prospects" (Longenecker, *In Stone and Story*, 41).

41. On conformity, see the commentary below on 2:16–17, 20–23.

42. See above on rhetography.

ment is composed of three clauses that focus on what *is* "according to Christ," initiated with "because" (ὅτι):

> because in him houses all the fullness of deity bodily
> and in him you have been made full
> who is the head of every power and authority

The causal conjunction *because* governs all three clauses. Analysis of the argument yields this structure:

> **Imperative:** Do not become captured through philosophy and empty deceit and things not according to Christ.
> **Rationale:** Because the fullness of deity houses *in* Christ bodily; because you have already been made full *in him*; because Christ *is* the head of every power and authority.
> **Implied Result:** There is no need for personal religious actions designed to acquire and attain to fullness. There is no need to look to any spirit or political powers or authorities for fullness of life. All things needed have already been achieved and supplied by Christ. The redemption, reconciliation, peace, and other benefits humans desire cannot be acquired through religious observances or ascetic actions imagined to be necessary for pleasing gods. Do not be persuaded to acquire benefit by means of personal merit.

All three clauses use present-tense verbs, indicating that the fullness of deity continues to house in Christ (κατοικεῖ),[43] that believers continue to be made full in him (ἐστὲ ἐν αὐτῷ), and Christ continues to be the head (ὅς ἐστιν ἡ κεφαλὴ), that is, the ruler of every power and authority. The perfect passive participle πεπληρωμένοι, "have been made full," explains the current and continuing state of the believers. They have already been given all they need.[44] The old attempt at self-sufficiency was always a delusion.[45]

---

43. On house and household language in Colossians, see the discussion of *alternative culture* in the introduction.

44. Sumney is correct to assert that "the basic issue in Colossians is soteriological, not christological" (*Colossians*, 134). The Son-image-fullness of God has made believers full of salvation "in him."

45. So, once again, "Do not put your trust in princes [ἄρχοντας], in mortals, in whom there is no help" (LXX Ps 145:3). Do not believe the old lie: "But the serpent

Humans are made full in Christ, not by trying to make the gods or any powers happy.

This step continues and develops the **ideological texture** that was taking shape as early as Col 1:9 with the declaration of prayers that the holy ones would be "filled [πληρωθῆτε] with the knowledge of his will in all spiritual wisdom and understanding." Here, with the warning about someone who will present an empty philosophy, they are told, in the intentional *repetitive texture* of the noun πλήρωμα and the verb πληρόω (1:9, 19), that they "have been made full" (or "have been filled," πεπληρωμένοι). This is the ideology or shared value that the Lycus believers are to get—that they have already been made full in Christ, in whom houses all the fullness of deity. The cosmic-precreational reality of the Son-Christ (1:15–20) undergirds this understanding. The point being made by the ideology is about continuing the "walk in him" (2:6) without being overtaken by the deceitful philosophy. The rhetoric intends to build trust and confidence in who Christ is and in what Christ has done for them. Christ is all they need. Nothing else—religion, politics, meritorious behaviors—can provide anything more or anything better. This ideology leads to the explanations of the next sentence, 2:11–15, and already has in sight the comprehensive statement of 3:11, "Christ all and in all." The answer to the philosophy is, "No, we have been filled already." This is an ideology of faithfulness to what had been heard in the proclamation by Epaphras and now in the more developed theology in the letter.

Step Three: God in Christ Has Done Everything You Need (2:11–15)

Rhetography

The visualization of the Lycus believers as people who have been made full in Christ opens the way for an argument, explanation, and visualization of how the filling was brought about. This progression describes the apocalyptic actions of God with vivid imagery in a new sentence at verse 11.[46] Christ is pictured in the emphatic "in whom" (ἐν ᾧ) at the begin-

---

said to the woman, 'You will not die, for God knows that when you eat of it your eyes will be opened, and *you will be like God*, knowing good and evil'" (Gen 3:4–5).

46. NA[28], UBS[4], and UBS[5] begin a new sentence at 2:11. The SBLGNT and earlier editions (e.g., UBS[3]) have a continuous sentence from 2:8 to 2:15. It is possible to read it either way. The rhetography of the sentence should be visualized as a whole, taking

ning of the sentence.⁴⁷ The image of the holy ones is elaborated graphically by presenting them as circumcised people in Christ (περιετμήθητε).⁴⁸ The result of the surgery of circumcision can be imagined, recognized by people of the Lycus as the Jewish covenantal sign (or at least as a Jewish peculiarity).⁴⁹ The circumcision here, however, is visualized differently because it is not performed in the usual physical way but "made without hand" or "not handmade" (περιτομῇ ἀχειροποιήτῳ).⁵⁰ It is a circumcision that envisions "the stripping off of the body of the flesh." This is not the physical flesh of the foreskin but the metaphorical cutting away of the life in darkness and the transfer into the Son's kingdom.⁵¹ The former life has been stripped away, and the life of fullness in Christ is now visible and practiced. This is "the circumcision of Christ" (τῇ περιτομῇ τοῦ Χριστοῦ) brought about by the apocalyptic work of God in the death of Christ. It is the action of redemption, forgiveness, reconciliation, and peacemaking that reenvisions what was set in the imagination in 1:12–15. While audiences recognize that the rhetograph describes what has happened to them and for them, they continue to see Christ at the center of the portrayal as the one *in whom* God—the deity who houses in Christ—brought about their circumcision. Christ's apocalyptic presence is the indicator of the reality of their nonhandmade circumcision.⁵²

---

the comprehensive visual effect into the mind. See Robert Farrar Capon's description of how the visuality of a juggler's performance is seen as a whole in *The Fingerprints of God: Tracking the Divine Suspect through a History of Images* (Grand Rapids: Eerdmans, 2000), 23–40.

47. This image continues the *repetitive ἐν αὐτῷ texture* that began in 2:6. Contra Talbert, it is not the instrumental "through him" (*Ephesians and Colossians*, 213).

48. The only instance of the aorist passive of this verb in the New Testament.

49. See below on **intertexture**.

50. NRSV and NRSVue are misleading with the interpretive rendering "with a spiritual circumcision." Art historians study *acheiropoiēta*, icons such as the image of Edessa, the veil of Veronica, and the shroud of Turin, traditionally imagined to have come into existence miraculously, not made by humans. See "International Workshop on the Scientific Approach to the Acheiropoietos Images," ENEA, https://tinyurl.com/SBL7106f.

51. The phrase "the body of the flesh" is unique in the Pauline letters to Col 1:22, 2:11. For discussion of flesh (σάρξ), see James D. G. Dunn, *The Theology of Paul the Apostle* (Grand Rapids: Eerdmans, 1998), 62–73.

52. The priestly action of circumcising is blended with the apocalyptic action of cutting away the former life.

Overlaid on and interwoven with the picture of circumcision is the picture of the burial of the audience members with Christ, which picture itself is interwoven with the image of their baptism (συνταφέντες αὐτῷ ἐν τῷ βαπτισμῷ). The nonhandmade circumcision, the stripping off of the body of the flesh, is seen together with the burial of believers with Christ's burial (their death is implicit here and comes explicitly into view in 2:13), visualized in the recollection of the concrete reality of their baptism.[53] The burial-baptism is followed by resurrection "in him" (ἐν ᾧ καὶ συνηγέρθητε). Death, burial, and resurrection are seen as a complex unity, a continuum, in and necessarily with Christ.[54] The actual raising (i.e., the enlivening, saving work) is brought about "through the faithful active energy of God who raised him from the dead" (διὰ τῆς πίστεως τῆς ἐνεργείας τοῦ θεοῦ τοῦ ἐγείραντος αὐτὸν ἐκ νεκρῶν).[55] The imagery is visually explained: it is the action of God, performed in the same way, that is, by the same energy, that God used in raising Christ out of death. The baptism and raising of humans are analogous to the reality of God's action and the nonhandmade circumcision of Christ.

There is an amazing blending of images in this picture. Physical circumcision is blended with nonphysical circumcision and with the cutting away of the former existence in darkness. Nonphysical circumcision is blended with believers' burial and resurrection with Christ brought about by God. The imagery of burial is blended with baptism. This blending produces a quite marvelous visualized space where the circumcision-stripping off of the body of the flesh–burial–resurrection sequence is seen comprehensively as a single portrayal. The comprehensive vision is located in Christ (in whom is the fullness of deity bodily) and brought about by the action of God. The imagery is complex, it has multiple blends of topoi, but the complexity presents a reality that people can grasp. It

---

53. See the death of Christ mentioned already in 1:20–22.

54. Contra a frequent interpretation, the pronominal phrase ἐν αὐτῷ in 2:12 should not be understood as "in which" (i.e., in baptism) but as a repetition of "in whom." Baptism stands here (and in Rom 6:4) for burial, that is, for *immersion*, and not for resurrection, that is, for *emersion* (see Dunn, *Epistles to the Colossians and to Philemon*, 160; Lincoln, "Colossians" 624). Baptism symbolizes union with Christ in death and burial. See 2 Cor 5:14, which envisions Christ's death as everyone's death.

55. The words διὰ τῆς πίστεως τῆς ἐνεργείας τοῦ θεοῦ are understood subjectively, through the faithful activity of God, not objectively, through faith *in* the activity of God. This fits the context where all the redemptive activity is performed by God in Christ.

SCENE THREE: DON'T BE DECEIVED. LIVE THE NEW REALITY   163

is understood precisely because it is a visualized, recognizable, remembered, apocalyptic picture.

The image of death becomes explicit in 2:13. The circumcised-baptized-raised humans remain in sight but now in their former condition—that is, prior to being raised with Christ—as dead, and following the circumcision imagery, they are viewed in their former condition of being uncircumcised.[56] The former condition of being dead and uncircumcised is seen simultaneously as being "in trespasses," that is, in sins that cross the line.[57] The entire picture implies that they are alive in a present view. This implication is immediately explicit in the image of humans having been "made alive with" Christ. They are alive, although in another view of the same tapestry they are seen to be dead. The image of being made alive "with him" corresponds to the continuing overlaid image of Christ and believers. The complexity of the rhetograph increases with the addition of the notion of the forgiveness of the trespasses that contrasts with "in trespasses and the foreskin of your flesh."

Next, the visualization in verse 14 brings the senders of the letter back into focus along with the audience with the reappearance of the plural pronoun *us*. The broader perspective on "we" and "us" pictures the forgiven senders and receivers as liberated people in a liberated setting where no authoritative record (χειρόγραφον, a chirograph, a handwritten record) or authoritative powers stand against them or make requirements of them. The record of demands (δόγματα) that stands against them is visibly erased, removed from their space of existence. The action of the erasure is described as accomplished by God's action of removing the record (αὐτὸ ἦρκεν ἐκ τοῦ μέσου, literally "he took it out of the middle")[58] by "nailing it to the cross" (προσηλώσας αὐτὸ τῷ σταυρῷ). The cross and nailing imagery obviously envision Christ, blending in the action of nailing as the metaphor for the erasure of the record of rules or violations that stood against people. In the imagery of verse 15, the powers and authorities have been disarmed and triumphed, in other words led away as defeated captives.

---

56. Lit. "in the foreskin of your flesh." The word ἀκροβυστία in 2:13, commonly translated as "uncircumcision," literally means "foreskin" or "prepuce," the flesh removed in circumcision.

57. παράπτωμα, literally "beside the corpse."

58. Accusing witnesses were stationed in the middle of the court in Mediterranean legal disputes. On this see Barth and Blanke, *Colossians*, 332.

The comprehensive, vivid continuum of apocalyptic actions, non-handmade circumcision–burial (baptism)–resurrection–making alive–forgiving–erasing–taking out of the middle–nailing–crucifixion–disgracing–triumphing, multiple actions all viewed simultaneously as a complex unity, comes together in a blunt focus on a central and crucial location and event: the crucifixion of the Son-Christ, in whom houses the fullness of deity. This focus is seen most closely and graphically in 2:15 in the aorist nominative middle participle ἀπεκδυσάμενος, translated here as a true middle-voice form with the reflexive sense "stripping himself."[59] Frequently translated and understood in active voice to refer to the stripping or disarming of the powers and authorities, reading it for the middle-voice participle it is presents God (who is the subject of the participle) and Christ, in whom deity houses bodily, as willingly stripping himself in an apocalyptic display of the exposure of the body housing true deity.[60] This startling action of God and the Son-Christ itself boldly disgraces the powers and authorities. The irony is vivid and emotionally profound. The nonhandmade circumcision, the stripping off of the body of the flesh, the making alive, the forgiveness, the triumph, the redemption, reconciliation, peace, and fullness were all accomplished by *the exposure of deity* in the body of Christ on the cross.[61] This imagery flies in the face of ancient

---

59. The middle-voice participle is not *deponent*, i.e., middle with active meaning. Arguably there are no *deponent* verbs in Biblical Greek. Aorist participles "normally implicate antecedent action ... before the action of the leading verb." On this see Campbell, *Colossians and Philemon*, xxv, 41. On deponency see Bernard A. Taylor, "Deponency and Greek Lexicography," in *Biblical Greek Language and Lexicography: Essays in Honor of Frederick W. Danker*, ed. Bernard A. Taylor et al. (Grand Rapids: Eerdmans, 2004), 167–76; Martin M. Culy, "Series Introduction," in Campbell, *Colossians and Philemon*, xi–xiii. On ἀπεκδυσάμενος as middle voice, see Maier, *Picturing Paul in Empire*, 100, who references Roy Yates, "Colossians 2:15: Christ Triumphant," *NTS* 37 (1991): 573–91. See the rather incomplete discussions in Dunn, *Epistles to the Colossians and Philemon*, 167–68; Wilson, *Colossians and Philemon*, 208, 211–12; Beale, *Colossians and Philemon*, 201–2, 210–11; Barth and Blanke, *Colossians*, 332–33.

60. Allowing himself to be stripped of clothing and dignity by Roman soldiers. Victims of Roman crucifixion were hung naked on crosses for all to see as part of the disgrace of being executed (Maier, *Picturing Paul in Empire*, 100). There was no discrete loincloth on Jesus as in artistic and devotional representations. Regarding the participle, there is no grammatical reason to presume a change of subject to Christ.

61. The repetition of the cognate forms ἀπεκδύσει (2:11) and ἀπεκδυσάμενος (2:15) indicates that everyone gets metaphorically stripped, humans and deity. This is theological development beyond what is stated in Phil 2:5–11.

Mediterranean and Roman imperial expectations of how things are done in a kingdom through power, military force, war, politics, legislation, executions, exile, oppression, slavery, appeasing the gods, triumphal processions, the Pax Romana.[62] Unlike divine emperors, the Son of the unseen God is seen giving himself over to human disgrace for the redemption of humans and the cosmos.[63] Jesus Messiah is enthroned not on an elaborate, elevated chair but on a cross with a crown of thorns.

All this subverts the gospel of empire because it shows that what appears to be weak is actually what is strong. This is how the kingdom of the Son of Father God (1:13) comes to preeminence and power in the world. Lycus Valley Christ believers are meant to understand *this philosophy*, already stated in 1:20, "and through him to reconcile all things to himself, making peace through the blood of his cross, whether things on the earth, whether things in the heavens." This is much bigger than the empire of Rome and much bigger than the local pressure to observe human traditions in the Lycus. The picture demonstrates that the empty, deceitful philosophy (2:8) is irrelevant because the powers to which it appeals are impotent. They, ironically, have been disgraced and triumphed (2:15), forced to walk in a procession presenting them as defeated and demoralized. The rhetograph makes the argument. Lycus believers should beware of the false, irrelevant philosophy and not be misled by it. God in Christ has provided everything. Nothing else is required to complete the picture.

Translation

> **2:11** In him also you were circumcised with a nonhandmade circumcision in the stripping off of the body of the flesh[64] in the circumcision of Christ, **2:12** buried with him in baptism in whom also you were raised through the faith of the power of God who raised him out of [the[65]] dead; **2:13** and you, being dead in[66] the trespasses and the foreskin of your flesh, he made you[67] alive with

---

62. Perhaps also modern expectations of the same kinds of things.
63. Emperors were, of course, frequently presented in statuary as heroic nudes. But not nailed to a cross in naked disgrace. See images in Maier, *Picturing Paul in Empire*.
64. NA^{28} indicates the variant τοῦ σώματος τῶν ἁμαρτιῶν.
65. NA^{28} indicates variant ἐκ τῶν νεκρῶν.
66. Some manuscripts do not have the preposition ἐν.
67. Some manuscripts have ἡμᾶς, "us."

him, forgiving us all the trespasses, **2:14** erasing the handwritten record of demands which is opposed to us, and he [himself] took it out of the middle, nailing it to the cross; **2:15** stripping himself, he disgraced the powers and the authorities in boldness, triumphing them in him.

Textural Commentary

This step is carried along rhetorically by internal *progressions* and by the connected *repetitive texture* of the "in him" (ἐν αὐτῷ) and "in whom also" (ἐν ᾧ καί) phrases focusing things locationally in Christ that began at 2:6. The repeated "in him" occurs five times (2:6, 7, 9, 10, 15), "in whom also" twice (2:11, 12), and "with him" twice (2:12, 13).[68] The "in him" and "in whom also" phrases are taken to be equivalent in meaning. Everything described and done according to these verses was done "in him" and "with" him. In other words, nothing was done apart from Christ, in whom the fullness of deity houses.[69] The lives of the holy ones, all that they are rooted and built on (2:6–7), is entirely focused and located in Christ. The complex series of actions by God done to them (nonhandmade circumcision, burial, baptism, raising, making alive) and for them (erasing, removing out of the middle, nailing, stripping, disgracing, triumphing) have been done "in" and "with" Christ, in whom deity houses. That the deceitful philosophy is "not according to Christ" is contrasted in the *argumentative texture* of verses 9–10: "*because in him* houses all the fullness of deity … and you are *in him* made full." The repetitions indicate that the holy ones are now so embedded in Christ that the fullness they have in him dominates. Six internal *progressions* present the actions in a systematic way, indicating the sequencing of envisioned ideas that blend together as priestly-apocalyptic actions to make the argumentative point:

- ♦ in whom you were circumcised—no longer bound by the body of the flesh, a metaphor representing the elemental, human, earthly,

---

68. Without a preposition but understood as "with him" in 2:12, and with a preposition in 2:13 (σὺν αὐτῷ), strengthened by the συν- compound verbs συνταφέντες, συνηγέρθητε, and συνεζωοποίησεν.

69. The ἐν αὐτῷ at the end of 2:15 is understood here as "in him" rather than "in it" as in many translations. God is the subject of the participle θριαμβεύσας, an action, like all described in this step, performed in Christ (see Wilson, *Colossians*, 211).

SCENE THREE: DON'T BE DECEIVED. LIVE THE NEW REALITY

dark realms and forces that drive people to become captives, imagining that the ideology and behaviors they demand are required
- buried with him in baptism—Christ's burial and the believers' burial with him blends with the cutting away of the body of the flesh. The cutting away (the circumcision of Christ) is understood concretely in the memory of their baptism.
- in him you were raised—the cutting away of the body of flesh now blends the stripping away of the flesh and their baptism with the faithful action of God in raising them with Christ
- you were made alive with him— the former life "in the trespasses and foreskin of your flesh" was dead existence, from which the believers "were made alive with" Christ. They were simultaneously forgiven (χαρισάμενος ἡμῖν) all trespasses
- erasing, removing, nailing—the first of two statements introduced by aorist participles that describe the simultaneous erasure of the record of demands that stood against people, pressuring them to perform
- stripping, disgracing, triumphing— Christ stripping himself, giving himself to death in the crucifixion, paradoxically disgraces the powers and authorities and triumphs them, that is, leads all rivals and empty philosophies away in a humiliating procession

Together these interwoven progressions form the *argumentative texture* that makes the point: believers have been made full in Christ.[70]

Case: (indicated in 2:6-7, 8-10) The letter recipients are likely to be faced with pressures from someone[71] aiming to persuade them to take on a philosophy that imagines that religious identity is affirmed in self-generated practices that are according to human tradition and not according to Christ. Against this it is argued that all the fullness of God is already present for them in Christ, in whom they are *already* full.

Rationale: In Christ "the body of flesh," life lived according to the elements of the world, in the darkness and death of "trespasses and the foreskin of your flesh," and pressured to conform

---

70. The argument is similar to what was seen previously in 1:15-20. Everything humans need is already provided in Christ.

71. The language of 2:20-23 suggests that the pressure has already started.

to religious identity defined by human demands and expectations, has been cut away, circumcised, stripped off, in the non-handmade "circumcision of Christ."[72] This cutting away has been accomplished by the action of God, who raised Christ Jesus, in whom and with whom humans also have been buried and raised. Christ's death, burial, and resurrection is their own death, burial, and resurrection, and they are now very much alive with Christ, and everything of the former body-of-flesh existence has been removed. Existence in the body of the flesh is characterized by the compulsion to obtain fullness through self-generated human performance, by the knowledge and guilt of unforgiven trespasses. It is pressured by the expectation of observance of the philosophy. It has all been removed, the expectations erased, nailed to the cross with Christ, who in unexpected and graphically dramatic fashion has disgraced the human traditions and powers that demand religious identity in the body of the flesh. The benefit of such fullness is neither acquired nor kept by human self-performance. The argumentative rationale focuses on what God has already done. Everything needed for fullness of life has been accomplished. All indictments of the flesh, of the cosmic-spiritual and political-spiritual powers, are irrelevant. Nothing else is required.

Result: This rhetorical argumentation demonstrates that Lycus Christ believers need not succumb to the pressure that attempts to impose what are claimed to be obligatory traditions and practices. Everything has been accomplished by God in Christ. They should have no uncertainty: the powers who promote and demand them are powerless.

This argumentation, set in apocalyptic rhetorolect, extends from the undergirding philosophy presented in 1:15–20. It demonstrates the overall wisdom intention of Colossians. The argument aims to affect audiences of the letter by showing that the human space they inhabit as believers has

---

72. Contra Lightfoot and many who have followed him over more than a century, 2:11 is not describing the "practical errors" of the Colossians who "do not need the circumcision of the flesh; for you have received the circumcision of the heart" (Lightfoot, *Colossians*, 183). Rather, the imagery of circumcision is argumentatively employed to demonstrate that the "body of the flesh" aspects of life have already been removed. The argument is not against the actual practice of circumcision (compare Galatians).

been radically altered. In the reconfigured new space into which they have been transferred, neither those who make the demands nor the powers imagined to be behind the demands possess real authority or credibility. Christ believers do not need to accept any impositions of the old space of the στοιχεῖα, regardless of how attractive and wise it may seem to be. They have all they need in Christ.

The *sensory-aesthetic texture* of these verses would have been discernible to Lycus believers, as it is still. There is a rich evocation of visual, tactile, aural, and emotional senses in the description and imagery of circumcision, cutting, burial, memories of baptisms, trespasses and foreskins, stripping and bodily exposure, disgrace, and triumphal procession. All of these strike the mind, blending together to arouse memories and emotions, to evoke agreement and the nodding of heads, bodily sensations, appealing to human qualities of being, personality, intellect, the affections, and social knowledge.[73] They have a feel and an appearance that are recognizable and that establish understandings. Some descriptions have sensory effects on human bodies and the sense of touch.[74] Included are the images and sensations aroused by cutting (circumcision) and stripping off the body of the flesh, burial, and baptism and the foreskin of your flesh.[75] Listeners immediately understand the physical meaning of the terms, sense the cutting of the surgery even though the circumcision is described as nonhandmade and the descriptions are metaphorical. Everyone, the believers and Christ, experiences stripping, either the body of the flesh or clothing. Some descriptions speak to the human sensory notions of death and life: death; burial; baptism, raising from death; death in trespasses and the foreskin of your flesh; nailing to a cross. To this is added the tactile impression of the handwriting of the record of demands (chirograph, v. 14).

These touch deeper senses that make for an intellectually and emotionally palpable rhetoric that focuses in on physical actions, their effects, and memories of them occurring in the past. Other descriptions suggest the possibility of reduced stress and mental relief in the forgiveness of trespasses and the removal of the record of demands people faced. What

---

73. The zone of emotion-fused thought (see Robbins, *Exploring the Textures of Texts*, 30–31).

74. The zone of purposeful action.

75. The noun ἀπέκδυσις (2:11) and cognate verb ἀπεκδύομαι [ἀπεκδύω] (2:15) may be neologisms created by the authors. See Albrecht Oepke, "ἀπεκδύω, ἀπέκδυσις," *TDNT* 2:318–19.

happened to Christ in his stripping of himself along with the nailing to the cross, the Son-image of God in whom the fullness of deity houses, touches the senses with shock and horror. Disgracing and triumphing the powers and authorities can elicit surprise but also the sensibility that they got what they deserved. It might evoke gratitude that God in Christ is victorious (see 2:7). Such a scene draws out the sensory-aesthetic texturing of sights, sounds, even smells, the removal of power, the rejection of authority, the emotion of shame, and the physicality of a procession in which prisoners are marched away ignominiously. The word θριαμβεύω is a verb of seeing and hearing, of observing the triumphal procession visually and audibly as it goes along through the streets.

Some words and grammar appeal to the senses of ear and sound.[76] The aural texturing of repetitions of the preposition ἐν produce melodic patterns that tie together and explain actions done to the believers:

<u>ἐν ᾧ καὶ</u> περιετμήθητε περιτομῇ ἀχειροποιήτῳ
  <u>ἐν</u> τῇ ἀπεκδύσει τοῦ σώματος τῆς σαρκός,
  <u>ἐν</u> τῇ περιτομῇ τοῦ Χριστοῦ
<u>ἐν ᾧ καὶ</u> συνηγέρθητε

The homoeoteleuton of the passive verbs emphasizes what was done "in him." The prepositional phrases explain the nonhandmade circumcision. The συν- compound verbs (συνταφέντες, συνηγέρθητε, συνεζωοποίησεν) reinforce the sense of being with and in Christ. The harmonic and coordinated sound of verb and noun forms for circumcision (περιετμήθητε περιτομῇ), enhanced by the sharply consonanted ἀχειροποιήτῳ, produces striking sounds. Each of the aorist participles (χαρισάμενος, ἐξαλείψας, προσηλώσας, ἀπεκδυσάμενος, θριαμβεύσας) conveys meaning of felt experiences.

What the sensory features do is to help press home the perception that humans have been made full in Christ, that the philosophy of human traditions and the elements of the world and behaviors being demanded are irrelevant now in Christ. Anything that can keep them from fullness in Christ has been removed. The Lycus holy ones should be conscious of this truth and beware of whoever promotes it. The linear progression describing what has been done to them and for them impresses on them that the things according to Christ are relevant and trustworthy.

---

76. The zone of self-expressive speech (see Robbins, *Exploring the Textures of Texts*, 30–31).

SCENE THREE: DON'T BE DECEIVED. LIVE THE NEW REALITY   171

Intertexture. While there are no quotations (recitations) from the Hebrew Bible or LXX in Colossians, there are intertextures with the world of texts and ideas outside the letter.[77] These are recontextualizations, reconfigurations, and thematic elaborations[78] of resources that are employed in 2:11–15 to shape the argument and impress the argumentative force on the mind. Like other things in Colossians, the intertextures indicate development of ideas and motifs seen in earlier Pauline letters. The Pauline description in Phil 2:5–11 of Christ Jesus, being in "the form of God" and "equality with God," who "emptied himself [kenosis] taking the form of a slave" "and became obedient to … death on a cross" is extended in Col 2 in the statement that all God's fullness houses in Christ (2:9) and that, being nailed to the cross, Christ stripped himself while simultaneously disgracing and "triumphing the powers and authorities."[79]

The first clear **intertexture** is about circumcision.[80] The practice and significance of circumcision has been clear in biblical texts since Gen 17:1–7, where Abraham and every male of his house underwent the surgery as a sign of the covenant between themselves and God. According to the Torah, male children born to Israelite mothers were to be circumcised eight days after birth (Lev 12:3). The practice was known among some gentile peoples such as the Colchians, Egyptians, and Ethiopians (Herodotus, *Hist.* 2.104).[81] Residents of the Lycus Valley were aware of the practice, so the term and allusion would have been understood by them. The argument does not indicate that male believers were being pressured

---

77. See Jerry L. Sumney, "Writing in 'The Image' of Scripture: The Form and Function of References to Scripture in Colossians," in *Paul and Scripture: Extending the Conversation*, ed. Christopher D. Stanley (Atlanta: Society of Biblical Literature, 2012), 185–229; Pizzuto, *Cosmic Leap of Faith*; Gordon D. Fee, "Old Testament Intertextuality in Colossians: Reflections on Pauline Christology and Gentile Inclusion in God's Story," in *History and Exegesis: New Testament Essays in Honor of Dr. E. Earle Ellis*, ed. Sang-Won Son (London: T&T Clark, 2006), 201–21; Gordley, *Colossians Hymn in Context*; Beetham, *Echoes of Scripture*.

78. Robbins, *Exploring the Textures of Texts*, 48–58.

79. On Phil 2:5–11, see especially Holloway, *Philippians*, 114–29. On "stripping himself," see above, especially on rhetography.

80. For some of these interpretations see Jeal, "Sociorhetorical Intertexture," 151–64.

81. See Strabo, *Geogr.* 17.2.5, which is nearly contemporaneous with the New Testament. Herodotus claims that "the Syrians of Palestine themselves confess that they learned the custom from the Egyptians," an apparent allusion to the Jewish practice.

to become circumcised, as has often been thought.[82] Rather, intertextural and **social intertextural** knowledge regarding circumcision is employed in 2:11 to shape rhetorical argumentation. The **intertexture** sets up the imagery for the holy ones to grasp that they have been circumcised with the nonhandmade circumcision, in turn described as the "stripping off of the body of the flesh."[83] Nonhandmade circumcision in the form of circumcision of the heart is a feature of the rhetoric of other Pauline texts (Rom 2:28-29; see Phil 3:3) and in Jewish canonical and noncanonical texts (Deut 10:16; 30:6; Jer 4:4; 9:25-26; Ezek 44:6-7; 1QS V, 5; Jub. 1.23; Philo, *Spec.* 1.305; Josephus, *A.J.* 12.241). The term *nonhandmade* occurs in Mark 14:58 and 2 Cor 5:1. *Nonhandmade* obviously contrasts with *handmade*, which implies humanly produced things. The word "handmade" (χειροποίητος) occurs in the LXX to refer to idols and to places of worship (Lev 26:1, 30; Isa 2:18; 16:12; 19:1; 21:9; 31:7; 46:6; Dan 5:4; 5:23; Bel 1:5). In the New Testament it refers to a sanctuary (Heb 9:24). These intertextures are more likely to indicate the intertextural knowledge of the authors than the recipients. The term "the foreskin of the flesh" is used only here in this word order (2:13). It reverses the wording "the flesh of your foreskin" used in the LXX (Gen 17:1, 14, 23-25; 34:24; Lev 12:3; Jdt 14:10), perhaps to emphasize that something unnecessary is removed. It may be echoed by "the passions of the flesh" and "the will of the flesh and the mind" in Eph 2:3.

The erasure of "the handwritten record of demands that stood against us" is often considered to refer to the removal of the effect of the Torah,[84] but Colossians does not mention or imply the Torah in its rhetoric. The terminology has many intertextural connections that make it clear that a metaphorical written document indicating and acknowledging obligation or indebtedness is envisioned (see Tob 5:3, 9:5). Similar terminology is found in a number of apocalyptic texts, referring to documents employed for passing judgment against persons because of their evil actions (1 En. 89.61-64, T. Ab. 12.7-18, T. Job 11.11, Apoc. Zeph. 7.1-8, 2 En. 53.2-3; see also Life of Aesop 122; Exod 32:32-33; Rev 20:12). The chirograph is to be understood here to refer to a metaphorical or virtual record of any kind

---

82. See above, n. 72.
83. A phrase unique to Col 1:22; 2:11.
84. See 3 Macc 1:3 and 4 Macc 4:24, where δόγμα might refer to the Torah; see also Philo, *Leg.* 1.55; *Gig.* 52.

that indicts and demands judgment against people.[85] Here the mentally envisioned record is erased in stark apocalyptic removal out of the middle of a court and nailed with Christ to the cross. The implication is that the expectation of judgment has been killed by the action of God in making people alive with and in Christ and in forgiving all their trespasses. Judgment against humans is quashed. The *historical intertexture* with the crucifixion of Jesus is clear, certainly in the imagery of the nailing of the *titulus* or indictment statement to the cross (Matt 27:37, Mark 15:26, Luke 23:38, John 19:19–22), but more particularly in the nailing of Jesus himself, in the judgment taken in his body, in the metaphorical "circumcision of Christ" (Col 2:11) that removed the "body of the flesh" and every call for judgment against humans.

The action of "triumphing them" (θριαμβεύσας αὐτοὺς, aorist participle with plural pronoun, 2:14) alludes to the Roman military tradition (Lat. *triumphus*) wherein the leaders (the powers and authorities) of a defeated nation, along with family members and friends, were forced to process in a humiliating and cruel parade that displayed them for public ridicule as defeated, weak, demoralized, and completely subjugated by the victorious general and his army. The New Testament intertexture is 2 Cor 2:14, where Paul envisions himself and other believers being "triumphed" (θριαμβεύοντι ἡμᾶς, "triumphs us"), being led in a dramatic Roman procession.[86] A triumph displayed the glory of the general and his army with depictions of battles, conquered territory, plunder, animals to be sacrificed, music, soldiers, the conquered king with his family and retinue, many decorative features, a range of associated sounds and odors, and cheering crowds.[87] All of this was meant to bolster the image of imperial Rome with its emperor and army by exhibiting itself as the great power

---

85. In SRI terms it is an *oral-scribal reconfiguration* of accusations and indictment. It is not, contra Lincoln, only the indictments of heavenly powers ("Colossians," 625–26). It includes indictments of all kinds, including those of cosmic-spiritual and earthly political-spiritual powers.

86. For a full sociorhetorical interpretation of 2 Cor 2:14–17 including extensive bibliography, see Oropeza, *Exploring Second Corinthians*, 161–96.

87. See the striking description of the three-day triumph of Aemelius Paulus described by Plutarch (ca. 46–120 CE) in Plutarch, *Lives*, vol. 6, *Dion and Brutus; Timoleon and Aemilius Paulus*, trans. Bernadotte Perrin, LCL (Cambridge: Harvard University Press, 1918), 31.1–37.3, at https://tinyurl.com/SBL7106g, and following chapters. See also the description in Oropeza, *Exploring Second Corinthians*, 191–92, who calls a triumph a "visual extravaganza."

and authority that brought peace and prosperity to the world. In both intertextures, however, 1 Cor 2:14 and Col 2:15, God, not Caesar or a Roman military general, is the subject of the triumph, the leader of the procession who disgraces the powers and authorities. In Colossians God is doing so not through political-military force but in the stripping and death of the Son-Christ, who is himself the very image (εἰκών) of God, in whom God reconciled and made peace, the one in whom the fullness of deity houses. The intertextual apocalyptic imagery makes the point: God in Christ has provided all things. The powers and authorities are impotent and irrelevant. It has all been done "in him" (ἐν αὐτῷ). Nothing else is required or wanted to make things right or keep them right. Do not be persuaded by the philosophy.

Residents of Colossae, Hierapolis, and the Lycus region would have understood the political language and imagery of a triumphal procession. It was a known, culturally understood event, a feature of their collective knowledge whether they had witnessed one or not. The mental visuality of this intertexture makes the triumphal procession of the grandly disgraced powers and authorities described in 2:15 stand out in bold relief. The true Pax is not the Pax Romana. It is the peace of Christ (1:20).

Social and cultural texture. The Lycus recipients of the letter lived in the dual sociocultural space of relatively important urban locations and of early Christian *ekklēsiai*. This space naturally carries with it expectations of the city-region, trust in Christ, and membership in the Christ community. The central argumentative rhetoric of the letter (2:6–3:4) envisions these people in a *challenge-riposte* cultural situation[88] where they face demands that they conform to an unnecessary, unhelpful, and dangerous philosophy of traditions, elemental realities, and behaviors. The social inclination to such pressures is to conform to the challenge. But they must be wary of it. The challenge emphasizes the social importance of engaging in expected, acceptable behaviors that satisfy perceived necessary religious praxis. By employing the topoi of these verses, the authors demonstrate that the believers already inhabit space impervious to the very kinds of challenges they face. They should not blend their new reality in Christ (an internal space) with a sociocultural space (an external space) that emphasizes their own achievements rather than the good things they already have in Christ.

---

88. On challenge-riposte cultural environments, see Robbins, *Exploring the Textures of Texts*, 80–81.

Ideological texture. It is clear that this step aims to remind and move people toward an ideology. It is an *ideology of fullness*. Things in Christ are different than they are in Mediterranean culture. The holy ones have already been made full in Christ, in whom houses the fullness of deity (vv. 9–10). This ideology generates the wisdom that humanly produced religious activities are meant to satisfy human demands for conformity. Details of the nature of the demands follow in the following rhetorical steps.

Sacred texture. This step is replete with sacred texture. It has a holy, divine nature because it intentionally and explicitly points its audiences to the actions taken by God in Christ on behalf of people.[89] It states repeatedly that the Colossian believers are located in Christ. It states that people have forgiveness of sins and are alive with the raised Christ Jesus. They cannot be connected with God in any other way. Humanly produced ways of thinking and behaving inhibit rather than help. The apocalyptic and sacred actions of God have brought about a holy relationship for people. God has made people alive with Christ in the sacred space of the Son's kingdom.

Rhetorical Force as Emergent Discourse

The three steps of this scene present a developed prophetic discourse that blends along the way with priestly and apocalyptic rhetorolects to produce understanding of the wisdom space that members of the Christ community inhabit "in him." The first step (2:6–7) envisions Paul as prophetic narrator or teacher who, in a tone and with wording similar to what was heard in 1:9–12 (walking, thanksgiving), encourages letter recipients to move ahead, confidently established in what they had received regarding Christ Jesus the Lord, sure of their faith, overflowing in thanksgiving as they walk along. This like saying, "You know who you are 'in him.' Behave accordingly." The suggestion that someone might attempt to deceive them has already been made (2:4). This rhetoric opens the third scene with a challenge to continue commitment to the gospel mystery and the maturity for which the authors work (1:28–29). The second step (2:8–10) continues in prophetic mode with the imperative and challenging warning "Beware." Christ believers will encounter danger as they walk along. This is a major piece of the rhetorical force of the discourse: "Watch out!

---

89. See Robbins, *Exploring the Textures of Texts*, 120.

Don't be captured." There is a deceptive, misleading philosophy that is not according to Christ, that opposes Christ. It is entirely about misguided humans and the elements of their chaotic, disordered, dark world (1:13), where they imagine they must make themselves qualified for a share (see 1:12) in whatever peace and benefactions the gods might provide. This false philosophy, the authors believe, stands against the true philosophy of the Son-Christ, who is the cosmic-precreational firstborn of creation in whom all things hold together. The believers are already full in him. He is the head of every power and authority. The force of the rhetoric is clear: Do not try to fill what is already full. Do not place your trust in humans and the way of the world. The way of the elements of the world is dangerous. It enslaves people to darkness and disorder and failing attempts to acquire fullness of life. Do not give in to it. The third step (2:11–15) explains how all of the priestly action needed to reconcile, forgive, liberate, and make peace has been accomplished already in the apocalyptic energy and actions of burial, making alive, raising out of the dead, forgiveness of trespasses, erasing the demands of the philosophy, in the self-stripping of deity, and the nailing to the cross. The inimical visible and invisible (1:16) powers and authorities have been disgraced and triumphed. These actions of God, seen together in a complex, unified imagery, make the crucial theology and reality of the passage understood: all has been done; nothing more is required.

The Christ believers are meant to grasp the ideas and images socially, culturally, and from experience. The force of the rhetoric moves the audience members to understand that they should indeed beware of the deceptive philosophy and reject it when its promoter demands observance of it. The misleading philosophy is untrue and irrelevant. The gospel of empire by which people were culturally conditioned to believe in the strength of political and military hegemony, the necessity to please and appease the gods, and to trust in the imposed peace of the Pax Romana is declared irrelevant by the weak, disgraceful stripping of the Son-Christ bodily, which is strength.[90] The religious powers to which the philosophy appeals are impotent. It is they who are defeated and demoralized. The new reality into which people are transferred has come in this seemingly weak yet strong way. This is much bigger than the empire of Rome and much bigger

---

90. See Paul's description of the power of weakness over strength in 2 Cor 11:16–12:10.

SCENE THREE: DON'T BE DECEIVED. LIVE THE NEW REALITY 177

than the local pressure in the Lycus to observe human traditions. The metaphorical stripping off of the foreskin in nonhandmade circumcision and the stripping of deity on the cross—the mystery proclaimed by Epaphras and Paul and received by the holy ones—provides everything. The reconciling task was completed.

The rhetorical force of these steps might be illustrated like this: Believers have been circumcised with the circumcision of Christ. Once being circumcised, why would they return to "the foreskin of your flesh" again? It's a foreskin. Once the surgery is done, would you keep the piece of removed, dead skin? Where would you keep it? What could you possibly do with it? No. It is stripped off and discarded, never wanted or seen again. The priestly-apocalyptic events mean that the philosophy is unnecessary. Wisdom is to live the new reality trusting, resting in what God has done in Christ.

Step Four: Do Not Let Someone Judge You (2:16–17)

Rhetography

Argumentatively, this step draws a conclusion (Μὴ οὖν τις ὑμᾶς κρινέτω) based on the preceding picturing. But rhetographically it pictures Paul at center stage again, calling to the holy ones to refuse to allow someone (τις ... κρινέτω, singular)[91] to judge them regarding their visible behavior of eating and drinking, or in their participation in a feast (or festival), a new moon observance, or Sabbaths. This recalls the imagery of step two (2:8–10), where virtual Paul calls for them to beware so that someone will not capture them (Βλέπετε μή τις ὑμᾶς ἔσται ὁ συλαγωγῶν). The view shifts from Paul to the readers/listeners, who are now to see themselves rejecting the demands of the judge (critic) who is visible and threatening them. It becomes clear as the picture is envisioned that the judge expects the Christ believers to practice the observances related to eating and drinking, participation in particular feasts, new moon rites (perhaps daily or

---

91. I.e., someone who is judging, criticizing, but perhaps not limited to an individual person. The singular indefinite pronoun τις and singular verbal forms in 2:4, 8, 16, 18 envision a person who is pressuring the believers to engage in various practices. There is no immediate reason to use plurals such as *opponents* or speak as if the *ekklēsia* had been invaded or infiltrated by an organized group, as do many interpreters.

monthly lunar rites), and in Sabbath practices. The pressure imposed by the judge to practice the observances should be rejected because, as the mental vision expands, the observances appear as "a shadow of the coming things" (ἅ ἐστιν σκιὰ τῶν μελλόντων), not the new reality of the present described in verses 8–15. The body casting the shadow is Christ's body, in whom believers now exist, brought into central focus once again (in the repetitive textures of τὸ δὲ σῶμα τοῦ Χριστοῦ, 1:18, 21, 24, and the "in him"/"in whom" language, 1:14–20, 2:6). The believers can visualize their present existence in full light rather than in the allusiveness of shadow. They are to see the shadow but are envisioned to be refusing to stand in it. They stand in light, not in the darkness of a shadow (see 1:12–13), and so are portrayed rejecting it, in the body.

The picture of shadow and body is very complex. The body of Christ casts the shadow, while at the same time the shadow alludes to Christ. The pressure to focus on the shadow (i.e., to accept the judge's demands to practice the observances) is to be rejected as irrelevant because the forces have been disempowered (vv. 10–15); thus the shadow itself, while indicating that a body casts it, is not or is no longer important. Christ and his body the *ekklēsia*, to whom the shadow alludes as coming, have arrived. Only the body itself[92] is now important as the focus of concern in this particular image. The precreational Son was figuratively already casting the shadow (1:15–19, 2:9), indicating protologically the presence of God, the redemptive activity of God in the created order, and the body-*ekklēsia*. Now 2:17 elicits the visualization of the bodily formed Christ, with whom the audience has been raised (2:12) and in whom they live, to convey the understanding that judgments regarding shadow observances are religiously inconsequential.

This step presents prophetic rhetoric that calls for rejection of the efforts of someone who would judge and restrict the Christ believers with particularized religious observances. The prophetic language blends into wisdom rhetoric that encourages audiences not to live in the shadow but in the reality of life in the body of Christ, into which they have been transferred. Blended visually are images of Paul, the Colossians, a judge, and Christ, along with images of observances that are to be rejected by the believers. This creates a tone-coloring[93] that audiences should discern. Since the Son/Christ has completed his work, the shadow is no longer required.

---

92. Cf. NRSV, "substance."
93. German *Klangenfarben*.

SCENE THREE: DON'T BE DECEIVED. LIVE THE NEW REALITY 179

Translation

2:16 Therefore do not let someone judge you regarding food and drink or[94] participation in a feast or a new moon or sabbaths, **2:17** which are a shadow of the coming things, but the body is Christ's.

Textural Commentary

This step begins with *repetitive texturing* that reintroduces, enhances, and expands the concern stated in Col 2:4 and the warning made in 2:8. Someone might deceive the believers with a plausible argument (2:4). Someone might attempt to capture them through philosophy and empty deceit (2:8). Someone might judge them regarding religious practices (2:16). These repetitions warning of threats prepare the way for the rhetorical texturing that begins in 2:16–17 and proceeds in steps to 2:23. The repetition occurs again at 2:18 (see below), warning that someone is attempting to deceive them by insisting on completely unnecessary and unhelpful practices. The repetitions display significant grammatical texturing. The verb παραλογίζηται in 2:4 is present subjunctive third-person singular; the verb ἔσται in 2:8 is future middle indicative third-person singular; the verbs κρινέτω in 2:16 and καταβραβευέτω in 2:18 are present active imperative third-person singular. This *grammatical progression* moves from the subjunctive "someone might deceive you" to the warning that in the (probably near) future "someone will [attempt to] capture you" to the imperatives "do not let someone judge you" and "do not let someone cheat you." What might occur at 2:4 becomes expected to occur as the argument progresses. By 2:20–23 it has occurred, since the present-tense verbs indicate that audience members have already succumbed to the pressure to restrict themselves from various physical practices.

The rhetorical **argumentative texture** overall is straightforward and clear. The historical issues that scholars spend massive amounts of time and space attempting to solve are focused on these verses and in the next two steps (vv. 18–19, 20–23). It is the inner rhetorical argumentation, however, that goes to the heart of what this part of the letter is designed

---

94. Some manuscripts do not have the word ἤ, "or."

to accomplish. What the rhetoric aims to accomplish becomes clear even though the precise nature of the philosophy remains opaque.[95]

> **Case:** Christ believers must not allow themselves to be judged regarding expectations for their observance (or lack of observance) of what appear to be a mixture of Mediterranean and Jewish religious traditions of eating and drinking, of participating in feasts, and new moon and Sabbath practices.
> **Rationale:** Since the believers have been filled in Christ, now living in the new reality—the forgiveness of trespasses, freedom from decrees and powers and authorities—all brought about by the completed apocalyptic actions that have made them alive with the raised Christ, they must not allow someone to judge them (i.e., intimidate them) so as to persuade them to think it necessary to engage in the practices. The practices are a shadow, not the reality of what was to come. That reality that casts the shadow has arrived and is Christ himself. The observances are irrelevant.
> **Anticipated Result:** Christ believers in Colossae and the Lycus Valley will not be intimidated in regard to these behaviors. They will recognize that the shadow nature of the practices is not the substance of the new reality and therefore will reject practice of them and reject the pressuring of the judge.

This argumentative texturing aims to shape the Lycus believers toward the growing, maturing, wisdom living the letter encourages. It is about the "walk in him" (2:6). Engaging in the practices about which they are being judged will not make them better people. The practices are repressive rather than bringing about the fruitfulness and growth the letter has in sight (1:6, 10).

The language in 2:16 about eating and drinking, participation in a feast, a new moon, or Sabbaths makes what appear to be obvious connections with several specifically Jewish practices. At this point many interpreters envision and reconstruct the "empty and deceitful philosophy" as pressure to engage in Jewish observances such as those mentioned. The judge or complainant is imagined to insist that the Jesus believers

---

95. Interpreters regularly use terms such as "might be," "could be," "possible," and "probable" to indicate that much is simply unknown.

SCENE THREE: DON'T BE DECEIVED. LIVE THE NEW REALITY   181

in Colossae behave visibly in what seem to be identifiably Jewish ways.[96] There are **intertextural** LXX links with eighth-century BCE prophets First Isaiah and Hosea (Isa 1:13–14, Hos 2:13 [11]), with exilic prophet Ezekiel (Ezek 46:1, 6), and with the postexilic texts 1 Chr 23:30–31, 2 Chr 31:3, and Ezra 3:4–5.[97] By the Second Temple period, daily prayers came to be coordinated with cycles of the luminaries including lunar cycles and new moon observations.[98] There was some level of awareness of Jewish beliefs and practices among the gentile audience members of the letter, as the reference to and imagery of circumcision in 2:11 indicates. How much, though, did the gentile residents of Colossae know about Judaism? Would they have immediately recognized the criticism? Perhaps even a little familiarity with the language and contexts calling for proper Israelite and Jewish practices would make it possible for a knowledgeable person living in the Lycus to pressure the Christ believers in such a way. Certainly Jews had been living in the Lycus Valley, possibly making for a broad if not deep familiarity with Jewish practices by the non-Jewish population.[99] It is unlikely, however, that any Jews lived in Colossae during the first century CE.[100] It might be that the language of 2:16 reveals more about the thinking and concerns of the authors of the letter than direct knowledge about residents of Colossae or that audience members in Laodicea and Hierapolis are in mind in 2:16.[101] Justin Martyr's mid-second-century *Dialogue with*

---

96. Might it have been thought that if people look Jewish, i.e., that they are messianic believers, members of a Jewish religion, that they should behave in Jewish ways? See the interpretation by Kahl regarding Galatians in *Galatians Re-imagined*, 210–27.

97. The words occur individually in many LXX texts. New moon observances (νεομηνία) are noted in the contracted form νουμηνία, e.g., LXX Num 29:6, 1 Esd 5:52, 9:17.

98. On this see Jeremy Penner, *Patterns of Daily Prayer in Second Temple Period Judaism*, STJD 104 (Leiden: Brill, 2012), 101–64. Penner takes Qumran texts into account. Prayers were sometimes imagined to be coordinated with the prayers of angels. Israelites were warned not to worship objects observed in the heavens (Deut 4:19, 17:3, Jer 8:1–2, 19:13, Zeph 1:5), but "new moons" does not have this worship in mind.

99. See Huttner, *Early Christianity in the Lycus Valley*, 67–79; see also Maier, *Picturing Paul in Empire*, 92–93; Kahl, *Galatians Re-imagined*, 211–15.

100. Cadwallader states, "There is simply no evidence for Jews at Colossae between [= from] the first and [= to the] twelfth century" ("On the Question," 131–32). See also Alan H. Cadwallader, "Colossae," Bible Odyssey, https://tinyurl.com/SBL7106h.

101. Cadwallader suggests that the Jewish-sounding terms might be "more of a rhetorical than historical construction" ("On the Question," 132).

Trypho, set in Ephesus (approximately 150 kilometers from Colossae), has Trypho encouraging Justin to become circumcised and to observe "the Sabbath, and the feasts, and the new moons of God" (Justin, *Dial.* 8.4). The first day of each month in the Jewish calendar, Rosh Chodesh, is marked by the new moon and a number of offerings (Num 28:11-15; see Num 10:10; Ps 81:3; 11Q5 XIX, 7; 11Q19 XLIII, 20; Josephus, *A.J.* 3.238).

But the **intertextures** are not limited to Jewish observances. There was a diverse ethnic, cultural, civic, business, ceremonial, and religious demography in the Lycus area, in Phrygia, and Roman provinces in Asia Minor.[102] A vast array of gods and goddesses have been identified as known at Colossae, including Zeus, Apollo, Artemis, Cybele, Men, Tyche, and Isis, as would have been practices associated with them. This indicates very complex **social and historical intertextures**.[103] Restrictions regarding eating and drinking were widely known in Phrygia, for example in the widespread Cybele cult, in order to induce mystical or visionary experiences.[104] Rites could involve chaotic dancing, mutilation, and even self-castration. It is possible that the phrase "food and drink" reflects the kinds of disputes and ideas indicated in Rom 14:13-23. There were dozens of religious, civic, and regular calendrical feasts/festivals and other observances celebrated in Asia Minor. Participation in these events was a social and religious expectation.[105] While Sabbath observance was distinctively Jewish, it was occasionally taken up by gentile "worshipers of God" (as in

---

102. Maier, *Picturing Paul in Empire*, 92-93, with references there.

103. Cadwallader provides "the list of gods for which we have evidence at Colossae," composed of twenty-two deities. He points out that human names often reflected belief in gods. In Philemon and Colossians, the names Tychicus (Tyche), Epaphras (Aphrodite), and Nympha indicate onomastic connections (Cadwallader, *Fragments of Colossae*, 68-69). See also the many gods and goddesses noted in Arnold, *Colossians Syncretism*; see also Maier, *Picturing Paul in Empire*, 92-93. See the essays in Harrison and Welborn, *First Urban Churches 5*, especially Alan H. Cadwallader and James R. Harrison, "Perspectives on the Lycus Valley: An Inscriptional, Archaeological, Numismatic, and Iconographic Approach," 3-70.

104. See Sumney, *Colossians*, 150-51. On the Cybele cult, see "Cult in Phrygia (Asia Minor)." Apuleius, in his second-century novel *Metamorphoses (The Golden Ass)* 11.5, has Cybele say, "The Phrygians, first-born of mankind, call me the Pessinuntian Mother of the gods."

105. Foster, *Colossians*, 281. See George H. van Kooten, *Cosmic Christology in Paul and the Pauline School: Colossians and Ephesians in the Context of Graeco-Roman Cosmology, with a New Synopsis of the Greek Texts*, WUNT 171 (Tübingen: Mohr Siebeck, 2003), 140-41.

Acts 16:13–14, σεβομένη τὸν θεόν, and Acts 18:7, σεβομένου τὸν θεόν). Juvenal (late first to early second centuries CE) satirized gentiles who observed the Sabbath, some who even became circumcised:

> Some who have had a father who reveres the Sabbath, worship nothing but the clouds, and the divinity of the heavens, and see no difference between eating swine's flesh, from which their father abstained, and that of man; and in time they take to circumcision. Having been wont to flout the laws of Rome, they learn and practise and revere the Jewish law, and all that Moses committed to his secret tome, forbidding to point out the way to any not worshipping the same rites, and conducting none but the circumcised to the desired fountain. For all which the father was to blame, who gave up every seventh day to idleness, keeping it apart from all the concerns of life. (*Sat.* 14.96–106)[106]

New moon observances seem to have been important non-Jewish observances, though the evidence comes from the second century (see *PGM* IV.2389; XIII.387).[107] The god Men was portrayed with "moon-shaped horns on his shoulders," which might be suggestive of new moon or other lunar observances.[108]

The complexity of literary, social, and historical intertextures is striking. Recent commentary makes a claim for intertextural allusions in Col 2:16 (and 2:18; see below) to temple imagery and theology associated particularly with Lev 20:25–26 and other texts.[109] The judge's pressures regarding food and drink are interpreted to allude to clean and unclean laws, including dietary rules that were followed to prevent uncleanness from entering the temple. Colossians, of course, never uses the word "temple" (ναός), and gentile residents of Colossae were unlikely to have made the connection, to have been interested in going to Jerusalem, or to have discerned a "heavenly temple"[110] corresponding to the Jerusalem temple in the rhetoric of

---

106. Wilson, *Colossians and Philemon*, 216.
107. See Arnold, *Colossians Syncretism*, 148–50, 215–17; Hans Dieter Betz, ed., *The Greek Magical Papyri in Translation* (Chicago; London: University of Chicago Press, 1986), loc. cit; also Foster, *Colossians*, 281–82.
108. Rosemary Canavan, "Unraveling the Threads of Identity: Cloth and Clothing in the Lycus Valley," in Harrison and Welborn, *First Urban Churches 5*, 87–88, with references there.
109. See Beale, *Colossians and Philemon*, 214–40, et passim.
110. Beale, *Colossians and Philemon*, 217.

the letter. Might someone have tried to persuade them to practice dietary rules for this reason?[111] It is impossible to know. It is similarly impossible to know whether 2:16 has in sight any of a range of Hellenistic philosophies that have been proposed.[112] There are many proposed parallels, but nothing is explicit anywhere in the text of Colossians, and none come without substantial, frequently overwhelming challenges. It is true, as John Stambaugh and David Balch point out, that "the average resident of a Greek city had a basic acquaintance with the classics, with tales of mythology, and with rhetorical principles, reinforced by the plays and mimes and recitations of bards at festivals, and by the lectures and discussions of rhetoricians and philosophers in marketplaces, gymnasia, and street corners."[113] But it is unlikely this went much beyond the basic acquaintance noted for most people, and more, clear, explicit evidence is not available. Perhaps many things could have been, but without sufficient, hard evidence, they serve mainly to arouse scholarly speculation and continue the debate.[114]

The observances are together described in verse 17 as "a shadow [singular] of the coming" (ἅ ἐστιν σκιὰ τῶν μελλόντων), with the shadow being cast by "the body of Christ" (τὸ δὲ σῶμα τοῦ Χριστοῦ). Translation requires a verb, probably drawn from the ἐστιν in the first clause, to be understood and inserted in the second, rendering it as "but the body *is* of Christ" or "the body *is* Christ's." There are few intertextural connections that help with understanding. In the New Testament the image of shadow in the Gospels of Matthew and Luke (Matt 4:16, Luke 1:79) points to the arrival (incarnation) of Messiah and the arrival of the kingdom of God. Hebrews

---

111. This view reflects the very common interpretation that the Colossian philosophy was fundamentally Jewish. A recent commentary taking this view is McKnight, *Letter to the Colossians*, 25–34. McKnight concludes that the opponents are Jewish "halakic mystics … or Torah-shaped transcendentalists" (32). Cf. Arnold, who finds these views inadequate ("Initiation, Vision, and Spiritual Power," 173–75).

112. So, for example, Pythagorean (Schweizer), Platonic (DeMaris), Cynic (Martin). See Eduard Schweizer, *The Letter to the Colossians* (Minneapolis: Augsburg, 1982); Richard E. DeMaris, *The Colossian Controversy: Wisdom in Dispute at Colossae*, JSNTSup 96 (Sheffield: Sheffield Academic, 1994); Martin, *By Philosophy and Empty Deceit*. See also Copenhaver, *Reconstructing the Historical Background*, 18–23.

113. John E. Stambaugh and David L. Balch, *The New Testament in Its Social Environment* (Philadelphia: Westminster, 1986), 122–23.

114. I recognize, of course, the importance, necessity, and value of comparative study. Scholars try to understand many difficult and speculative things by comparing them to what is known (see Cadwallader, "On the Question," 105–51).

8:5 views the holy sanctuary as a shadow of the better heavenly one, and Heb 10:1 envisions the law/Torah as a shadow of the coming realities associated with the arrival and priestly role of Messiah. Some interpreters have imagined that Col 2:17 has in mind apparent Jewish observances that foreshadow the coming of Messiah at the parousia. The evidence for these interpretations is very thin. What 2:17 presents is a *rhetoric of shadow* where the shadow represents being in darkness. Believers have already been told that they have been "transferred out of darkness" (1:13) and are already in the kingdom of the Son/Christ. To give in to the judge would be to live in the shadow, to return to the darkness of the chaos of the created order of the στοιχεῖα, and would be to succumb to pressure designed to impose social control. The new reality in the imagery of Colossians is that the believers themselves are the body of Christ, the *ekklēsia*, the assembly of Christ believers (1:18, 24; see 1:19, 3:15).[115] They themselves are the reality or substance that casts the shadow. The shadow alludes to the light of being in Christ. They should not reenter the shadow of their former existence apart from the precreational Son of God's love. Reverting to a do-it-yourself religious practice would be a serious mistake.

From a sociorhetorical point of view, where the rhetoric and rhetorical force of texts are in focus, it is crucial to ask what rhetorical language is being employed and what generated (or is the exigence of) the rhetoric more than what problem or kind of historical problem lay behind things. The directive of 2:16 is a prophetic texture that merges into a wisdom texture that has a slight apocalyptic tone.[116] The prophetic rhetoric urges the Christ believers to reject criticism that aims to make them feel inferior because they do not practice the specified and expected religious observances (and other religious observances, 2:18). The wisdom texture urges the believers not to live in the shadow of coming things but in their present reality as the body casting the shadow (2:17). The slight apocalyptic tone is seen in the way the shadow alludes to "the coming things" (τῶν

---

115. As noted in the rhetography section above (see, e.g., Sumney, *Colossians*, 152–53). Light is shining in the present time and space on the *ekklēsia*, thereby demonstrating that the practices demanded belong to the realm of shadow rather than the realm of "the inheritance of the holy ones in the light" (1:12).

116. Prophetic texture or discourse because it proclaims and urges belief and action. Wisdom texture or discourse because it envisions good behavior in the space of actual living. Apocalyptic because it envisions and reveals the action of God that provides benefits to humans.

μελλόντων). This rhetoric points us to what people in a Lycus Valley town such as Colossae were familiar with in their **social and historical intertextural** setting under Roman domination and provides a more secure, contextualized footing for interpreting the verses.[117]

What social, cultural, and religious influences were doing generally was encouraging assimilation and enculturation toward "Roman conformity."[118] Differing cultures were heading toward, being pushed toward, a more integrated demography in the Roman context. At the same time, Colossians presents an image of conformity focused on the actions of God, "who rescued us out of the jurisdiction of darkness and transferred us into the kingdom of the Son of his love" (1:13), the Son who has brought about reconciliation "in the body of his [own] flesh" (1:20, 22).[119] The unity of the Christ believers was founded on the work and rule of Christ himself, not on conformity to Roman cultural and behavioral context. The religiocultural imperial context that expected recognition of a vast range of deities (including the imperial cult) and Roman power and exclusivism criticized people who did not engage in practices imagined to be proper to religious profession and civic good.[120] Living in such a context of ideas, beliefs, and expectations lies behind the imperative "do not let someone judge you." It is not just that the critic demands the observances but that believers are being pressured to behave in ways acceptable to the critic. Whether they are Jewish or gentile observances makes little difference to the rhetorical argumentation and overarching reality. The Colossian believers might themselves not even have known the differences between or among them.[121]

---

117. Recall the analysis of Roman imagery, iconography, religion, and political language and expectations earlier in the commentary on Col 1:3–23.

118. Maier, *Picturing Paul in Empire*, 93–94, quoting Cadwallader, "Greeks in Colossae," 224–41. Roman conformity included economic, architectural, family/household, symbolic, military, judicial, and other aspects of life.

119. See Maier, *Picturing Paul in Empire*, 93.

120. On acculturation in the Lycus region, see Rosalinde A. Kearsley, "Epigraphic Evidence for the Social Impact of Roman Government in Laodicea and Hierapolis," in *Colossae in Space and Time: Linking to an Ancient City*, ed. Alan H. Cadwallader and Michael Trainor (Göttingen: Vandenhoeck & Ruprecht, 2011), 130–50. The situation in the *ekklēsia* in Colossae was, contra the view of many scholars (recently Johnson) not like that indicated in Galatians. See Luke Timothy Johnson, *Constructing Paul* (Grand Rapids: Eerdmans, 2020), 1:215.

121. For this suggestion see Wilson, *Colossians and Philemon*, 222. This also is true for 2:18.

The pressure was to fit in to particular socioreligious categories and to satisfy the critic. The believers are being exhorted to go against the human tendency to be accommodating to their critics. This is the wisdom they should take on. They should not enter the shadow.

Step Five: Do Not Be Cheated by the Self-Important Complainant (2:18–19)

Rhetography

The call to reject the pressure to conform to shadow practices continues with a second argument, but it shifts in this step (using the same grammar) from the previous images of attempts at capture (2:8) and judgment (2:16) to the image of attempts to cheat, rob, disqualify, or deprive the Christ believers of a possession (μηδεὶς ὑμᾶς καταβραβευέτω).[122] Paul is envisioned in direct sight again, calling for the Colossians to reject the efforts of someone (μηδεὶς ... καταβραβευέτω, once again singular) attempting to cheat them, someone arrogantly wishing to manipulate their particular moral and religious behavior, rather than maintaining correct focus on the head, the Son-Christ. The unnamed cheater-defrauder is visible in the rhetograph. This person appears as one who takes an implicitly perverse pleasure in promoting the humility, worship, and religious visions of people like the Colossians believers, doing so without genuine cause but only for conceited self-satisfaction (εἰκῇ φυσιούμενος)[123] based on "the mind of his flesh" (ὑπὸ τοῦ νοὸς τῆς σαρκὸς αὐτοῦ), that is, from self-interested motives. For the Colossians to be seen practicing the desired behaviors would make them appear to be very religious, but it would be merely an appearance, an artifice, subtly intended for the pleasure of others, a deception against them.[124] The cheater-defrauder is envisioned as a moralizer of the worst sort, a moral, behavioral, religious power figure who does

---

122. καταβραβεύω, a *hapax legomenon* in the New Testament, meaning "cheat, rob, defraud, disqualify," perhaps "take the prize from," is used in parallel to κρίνω in 2:16. See the cognate βραβεύω, "rule, act as judge, umpire," in 3:15. Exactly the same grammar is used in 2:16 (Μὴ οὖν τις ὑμᾶς κρινέτω) and 2:18 (μηδεὶς ὑμᾶς καταβραβευέτω): negative pronoun followed by a third-person singular imperative verb.

123. Literally "puffed up without cause." See below in textural commentary on the urge to seek status.

124. The "empty deceit" noted in 2:8.

not have the interests of the people at heart. This person has a need for recognition as a power figure, seeing himself as one who thinks he knows what other people should do. The tone-coloring of the rhetography portrays this shrewd person very negatively, darkly. The readers/listeners are viewed brightly, rejecting the pressure.

While the false piety gives the impression of practicing humility and worship like the angels, and the experience of entering visions appears to be attractive because people practicing these things are imagined to be visibly adding to their redemption, helping themselves, the actual visible result is seen in the conceited, self-important "puffing up"[125] of the deceiver. The arrogance is presumptuous and is social, not spiritual or genuinely religious pressure. This person is not "holding to the head" (οὐ κρατῶν τὴν κεφαλήν), a statement that refocuses vision on Christ while indicating that the deceiver does not understand Christ as the one in whom God's fullness dwells, who thinks that trying to be like angels is more important than Christ. The rhetograph here moves to head and body imagery that takes over the central space of the picture. The head (Christ, 1:18) is now centrally in sight, and it is out of this head that the entire body (the *ekklēsia*, 1:18) is nourished for the growth in all its united parts.[126] This body, in a nice turn of phrase, "grows the growth from God" (αὔξει τὴν αὔξησιν τοῦ θεοῦ),[127] visibly supported and held together by its ligaments and sinews. This is a strong, growing body. The problem visualized in the picture is that the deceiver is not "holding to the head," not appropriately honoring and trusting the head, thereby presenting as a dangerous person to the Colossian believers. The believers are viewed as standing against the deceiver, refusing to be taken in.

This step continues the view of Paul in prophetic space and, like the previous step, has a wisdom concern. Paul does not want believers to be cheated by the selfish actions of a false teacher who demands adherence to his choice of particularized behaviors. The behaviors appear to be pious and important, but the picturing shows that their net result is the loss of something crucial, and it envisions the artificial inflation of the promoter of the observances. Virtual Paul will not stand for the self-righteous moralizing religion promoted by a deceiver. Christ believers should avoid it too. Blending of the attractive space of the behaviors with the space of the

---

125. φυσιόω, "inflated self-importance," "arrogance."
126. The body is Christ's; see 2:17. *Repetitive texture*, τὸ σῶμα.
127. With τοῦ θεοῦ understood as an ablative, from God.

deceiver produces a third space where both the behaviors and the deceiver are rejected.

Translation

> **2:18** Do not let anyone cheat you by insisting on humility and worship like the angels, which things he has seen when entering in, made arrogant without cause by the mind of his flesh, **2:19** and not holding to the head, out of which all the body, being supplied and united through the [its] joints and ligaments, grows the growth from God.

Textural Commentary

This step extends and enhances the *repetitive texturing* of warnings woven into the argumentation. It emphasizes the deceitful nature of the disrupted, chaotic, earthly nature of the philosophy and the deceitful and misguided intentions of the one making demands. The demands from the unnamed person are willful and insistent. The selfish, arrogant demands reveal a fleshly mind that has no grasp of the good that God does in the world. This person is more interested in denigrating people he wishes to control than in being helpful. The grammar and syntax in this step are very complex, and terms are difficult to define, despite the intense work of many scholars. There are many interpretations that address these complex verses. As in verses 16–17, *argumentative texture* and **intertexture** will help us with understanding the shape of the rhetoric.

The rhetorical argument is very much like that of the previous step four, verses 16–17. The inner texturing is clear, despite the difficult exegetical issues. The argument is based on the imperative "Do not let someone cheat you" (μηδεὶς ὑμᾶς καταβραβευέτω).

> **Case:** Believers must not allow someone to cheat them out of the new reality they have as members of the body-*ekklēsia* by insisting on devotion to certain religious, mystical observances that come from the realm of human traditions and are not according to Christ (see 2:8).
> **Rationale:** The observances are demanded by someone who is "arrogant without cause," who sees things through his fleshly mind and is not "holding to the head" of the body, to the Son/

Christ, out of whom the body grows. By implication, the practices will do nothing good or useful for the believers. They cannot provide the growth that comes from God.

Anticipated Result: The believers will remember the Son-Christ, who is head of the body, their trust in him, and will reject the imperious demands.

The pressure imposed on believers described in 2:18, like that indicated in 2:16, comes in the form of a complaint or series of complaints. It is apparent that the Christ believers have not been meeting social expectations (**social intertexture**) in their religious practices. The upshot of this is that someone willfully insists that they practice "in humility and worship like the angels, things he has seen while entering in" (a literal, stilted translation of ἐν ταπεινοφροσύνῃ καὶ θρησκείᾳ τῶν ἀγγέλων, ἃ ἑόρακεν ἐμβατεύων). The complainant wants religious practice to conform to the social conventions he finds acceptable and expected in his religiocultural milieu. In Roman-dominated contexts, people were expected to be visible participants in public observances. The believers are imagined not to be worshiping or experiencing religion in expected and acceptable ways. But the complainant is described as "arrogant without cause by the mind of his flesh" ("his fleshly mind"), as one who does not understand the connections of the head (Christ) and the body (*ekklēsia*) for growth. This suggests that the complainant is an outsider, not a Christ believer and member of the *ekklēsia*. It is likely that the complainant was concerned to acquire or increase his status in the city by gaining control over other people.[128] This compulsion for status is embedded in the "empty deceit" of the "philosophy" (2:8).

The conformity demanded is difficult to understand. Grammatical and syntactical threads and word meanings are convoluted and difficult to translate. The complainant desires (θέλων) recognizable religious practice. Intertexturally the verb θέλω (used in this form in the New Testament; elsewhere ἐθέλω) indicates wish, will, purpose, desire, resolution or determination, insistence. In the LXX it can indicate pleasure or delight (e.g., 1 Kgdms 18:22, 2 Kgdms 15:26, 3 Kgdms 10:9). Here it is not too much to

---

128. The Greek grammar makes the masculine pronoun correct usage. On the urge to acquire or capture status in the ancient Mediterranean, see Longenecker, who refers to it as "the 'fire in the bones' that drove the machinery of the world that the early Jesus-movement was infiltrating" (*In Stone and Story*, 20).

say that the complainant *insists* that the believers practice what he wants. Humility (ταπεινοφροσύνη) was not an admirable quality in ancient Mediterranean tradition, where it was imagined as a characteristic of persons of very low social status.[129] Even so, in the New Testament the term occurs in passages describing qualities believers should display (Acts 20:19, Phil 2:3, Eph 4:3, 1 Pet 5:5). The rhetoric here, however, in the balanced dative prepositional phrase ἐν ταπεινοφροσύνῃ καὶ θρησκείᾳ τῶν ἀγγέλων,[130] indicates that both *humility* and *worship* should be read as governed by the preposition *in* and refer to the angels' own humility and worship. In this case the wording means "in humility and worship *like* the angels."[131] This interpretation, rather than separating off the internal genitive phrase θρησκείᾳ τῶν ἀγγέλων, takes into account the entire dative phrase, which functions as a dative (or instrumental) of manner.[132]

The genitive phrase "worship of angels" has generated massive and varying interpretation. If separated off from the full dative phrasing, the words θρησκείᾳ τῶν ἀγγέλων are read by some as an objective genitive where the angels receive worship, by others as a subjective genitive where the angels are the practitioners of worship, and, as at least one scholar has suggested, as a genitive of source (an ablative) where worship is *from* the angels.[133] Data from much later times can be found to support each of the grammatical possibilities.[134] The word θρησκεία typically refers to the worship of God or another deity (e.g., Wis 14:18, 27; Jas 1:26-27), never

---

129. See Sumney, *Colossians*, 155.

130. Balanced in the melodic flow of ἐν ταπεινοφροσύνῃ (seven syllables) and θρησκείᾳ τῶν ἀγγέλων (seven syllables) and in the *homoioptoton* of the dative nouns.

131. See Sumney, *Colossians*, 154-55, who calls it "worship with the angels." As Sumney points out, it would not be imagined that the phrase "worship of the church" indicates that the church is to be worshiped, so here the "worship of angels" does not mean that the complainant demands that angels are to be worshiped (11). See the intertextural references in Sumney and in Talbert, *Ephesians and Colossians*, 217-19.

132. Daniel B. Wallace, *Greek Grammar beyond the Basics: An Exegetical Syntax of the New Testament* (Grand Rapids: Zondervan, 1996), 161-62; BDF §198.

133. Martin, *By Philosophy and Empty Deceit*, 150-60. The subjective genitive view is promoted by Fred O. Francis, "Humility and Angelic Worship in Col. 2:18," *ST* 16 (1962): 109-34, repeated in Francis and Meeks, *Conflict at Colossae*. This view has been followed by many interpreters.

134. See Talbert, *Ephesians and Colossians*, 218-19. There are many reconstructions of the historical connections of 2:18. All are tentative, none of them are finally definitive (see Wilson, *Colossians and Philemon*, 61-63). A major problem with interpretations is the desire of scholars to identify a single and most probable solution to

to worship by God.¹³⁵ The rhetoric of the wording, however, indicates that the complaint is about Christ believers' perceived shortcoming in practices. The complainant imagines that the believers should practice humility and worship *in the manner of the angels*. This would be actions that correspond with what was imagined to occur in the cosmic realm. The letter does not offer more information.¹³⁶

Yet more difficult is the following "which things he has seen while entering in" (ἃ ἑόρακεν ἐμβατεύων). Like "worship of the angels," these words have received multiple, widely varying interpretations. The third-person singular ἑόρακεν pretty clearly refers to the someone here called the complainant. The verb ἐμβατεύω, "to enter in," is a *hapax legomenon* in the New Testament, here as the present nominative participle ἐμβατεύων. In the LXX it occurs in Josh 19:51 and 1 Macc 12:25, where it refers to invading or taking possession of land/territory. In 2 Macc 2:30 ἐμβατεύω is employed to describe entry into study of a text in order to prepare an abridgement. The rhetoric is clearly about "entering in." What has the complainant entered in his own religious practice and which he insists Christ believers must also experience?¹³⁷ Entering mysteries?¹³⁸ Entering the (or a) heavenly realm? Entering visionary experiences?¹³⁹ Entering temples or other holy places?¹⁴⁰ The text of Colossians does not say.

---

the philosophy. Copenhaver's *Reconstructing the Historical Background* is an exception in claiming two solutions, one for 2:16–17 (Jewish) and another for 2:18–19 (Apollo).

135. See the cognate form θρησκός in Jas 1:26.

136. There are many interpretations that aim to explain "worship of angels" in the objective genitive sense (e.g., Arnold, *Colossians Syncretism*, 11–102). Beale, for a recent example, points to "some evidence" for "idolatrous" worship of angels in Asia Minor (*Colossians and Philemon*, 224–27). He also cites Rev 19:10, where John attempts to worship (προσκυνῆσαι) the angel. For historical and archaeological information about angels and Colossae including the objective worship of angels, see Cadwallader, *Fragments of Colossae*, 180–98.

137. See Copenhaver, *Reconstructing the Historical Background*, 212–26. For a summary of views, see Beale, *Colossians and Philemon*, 227–29.

138. See Longenecker, *In Stone and Story*, 92.

139. Sumney, *Colossians*, 156 et passim.

140. As noted previously (n. 109), Beale interprets "entering in" as allusion to entering a temple: "This commentary has been at pains to detect probable OT allusions to a temple idea at a number of significant points in chaps 1 and 2, both with respect to Christ as the temple (1:19; 2:9) and believers as the temple (1:9, … 2:10a; … 1:22, 23; 2:7,11)" (*Colossians and Philemon*, 234). See also Lincoln, "Colossians," 567, 632; Talbert, *Ephesians and Colossians*, 219–20. They hypothesize a complainant who

In the dominating Roman imperial context of Colossae, the Lycus, and nearby regions, it was socially and religiously important to be seen recognizing and participating in appropriate observances. The Roman influence was unmistakable.[141] People living in the Lycus Valley and Colossae would, in their visual imaginations, see this vivid Roman influence in things such as "coins, inscriptions, statues, and reliefs that were widely dispersed" in the area.[142] Relatively nearby was the city of Aphrodisias, where the temple complex called the Sebasteion (or Augusteum) made Aphrodite and the Divini Augusti (the divine emperor cult) visible.[143] Residents of Colossae would be aware of this imagery and regular observances that called for at least nominal participation in religious-civic events that honored the deities. When people of the new Christ faith did not participate by "entering in" to these expectations, it would very likely be noticed. Conformity to Roman power and expectation was the right thing to do. The Roman imperial context and connections of language have been clear from nearly the beginning of the letter.[144] This rhetoric of worshiping like the angels

---

has entered a synagogue, noticing there practices the Christ believers were not observing. Copenhaver, following Dibelius, claims an allusion to entering mysteries at the Apollo temple at Claros (*Reconstructing the Historical Background*, 212–26). See the descriptions of cults and sanctuaries in Huttner, *Early Christianity in the Lycus*, 42–66.

141. On this see especially Maier, *Picturing Paul in Empire*; Maier, "Reading Colossians in the Ruins," 212–31; Maier, "Paul, Imperial Situation, and Visualization," 171–94; Maier, "Salience, Multiple Affiliation," 153–69.

142. Maier, "Paul, Imperial Situation, and Visualization," 192. See also the summary description of the Roman context of then Lycus Valley in Janice Capel Anderson, *Colossians: Authorship, Rhetoric, and Code*, TCSGNT (London: T&T Clark, 2019), 55–59.

143. See especially Maier's essays "Reading Colossians in the Ruins" and "Paul, Imperial Situation, and Visualization." Aphrodisias was within traveling distance and cultural distance from Colossae, much closer than, say, Claros, and vastly closer than Jerusalem. There were sebasteia in a number of locations, including Antioch of Pisidia, Ankara, Sebaste/Samaria, and Cartagena. See also Huttner, *Early Christianity in the Lycus*, 59–66. On Aphrodisias, see "Aphrodisias Excavations," Aphrodisias Excavations Project, https://tinyurl.com/SBL7106i, and Aphrodisias homepage, https://tinyurl.com/SBL7106j.

144. Angela Standhartinger points out that while Jewish and other cultic and philosophical views and practices that many have suggested and promoted cannot be ruled out, the evidence for them is not clear. See Standhartinger, "A City with a Message: Colossae and Colossians," in Harrison and Welborn, *First Urban Churches* 5, 247–50.

and "entering in" to the dominant polytheistic, imperial, multiple practice culture is what someone might complain about. But the verses claim that the complainant is arrogant because of his fleshly mind, is not holding to Christ the head of the body, of which believers are members, the head who supplies the nourishment that "grows the growth from God" (2:19).

The complainant does not understand the nature (and grace) of the Christ belief. What he wishes to impose on the believers is the do-it-yourself approach to religion that is about pleasing the gods and the expectations of the sociocultural powers. To succumb to the pressure of this kind of salvation by works would be to move into the shadow and the realm of the mind of the flesh. Colossians has already made clear that Father God in the precreational Son-Christ has transferred those members of the body into the new reality of the light. It has been accomplished by Father God and the Son. The powers have been made irrelevant. For the believers to succumb to the pressure to practice the observances described in 2:16 and 18 would be to allow themselves to be deceived and deprived of what they possess. The rhetorical point is like the great wisdom rhetoric of Scripture: humans cannot construct their own access to the tree of life (see Gen 3:22–24). You cannot build your own tower to heaven (see Gen 11:4–9). Do not be persuaded to try.

Step Six: You Died with Christ; Do Not Submit to Useless Rules (2:20–23)

Rhetography

This step begins with an apocalyptic image and shifts to a wisdom image. The apocalyptic rhetorolect "If you died with Christ from the elements of the world" reenvisions images already evoked by 2:8–10 and 2:11–15, where the audiences appear in apocalyptic space as people who are full in Christ and who are raised and alive with him and exist beyond the power of all cosmic and human (i.e., created) authorities Christ has disgraced and triumphed.[145] In this step, the readers/listeners are reapprised of the image of their separation from (ἀπό) the adversarial, disordered, and chaotic "elements of the world" by means of their death with Christ.[146] This brings Christ's body, the stripping, the nailing, his death on the cross,

---

145. Looking ahead, the Εἰ ἀπεθάνετε σὺν Χριστῷ clause that begins step six here is paralleled by Εἰ οὖν συνηγέρθητε τῷ Χριστῷ at the beginning of step seven in 3:1.

146. See the textural commentary, below, regarding the grammar of 2:20.

SCENE THREE: DON'T BE DECEIVED. LIVE THE NEW REALITY   195

and the condition-altering effects of these things back into central view, along with the audience's own portrayal in the images. They are visualized as having died with Christ and therefore now exist in him, nourished from his head, free from the former life scene where sin and the things of the disordered cosmos prevailed. This apocalyptic imagery reiterates the impotence and irrelevance of the defeated powers and authorities and enhances the view of the Christ believers rejecting pressures from whoever is attempting to deceive them and bind them to things of the present world. The image evokes a question that visualizes the ongoing existence of the audiences: they have died with Christ, so why do they obligate themselves to follow rules like people "living in the world" (τί ὡς ζῶντες ἐν κόσμῳ δογματίζεσθε)?[147] Why were they just previously visualized to be rejecting the pressure to defer to the insistence of a complainant and are now seen to be practicing specific and unhelpful human commands and teachings (κατὰ τὰ ἐντάλματα καὶ διδασκαλίας τῶν ἀνθρώπων)?[148] The active rejection seems forgotten and is replaced by self-obligation (δογματίζεσθε) to restrictions[149] that creates a disorienting angle on the picture: since people are presented as free from dangerous and restrictive pressures and powers, why are they living with particularized restrictions? "Do not handle, do not taste, do not touch" (Μὴ ἅψῃ μηδὲ γεύσῃ μηδὲ θίγῃς).[150] The believers are now observed in a narrow, forbidding shadow where they are being very cautious, avoiding participation in anything that might be thought to be questionable according to present-age, elements-of-the-world ideologies. The rhetograph portrays a puzzling and biting irony: rejection of the things of the disordered world with simultaneous obligation to them. Viewers of the picture are to ask why it is so. The very actions that they are seen to be obligated to reject are distinctly visualized as being performed with a view toward destruction (ἅ ἐστιν πάντα εἰς φθορὰν τῇ ἀποχρήσει).

Someone is observed, somewhere just away from the center of the visualization, calling out, "do not handle, do not taste, do not touch." This is meant to stir up rhetorical concern and questioning: Why are Christ

---

147. Note repetitive texturing of word κόσμος.
148. Which repeats the idea of "the traditions of humans" in 2:8.
149. On this view, δογματίζεσθε is a true middle form, from δογματίζομαι, not the permissive passive form of δογματίζω. See grammatical analysis below.
150. This language points to an actual person who is pressuring the Colossians. Someone is saying "Don't handle, don't taste, don't touch." But at the same time there are Colossian believers who obligate themselves to such restrictions.

believers seen inserting themselves into obligations and restrictions? The reasoning for refusing it is clear. They visualize themselves as having died with Christ, as raised with Christ, as circumcised with the circumcision of Christ. The shadow is only a shadow, not real substance. They live in the kingdom of God's Son (1:13). There is no need for them to be seen living with the narrow restrictions. It reminds them of the filling that already occurred according to 2:10. Do not try to fill what has already been filled.

Overlaid on this imagery, paradoxically and simultaneously again, the restrictive obligations appear to present a logic (λόγος) that has wisdom in the ways that they provide the false security of self-imposed piety, humility, and unsparing treatment of body. The people who are seen to observe the restrictions appear, from a human point of view, to be very religious and very cautious of the *body* dangers of handling, eating, and touching.[151] *Body* here is envisioned in a very questionable light as part of the cosmos that requires restrictions. The picture portrays, however, the reality that these restrictions have no value. Though they seem to indicate appropriate religious observance, they do not prevent fleshly desire.[152] The vision of true value is found in the dying, rising, crucifying, nailing, baptizing, circumcising images of Christ that they saw previously. The pressure to observe the restrictions is a visual reminder of the deceiver seen in 2:18. Self-imposed or deceiver-imposed observances are ineffective. They do not keep people *in*. The visible action of Christ and the unity of believers with and in him is what works in this picture.

This step moves from apocalyptic space, where believers in Christ are once again observed to have died with him, to wisdom space, where restricting certain behaviors is seen to be ineffective. Although the restrictions appear to be attractive, they have no value. Virtual Paul wishes for audiences to continue their resistance to the pressure to conform to humanly contrived rules—just as in the imagery of 2:8–10 and 2:11–16—and to know that the apocalyptic actions of Christ, who exists precreationally, are what has freed them from all authorities and obligations.

---

151. Handling, eating, touching are metaphors for participation in behaviors of many kinds.

152. Or they produce fleshly desire. See the textural commentary regarding the translation difficulties of this phrase in 2:23. Perhaps this raises the question of what *does* prevent fleshly desire. Aging? Illness? Injury? Emotional trauma? Depression? Death? We shall all be dispossessed of many things.

Translation

2:20 If you died with Christ from the elements of the world, why do you obligate yourselves to rules like those living in [the] world? **2:21** Do not handle, do not taste, do not touch, **2:22** which things are all going to destruction by means of use, [being] according to human commands and teachings, **2:23** which very things have indeed a logic of wisdom in self-generated piety and humility and[153] harsh treatment of body, though not with any value against the indulgence of the flesh [or: though not with any value: they lead only toward gratification of the flesh].

Textural Commentary

Like the two previous steps, these verses have some very difficult grammatical, syntactical, and lexical texturing that needs careful analysis in order to understand the rhetoric. Although this step does not open with another imperatival statement, *repetitive texturing* stands out with the question regarding the obligation the believers feel to submit to rules (τί ὡς ζῶντες ἐν κόσμῳ δογματίζεσθε; Μὴ ἅψῃ μηδὲ γεύσῃ μηδὲ θίγῃς, 2:20–21).[154] Similarly, the phrasing of verse 22 ("according to human commands and teachings") is much like that of 2:8 ("according to human tradition"). The imagery of dying with Christ is implicit in 2:12–13 and is repeated here in explicit words. These repetitions emphasize the orchestrated rhetorical flow of language and ideas. The first words of the step, "If you died with Christ," anticipate the next progression, "If therefore you were raised with Christ," at 3:1.

Argumentation continues in the mode of prophetic discourse that shifts to wisdom rhetoric. The difference compared to the two previous steps is that the rhetorical argument does not begin with imperatives but with a question: "If you died with Christ ... why do you obligate yourselves to live" in particular, unhelpful ways? Believers are alive, raised with Christ, forgiven, and the flesh has been cut away (2:11–13). Why do they live as if these things were not true, not realized?

---

153. Some manuscripts omit καί.
154. This is the NA[28]/UBS[5] version. SBLGNT places the question mark (;) at the end of 2:21.

Case: As was already made clear in step three (2:11–15), the Christ believers have died with Christ from the disordered, chaotic, empire-focused, material world, but they now feel obligated to conform to the religious-social contexts in which they live and are submitting to rules such as "do not handle or taste or touch." This leads to the rhetoricized question, "Why are you reobligating yourselves to the elements of the cosmos like persons living in the world?" The question calls for a clarifying rationale even as it already implies a rationale. To ask the question is to indicate—in effect to remind—that the self-obligation is an unnecessary mistake.

Rationale: If they have died to the elements of the cosmos, indeed since it is true that they *have* died with Christ to them, signified in their baptism, why now do they obligate themselves to conform to the pressure to engage in the elemental, worldly observances? The implied rationale in the question is that there is no such obligation. This rhetoric of reasoning is as much to say as, "You are not part of this. Why have you given in? Why do you live in the shadow?" Like the elements, powers, and authorities that have been disgraced and triumphed in the apocalyptic actions of Christ, in whom they have been made full, restrictions such as "do not handle, do not taste, do not touch" along with others are now irrelevant. They are in fact ineffective. They will not, in some pietistic sense, make them better people. They will not appease the gods. They will not last; indeed, they are destroyed as they are used (ἅ ἐστιν πάντα εἰς φθορὰν τῇ ἀποχρήσει). They will not provide entrance to some genuine religious experience. They are human commands and teachings rather than from the domain of Father God and his Son. They look impressive, look to be deeply religious, wise, and logical from a human point of view, but they are self-generated, useless, harsh things that have no value. Believers already have all they need.

Anticipated Result: The believers will no longer be self-obligated and will give up the useless observances.

On the grammatical-syntactical level, 2:20 is difficult to translate. The verb δογματίζεσθε is typically understood as a "permissive passive" of δογματίζω.[155] It should be read as the true middle-voice verb δογματίζομαι,

---

155. Derived from δόγμα, "law, rule"; as a verb, "to obey rules, decree, ordain." See Dan 2:15, Esth 3:9, 2 Macc 10:8, 15:36, 3 Macc 4:11, 1 Clem. 20.4, 27.5.

hence meaning "you obligate yourselves." The preposition ἀπό, following the compound verb ἀποθνῄσκω, is considered by some interpreters to be connected with δογματίζεσθε.[156] It is more likely that ἀπό is intended to make dying with Christ *from* the elements of the cosmos more emphatic.[157] Either way, the point is that believers in Colossae had already given in to the pressure to conform to the point where, rather than being obligated passively by the complainant, they were actively obligating themselves to consciousness of restrictive religious rules such as "don't handle, don't taste, don't touch." They imagined themselves to be obligated to the disordered, chaotic world even though they are not so obligated in the new reality of Christ. The rhetoric of verse 22, employing the relative pronoun ἅ, "which things," has in view the behaviors to be rejected by the prohibitive subjunctive forms "do not handle or taste or touch" as antecedent[158] (i.e., the behaviors themselves, not the prohibiting statements) and goes on to say that they (the handling, tasting, touching) "all go to destruction with use" (πάντα εἰς φθορὰν τῇ ἀποχρήσει). This puzzling language (ἀπόχρησις, "consumption, use, full use"; a *hapax legomenon* in the New Testament) indicates that refusals to handle, taste, or touch are manifestly unnecessary, in fact useless, because they will not last, they are used up or consumed as they are practiced and have no further significance. This points again to the recognition in Colossians that the powers and authorities have been made irrelevant.

The remaining grammatical-syntactical difficulty involves the uncertainties about how to translate and interpret the final phrasing of verse 23, οὐκ ἐν τιμῇ τινι πρὸς πλησμονὴν τῆς σαρκός. Pretty clearly the wording plays off the particle μέν used earlier in the verse, so could be rendered as "*but* not with any value against the gratification of the flesh," where πρός

---

156. On these interpretations, see the detailed grammatical analysis in Martin, *By Philosophy and Empty Deceit*, 35–43. Martin offers the wooden translation "If you died with Christ, are you decreeing anything for yourselves from the elements of the cosmos as if you were living in the cosmos?" (42). One could wonder what native speakers of Greek living in Colossae or Phrygia would have heard and understood from the wording.

157. Archibald T. Robertson, *Grammar of the Greek New Testament in the Light of Historical Research* (Nashville: Broadman, 1934), 559. See Wallace, who points out that in Koine the genitive of separation, "a common idiom in the Attic dialect … has been replaced, by and large, by ἀπό + genitive" (*Greek Grammar*, 360–62).

158. Typically, μή followed by the aorist subjunctive, as here (Wallace, *Greek Grammar*, 469).

means "against." But the wording could also be rendered as "but not of any value leading toward gratification of the flesh," where πρός is understood to mean "toward." It is difficult to decide between the opposite meanings. Are the behaviors without value because they do not inhibit fleshly desires, or are they without value because they stimulate fleshly desires? A sure decision about one or the other version of this rhetoric is not fully discernible and is probably not necessary. Both ways may be true. Either way, the refusals to handle, taste, or touch are restrictions that have no value. They do not work for the good of the Christ believers. The self-obligation would be for the gratification of the complainant.

The self-generated efforts to avoid handling, tasting, and touching (and many other things unnamed) are unnecessary not only because they are headed for destruction but because they fit in the category of "human commands and teachings" (2:22). This statement is governed by the same pronoun ἅ at the beginning of verse 22. The warning in 2:8 to beware of things "according to the tradition of humans" (κατὰ τὴν παράδοσιν τῶν ἀνθρώπων) is reconfigured here to oppose what is "according to the commands and teachings of humans" (κατὰ τὰ ἐντάλματα καὶ διδασκαλίας τῶν ἀνθρώπων). This is expanded, in turn, with the specifying qualitative use of the relative pronoun ἅτινα ("which very things") in verse 23.[159] In other words, the precise self-obligation to avoid things such as handling, tasting, and touching gives a sense of reason, self-generated piety (worship), and harsh treatment of body, while in truth has none of these values at all.

That the self-obligated avoidances are "according to the commands and teachings of humans" points to the important **intertexture** of 2:22 with Isa 29:13.[160] The authors of Colossians, if not the believers in Colossae, indicate awareness of the same kind of LXX language that is creatively inserted here. Isaiah 29:13 anticipates the judgment of Jerusalem because "they worship pointlessly, teaching human commands and teachings" (μάτην δὲ σέβονταί με διδάσκοντες ἐντάλματα ἀνθρώπων καὶ διδασκαλίας). Colossians 2:23 goes on to describe the "self-generated piety" with the striking word ἐθελοθρησκία, that forms a *repetitive texture* with θρησκεία in 2:18. Observing the rules of verse 21, like worshiping in the manner of the angels, is to follow the things of the created order, is generated by human traditions, and has no value for the believers' religious practice. Interestingly,

---

159. See Wallace, *Greek Grammar*, 344.
160. See Sumney, *Colossians*, 163–64.

the word ἐθελοθρησκία is reconfigured from ἐθελοθρησκεία (note that the ε is dropped to form the -σκία ending).[161] The rhetorical allusion is made thereby to the σκία-shadow (see above on 2:17). To produce self-generated, human worship/piety is to reenter the shadow.

Ideological texture. Texts present ideologies and create ideologies. Ideologies are textures of rhetoric that shape how people understand the contexts in which they live and with which they interact. It is about how they walk (2:6). These steps in the rhetorical movement of Colossians are pieces of the overall wisdom ideology the letter presents. The letter recipients were encouraged to continue to live faithful and productive lives as Christ believers and members of the body-*ekklēsia* (e.g., 2:2–3). The ideology of "the mystery of God—of Christ—in whom are hidden all the treasures of wisdom and knowledge" (2:2–3), which the letter creates and explains, is the worldview the believers have come to and from which they must not allow themselves to be persuaded to deviate. The fullness of deity dwells in Christ bodily, and in Christ they have been filled (2:9–10). What they must not take on or, correctly stated, what they must not reenter, is an ideology that conceptualizes that the maintenance of religious and social life in the city is necessary and more important than life in the new reality in Christ. That ideology conceptualizes that acceptance *depends on* the practice and visibility of things such as eating and drinking, participation in festivals/feasts, Sabbath observance, worship practices in the manner of angels, entering and giving honor in polytheistic and politically oriented places of worship, or in not handling, tasting, or touching certain things, and that all this is more important than trusting in Christ. To reenter that ideological realm would be to revert to a do-it-yourself ideology (or theology) that imagines that personal performance—a works theology—must be maintained rather than trusting the apocalyptic, forgiving, reconciling actions of Christ. This could only imply that Christ is insufficient and does not fill believers full. What 2:16–23 develops is an *ideology of rejection*. Live within the new reality of the cosmic-precreational Son of Father God. Other cosmos realities are *irrelevant*. Whatever judges unfairly, deceives, encourages self-obligation against what Christ provides, distracts, inhibits by means of human commands and teachings according to the disordered way of the cosmos is to be rejected.

---

161. See Sumney, *Colossians*, 165.

Rhetorical Force as Emergent Discourse

The rhetoric of Colossians reshapes the imagery and storyline of Lycus Valley human expectations for the believers. The reshaping explains how things are different from the experienced and expected reality of the Roman-dominated social and religious environment. Believers have been transferred to the new reality of the Son's kingdom. They live now in the reconciled creation (1:20) as people reconciled in the body of the Son- Christ's own flesh to be "holy and without blemish and above reproach" (1:22). The judge-deceiver-cheater of 2:16, 18, 20 wishes to force the old ways of the world on the believers for selfish, controlling reasons. But Paul and his writers know it is not possible to enter the domain of Father God by performing whatever were perceived to be actions or works or euergetisms that would gain favor. That would be the way of the constructed realm of powers and authorities who offered not grace but demanded human efforts to please the gods including the divine Caesar. Humans cannot enter the cosmic-precreational domain of God and his Son by their own efforts, not since Gen 3:22–24, when they were prohibited from "reaching out the hand and taking from the tree of life, eating, and living forever."[162] Conformity to life in Roman Asia Minor meant assimilating to varied and confusing social-religious practices. In Colossae and other Lycus Valley locations such as Laodicea and Hierapolis, Christ believers were being criticized regarding religious behaviors they were expected to practice and, according to 2:21, behaviors from which they were expected to abstain.

The rhetorical force of 2:16–23, following up on what went before (1:12–2:15), impresses the mind with the new reality that reconciliation is brought about only by God in Christ and that Christ is "the hope of glory" (1:27, 3:4). Human efforts cannot make things right in the disordered, chaotic cosmos. Christ has reordered the disorder not by the power of an empire but by the power of death and resurrection. The Roman salvation is no real salvation at all. The rhetoric describes a new imaging of the cosmos. So the believers are not to be persuaded to reenter the shadow. They have died with Christ and must not obligate themselves to the false, deceptive reality.

---

162. Lightly paraphrased from Gen 3:22. In this sense Gen 3 is a wisdom text, presenting the wisdom of the ages given by ancient sages.

Step Seven: You Were Raised with Christ; Seek the Above Things (3:1–4)

Rhetography

This pictorial step moves ahead from the preceding vision in a parallel but directionally opposite motion.[163] The parallel picturing is indicated explicitly in the language employed in 2:20 and 3:1, both of which begin with the conditional εἰ followed by the preposition σύν.[164] The directional movement is envisioned as dying with Christ in 2:20, while the action in 3:1 is envisioned as being raised with Christ (Εἰ οὖν συνηγέρθητε τῷ Χριστῷ).[165] Believers are pictured being raised out of death with Christ in a way that impresses the vision on the mind as the apocalyptic, argumentative base (as in 2:20) for the prophetic and wisdom statements that follow. The Colossian holy ones are once again observed in the action portrayed in 2:12–13. Their raised and living location with (and in) Christ is clearly in sight. This apocalyptic, raised positioning places them in a location where they can be encouraged to see themselves seeking "the above things" (τὰ ἄνω ζητεῖτε). This view looks up to the highest possible location, to where Christ is sitting at the right hand of God (οὗ ὁ Χριστός ἐστιν ἐν δεξιᾷ τοῦ θεοῦ καθήμενος). The mental vision is drawn upward, from seeing the image of the believers being moved from death to life in resurrection with Christ to seeing Christ in exalted position alongside God. The prophetic statement "seek the above things" in this way pushes visioning upward to exalted space.

By almost obvious contrast given what has gone before in Colossians, the exaltation of Christ is not the exaltation of Caesar or of anyone or anything in the created order of heaven and earth. Caesar is not visualized sitting on Jupiter's throne. Christ alone is seated at God's right hand, alone the Son of Father God and the one with whom believers have also been raised.[166] The wisdom directive then elicits a parallel wisdom rheto-

---

163. The chapter and verse division at 3:1 helps us find our place in the text but suggests an unhelpful division in the rhetorical flow of language and ideas.
164. Where σύν stands independently in 2:20 and in the compound συνηγέρθητε in 3:1.
165. Dying is active; being raised is passive.
166. It is instructive to compare this rhetoric with what is developed and observed in Eph 2:4–6, "But God ... made us alive together with Christ ... and raised us up with him and seated us with him in the heavenlies in Christ Jesus."

graph that portrays a thinking rather than seeking image where listeners observe themselves thinking "the things above" (τὰ ἄνω φρονεῖτε) rather than thinking about things of the earth (μὴ τὰ ἐπὶ τῆς γῆς). The visualization does not (yet) make explicit the above things that are to be sought and thought about, although it does show Christ sitting on the preeminent right side of God. The nature of the imaging, however, clearly colors the above things as good, as things that should not be resisted and that pose no danger to the audiences. The above things are also set in visual contrast to the on-the-earth things. The downward view that thinks about and visualizes the things on the earth, observes images of evil things in the imagination—things made explicit when the contrasting behaviors listed in the next section (3:5–17) come into sight[167]—and, though the downward view is possible, it is not a view that should be taken.

The wisdom exhortation to seek and think of the above things is continued with a visual and apocalyptic rationale in the next two clauses that reenvision something the audiences have already seen, that is, that they have died and that their lives are now hidden with Christ in God (3:3). This brings into the foreground yet again the image of dying with Christ (see 2:12–13) and now embellishes the visual nature of the raised life believers now live in Christ (and Christ in them) by adding to the picture the vision of their having been hidden with Christ, who is in God (καὶ ἡ ζωὴ ὑμῶν κέκρυπται σὺν τῷ Χριστῷ ἐν τῷ θεῷ).[168] This is a complex image that does not visibly portray the believers, although they know that they are there, hidden in the picture, but it does portray Christ in a new way, located "in God."[169] This visioning, however, anticipates future moments when both Christ and believers will be clearly seen (ὅταν ὁ Χριστὸς φανερωθῇ ... ὑμεῖς σὺν αὐτῷ φανερωθήσεσθε).[170] Christ is "your life" (ἡ ζωὴ ὑμῶν), your own existence, matching the previous imagery of believers "in Christ" and "with Christ." The visual imagination is filled with pictures of believers and Christ together presented in a glorious way. This contrasts dramatically

---

167. Where specified evil behaviors that are visible "on the earth" are to be "put to death."

168. Strikingly, the visualization of being raised from death is coordinated with having been hidden.

169. Unseen God has been called into imagination a number of times in the rhetoric so far, 1:1–3, 6, 10, 15, 19–20, 25, 27; 2:12–13, 19; 3:1.

170. Note that the verbs are forms of φανερόω, "make known, cause to be seen, show." See the full explanation in textural commentary, below.

SCENE THREE: DON'T BE DECEIVED. LIVE THE NEW REALITY

with the high-pressure, threatening, shadowy, dark images of judgment, complaint, and deceit presented in the preceding steps (2:16–23).

This step offers a blended apocalyptic-wisdom-apocalyptic sequence. The apocalyptic reality of being raised with Christ presents the visual case for the wisdom behavior of seeking and thinking about the things above. The space above is the apocalyptic location of Christ, sitting at the right (side) of God. The apocalyptic reality is blended with wisdom reality to produce a third space where the raised yet hidden life in Christ is responsibly lived out alongside pressures against it, always seeking and thinking about the above things. This new space—which has subtly been in view since nearly the beginning of the letter—is anticipated to be more fully visible as things go along. It imagines the ongoing existence of the believers. The constant is that believers are always "with" (σύν) Christ.

Translation

> **3:1** If therefore you were raised with Christ, seek the above things where Christ is seated on the right hand side of God. **3:2** Think about the above things, not the things on the earth. **3:3** For you died and your life has been hidden with Christ in God. **3:4** Whenever Christ—your life[171]—is made visible, then you also will made visible with him in glory.

Textural Commentary

This *progression* completes the persuasive force of the language of 2:16–23, in fact of the rhetoric that began its work already in Col 1:3 that drew the eyes and thoughts upward to "the hope stored up in the heavens" and was expressed in "the word of the truth of the gospel" (1:5).[172] The focus is on the believers in their direct relationship with the raised Christ—"who is the image of the unseen God [1:15] ... firstborn out of the dead [1:18]"— implied from the outset of the letter as raised and living with resurrection explicit in the *repetitive texturing* of 2:12–13 and now in 3:1, "raised with Christ." Christ is seated at the right side of God, an **intertextural** thread

---

171. Some manuscripts have ἡ ζωὴ ἡμῶν, "our life."
172. Some, e.g., Barth and Blanke interpret 3:1–4 as the beginning of a new section rather than a continuation and completion of the preceding rhetoric (*Colossians*, 391–92).

to Ps 110:1.[173] Just as Christ died and was raised, so his followers, who were "dead in the trespasses and foreskin of [their] flesh," have died (3:2, repeating "died with Christ," 2:20), have been "raised with Christ" (3:1), and now with Christ—"your life" (3:4)—have been hidden with Christ in God.[174] The movement of Christ and believers is clear: Christ died and was raised, and believers have died and been raised with him, their death and resurrection with Christ signified in their baptism. At the same time that it completes the exhortations of 2:16-23, the rhetoric of being raised with Christ induces the imperatives to seek (ζητεῖτε) and think (φρονεῖτε) about the above things, and also functions to introduce the imperative "therefore" (οὖν) *progressions* that follow in 3:5 ("therefore put to death," aorist active imperative) and 3:12 ("therefore clothe yourselves," aorist middle imperative), with more imperatives implied and expressed through to verse 17.

The rhetoric and rhetography have a goal in sight. The apocalyptic image of being raised with Christ, presented grammatically as a conditional statement ("*If* therefore you were raised...") but understood as a completed reality, is aimed at a wisdom result.[175] The apocalyptic raising *with* Christ envisions the new reality *in* Christ and encourages seeking and thinking about the above realm, where Christ is seated at the right of God, rather than the earth realm of the defeated and irrelevant στοιχεῖα (see 2:8, 20). Jesus-followers are to be oriented toward[176] the new reality of living in the Son's kingdom (1:13, 4:11). The nature of this wisdom is expanded (*ekphrasis*) in 3:3-4 and more fully in 3:5-4:6.

So the first two verses in this step draw together much of what has been stated in the letter to this point. Here is "the truth of the gospel which comes [τοῦ παρόντος] to you" (1:5): believers have been raised with Christ, having previously died, and in their collective life—indicated in the singular forms ἡ ζωὴ and κέκρυπται—have been hidden with Christ in God. They are completely secure with Christ. This draws to a fair conclusion concerns about the pressures they face from the complainant and from the

---

173. This intertexture, frequent in the New Testament, might or might not have been recognized by the Lycus Jesus followers.

174. Note the graphic use of prepositions σύν and ἐν.

175. Apocalyptic discourse typically has wisdom, i.e., the life of good and productive behavior, in view. Where this goes, eventually, is to 3:11, "but Christ all and in all," ἀλλὰ τὰ πάντα καὶ ἐν πᾶσιν Χριστός. See below.

176. See Barth and Blanke, *Colossians*, 395.

SCENE THREE: DON'T BE DECEIVED. LIVE THE NEW REALITY   207

pressures to conform to life as understood in their urban, Roman-influenced contexts. It is as much as to say, "Don't worry, don't be pressured, don't give in. Don't be misled and captured by the various στοιχεῖα τοῦ κόσμου. The powers are in fact defeated and impotent. You are secure with Christ in God." This rhetoric anticipates reasonable questions: What happens now? What do we do now? How should we live our lives in this new reality? There are textured answers: (1) seek the above things, (2) think about the above things, and (3) whenever Christ your life is made visible, then you will be made visible with him in glory. Being raised with Christ and seeking and thinking about the above things are elevated, sublime (ὕψος) ideas.[177] They are notions and realities that capture the imagination, drawing people to look up or to imagine the elevated, sublime domain where Christ sits at the right hand of God. Seeking and thinking about such things, the things of Christ and Father God, may by now be stated straightforwardly enough, since the letter has already made clear that the Son-Christ of the above domain works at creative and sustaining activity (1:16–17), that all the fullness of deity houses in him (2:9), and that his death and resurrection have defeated the powers.

Much more difficult to interpret and understand is the rhetoric of verses 3–4. What is the meaning and rhetorical force of the clause "Whenever Christ your life is made visible"? What is the meaning and rhetorical force of the next clause, "then you also will be made visible with him in glory"? The ideas overall are presented in a *past–present–whenever–then* rhetorical sequence. Already in the *past* believers died and were raised with Christ. In the *present* they are hidden[178] with Christ (who is their life; ζωή, their existence). *Whenever* (ὅταν) Christ may be made visible (φανερωθῇ, aorist subjunctive passive; "made visible; brought to light; made to shine; manifested; illuminated"), *then* (τότε) his followers themselves "will be made visible in glory" (φανερωθήσεσθε ἐν δόξῃ, future passive). A key notion is that what is hidden will be brought to light, become visible, become seen—it will *shine*. Another emerging question is to ask what is meant by "in glory." This sequencing is understood by almost all interpreters to anticipate the revelation of Christ at his parousia and the

---

177. The term *sublime* suggests things that are evocative, that transport the mind and the senses toward understanding. On the rhetoric of the sublime, see Jeal, *Exploring Sublime Rhetoric*.

178. They continue to be hidden, κέκρυπται, perfect passive.

revelation of believers with him in the heavenly realm.[179] But the rhetoric is more subtle and allusive than what is too quickly imagined to be solely a direct, clear, and focused reference to the expected return of Christ. All this requires careful analysis of **inner texture**.

Argumentatively, Col 3:4 is constructed as a ὅταν/τότε, whenever/then temporal statement. That is, "whenever" some specified event may occur, "then" another event will (or is expected) to occur.[180] The temporal conjunction[181] ὅταν is an elision of ὅτε, "when," and ἄν, a conditional particle generally directly untranslatable but having a conditional nuancing effect. It has a contingent, temporal, and often repeatable force meaning "whenever."[182] The context makes this meaning clear because ὅτε, "when," is employed in 3:7 to form a structural and argumentative counterpoint to the preceding word ποτέ, "then" (ἐν οἷς καὶ ὑμεῖς περιεπατήσατέ ποτε, ὅτε ἐζῆτε ἐν τούτοις).[183] In other words, the distinction between the words ὅταν (used again in 4:16) and ὅτε was clearly understood by the writers. A similar distinction occurs in Colossians where the pronoun ἅ, "which things," in 2:22, becomes ἅτινά, "whichever things," in 2:23.[184] The change in pronoun indicates a different shade of meaning. Our authors knew how to shape words carefully and creatively.

The words typically employed to refer to the future return of Christ, the nouns παρουσία and ἀποκάλυψις and the verb ἀποκαλύπτω, do not occur in Colossians, nor does the noun ἐπιφάνεια, which does appear in 2 Thessalonians and in all three Pastoral Letters.[185] The cognate form of παρουσία, the verb πάρειμι, occurs (as the participle παρόντος) in 1:6.

---

179. An exception is Gerhard Swart, "Eschatological Vision or Exhortation to Visible Christian Conduct? Notes on the Interpretation of Colossians 3:4," *Neot* 33 (1999): 169–77. While this article is noted by some, it is usually quickly dismissed.

180. See Wallace, *Greek Grammar*, 479. The demonstrative adverb τότε refers to subsequent time.

181. Or adverbial conjunction of time (see Wallace, *Greek Grammar*, 677).

182. BDAG, 587.

183. The particle ποτέ refers to preceding time.

184. See the translation of 2:23 above, where ἅτινά is rendered as "which very things." The more awkward sounding and archaic "whichsoever things" conveys the idea clearly.

185. Colossians 3:6 states that "the anger of God comes on the sons of disobedience," but unlike other Pauline letters, there is no wording in the letter regarding the "day of the Lord" (1 Thess 5:2, 2 Thess 2:2), the "day of Christ" (Phil 1:6), or judgment (Rom 14:10, 2 Cor 5:10).

What *is* employed in Col 3:4 are forms of the verb φανερόω. It is assumed (presumed?) by interpreters, often without argument or simply by default, that here φανερόω functions as a synonym or alternative for παρουσία or ἀποκαλύπτω.[186] It seems correct that 3:4 refers to the parousia, even if it is not explicit with the usual and expected words. It is not as clear a reference to the parousia as some interpreters claim. Lexical and syntactical meaning is more allusive in the larger context.

φανερόω and ἀποκαλύπτω have differing nuances of meaning. There is no concept of the prefixes *re-*, *dis-*, or *un-* with φανερόω as there is with ἀποκαλύπτω. The compound verb ἀποκαλύπτω (ἀπό + καλύπτω) means "dis-cover, un-cover, un-veil," hence in typical English translation "reveal," from Latin *revelare* (*re* + *velum*), "uncover, unveil, lay bare." The verb φανερόω, employed four times in Colossians (1:26; 3:4 [twice]; 4:4), is variously translated in the New Testament but has its roots of meaning in the conception of light and visibility and so can be translated with terms such as "manifest,"[187] "make known," "make visible," "cause to make visible," "appear," "make clear," "bring to light," "set in a clear light."[188] It is cognate with the range of φαν- words including the verb φαίνω.

The syntactical force of the clause ὅταν ὁ Χριστὸς φανερωθῇ (i.e., ὅταν with the subjunctive φανερωθῇ) indicates that Christ is to be made visible at an undefined future time. The anticipated visibility is a certainty and the clause is temporal, but the actual time of it is not indicated. Given what is known from elsewhere in the Pauline letters and given the typical understanding of linear time, it seems natural and correct to assume the clause has the parousia in view. The future time of Christ's becoming visible in the parousia is unknown. Still, it is not at all explicit. There is something else at play.

---

186. Margaret MacDonald suggests that "the attempt to draw a contrast with what is hidden probably leads to the choice of *phaneroō*—a more natural choice to create the antithesis of hiddenness and revelation" (*Colossians and Ephesians*, 129). It is not made clear why ἀποκαλύπτω would not have the same effect. For φανερόω and cognate forms, see Rudolf Bultmann, "φανερόω," *TDNT* 9:1–10.

187. Cf. the Latin *manifestatio*, "a showing."

188. In the NRSV and NRSVue φανερόω is translated in 2 Cor 5:10 as "appear," and in the next verse, 5:11, as "well known." In Rom 1:19 it is given as "shown" in the NRSV and "made it plain" in the NRSVue. In 1 Cor 14:25 the adjective form φανερός is translated as "disclosed." In Mark 4:22 it is translated as "disclosed," and in Mark 14:64 is interpretively translated as "decision." See below on **intertexture**.

The following clause, τότε καὶ ὑμεῖς σὺν αὐτῷ φανερωθήσεσθε ἐν δόξῃ, also a temporal clause, specifies that "then," when Christ is made visible, his followers who are hidden with him in God will also be made visible. It is easy to assume that this refers to the parousia, when believers will be visible in the heavenly domain with Christ and God in glory. It is not stated who, apart from the believers and Christ, will see all this. Will the defeated powers see it? Will persons who are not Jesus-followers see it?

The phrase "in glory" is frequently imagined in a locative sense, that is, that glory is the space of the above realm. Yet the notion of being made visible does not suggest transportation to another domain, whether at the parousia or at any time. Glory points to the idea of the majestic, to splendor, dignity, radiance, and honor.[189] It evokes awe and wonder. Glory is a *condition*, the visible presence, not a heavenly or eschatological location. Glory belongs to Father God and his Son. To be in glory is to be made visible with Christ (σὺν αὐτῷ) when he is made visible. It is to appear in honor and splendor with Christ. The phrase is to be understood as a dative of manner, that believers will be made visible, will be in light in the manner of glory, in a glorious, we may say radiant way, whenever Christ is made visible.[190] This way of thinking about glory has been in sight in the repetitions of the word *glory* earlier in Colossians: the "power of his [the Lord's] glory" (1:11) and "the wealth of the glory" of the now-made-known "mystery among the nations, which is Christ in you, the hope of glory" (1:27). These verses have in view the power, majesty, splendor, and honor of Father God, the Son, and humans.

The forward-looking view of 3:4 evokes a vision not only—not even primarily in the context—toward the parousia. As noted above, the seeking and thinking about above things introduces the behavioral imperatives and progressions that flow to verse 17 and indeed all the way to 4:6. This is the allusive, subtle, and forward-looking wording in 3:3–4 about believers who are hidden with Christ being made visible with Christ in a glorious way *whenever* Christ is made visible. The repetitive force of the conjunction ὅταν must be taken seriously. This is the wisdom direction for the believers who are hidden with Christ in the present (3:3). Recall

---

189. See Gerhard Kittel, "δόξα," *TDNT* 2:232–37, 247–55. It *can* refer to an eventual judgment (e.g., Rom 2:7, 10) but also to honor, dignity, or notable appearance of God or of humans in the present (e.g., Rom 3:23, 4:20, 1 Cor 2:7, 11:7, 2 Cor 6:8, 8:23, Phil 1:11, 3:19, 1 Thess 2:20). See especially 1 Cor 15:40–43.

190. Campbell, *Colossians and Philemon*, 50.

that the letter as a whole has in sight the productivity and maturation of Jesus-followers in Colossae. Life is different now, in Christ. Believers have been transferred to the new reality of life lived faithfully (1:21–23). In the new reality, whenever the hidden Christ is made visible, is brought to light, then the believers are also brought to light, to shine gloriously, honorably in the world. Christ shines when his followers "put to death the earth things," that is, the behaviors of self-interest that draw God's wrath (3:5–9), and where they have put on "the new person" who ("who," since the garment put on is a person, ἄνθρωπον, 3:10)[191] is continuously being renewed (3:10), who no longer belongs to the earth, and where "Christ [is] all and in all" (ἀλλὰ τὰ πάντα καὶ ἐν πᾶσιν Χριστός, 3:11).

Intertexture. The rhetoric of Christ exalted and located (sometimes "seated") at the right hand of God occurs frequently in the New Testament, reflecting the resurrection and ascension (Luke 20:42; 22:69; Acts 2:33–34; 5:31; 7:55–56; Rom 8:34; Eph 1:20; Heb 1:3, 13; 8:1; 10:12; 12:2; 1 Pet 3:22). The descriptions of the Son-Christ in Colossians make the exaltation motif in 3:1 unsurprising. Similarly, the resurrection motif in 3:1 naturally leads to "the above things" motif in contrast to "the earth things," ideas developed elsewhere in New Testament thinking (e.g., John 3:3, 31; 8:23; 11:41; 19:11; Gal 4:26; Eph 1:20–21; 4:10; Heb 7:26). The language of being hidden (κέκρυπται) with Christ in God, while unique to Col 3:3, nevertheless has threads of connection with the mystery that had been hidden (ἀποκεκρυμμένον) from the ages and generations but is now brought to light (ἐφανερώθη, 1:26).[192] The hidden mystery that extends from the ages and generations points to the cosmic-precreational source of what was to come to light in the gospel (see Matt 13:35, Luke 10:21, 1 Cor 2:7, Eph 3:9, Heb 11:23). The language and idea of hiddenness occurs again in 2:2–3, stating that in Christ are "all the hidden [ἀπόκρυφοι] treasures of wisdom and knowledge." It is with this same Christ, their life, that the believers are hidden, in whom they are made full (2:10) and with whom—emphasized for a second time as their life, ἡ ζωὴ ὑμῶν—they will be brought to light (3:4). And Christ, with whom they are hidden, "(is) all and in all."[193] The intertextural connections of hiddenness in Colossians lead to this "all and in all" Christ alluded to in the language

---

191. See Jeal, "Clothes Make the (Wo)Man" (esp. 407–9).

192. Aorist passive of φανερόω. ἀποκεκρυμμένον is a perfect participle from the extended compound verb ἀποκρύπτω, "conceal."

193. Or "is all things and in all things." Once again it is clear that Christ provides

of 1:13–20 and 2:9. All the fullness of deity houses in the one with whom believers are hidden and brought to light. The glory of this shines out in the rhetoric of 3:11.

The occurrence of φανερόω in Col 3:4 relates intertexturally most directly in the context to its nearest occurrence in 1:25–27, which envisions Paul fulfilling (πληρῶσαι, 1:25) "the word of God," speaking and working on behalf of the formerly hidden mystery "now brought to light" (νῦν δὲ ἐφανερώθη, aorist passive) as "Christ in you, the hope of glory." This now-manifested mystery has a clear view to "every person as mature in Christ" (1:28). The "riches of the glory of this mystery" (τὸ πλοῦτος τῆς δόξης τοῦ μυστηρίου τούτου, 1:27) occur in the present and anticipate, hope for, "glory." The nearest and most striking intertextures outside Colossians are those in 2 Cor 4:7–12 and Eph 5:6–16. The similarity of language in Col 3:4 and 2 Cor 4:10–12 is particularly notable in the aorist subjunctive use of φανερόω (φανερωθῇ, "made visible").[194] The continuous action of making the body of Christ visible (πάντοτε, 2 Cor 4:10; ἀεί, 4:11) suggests the reconfiguration of ideas in the repetitive actions of the hidden Christ and believers being made visible indicated in Col 3:4. The repetitive visibility reaches its zenith in behavioral reality, in the recognition that Christ is all and in all. The more developed intertexture of Eph 5:8–14 extends beyond Colossians in the way it reconfigures the movement from darkness to light (φῶς; see Col 1:12–13) and the exposure of things done in a hidden (κρυφῇ, "secret") manner, so that all things disgraced by the light are *made visible* (Eph 5:13). "For everything that becomes visible is light" (πᾶν γὰρ τὸ φανερούμενον φῶς ἐστιν, 5:14). Christ will shine (ἐπιφαύσει, future)[195] on those who wake to this.

The *past-present-whenever-then* sequencing exudes an impressive *sensory-aesthetic texturing* in the ways it interweaves being raised with Christ, drawing sight lines to the above things, death with Christ, life hidden with "Christ your life," and being made visible with Christ. There is a strong appeal to the body and physicality and to the emotions. Audiences are drawn into the picturing and into participation by quite personal sensibilities.

---

what Rome, Caesar, and the seen and unseen powers cannot: life. The emperor is not "your life."

194. Which the NRSV and NRSVue translate as "made visible." On the connections, see Swart, "Eschatological Vision or Exhortation."

195. From φαῦσις, "light, illumination."

Rhetorical Force as Emergent Discourse

What comes into view in 3:1–4 is a deepened and clearer vision of the new reality. This is the reality of life "raised with Christ," who "is seated on the right side of God" and with whom in their collective life (ἡ ζωὴ ὑμῶν) the believers are "hidden in God."[196] The *past-present-whenever-then* rhetorical sequence becomes visualized all of a piece, together, even though we humans tend to imagine sequencing according to linear time. Life transcending linear time is envisioned.[197] This is a development in Colossians that even the authors may not have grasped in a full way. Believers are raised persons who are hidden with Christ in God, Christ is their life, and whenever in this new reality Christ is shining, even out of hiddenness, they are shining, too.[198] The shining is itself visible in the identifying clothing of the new person, which person "is being continuously renewed in knowledge according to the image of the one who created it" (3:10).[199] In this holistic, shining new reality, the usual kinds of human ethnic, religious, physiological, geographical, and social distinctions and limitations ("where there is not Greek and Jew, circumcised and foreskin, barbarian, Scythian, slave, free") are irrelevant. In the new reality "Christ (is) all (things) and in all (things)" (ἀλλὰ τὰ πάντα καὶ ἐν πᾶσιν Χριστός, 3:11). All is subsumed in Christ.

On this reading, in Col 3:4 future linear time and the parousia, even if in implicit allusion, are at best secondary. The primary and explicit point made by the rhetoric is that in the new reality in Christ believers will shine (φανερωθήσεσθε) in a glorious manner whenever Christ shines (ὅταν ὁ Χριστὸς φανερωθῇ). "Christ all and in all"; "he is before all things, and all things hold together in him" (1:17). Whenever goodness shines forth in the world (e.g., 3:12–17), "above all in love, the bond of maturity" (3:14), then Christ is shining. The "peace of Christ rules"[200] in hearts (3:15).

---

196. Being "hidden" indicated by κέκρυπται, perfect passive, hence they have been and continue to be hidden.

197. On nonlinear time (or time as a field) and its christological implications, see the discussion in Campbell, *Pauline Dogmatics*, 709–11; see also Haught, *God after Einstein*; Haught, *New Cosmic Story*.

198. See Mary Oliver's poem "On Thy Wondrous Works I Will Meditate (Psalm 145)," in *Devotions: The Selected Poems of Mary Oliver* (New York: Penguin, 2017), 134–38, §6.

199. On clothing as identification, see Jeal, "Clothes Make the (Wo)Man."

200. More literally "acts as an umpire" (βραβεύω) in your hearts.

This is what is developed further in Eph 5:6–16, where "Christ will shine [ἐπιφαύσει] on you."

Step Eight: Life in the New Reality (3:5–17)

Rhetography

Now the believers, who have died and been raised with Christ, who are seeking and thinking of "the above things," are "hidden with Christ in God," and anticipate being "made visible" (shining) with Christ, are observed living, actually *being* visible, in the new reality. Virtual Paul speaks to them from prophetic space as a teacher in what is imagined, visualized, and heard to be a logical, hortatory, challenging tone. Lycus Valley Christ believers, now feeling encouraged to ignore the irrelevant pressures placed on them, are listening, their imagined faces and bodies responding to what they hear, perhaps some heads nodding (or shaking), some emotions, anticipation, some worry, and, by now in the rhetorical flow of the letter, deepened understanding of filiated living in Christ.[201] The focus is concentrated on the second-person plural "you" Christ believers, who are presented with wisdom, that is, behavioral information that, given the instruction they have already heard about the pressures they face (2:4–23), will move them to visualize themselves as people raised with Christ who will accept the advice. In the overall imagery there are two imperative movements. The first is "put to death" or "kill" (νεκρώσατε οὖν, 3:5) and the second "put on" or "clothe" (ἐνδύσασθε οὖν, 3:12). Internally there are additional imperatives.

The behaviors to be killed are "the things of the earth" (lit. "the parts on the earth," τὰ μέλη τὰ ἐπὶ τῆς γῆς), earthly, earthy practices that should no longer be considered (as 3:2 urges). Many behaviors practiced in ancient Mediterranean locations such as Colossae were earthy and antithetical to the above things. Mentioning them indicates that they were regularly practiced in Colossae and that Christ believers—or some of them—engaged in them. The visualized action of killing personifies them, treats them as living things that should no longer live. The image of killing is expanded (*enargeia*) with a complex vision of earth behaviors that should be destroyed: fornication (πορνεία), uncleanness (ἀκαθαρσία), passion (πάθος), lust (ἐπιθυμίαν

---

201. See discussion of filiated culture under "Alternative Culture" in the introduction.

κακήν, "evil desire"), and greed, the latter described as idolatry (πλεονεξία ἥτις ἐστὶν εἰδωλολατρία).²⁰² These behaviors are shockingly rhetographic, the pictures making their own argumentation in the way they evoke visualizations of highly sexualized, sensory, self-indulgent activities. While naming them might evoke opposing visions of good behavior, people were well aware that the bad behaviors were commonly practiced.²⁰³ These earth behaviors are envisioned as bringing about the "anger of God" on their practitioners, who appear as "the sons of disobedience,"²⁰⁴ a metaphor picturing persons who live in blatant rebellion against what is good, persons recognizably deserving of God's anger. The disobedience sounds inbred, a familial, hereditary flaw in the symbolic sons.²⁰⁵ The rhetorical implication is that listeners to this language see and agree with the description of behaviors that are "the things of the earth." Driving the ideas home, verse 7 offers a view of the Christ believers' own past, making things personal: "in which *you* also walked [περιεπατήσατέ] *then, when you* were living [ἐζῆτε] in these things." The manner of life *then* contrasts with life in the manner of *glory* (3:4). Killing off the earth behaviors is a good thing. It is as if they are personified, living, leering, greedy, wholly self-interested στοιχεῖα creatures who demand worship and as such must no longer live among the believers.

Playing off structurally and rhetorically from their past ("then," πότε, v. 7), verse 8 shifts the imagery from killing to the present with the imperative "but now put away from yourselves" (νυνὶ δὲ ἀπόθεσθε) what seem to be less salacious and idolatrous but no less disagreeable, divisive behaviors: anger, rage, evil, blasphemy, obscene speech, lying (ὀργήν, θυμόν, κακίαν, βλασφημίαν, αἰσχρολογίαν, 3:8; μὴ ψεύδεσθε, 3:9).²⁰⁶ This putting away is expanded with undressing and dressing imagery.²⁰⁷ The

---

202. For meanings of these terms see textural commentary.

203. On social practices in the Roman Mediterranean see Longenecker, *In Stone and Story*; Harry O. Maier, *New Testament Christianity in the Roman World*, EBS (Oxford: Oxford University Press, 2019).

204. A Hebraic idiom. For textual variant, see n. 215 below. On the usage of the word *comes* (present-tense verb ἔρχεται), see below on textural commentary.

205. The metaphor is more of a rhetorical profanity than a term carrying theological meaning.

206. The then/now shift and the imperative "put off" presumes that believers in Colossae did engage in the bad behaviors.

207. In participles of attendant circumstances, i.e., coordinated with ἀπόθεσθε. The imperative is "put away" with "stripping off of yourselves" and "putting on yourselves" (clothing yourselves).

old person (ἀπεκδυσάμενοι τὸν παλαιὸν ἄνθρωπον) with its earth practices has been stripped off, and the new person (ἐνδυσάμενοι τὸν νέον) of the above domain—whose practices are noted in verses 12–17—has been put on.[208] The change of clothing alters both how people are identified and their actual identity. The new clothing reconfigures what is seen, thereby reshaping what is perceived. The change of clothing also indicates change of intention and change of behavior because humans wear different kinds (or forms or fashions) of clothing for differing purposes, and they are inclined to behave in ways that accord with their clothing. The goodness of undressing and redressing is made clear in the continuous renewal of knowledge, of the development of a reconstituted mind directed toward the one who created it (v. 10).[209] The one who created human minds is, of course, God, who made humans according to his image and likeness (Gen 1:26).

The *killing–putting off–stripping off–putting on* sequence is visualized as a unit, effectively as a single action of a single moment that initiates continuously renewed (present passive) knowledge that accords with the image of creator-God. The key rhetorical notions are change and renewal. In the renewal, earthly distinctions recognizable in the Roman Mediterranean contexts employed to identify, separate, and disempower people are no longer relevant. What people are by ethnic origin (Ἕλλην καὶ Ἰουδαῖος), by natural or altered physiology or identifying mark (περιτομὴ καὶ ἀκροβυστία), by non-Roman geographic ethnicity (βάρβαρος, Σκύθης), or by social status as slave or free person (δοῦλος, ἐλεύθερος) is removed.[210] In stark contrast, all things, all distinctions, all things of the earth domain, are subsumed in Christ: "but Christ all and in all" (ἀλλὰ τὰ πάντα καὶ ἐν πᾶσιν Χριστός, 3:11).[211] Christ is envisioned as the distinctive identifying clothing—the new person who has been put on. Christ is everything to the

---

208. This view of clothing as a person is unique in the New Testament. Translations such as NRSV and NRSVue, which read "the old self" and "the new self," are misleading since they imply that the new clothing is one's own self. **Intertexture** indicates that the clothing in view is Christ himself (Rom 13:14, Gal 3:27; see also Eph 4:24). The aorist middle participles indicate they have already unclothed and reclothed themselves. They are already hidden with Christ in God. See Jeal, "Clothes Make the (Wo)Man."

209. See Jeal, "Starting before the Beginning."

210. For details see textural commentary below.

211. See Dunn, *Epistles to the Colossians and to Philemon*, 225–26. The nominative Χριστός is placed in an emphatic position.

cosmos and to those who trust in him. Constructed differences between people, contra the common social, cultural, religious, and political standards of the day (of any day), are irrelevant. This is a visible inversion of Roman and Mediterranean social and cultural realities, where a hierarchical structure of power and wealth at the top and slaves (as effectively nonpersons) at the bottom was accepted as normal and good.[212]

The second major imperative (3:12) once again envisions people putting on clothing (ἐνδύσασθε οὖν, 3:12), but now not clothing that is a person but the clothing of good behaviors of the above realm. Evil, disobedient practices have been killed and put away and are now seen being replaced by the kinds of worthy, fruitful, and growing good works already envisioned in the letter at 1:10. Those clothing themselves are beautifully presented as chosen, holy, and beloved persons, in other words, now fully alive, having been raised with Christ. Garment items are listed: viscera of compassion (σπλάγχνα οἰκτιρμοῦ); kindness (χρηστότητα); humility (ταπεινοφροσύνην); gentleness (πραΰτητα); patience (μακροθυμίαν); putting up with and forgiving one another (ἀνεχόμενοι ἀλλήλων καὶ χαριζόμενοι ἑαυτοῖς); if someone has a complaint against another, forgive the offense; just as the Lord forgave you, so you should forgive.[213] The overgarment, thus the most immediately visible and identifying, indeed the most important, clothing to be put on is love (ἐπὶ πᾶσιν δὲ τούτοις τὴν ἀγάπην, 3:14). As the outer garment, love covers and holds the other items together, metaphorically the "bond of maturity" (σύνδεσμος, "fastening, connector, binder"; τελειότης, "maturity"). The Jesus-followers are directed, in two first-person imperatives, to allow "the peace of Christ" to be the "judge," or, better, the "umpire" or "arbitrator" (βραβευέτω, third-person imperative) in their hearts and to allow the word of Christ to house in them (ἐνοικείτω, third-person imperative) richly. The regularly arbitrated peace will support the one body of believers. In this one-body context they should be thankful (3:16). In the context of allowing the word of Christ to house in them, they should practice wisdom audibly, even musically, using words in the forms of teaching, admonition, and singing. In what might seem like an additional feature of the outer garment, they should "do all things" in the name of Lord Jesus,

---

212. See the discussion in Jeal, *Exploring Philemon*, 138–52, 157–63; Longenecker, *In Stone and Story*, 183–97.

213. The wording here is awkward, more directly literally "if anyone has against someone a complaint, just as the Lord forgave you, so also [should] you."

through him giving thanks to Father God (3:17). Doing all in the name of Jesus is one way in which the peace of Christ arbitrates.

The imagery cast on our imaginations moves us to think that the Lycus Valley Christ believers took this rhetoric seriously, that they did kill off and put away bad behaviors and put on good ones. In all this they recognize Christ all and in all, that the distinctions they live with in their locations are not any longer relevant, their own desires and self-interests are rejected in favor of the good of others. Above all love. Allow the peace of Christ to umpire and the word of Christ to house. In a striking image, they are themselves the house in which Christ dwells.

From prophetic space this step proclaims wisdom to be practiced. Once again, things are different in the new reality. Humans have been raised with Christ, are hidden with Christ in God, and are to be made visible with Christ. They should therefore kill off evil and deleterious practices, clothe themselves with the new person, demonstrate genuine love and care for people, and above all clothe themselves with love. This is blended prophetic, wisdom, and apocalyptic discourse that envisions the household social reality in Christ in which believers exist. In this new reality we observe them singing and giving thanks to Father God (3:16–17).

Translation

> **3:5** Therefore put to death the things (members)[214] of the earth: fornication, uncleanness, passion, lust, and greed which is idolatry, **3:6** because of which the anger of God comes on the sons of disobedience,[215] **3:7** in which you also walked then, when you were living in these things.[216] **3:8** But now also put away from yourselves all (these) things: anger, rage, evil, blasphemy [slander], obscene speech out of your mouth. **3:9** Do not lie to one another, having stripped off of yourselves the old person with its practices **3:10** and having put on yourselves the new person which is being renewed in knowledge according to the image of the one who created it, **3:11** where there is no longer Greek and Jew, circumcised and foreskin, barbarian, Scythian, slave, freeperson, but Christ (is) all and in all.

---

214. Some manuscripts read μέλη ὑμῶν, "your things."
215. Some manuscripts omit ἐπὶ τοὺς υἱοὺς τῆς ἀπειθείας.
216. Some manuscripts read αὐτοῖς rather than τούτοις.

3:12 Put on, therefore, as God's chosen, holy, and beloved ones, viscera of compassion, kindness, humility, gentleness, patience, **3:13** enduring with one another and forgiving each other; if someone has a complaint[217] against another, just as also the Lord[218] forgave you, so also you (should forgive). **3:14** But above all these (put on) love, which[219] is the bond of maturity. **3:15** And let the peace of Christ umpire in your hearts, in which also you were called in one body; and be thankful. **3:16** Let the word of Christ[220] house in you richly, in all wisdom teaching and admonishing each other, singing psalms, hymns, spiritual songs in gratitude in your hearts[221] to God;[222] **3:17** and all that you might do in word or in work, (do) all in (the) name of Lord Jesus,[223] giving thanks to Father God[224] through him.

Textural Commentary

Argumentative texture. Argumentation in this step functions overall on the opposing metaphorical movements of killing (i.e., doing away with) and dressing (i.e., putting on).

Case: audience members are directed (perhaps "admonished" or "put in mind," νουθετέω, as 3:16 suggests), to kill behaviors of the earth domain that people practice. The listeners can look back to their own past and recall that formerly they walked in, lived in, the indulgent, disordered, and deleterious behaviors. They must put away well-known divisive power-emotions and language. Implicitly but still clearly, they are to recognize that Roman imperial, sociocultural, and political power has been defeated and made irrelevant by Christ. They must clothe themselves with all manner of good and unifying actions, some of which (e.g., "put-

---

217. Some manuscripts read μέμψιν (μέμψις), "reason for complaint."
218. Some manuscripts read Χριστός.
219. Some manuscripts read ὅς or ἥτις rather than ὅ.
220. Some manuscripts have θεοῦ.
221. Some manuscripts have the singular τῇ καρδίᾳ.
222. Some manuscripts have τῷ κυρίῳ, "to the Lord."
223. Some manuscripts read Ἰησοῦ Χριστοῦ.
224. Some manuscripts read θεῷ καὶ πατρὶ.

ting up with and forgiving one another") could be tedious and exhausting. Above all, they must put on love. The case presented envisions a caring morality. The peace of Christ is to be the arbitrating force among believers as they live in the body of Christ, into which they were called. The word of Christ houses itself in them in wisdom. All is to be done devotedly in the name of Lord Jesus. They must respond to all these things in thanksgiving to Father God.

Rationale: Reasoning is based on the new reality—on the presented facts—that the believers have been raised with and are therefore alive with Christ. They now think about the above things. The transferal to the new reality mentioned earlier in the letter has been accomplished. Pressures to conform to powers and authorities and to complaints raised have been reduced to irrelevance. Things are different now. Their former way of life (ποτέ) is not what it is now (νυνί). Believers wear new clothing (a person) that identifies them in a new way. In fact, the cosmos is not the same. Human believers have been made full (2:9–10) in the preeminent Son-Christ, who is himself the image of the unseen God (1:15) and through whom all things on the earth and in the heavens have been reconciled (1:20). This same Son-Christ is securely seated at God's right hand, and life is hidden with him in God (3:1–2). This is to say that a fundamental, foundational difference has occurred. All powers, oppressions, and distinctions have been replaced by the kingdom of God's Son. The goodness of the Son-Christ, who is "all and in all," has arrived. All this argues that in the new reality selfish, divisive, and morally dangerous behaviors must be discarded, and caring, forgiving, loving, and Christ-centered (3:15–16) characteristics taken on. All this is what chosen, holy, beloved (rather than enslaved) persons should do. In this completely secure reality—which is understood by faith—people must live with the understanding that Christ is all and in all.

Anticipated Result: Christ and Christ followers will be made visible behaviorally and faithfully in their Lycus Valley contexts. They will get along well together, live peaceably, endure one another's failings, being bound together by love. They will live wisdom lives where they teach and admonish one another, singing in their hearts to God. Shining gloriously.

Inner textures. Here there are textures of bad and good behaviors. The blended prophetic-wisdom discourse of this step, beginning with the striking rhetoric of the imperative verb νεκρώσατε, "kill," used only here in the Bible,[225] makes completely clear that the sexual practices of the *repetitively* mentioned "earth" (1:16, 20; 3:2, 5) are not to be practiced, certainly not by believers. The sexual topoi are equally striking. The occurrence of the word μέλος, properly understood as limb or member of a physical body, signals that sexual bodily practices are in mind.[226] Fornication (πορνεία) is a broad term referring to sexual immorality including intercourse with prostitutes, but here, given that Colossians stands within the Pauline letter tradition aimed at Christ believers and the focus on wives and husbands in the following household code (3:18–19), the term indicates extramarital sexual relations.[227] The second term, "uncleanness" or "impurity" (ἀκαθαρσία), refers to immoral sexual activity. There are a number of **intertextures** in the Pauline corpus that indicate this sexualized meaning, connecting it with πορνεία (2 Cor 12:21; Gal 5:19; Eph 4:19; 1 Thess 4:3, 7; see Rom 1:24, 6:19).[228] The third term, "passion" (πάθος), points to emotions, here sexual emotions, that have gotten out of control. The three uses of the word in the New Testament place it in relation to sexual desire (Rom 1:26, Col 3:5, 1 Thess 4:5). "Evil desire" (ἐπιθυμίαν κακήν) is "lust," strongly emphasized by the adjective. Like the preceding "passion," this idea alludes to wicked sexual yearnings that should not be imagined or fulfilled. The final term in the list is "greed" or "covetousness," defined as "idolatry" (πλεονεξία ἥτις ἐστὶν εἰδωλολατρία). Greed is the urge and desire to obtain more than what is needed, deserved, or rightful, even if acquiring more and more is seen as an indicator of success.[229] It is desiring and aiming to acquire too much,

---

225. Forms of the cognate noun νεκρός, "death," occur in Col 1:18, 2:12–13. See Rom 8:13, "kill the practices of the body," where the imperative for "kill" is θανατοῦτε.

226. Andrew T. Lincoln, "The Household Code and Wisdom Mode of Colossians," *JSNT* 74 (1999): 107.

227. See Sumney, *Colossians*, 189.

228. There were lists of vices and virtues available in the ancient Mediterranean. See Abraham J. Malherbe, *Moral Exhortation: A Greco-Roman Sourcebook*, LEC 4 (Philadelphia: Westminster, 1986), especially 138–41. See also Talbert, *Ephesians and Colossians*, 227. But Col 3:5–17 is not merely copying in a list of things to avoid or practice. The rhetoric works on the foundation of the new reality where believers have been raised with Christ, as hidden in him, and display the life of glory.

229. Achieving success was a major social goal in the ancient Mediterranean (see

when what is desired—or when persons are sexually desired or when sex itself is desired—is only for one's own gratification (see Exod 20:17).[230] It is selfish, idolatrous, and obsessive because the things desired become gods, that is, things prioritized above Father God and his Son as objects to be used solely for personal indulgence.[231] It is dehumanizing. The Pauline intertextures help make this clear (Rom 1:29, Eph 4:19, 5:3, 1 Thess 2:5). Sexual intercourse is presented in the New Testament as appropriate to and properly limited to marriage. The sexual activities mentioned in this step envision practices outside that relationship. People who are seeking the above things must kill them off. They carry the earthy odor of being out of control, chaotic, not of the sacred space of the above things where Christ is seated.

The chaotic sexualized space draws the anger of God (v. 6). The anger of God is not presented as a reason for rejecting the practices but is what the chaotic, out-of-control living brings about. Still, the rhetoric is threatening in the implication that the behaviors should be killed to avoid anger. This texture of God's anger and judgment does not here envision the parousia or final judgment, but some **intertextures** clearly tie them to exclusion from the kingdom of God (e.g., 1 Cor 6:9–10, Gal 5:19–21, Eph 5:3–5). The present-tense verb "comes" (ἔρχεται) indicates that the anger is coming in the present, presumably in the range of effects the chaotic practices bring about in people's lives. God's wrath here and elsewhere is not about a vindictive wish to punish or cause pain but about justice. The connected phrase "on the sons of disobedience" is questioned textually but may well be original.[232] The terminology "the sons of" is a frequent **intertexture** in Hebrew literature, for example in the Old Testament, "sons of the prophets" (2 Kgs 2:3, 5, 7, 15; see Amos 7:14), "sons of men/man" (Ps 145:12; Prov 8:4; Eccl 2:3, 8; 3:10), "sons of the stranger" and "sons of the

---

especially Longenecker, *In Stone and Story*, 52–65). Greed as an idol leading to success reminds of the adage "Wealth might be a curse, not a blessing" (see Jas 5:1–6).

230. See Lincoln, "Colossians," 642.

231. More on all of these terms can be found in the literature.

232. Hebraic idiom. Belonging to the group or category of disobedient persons. Textual variant: P[46] and B (Codex Vaticanus) do not have "on the sons of disobedience." The words occur in Eph 2:2, 5:6 (see also Heb 3:18, 11:31); some think they have been assimilated here. However, the plural ἐν οἷς καὶ ὑμεῖς in 3:7 seems to have it as antecedent, suggesting it is genuine. See Barth and Blanke, *Colossians*, 405; Dunn, *Epistles to the Colossians and to Philemon*, 210 n. 4; Sumney, *Colossians*, 192–93.

SCENE THREE: DON'T BE DECEIVED. LIVE THE NEW REALITY   223

alien" (Isa 56:6, 61:5), and "sons of the living God" (Hos 1:10).²³³ The New Testament employs the terms "sons of thunder" (Βοανηργές, from Hebrew בְּנֵי רֶגֶשׁ, Mark 3:17) and "sons of disobedience" (Eph 2:2) with exactly the same wording in Eph 5:6. The pointed "sons of" nuancing of Col 3:6 has the *sensory* effect of moving people to see practitioners of the behaviors in a particularly dark, shadow-like space that is not part of the raised life envisioned.

Many interpreters describe the then/when (ποτε/ὅτε) clauses of verse 7 as chiastic rhetoric that works by means of the second clause reversing the movement²³⁴ of the first:

ἐν οἷς καὶ ὑμεῖς περιεπατήσατέ
ποτε,
ὅτε
ἐζῆτε ἐν τούτοις·

The *sensory-aesthetic* rhetoric turns on the intersection of ποτε and ὅτε, making the former walk synonymous with the former life. The point could have been made using just one of the verbal ideas. The nice turn of phrasing is, however, more and different from chiastic.²³⁵ It is a repetitive and melodic expansion. Repetitive sound features are clear in homoeoteleuton—the highly *sensory* -τε word endings in περιεπατήσατέ, ποτε, ὅτε, and ἐζῆτε and the pleasing repetition of sounds and ideas that impress readers and listeners with the contrast of the actions of the former life with present reality of life hidden with Christ in God. While the first clause employs an aorist verb ("you walked"), the second nuances and enhances the idea with an imperfect verb ("you were living"). **Intertexturally**, the metaphor of walking to describe living is a common motif in the Pauline letters (e.g., Rom 6:4; 13:13; 2 Cor 5:7; Gal 5:16; Eph 2:2, 10; 5:2; see Mic 2:3; 4:2, 5), configured here explicitly with the verb "live" (ζάω).

---

233. Examples can be found in Georg Fohrer, "υἱός," *TDNT* 8:345–48; see also Eduard Lohse, "υἱός," *TDNT* 8:358–59.

234. There is no reversal here, only an expansion of what occurred "then."

235. In fact chiasmus is not mentioned in the ancient handbooks of rhetoric. Many claims of chiasmus (criss-cross structure) in New Testament texts seem to me unconvincing. The nearest rhetorical figure in the handbooks is *antimetabolē* (*commutatio*), where ideas are transposed by reciprocal but contrary notions using the same word stems (Rhet. Her. 4.28). See Jeal, *Exploring Philemon*, 74 with n. 21.

Rhetorical force. The rhetoric of 3:5–7 makes clear that the recipients of the letter had practiced and some still do practice the sexual sins that are described. Given what we know about life in cities in the empire, it is likely that some attended brothels, and certainly people were familiar with the ideas and nuancing.[236] They are graphically and dramatically directed to kill them. People can make choices about the behaviors.[237] The force of the rhetoric could not be missed.

The texture of verses 8–9 moves away from the then/when former practices of the recipients lives to the present ("but now," νυνὶ δὲ), led less strikingly but clearly enough by the imperative "put away from yourselves" (ἀπόθεσθε) the intensely emotional and more visible and audible anger, rage, evil, slander, obscene speech, and lying.[238] Each of these behaviors, while different in nature from the sexualized practices of verse 6, is connected in how they are chaotic, disordered, self-indulgent, and demonstrate loss of control. They are deeply *sensory* in the ways that all of them have emotional and physical/physiological effects and implications. Readers and listeners to the verses can experience *virtually* the rising blood pressure, the flushed, heated faces, the frenetic body movements that indicate rage and punctuate slanderous words. They recognize virtually the expressions of obscenities and the subtle, intentionally deceptive speech of lies. "Anger" (ὀργή) and "rage" (θυμός) are close to each other in meaning, forming a hendiadys (without the conjunction *and*), though the notion of rage is more intense, perhaps more sudden or reactive in nature, an outburst.[239] The human anger and rage in view here is not the anger of the justice of God observed in 3:6. The word "evil" (κακία) means malicious wickedness. It aims to harm people and things; it is destructive. "Slander," often given in the untranslated form "blasphemy" (βλασφημία), is an arrogant, haughty use of language. Slander aims to set oneself above others, to assume superiority while simultaneously making others inferior. It echoes the old attempt to set self above God, the arrogance to become God. The term βλασφημία occurs vividly and repetitively in Revelation,

---

236. Longenecker, *In Stone and Story*, 185–87, 202–7.

237. In other words, people do not have to engage in sexual intercourse in the improper ways. They can choose not to follow up on their thoughts, inclinations, or urges.

238. The "zone of self-expressive speech" (Robbins, *Exploring the Textures of Texts*, 31).

239. See Sumney, *Colossians*, 196, and the intertextural references there.

SCENE THREE: DON'T BE DECEIVED. LIVE THE NEW REALITY   225

where the first beast shouts slanderous words against God (Rev 13:1, 5–6; see 17:3). Christ believers must put away shameful, base, disgraceful, "obscene speech" (αἰσχρολογία).[240] This kind of talk denigrates, reducing things to a dirty level. Believers may not lie to one another (μὴ ψεύδεσθε εἰς ἀλλήλους). Life and language among believers and in the world are to be honest. Lying is an attempt at coverup and manipulation. The rhetoric of these emotional speech descriptions reminds believers and emphasizes to them that there is no goodness, no edification in these behaviors. They are always destructive, divisive, and denigrating.

Now in Col 3:9–10 emerges the "having stripped off and put on" clothing topos. Unlike the preceding imperative verbs, middle-voice participles are employed not to command but to emphasize what has already happened: the Lycus believers have stripped off of themselves the old person and its practices (ἀπεκδυσάμενοι τὸν παλαιὸν ἄνθρωπον σὺν ταῖς πράξεσιν αὐτοῦ) and have put the new person on themselves (ἐνδυσάμενοι τὸν νέον).[241] They must live up to, hold on to, this picture of what occurred. This language and idea follow up on the *sensory-aesthetic* nature of putting away from themselves the emotionally charged behaviors. The clothing in this case is counterintuitively a person (ἄνθρωπος; see Rom 13:14, Gal 3:27, Eph 4:22–24).[242] Clothing protects bodies, but it also identifies them, makes wearers and their activities recognizable. Differing forms and styles of clothing are appropriate to differing activities. So dressing, undressing, and redressing have rhetorical connotations that indicate many things about them.[243] In other words, people are shaped and reshaped by the rhetoric of clothing. Putting on the new person as clothing indicates that things are different now, that there is a refashioned body with new roles to fulfill. The redressed body displays the new reality. Clothing is a very bodily thing, so is very highly sensory, felt on the body, and aesthetic, displayed on the body. It represents purposeful,

---

240. A *hapax legomenon* in the New Testament. This compound word is based on αἰσχρός, "shameful, disgraceful, abusive, ugly."

241. There is no explicit indication that this rhetoric refers to baptism. Undressing and redressing was not associated with baptism until the second century.

242. Not a new "self," as in NRSV (and others), or "nature," as RSV. In these texts the new person is Christ, not the believers. For a full treatment of these passages see Jeal, "Clothes Make the (Wo)Man," 394–414.

243. Such as work, profession, activity, social status, location, cultural connections, gender, age, mood.

embodied, self-conscious action.[244] Clothing brings about an altered way of thinking, a changed mind oriented toward the new situation. A change of clothing indicates a changed condition, a changed activity, a transformation. Changed clothing *creates*.

Redressing here parallels the killing of 3:5. The stripping repeats and continues the texturing already seen in 2:11, 15 and anticipates the "put on" imagery of 3:12, 14. Its bodily function reflects the *repetitive texturing* of "body," observed in 1:18, 22, 24; 2:11, 17, 19, 23. The old clothing is replaced by redressing with caring, unifying actions toward people (above all love by the time the rhetoric progresses to 3:14). People identify with the form of clothing they wear. New clothing indicates and demonstrates a new reality. You should not practice behaviors that do not accord with the reclothed form or fashion of clothing with which you present yourself.

A more developed **intertexture** with 3:5–10 is the exhortation in Eph 4:29–5:5, where the use of unedifying language and disordered sexuality is rhetoricized and contextualized with the directive not to "grieve the Holy Spirit," in whom believers were "sealed" (4:30), and with walking in love as did Christ, who offered himself to God as a sacrifice on our behalf (5:2).[245] The chaotic, disordered walk of life is out of step (see Gal 5:16–26) with the leading of the Holy Spirit, and it does not correspond to Christ's sacrificial, outward-moving love.

The practice and effects of the earthy, chaotic, selfish, and self-indulgent behaviors of the old, unraised person are completely deconstructed by the **ideological, social, historical, and sensory-aesthetic textures** woven into the language of Col 3:11. The rhetoric of killing the sexualized practices of the former life (walk), putting away chaotic and divisive language, and creating a changed appearance and identity by removing the clothing of the old person and reclothing with the new comes to a focused, even climactic high point in the lived household space. This is a space where (ὅπου) ethnic, religious, physiological (and physiognomic), geographical, and social differences are not (i.e., no longer) relevant and may not be permitted to cause or allow for mistreatment and division. The quite emphatic "where there is no" (ὅπου οὐκ ἔνι) insists that in the new reality these differences must not be allowed to separate people. Believers

---

244. The "zone of purposeful action" (see Robbins, *Exploring the Textures of Texts*, 31).

245. Literally "handed himself over as an aromatic fragrance." The word "grieve" in Greek is λυπέω, "give pain, distress, grieve, irritate, insult."

with renewed knowledge in their new clothing (3:10) must recognize they now inhabit space

> where there is no
> Greek and Jew,
> circumcision and foreskin,
> barbarian, Scythian,
> slave, free,
> but Christ all and in all.

Social and historical textures dominate here as they have in many ways from the outset of the letter. It is Christ who has been raised and who sits at God's right hand, not Caesar. It is Christ who is to be made visible, not Caesar. Believers are reminded that they have been raised with Christ and been hidden with him—again not with Caesar. It is the kingdom of God's Son into which believers have been transferred, we recall from 1:13, not Caesar's empire. So it is not the dominating Roman imperial personages and powers familiar to Lycus Valley residents with all their social and economic (οἰκονομία, "household management"; see 1:25)[246] demands (and benefits) that in overt and subtle ways support the self-indulgent "things on the earth" rather than "the above things." The Lycus Jesus-followers would readily recognize these political allusions. The superiority, domination, and expansionism that Rome considered it rightfully imposed was made irrelevant—despite the pressures it exerted on people, including the believers.[247] What was important to Rome was territorial expansion and the conformity of dominated people for the sake of imperial power. Colossians 3:11 is, in its own only slightly subtle way, pointing out to audiences under Roman imperial influence that the power over all people from all social levels and locations is "Christ all and in all." Life in the kingdom of the Son and the οἰκονομία of God transcends the structures and expectations believers face in their social lives in the Lycus.

The no longer relevant Roman-style ethnic-social-political-geographical distinctions are displayed in the series of antithetical bina-

---

246. Recall that in Col 1:25, God's οἰκονομία is explicit.
247. See especially Harry O. Maier, "A Sly Civility: Colossians and Empire," *JSNT* 27 (2005): 323–49; Maier, "Barbarians, Scythians and Imperial Iconography," 385–406; Maier, *Picturing Paul in Empire*, 63–102; Maier, "Colossians, Ephesians and Empire," 185–202.

ries. The antithetical rhetoric (antithesis, Rhet. Her. 4.15.21) is led and shaped by the "where there is no" dependent clause, which makes the contrast with the practices that have been put away and moves forward with the presentation of the reclothed persons who are "being renewed in knowledge according to the image" of the creator. Reclothing and the removal of the behaviors of the former walk now mean that the distinctions, imagined as negative stereotypes of people—implicitly the Christ believers, but certainly all persons, even distant Scythians—do not now limit people according to the categories listed (and, we may assume, any like negative categories or features). So it is not only the chaos and division caused by the various evil behaviors that are to be killed and put away, according to 3:5–10; it is also the social and religious chaos and division generated by being Greek (= gentile) or Jew, circumcised or having a foreskin (both terms may have been pejoratives; see Acts 11:3, Eph 2:11), by being distant and uncivilized barbarians or Scythians,[248] by being a slave or a free person. The binaries are oppositional in the sense that they illustrate the social, cultural, and economic-political prejudices and inequities of the earth realm where Rome dominated against the way things are in the new reality of the raised Christ-king and the above realm.

The final line of verse 11 presses the oppositional point home: "but Christ all and in all." There is no brutal, dominating force like Caesar and Rome in the body of Christ. This language presents the climax to the *progressions* that have gone before: all things are held together in the Son (1:17); reconciliation has been accomplished in his body through death (1:22); in Christ are all the treasures of wisdom and knowledge (2:3); in Christ houses all the fullness of deity bodily, people are made full in him and (2:9–10); Christ triumphs the powers and authorities (2:8–15); believers are raised with Christ, and with him they shine (3:1–4); and Christ all and in all (3:11).

---

248. On the terms related to circumcision, see Markus Barth, *Ephesians*, AB 34 (Garden City: Doubleday, 1974), 1:254–55, with notes there. The term *Scythian* has generated much debate. Both barbarians and Scythians were imagined as far distant "vanquished peoples pacified by imperial rule." Scythians lived on the edge of the empire, far away from the supposed civilized conformity of the empire, where they were thought to live in "absolute moral turpitude and indecency" (Maier, "Colossians, Ephesians, and Empire," 195; see also Maier, "Barbarians, Scythians and Imperial Iconography," 391–95; Maier, *Picturing Paul in Empire*, 92).

The set of binaries is adequate in itself to convey the idea, without extending the list. Many interpreters quickly observe (and as quickly pass over), however, that the pairs, unlike Gal 3:28, do not include "male and female."[249] Why does the developed, egalitarian rhetoric of Colossians not include the male-female binary? The basic answer to this question is that we do not know, and the text says only what it says. There may be no satisfying answer to the question. We cannot know the mind of the authors from our modern distance; it is their letter, not ours. Of the three Pauline passages that have similar description (1 Cor 12:13, Gal 3:28, Col 3:11; see Rom 10:12), only Gal 3:28 uses the male-female word pair ("there is no male or female"). It seems unlikely that male-female is not included because it was considered less important than, say, Greek-Jew, particularly given that the household wisdom presented beginning in the next step opens with a word to women (3:18). It may be that the gendered binary is not included because it is of a different kind, not imagined by the authors to have the geopolitical contextualization of those listed.[250] Certainly there is an overall political ideology in sight, not a gender ideology, as political and global as gender issues are seen by modern readers. Interpreters regularly point out that the first two pairs join terms with the conjunction καί, while the second two binaries do not. Consideration of *sensory-aesthetic texture* suggests a possible resolution. The rhetorical figure asyndeton, the omission of conjunctions, has the aesthetic effect of increasing the sense of speed of wording and intensifying the sense of emotion.[251] Omitting conjunctions "stimulates dramatic delivery" (Demetrius, *Eloc.* 192–195).[252] As the pace quickens, the emotional force of the language increases to drive the point home (Longinus, *Subl.* 19–21).[253] This effect is observed in Col 3:11:

---

249. For general discussion, see Foster, *Colossians*, 337–43.

250. On Roman geopolitical contextualization, see Maier, "Colossians, Ephesians, and Empire," 195.

251. On asyndeton, see David E. Aune, *The Westminster Dictionary of New Testament and Early Christian Literature and Rhetoric* (Louisville: Westminster John Knox, 2003), 66–67, with examples there. See also Jonathan Thiessen, "The Sublime and Subliminal in Romans 2–3," in Jeal, *Exploring Sublime Rhetoric*.

252. Interestingly, the Greek word for "connecting particle" or "conjunction" is σύνδεσμος, "bond, fastener, chain," which appears at Col 2:19, 3:14, Eph 4:3.

253. Asyndeton occurs in a number of vice and virtue lists in the New Testament, e.g., in the Pauline letters at Rom 1:29–31, 1 Cor 3:12, 7:27, 14:24, 15:1–2.

ὅπου οὐκ ἔνι
Ἕλλην καὶ Ἰουδαῖος,
περιτομὴ καὶ ἀκροβυστία,
βάρβαρος, Σκύθης
δοῦλος, ἐλεύθερος,
ἀλλὰ [τὰ] πάντα καὶ ἐν πᾶσιν Χριστός.

The rhetorical pace increases, intensifying the geopolitical drama toward the climactic ἀλλὰ [τὰ] πάντα καὶ ἐν πᾶσιν Χριστός. The rhetorically *disconnected* flow of nouns in the third and fourth pairs quickly draws readers and listeners along again to consciousness that Christ, not Caesar and imperial force, is the sustainer of all things. This effect is enhanced by the absence of verbs, which invites listeners to imagine vocalizing, "here or there, this or that, it doesn't matter." In other words, sometimes saying less implies more.[254]

This verse reveals and establishes an **ideological texture**, a reshaped worldview where the common and virtually universal distinctions among people living in the Roman world are not relevant ways of viewing them. The distinctions must not be thought of as barriers to fellowship and participation. In the body-household of Christ, people may not set themselves higher than their neighbors. The distinctions continue to exist, of course, because there were Greeks and Jews, some were circumcised and some were not, some people were from distant lands, and many persons were slaves, some freed. But ideologically and contextually there must be no barriers to the reconciliation (ἀποκαταλλάσσω) that has been in view from 1:19–22. What the Son-Christ has done, in what amounts to a moment of time in death, resurrection, and exaltation to Father God's right hand, has affected all things. The cosmos is a different place. This all-encompassing ideology of reconciliation and Christ all and in all generates the rhetoric of holding things together that functions in Colossians. It is the ideology of the new reality. An **intertextural** way of saying this is found in the language of 2 Cor 5:16–17, "From now on, therefore, we regard no one according to the flesh ... so if someone is in Christ there is new creation.

---

254. Some, e.g., Douglas A. Campbell (followed by Talbert, *Ephesians and Colossians*, 229) suggest that 3:11 forms an elaborate chiasm based on the view that *Scythian* is to be understood as "slave," with the chiastic structure Greek–Jew–slave–free. See Campbell, "Unravelling Colossians 3:11b," *NTS* 42 (1996): 120–32. This seems unlikely, given my analysis here. See comments on chiasmus and 3:7, above.

The old has passed away. Look! The new has come to be!"²⁵⁵ There is, must be, in the body-household of Christ, freedom from geopolitical-social divisive boundaries, prejudices, practices, and ideologies.

The second major imperative section, which begins at 3:12, brings resolution to the climax of 3:11.²⁵⁶ The exclusive vision of "Christ all and in all" leads here to completion of the *argumentative texture* employing the clothing imagery through to verse 14. The believers, having killed and removed the practices and ideology displayed by the clothing of the old person, and having reclothed themselves with the new person, must "put on" (ἐνδύσασθε), reclothe themselves, with all manner of good and unifying behaviors that display the change and that function to hold the body-household-*ekklēsia* together. Clothing themselves in this way displays maturity (τελειότης, 3:14), an overarching goal of the entire letter. In parallel lines, verses 15–16 shift the argument from clothing texture to first-person imperatives (βραβευέτω, "let the peace of Christ be the *umpire* in your hearts,"²⁵⁷ and ἐνοικείτω, "let the word of Christ *house* in you richly") that call for the peace and word of Christ to be internalized, which things become characterized in an embedded caring and vocalized morality. The peace of Christ is the arbitrating power among believers. The word of Christ houses itself in them in wisdom.²⁵⁸ So the climactic "Christ all and in all" resolves into a **cultural texture** that strongly contrasts with the self-indulgent, personalized, and divisive practices people regularly observed. In the **ideology** of the new reality, Christ is the umpire, and the word of Christ houses in people. Life practices are directed outward toward the good of others, and they shine in worship and thanksgiving. It would by now seem natural for Lycus Valley audiences reading or listening to the letter to recognize that it is Christ who guides this alternative culture in the midst of the dominating culture that calls for conformity to power and idolatrous greed.

Sensory-aesthetic texture dominates 3:12–17, with features that relate to minds and bodies. The Christ believers are to imagine themselves as "God's chosen, holy, and beloved ones" (ὡς ἐκλεκτοὶ τοῦ θεοῦ ἅγιοι καὶ

---

255. My translation. For sociorhetorical interpretation of these verses, see Oropeza, *Exploring Second Corinthians*, 357–71.
256. See above on rhetography.
257. βραβεύς, "one who ensures the rules of a competition are enforced."
258. The same dative form of wisdom, σοφίᾳ, occurs in 1:9, 28; 3:16; 4:5.

ἠγαπημένοι, v. 12).²⁵⁹ This description blends with the sensory features to form a **sacred texture** because the nominative forms and the participle name them as such by God's action. As such persons in Christ, they are to practice behaviors that directly affect and employ overlapping body zones of emotion, action, and speech:²⁶⁰

> **Emotion:** *Viscera* of compassion (σπλάγχνα οἰκτιρμοῦ, v. 12); kindness (χρηστότητα, "friendliness"); humility (ταπεινοφροσύνην); gentleness (πραΰτητα, "courtesy"); patience (μακροθυμίαν, "long-suffering, steadfastness, toleration, endurance"); enduring one another ἀνεχόμενοι ἀλλήλων, "putting up with"); forgiveness (χαριζόμενοι, "giving freely"); the peace of Christ; the word of Christ; hearts (καρδίαις, v. 15, repeated in v. 16).²⁶¹
> **Speech:** Teaching (διδάσκοντες); admonishing (νουθετοῦντες, putting in mind); singing (ᾄδοντες).
> **Action:** All of the emotional senses become enacted bodily: "Do all that you may do in word or in work in the name of Christ Jesus; giving thanks to Father God through him" (v. 17).

Above all these, people in the new reality must put on love (ἀγάπη, v. 14), the epitome of good behaviors. Love is the bond or fastener of maturity.

---

259. The three words *chosen, holy,* and *beloved* are used together only here in the New Testament. To be chosen (elect) is **historical intertexture** with the HB notion of Israel as the chosen people of God. "Beloved," ἠγαπημένοι, is a perfect passive participle indicating that believers have been and continue to be loved by God ("the ones being loved by God"). The participle is used only here and in 1 Thess 1:4 and 2 Thess 2:13; elsewhere ἀγαπητός appears, as in Col 1:7; 4:7, 9, 14.

260. See the descriptions of taxonomies of body zones in Robbins, *Exploring the Textures of Texts*, 30–31.

261. σπλάγχνα is often translated into English as "heart" but actually means intestines, bowels, guts. Compassion (οἰκτιρμός) is to be felt "in your guts" (see *TLNT* 3:273–75). In the ancient Mediterranean ταπεινοφροσύνην was imagined to be weakness, abasement, hence an undesirable quality. See Walter Grundmann, "ταπεινοφροσύνη," *TDNT* 8:1–6. Paul seems to have coined the word ταπεινοφροσύνη. See Eve-Marie Becker, *Paul on Humility*, trans. Wayne Coppins, BMSSEC (Waco, TX: Baylor University Press, 2020). Paul came to recognize that humans, Christ believers, have much about which to be humble. They are in fact weak, unable to save themselves. The compound word μακροθυμίαν (μακρός + θυμός) may have a distant etymological connection with the notion of withholding rage, i.e., a boiling, smoking wind/spirit, for a long time.

While in the section above on rhetography love was envisioned as an overgarment holding the new clothing together, the word σύνδεσμος might suggest that it is a belt for holding things together.[262]

Engaging in these highly sensory emotions and behaviors easily makes for much stress and takes much time, but they are presented as the way forward in contrast to the behaviors of the old walk. To all this thinking, emotion, and action the believers are called in one body (εἰς ἣν καὶ ἐκλήθητε ἐν ἑνὶ σώματι). This is, in the context of the letter, the body of Christ-*ekklēsia* (1:18, 22, 24; 2:17, 19). This is **sacred texture**: God called them into this body where they do good things for one another in the name of the Lord Jesus, where they sing in their hearts to God[263] and give thanks for it all. It is, in stark contrast to the way of life epitomized by Roman imperialism, the way of life in the Son's kingdom. This is the caring morality of the *ekklēsia*.

Rhetorical Force as Emergent Discourse: Holding Things Together

The reason for behaving in ordered and productive ways is that it is the right thing to do. While it is true that the disordered, disobedient life draws the anger of God (3:6), the fear of judgment is not what motivates people to kill bad behaviors and put them away from themselves. It is, rather, now right to do these things because the believers have been raised with Christ, are hidden with him in God, and seek and think about the above things. It is for them now to live visibly—to shine in a glorious manner—as the caring body of Christ-*ekklēsia* in the recognition and deeply embedded understanding and trust that Christ and no one else is all and in all. The rhetorical force aims to persuade people "above all these things" to "put on love" (ἐπὶ πᾶσιν δὲ τούτοις τὴν ἀγάπην, 3:14). Presenting Christ and love above everything else (not to mention humility) seems a strange thing in human societies, certainly in the imperial sociocultural-political environment of the ancient Mediterranean, where concerns of power and the flesh typically dominated. It is as if Colossians has reconfigured and developed ideas (and words) similar to what is observed in 2 Cor 10:1–5, which concludes with the claim that "we take every thought captive to obey Christ" (10:5).

---

262. Though the word does not seem to be used this way in biblical texts (Sumney, *Colossians*, 218). See also n. 252 above and Col 2:19.

263. See the more developed language of Eph 5:18–20.

In other words, the rhetorical force of Col 3:5–17 is to persuade the Lycus Valley *ekklēsiai* to hold the communities together with Christ, reconciliation, good, orderly, and productive behavior, and above all love. This is the culture and politics of the new reality into which they have been transferred. The power that conquers, divides, and humiliates people has been defeated and made irrelevant by Christ. The idolatrous culture greedy for the power, self-importance, and desire that imperial and political forces generate and promote is denied. The obvious dominating imperial-political-economic power—which people lived with day by day—has been overturned by Christ. The new behavior in its new clothing lives with the peace of Christ ruling and the word of Christ housed in it. The new way of living demonstrates the goodness in teaching, worship, and gratitude. This is wisdom and maturity of the new reality, inhabiting a sacred space.

Step Nine: Household Wisdom (3:18–4:1)

Rhetography

The rhetography of Colossians has portrayed a filiated culture from the beginning of the letter. Family and household are pervasive images that are cast in the imagination both explicitly and obliquely throughout the letter.[264] Recipients of the letter are called "holy and faithful brothers" already at 1:2, and Timothy is named "brother" at 1:1. In the rhetoric of personalities at the end of the letter, both Tychicus and Onesimus are called "beloved brother" (4:7, 9) and believers in Laodicea are termed "brothers" (4:15).[265] God is presented as the interpersonal "Father God" (1:2, 3, 12; 3:17) who has a Son whom he loves (1:13). Christ believers are consistently envisioned in these filiated, familial terms. Mediterranean people recognized that towns and cities were composed of households that in turn were composed of families. The family-household was understood ideologically as fundamental and normal.[266] It was composed of wives, husbands, children, slaves, and often other persons. Houses functioned as more than family residences; they were also places of business, gatherings,

---

264. On this see the discussion of *alternative culture texture* in the introduction.

265. The masculine plural "brothers" (ἀδελφοῖς) was employed generically and includes "sisters" and all filiated persons.

266. See Campbell, *Pauline Dogmatics*, 52–53; Longenecker, *In Stone and Story*, 198.

and often places for the manufacture and sale of goods.[267] Believers met in Nympha's house in Laodicea (4:13), and it is virtually certain that they assembled in a house (or several houses) in Colossae and Hierapolis.[268] Paul is portrayed as the servant (διάκονος) given "the household management" (οἰκονομία) by God (1:25).

The household—the normal location of the family—is visualized in noun and verb forms (οἰκ- words) in Colossians.[269] The repetitiveness of these terms (*repetitive texture*) reinforces the vision of the body-*ekklēsia* as a filiated, household community. So the shift to a vision of specifically domestic relations in the household wisdom of 3:18–4:1 fits appropriately in the larger picturing of the letter.[270] Picturing what would be imagined as orderly family-household living continues the portrayal of killing and putting away the disorder and chaos of Mediterranean life and putting on the good behaviors portrayed in the preceding verses (3:5–17). Household living should be good for all. Disordered family-household conditions are not appropriate for Christ followers. There is no change of overall rhetographic vision. It is all *familiar*. The Lycus audiences will envision themselves living life in the ways described. There were, of course, many exceptions. Paul the apostle, along with various others such as many of his coworkers, was not a householder, house dweller, or family member in the usual way. Perhaps many persons (e.g., the unmarried, widowed, elderly, homeless, orphaned, military personnel, the impoverished, itinerant workers, etc.) did not or could not fit into the household wisdom description of 3:18–4:1.

The direct hortatory wisdom rhetoric brings typical—hence to Mediterranean audiences recognizable and understandable—domestic life into

---

267. See Maier, "Household and Its Members"; Bruce W. Longenecker, "Family and Solidarity," in *In Stone and Story*, 198–211; also John S. Kloppenborg, *Christ's Associations: Connecting and Belonging in the Ancient City* (New Haven: Yale University Press, 2019), 24, 204–5. Kloppenborg notes, "Many associations employed familial language to describe internal relationships even though members were not necessarily related by birth or by adoption" (204). See also Huttner, *Early Christianity in the Lycus*, 142–45.

268. The households in view are in urban locations. There is no view of rural, industrial, or military locations.

269. See *alternative culture texture*.

270. Even though the flow of the letter, as many interpreters point out, can be understood with only slight awkwardness if 3:18–4:1 is omitted. See below on *textural commentary*.

view. Virtual Paul continues to be present and his voice continues to be heard, calling to and touching the senses. The believers are observed listening, but now the view is altered from seeing them doing everything in the name of the Lord Jesus (3:17) to envisioning them distinctly at home. The domestic life is also visible to nonbelievers, in other words to the neighbors. The vocative nouns evoke picturing of wives, husbands, children, fathers, slaves, and masters in a series of individual images, yet images that blend together in households. The call for the domestic ways of relating to one another simultaneously evokes contrasting mental images of undesirable and disordered behaviors. The visual ordering would strike some as unusual. Husbands or patres familias typically appeared first in descriptions of household management.[271] Here wives appear first. This would be noticed as an alteration to the usual Greco-Roman description.

Wives come into view first. Because the words αἱ γυναῖκες, ὑποτάσσεσθε τοῖς ἀνδράσιν are typically translated as "wives be subject to your husbands," "be in subjection to your husbands," or "submit yourselves to your husbands," the wives (and women) have been envisioned as necessarily in imposed subservient, servile familial and household roles.[272] Male domination is imagined and was real. The imagery of subjection and servility evokes for many modern interpreters the imposition of the oppressive and repressive hierarchical structure that has harmed wives and women for centuries. Wives are directed to subject themselves to the husbands and are visualized doing it because it is "proper in the Lord," that is, in the body of Christ. The middle imperative ὑποτάσσεσθε for many conveys the idea of "placing yourselves under" the husbands but is much better understood as "fitting in" or "fitting yourselves in."[273] This does not remove the hierar-

---

271. See, e.g., the analysis of household management described by Arius Didymus (first century CE) in David L. Balch, "Household Codes," in *Greco-Roman Literature and the New Testament*, ed. David L. Balch, SBLSBS 21 (Atlanta: Scholars Press, 1988), 40–45. See also the descriptions by Hierocles (second century CE) in Malherbe, *Moral Exhortation*, 83–104.

272. The Greek words γυναῖκες and ἄνδρες do not distinguish between wives and women or between husbands and men. The household context, however, indicates that wives and husbands are portrayed.

273. On ὑποτάσσω/ὑποτάσσομαι as "fitting in," see Martin, "Translating ὑποτάσσεσθαι in First Peter"; Martin, *Apostolic Confirmation and Legitimation*, on 1 Pet 2:13–3:7. See textural commentary, below. Many interpreters understand ὑποτάσσεσθε as middle voice (from ὑποτάσσομαι), the view taken here. See, for example, Gerhard Delling, "ὑποτάσσω," *TDNT* 8:43, 45; Barth and Blanke, *Colossians*, 433; Dunn, *Epis-*

chical household structure of the day, but it also does not evoke the vision of a servile, subservient, degrading, and unquestioning relationship where wives must capitulate to disordered power imposed by their husbands. In context the husbands *love* the wives (3:19). The wives' action of "fitting in" is volitional: they decide for themselves to act. They are observed actively fitting themselves into the traditional and socially expected family-household role where husbands were the dominant figures. It does not make for an egalitarian situation but does provide a level of household and family order. Unfair, disrespectful, and harsh treatment by husbands is contextually excluded, so the active fitting in of Christ-believing wives necessarily implies that they can resist or refuse to fit in when they are mistreated or when situations are not "proper in the Lord." Wives are seen, and apparently saw themselves, in a gendered hierarchy and household structure.[274] Everyone felt the pressure to adhere to social structures and expectations. Fitting in with husbands seemed normal to people in the ancient Mediterranean, who were culturally conditioned to think that male authority was obvious.[275] Husbands and the autocratic paterfamilias, normally the senior male of the household, were recognized as authoritative. Married women Christ believers are directed—not forced—to fit themselves into the hierarchy and structure of the place where they lived.[276]

Husbands appear second. They hear the directive to love their wives, mentally visualize themselves practicing love, and are seen putting the love into practice. This is love made visible in active care for the wives. The implication is that such caring was frequently not practiced, that wives

---

tles to the Colossians and to Philemon, 247; Beale, *Colossians*, 316. Middle and passive verbs, of course, have the same form.

274. Things were different in the capital, Rome, from places such as Colossae. Beard states, "It is clear, however, that Roman women in general had much greater independence than women in most parts of the classical Greek or Near Eastern world, limited as it must seem in modern terms" (*SPQR*, 307). Women were not meant to be publicly invisible.

275. There were known exceptions. For an overall description, see Jerry L. Sumney, "Excursus 3: Reading the Household Code," in *Colossians*, 230–38; Foster, *Colossians*, 366–72. See below, textural commentary.

276. The listening audience in Colossae may well have included married slaves, persons married to nonbelievers, some of them with children, some without, illegitimate children of slave owners, children alone, orphans, nonbelievers, homeless persons, people of varying social and economic status, etc. (see McKnight, *Colossians*, 343–44).

were dominated rather than loved. No rationale is given for the loving behavior, though it might be assumed that it is proper just as submission or fitting in is proper for wives. Perhaps love itself as an overt demonstration of care is the rationale. Marriage is here viewed as a reciprocal relationship. The additional directive, "do not be embittered toward them," presents husbands refusing, perhaps mentally but with visible result, to hold resentment or grudges against wives.[277] Husbands visualize themselves behaving in active, supportive ways toward their wives. They do not mistreat or harm wives in any way.

With the directive to obey their parents, children are imagined doing so. This obviously implies that children do not always obey their parents. The parents may be but are not necessarily the wives and husbands already in view. Some children in *ekklēsiai* might not have believing parents. The authors, by their employment of this rhetoric, imagine children—perhaps children of any age, including adults—conforming to this call and reasoning. It was an aspect of the social fabric they understood. The children see and recognize their location "in the Lord."

Next are observed fathers, who are directed not to provoke their children. They nurture their children. They are consciously avoiding being provocative. The rationale for nurturing the children is to prevent them from becoming discouraged or disheartened.[278] The children therefore appear in the imagination as encouraged, nurtured, eager persons.

The longest, most complex, and most graphic rhetoric in this step concerns slaves (3:22–25). Virtual Paul's call to slaves creates an image of them obeying their "flesh masters" (τοῖς κατὰ σάρκα κυρίοις) in every way. These are human masters who stand in contrast to the true master, the Lord Christ (3:25), who is still visible in the rhetograph. For the slaves, though, the picturing of their obedience expands as it continues to be visualized. They are not, deceitfully, "eye-slaving" as "people-pleasers" (μὴ ἐν ὀφθαλμοδουλίᾳ ὡς ἀνθρωπάρεσκοι)[279] "but in singleness of heart fearing the Lord," presumably the Lord Jesus. The slaves in sight are seriously devoted

---

277. This suggests that the authors knew something of how many men behave toward their wives or other women. The passive-voice verb πικραίνεσθε does not mean "do not make *them* [i.e., the wives] bitter," "do not be harsh with them," or "never treat them harshly" (as NRSV and NRSVue). Husbands (men) are the subject of the verb.

278. The verb ἀθυμῶσιν (ἀθυμέω) is a *hapax legomenon*.

279. Rhetographic terms that portray self-evidently what they represent metaphorically.

SCENE THREE: DON'T BE DECEIVED. LIVE THE NEW REALITY 239

to the Lord Christ. They, like other household members, are located in the Lord, and they indicate by their actions that they obey the flesh masters because of their convictions about Christ.[280] The rationale is like those of 3:18, 20. The Lord Jesus is in sight in the family visualization, and all that slaves do, like the advice given in 3:17, is done with the Lord's presence in mind. The tasks that the slaves are observed performing are worked out of their very souls (ἐκ ψυχῆς ἐργάζεσθε)[281]—they put all they have into the work, devotedly, energetically—as if they were working directly for the Lord rather than for their flesh masters. This is strongly emphasized for slaves who know that they will receive "the reward." As the slaves look upward with the other members of households (3:1–4), they can envision shining with Christ in glory.

The point is driven home in the visualization of their active slaving; they "slave in the Lord Christ" (τῷ κυρίῳ Χριστῷ δουλεύετε).[282] Though it appears curious when compared to the picturing of wives, husbands, children, and fathers, the slave doing something wrong will receive back in kind (ὁ γὰρ ἀδικῶν κομίσεται ὃ ἠδίκησεν; note the repeated verb ἀδικέω, "to do wrong"). Slaves are thus household members who are explicitly warned of the consequence of doing wrong things. As they look upward toward their inheritance they also see, by contrast, a portrayal of themselves experiencing the same kind of wrong done to themselves.[283] Probably they imagine this as a warning. Slaves are seen here in socially lower status than the other household members. This would not seem surprising to residents of Colossae. It is followed, however, with the statement that "there is no partiality" (καὶ οὐκ ἔστιν προσωπολημψία). Perhaps this offers an image of comfort, of amelioration to the picture by indicating that the pressure is not only on slaves.

The vision of slaves is followed immediately with a word to slave masters,[284] in a short and direct statement that they must provide (παρέχω, 4:1) *the right thing* (δίκαιος, what is just) and *the equal thing* (ἰσότης) to slaves. This is a new social portrayal for slaves. The visual rationale for equal treatment of slaves by masters is found in the portrayal of the mas-

---

280. They are, in other words, "fitting in."
281. Out of their "livingness" (cf. Latin *anima*).
282. The verb δουλεύω means "to slave." The locative "in the Lord Christ" is used here because it matches the repetitive "in the Lord" of 3:18, 20.
283. κομίσεται is middle voice, hence "he will receive himself."
284. Perhaps including household slave owners and slave overseers/managers?

ters' own master/Lord, who is in heaven. The obvious image is of the Lord Jesus, the same one seen as Lord of the other household members, who sits in heaven (the above realm) and in whom all the family is hidden and to whom they all look for glory (3:1–4). The masters know this and should keep the image in their minds, with the responsibility the imagery implies. Viewers may well wonder, however, how enslaved humans can possibly be treated with justice and equality yet remain as enslaved persons.

These verses cast familiar yet simultaneously unusual and striking visual imagery on the minds of readers and listeners. People were socially and culturally conditioned to believe that male priority and domination, self-serving relationships, authoritarian control of children, and oppressive slavery were normal and reasonable. There was a long philosophical history that supported the sociocultural views extending back to the time of Aristotle (see *Pol.* 1.4, 6, 13).[285] The household wisdom in this step addresses wives first, calls for frequently disordered, resentful husbands to love them and to nurture their children, and urges slaves to work honestly rather than deceitfully and slave masters to treat their slaves righteously. This is the beginning but not the completion of revolutionary change in the households of Christ believers and in cities in which they live. The hierarchical structures remain. But certainly notable, perhaps astonishing social change is envisioned that demonstrates more caring, encouraging relationships.[286]

This step provides a distinct shift of focus to the inner-familial households of believers in Colossae and the Lycus towns Laodicea and Hierapolis. Households are where families lived in their daily lives, including work, business, and social and personal interaction.[287] This is blended prophetic and wisdom discourse that has wisdom living in wisdom space as its goal. Virtual Paul is seen speaking, calling out, to members of households to behave in their various roles in ways that reflect their existence and space "in the Lord." The master/Lord Christ in heaven is in mind (4:1), like the emperor is on his throne, but transcending the emperor and Roman ethos and systems. While ordinary Mediterranean wisdom might look to Rome and the emperor and to traditional Greco-Roman household conventions, the rhetoric of this step looks to the Lord Jesus, to believers' location in

---

285. See below on textual commentary. For discussion see Jeal, *Exploring Philemon*, 147–48.

286. As Maier, *New Testament Christianity*, 150.

287. Though, again, not everyone lived in these family-household situations.

him, and to his location in heaven to govern their domestic lives. Nevertheless, the picture presents households and family relationships that, though having a few striking alterations, look remarkably like the usual Roman-Mediterranean domestic order.[288] The imagery of this step has parallels with the imperial household.[289] A distinct hierarchy that maintains distinctions among and between members of households is envisioned and is presumed to be acceptable. Despite the urging to reject religious and social pressures (as in 2:6–23), believers here are encouraged to fit in to household structures that seem to preserve certain injustices. Why submit to such things of the earth (3:2)?[290] Would some have objected? Would some have wondered about earlier Pauline statements such as "there is no longer slave or free, there is no longer male and female; for all of you are one in Christ Jesus" (Gal 3:28)?

Translation

> 3:18 Wives, fit yourselves in with the husbands[291] as (is) proper in (the) Lord.
> 3:19 Husbands, love the wives[292] and do not be embittered toward them.
> 3:20 Children, obey the parents in all things, for this is well-pleasing in (the) Lord.
> 3:21 Fathers, do not provoke your children, so that they may not be discouraged.
> 3:22 Slaves, obey in all things those who are masters according to the flesh, not in eye slavery as people pleasers, but in singleness of heart, fearing the Lord.[293] 3:23 Whatever you do, work out of (your) soul, as to the Lord and not (to) humans, 3:24 know-

---

288. Maier, *Picturing Paul in Empire*, 38 et passim, describes this as "hybridity," an "entangled history" (94–99). See also Maier, "*Histoire Croisée*," 93–94. There are boundaries but also entanglements across boundaries (94).
289. See Maier, *Picturing Paul in Empire*, 94–99.
290. I.e., to the στοιχεῖα or elements of the world.
291. Some manuscripts have ἀνδράσιν ὑμῶν, "your husbands," or ἰδίοις ἀνδράσιν, "your own husbands."
292. Some manuscripts read γυναῖκας ὑμῶν, "your wives."
293. Some manuscripts read θεόν, "God," suggesting κύριον refers to God, not the κύριον slave master.

ing that you will receive[294] the reward of the inheritance from the Lord. You slave in the Lord Christ. **3:25** For the one who does wrong will receive what he did wrong, and there is no partiality. **4:1** Masters, provide yourselves the right thing and equality to slaves, knowing that you also have a master in heaven.[295]

Textural Commentary

These verses are termed "household code" by most modern interpreters. The idea of code is understood, of course, but it is better to refer to the verses as a taxonomy, a list, a series of household exhortations (παράκλησες) or as household wisdom. The term *code* suggests something legal, that is, requirements that call for restrictions and penalties (or punishments or oppression) when they are violated. The verses, along with the yet more developed Eph 5:21–30 and others, have often been mistakenly interpreted and unfairly applied this way. While the exhortations draw on traditional Greco-Roman notions,[296] the rhetoric is not shaped as a set of legal rules that must be rigorously observed in perpetuity. These verses form a **social and cultural texture** interwoven with threads of related fabrics. The frequently employed German term *Haustafel* is helpful for grasping the rhetoric about family members of households, but the term used in earlier in Colossians, οἰκονομία, "household management" (1:25), conveys the idea quite clearly. In SRI terms, this is wisdom discourse. Argumentatively, the behaviors are described by such terms as "proper" (ἀνήκω, fitting, 3:18), "well-pleasing" (εὐάρεστος, 3:20), and "right" or "just" (δίκαιος, 4:1).

Study of **social texture** demonstrates that many people, certainly many Christ believers in Colossae, did not fit into the categories described in 3:18–4:1 in a neat, one-to-one way.[297] It is important to note that *economics*, a word derived from οἰκονομία, is actually *not* about the management

---

294. Some manuscripts have λήμψεσθε, "receive," rather than ἀπολήμψεσθε, "receive from."
295. Some manuscripts have οὐρανοῖς, "heavens," plural.
296. E.g., the *mos mairoum*, unwritten ancestral traditions, and written description like those referenced in n. 271, above.
297. See Maier, *New Testament Christianity*, 137–38; see also Margaret Y. MacDonald, *The Power of Children: The Construction of Christian Families in the Greco-Roman World* (Waco, TX: Baylor University Press, 2014).

of wealth but of *scarcity*.²⁹⁸ It is about people getting along as best they can with the tensions of life. This was certainly the case in the ancient Mediterranean. Well more than 90 percent (perhaps as much as 97 percent) of the urban Mediterranean population lived in levels of poverty. Day-by-day life demanded unrelenting hard work for mere subsistence.²⁹⁹ Goods of all kinds were regularly in short supply. Power was held by the small percentage of elite landowners. Paul the apostle, for example, did not himself practice the behaviors of the *Haustafel*, being unmarried (1 Cor 7:7, 9:5; see 7:7) and, at least in some situations, recommending against marriage (1 Cor 7:8, 26–35). Peter was married (1 Cor 9:5; see Mark 1:30) but seems also to have been an itinerant preacher for much of his life. Paul speaks of having children (e.g., Timothy, 1 Cor 4:17; Onesimus, Phlm 10; see 1 Cor 4:14, Gal 4:19) and certainly of "brothers" (see above on rhetography), but these are not biological family members residing in traditional households but rather fellow believers whom Paul nurtured. Paul must have resided in houses³⁰⁰ when he lived for extended periods in some cities but was not himself a householder as such. He was for much of his life an itinerant. Still, it seems clear that Paul respected and supported traditional Greco-Roman and Jewish household structures. But the *Haustafel* was not meant to be an inviolable pattern that must be followed.

Much interpretation focuses on identifying perceived sources of the household discourse.³⁰¹ The concern here, however, is not sources as such

---

298. "Economics is the study of choice under scarcity," according to Michael Ryan Moore. See Moore, "What Is Economics? A Lesson on Choice and Scarcity," Wharton Global Youth Program, University of Pennsylvania, https://tinyurl.com/SBL7106k.

299. See Carter, *Roman Empire and the New Testament*, 100–118. See the detailed information in Stephen J. Friesen, "Paul and Economics: The Jerusalem Collection as an Alternative to Patronage," in *Paul Unbound: Other Perspectives on the Apostle*, 2nd ed., ed. Mark D. Given, ESEC 25 (Atlanta: SBL Press, 2022), 41–78; Walter Scheidel and Stephen J. Friesen, "The Size of the Economy and the Distribution of Wealth in the Roman Empire," *JRS* 99 (2009): 61–91.

300. In houses in urban locations such as *insulae* or *tabernae*, not houses as modern suburbanites imagine them.

301. See, e.g., James E. Crouch, *The Origin and Intention of the Colossians Haustafel* (Göttingen: Vandenhoeck & Ruprecht, 1972); see also the analysis and bibliography in Balch, "Household Codes." Many more studies of sources are listed in the commentaries. Longenecker notes, "Most ancient codes that regulated behavior within households addressed only those with inferior status in the household. The Colossian code, however, broke out of that restriction and placed even masters within the frame of regulation" (*In Stone and Story*, 194).

but the sociorhetorical analysis of what the passage *does* to its audiences in its Lycus, Greco-Roman, and Christ-believing contexts. The household-management exhortations connect well with the preceding rhetoric that emphasizes the lordship of Christ.[302] There is no change to the general vision of seeking and thinking about the above things rather than the earth things that lead to disorder. It was not simply copied arbitrarily from another source and pasted in. The leading and striking *repetitive texture* is in six vocative nouns[303] followed by imperatives that directly address specific members of households: (1) Αἱ γυναῖκες, ὑποτάσσεσθε; (2) Οἱ ἄνδρες, ἀγαπᾶτε; (3) Τὰ τέκνα, ὑπακούετε; (4) Οἱ πατέρες, μὴ ἐρεθίζετε; (5) Οἱ δοῦλοι, ὑπακούετε; and (6) Οἱ κύριοι ... παρέχεσθε. This rhetoric calls out to each member in the same way with two variations: wives and slave masters are addressed with middle-voice verbs (ὑποτάσσεσθε, "fit yourselves in"; παρέχεσθε, "provide yourselves"). The grammatical structure places emphasis on the personal action of the specified persons as subjects of the verbs more than on the actions the verbs describe.[304] The emphatic repetitions of direct address have a sensory effect (*sensory-aesthetic texture*), moving listeners to look up, to pay attention as specified members of the body-*ekklēsia*-household rather than together as a less visible, generalized whole.

Despite modern concerns, wives in the Lycus Valley would not be surprised at being encouraged to fit in with their husbands. To do so was part of the **sociocultural** and household fabric of the time. The verb τάσσω and its cognate and compound forms are about order and arrangement.[305] The compound form ὑποτάσσω literally means "order or arrange under" (ὑπό, "under" + τάσσω, "place, order, arrange"), but the middle-voice ὑποτάσσεσθε requires the subject of the verb to act. The subject of ὑποτάσσεσθε, that is, the wives, provide the energy and will to fit in with their husbands. They are not passive. This contrasts with the connotations of ὑπακούω (listen

---

302. Contra, e.g., Dunn, *Epistles to the Colossians and to Philemon*, 242. On the connections see especially Lincoln, "Household Code," 94–95. Lincoln points out that if 3:18–4:1 were omitted, the syntactical flow would not be disrupted (though it would sound awkward with the close repetition of "thanksgiving"), "But, on the other hand, there is nothing awkward about the paraenesis if the passage is retained."

303. Although these are articular nouns in the plural, they function as vocatives, direct address, not as nominatives.

304. Wallace, *Greek Grammar*, 415.

305. Delling, "ὑποτάσσω," 27–48.

and obey), the word used as the directive to children and slaves in the following verses (3:20, 22). Christ-believing wives are *not* urged to obey commands as were children and slaves. For wives to fit themselves in was to live thoughtfully in the leveled structure of typical households. It was to fit into sociocultural expectations as they were understood, but not with a wholesale subjection.[306] Many slaves were married. Many marriages were not formalized; it was presumed that people were married if they declared that they were. A leading purpose of marriage was the production of legitimate children.[307] Love and affection were often secondary matters. Marriage had a presumed structure but also had to do with social status, social respectability, emotional stability, and protection.[308]

Husbands dominated families and households, and wives (and women generally) faced restrictions, but wives also had management responsibilities that supported the functions of the home.[309] They are not to be envisioned without any authority of their own. Certainly they had authority over their families and many activities in their households.[310] Wives could be responsible for managing the work of slaves.[311] As part of fitting in, they were expected to recognize their husbands' deities and participate in ritual practices.[312] Many had public roles and visibility outside the home including giving speeches, engaging in business, and slave ownership.[313] Some had distinct leadership roles in the *ekklēsia*, including

---

306. See classicist Hart, *New Testament*, 402 note g.
307. The word *matrimony* derives from *mater*, "mother." See Susan Treggiari, *Roman Marriage* (Oxford: Oxford University Press, 1991); Beard, *SPQR*, 303. On husbands and wives, see Beard, *SPQR*, 303–13. Beard points out that marriage of girls often occurred at age fourteen or fifteen, that "at least one in fifty women were likely to die in childbirth," and that "half the children born would have died by the age of ten.... Life expectancy at birth was probably as low as the mid twenties" (316). See the discussion of marriage in Longenecker, *In Stone and Story*, 203–5.
308. See again *alternative culture texture* in the introduction.
309. See Maier, *New Testament Christianity*, 150–55.
310. Women had power in the household. Sumney points out that women functioned as patres familias (matres familias) in households where there were no males (*Colossians*, 232). A wife had complete authority over things inherited from her own father (Maier, *New Testament Christianity*, 147).
311. The feminine form for "master," κυρία, could be applied to wives in this function (see LXX Gen 16:4, 4 Kgdms 5:3, Isa 24:2; see also 2 John 1, 5).
312. Sumney, *Colossians*, 232–33.
313. Maier, *New Testament Christianity*, 152. Though these more public roles could be considered an intrusion into male domains.

Nympha, named in Col 4:15. Elite wives had critically important roles in the imperial families, where emperors from Augustus onward "made blood the key qualification for succession" of their dynasties, even as they were often frustrated by the absence of male heirs.[314] While women and wives had no formalized political roles, many became influential in political, social, and religious affairs when it was observed that they could promote imperial and local interests.[315] Many found ways to assert power in their communities.

Life was difficult, tragedies were common, but the household could offer some comfort. Fitting in, however, did not protect wives from mean-spiritedness, violence, or unfaithfulness. The exhortation to husbands not to be embittered is telling in this regard. Fitting in also did not protect them from the massively widespread poverty and scarcity, which meant that women had to function in roles outside the house.[316] What it did offer was a level of order that was not easy to acquire elsewhere. The hierarchy is visible, palpable, certainly to modern interpreters.[317] Still, wives are portrayed first in the rhetograph, prior to other members of the household, prior to the husbands, so they are clearly *the first persons seen* in the house portrayed in this step, are recognizable for the women that they are, and in this way stand out distinctly.

The expressed *argumentative texture* for the directive for wives is that fitting in with husbands is "proper in the Lord" (ὡς ἀνῆκεν ἐν κυρίῳ). The imperfect verb ἀνῆκεν (from ἀνήκω, "appertain, be fit, fitting, proper") suggests the process of fitting in, not its completion, as proper. Orderly household living is a process rather than a completed state.[318] The pro-

---

314. See especially Guy de la Bédoyère, *Domina: The Women Who Made Imperial Rome* (New Haven: Yale University Press, 2018), 50–51 et passim. "Not one of the Julio-Claudian emperors was succeeded by his son.... It was the female route that legitimized the claim to dynastic descent by the successive male rulers" (51–53). In 65 CE Nero murdered his own wife, Poppaea Sabina, who was pregnant with their unborn child. The mythological female deity Venus Genetrix was considered to be the divine ancestor of the Julio-Claudian dynasty and the Roman people.

315. There are many examples. See de la Bédoyère, *Domina*, appendix 3 (466–74) for a list of "Key Female Personalities." Wives were not, though, treated at all as equals with their husbands (75–80).

316. Maier, *New Testament Christianity*, 135–36.

317. See the comments below in textural commentary.

318. Colossians 3:18 does not present a perfect, completed household situation. And it is not a rule for household living.

cess recognizes the sociocultural convention of male authority. There is, however, an important **intertexture** with the later and more developed Eph 5:21–22. Following a series of statements employing participles (5:15, 19–20), Eph 5:21 calls for mutual fitting in, employing the participle ὑποτασσόμενοι with the reciprocal pronoun ἀλλήλοις ("*fitting in with one another* in fear of Christ").[319] All members of the body-*ekklēsia*-household are to be submissive to the others. The fitting in here is about all members functioning *together* in their "walk" (note the repetitive περιπατεῖτε at 5:2, 8, 15). Ephesians 5:22, according to the best manuscript evidence, does not have a verbal form.[320] It relies on the participle of verse 21, literally stating simply, "the wives to their own husbands as to the Lord" (αἱ γυναῖκες τοῖς ἰδίοις ἀνδράσιν ὡς τῷ κυρίῳ). Colossians 3:18, by contrast, employs the middle imperative ὑποτάσσεσθε. The intertexture of language and rhetoric indicates that Colossians is moving toward or already assumes the reciprocal *mutual* submission described in Ephesians. The developed Eph 5:22 also has "as to the Lord" (ὡς τῷ κυρίῳ), nuancing more about the relationship and the argument by indicating that they are understood in the same manner as believers' recognition of Christ as Lord. Wisdom 8 portrays wisdom (the feminine σοφία) as the wife of the king who manages all things well (καὶ διοικεῖ τὰ πάντα χρηστῶς, 8:1), employing the compound verb διοικέω (διά + οἶκος, lit. "to manage a house").[321] A few verses later she is described performing the same household management when she works with a view toward persuading people and nations to proper regard for her king-husband (διοικήσω λαούς καὶ ἔθνη ὑποταγήσεταί μοι, 8:14). The wise woman supports the husband of the orderly household by bringing others into fitting roles (ὑποταγήσεταί, future passive of ὑποτάσσω). The intelligent, holy σοφία, "the breath of the power of God, and a pure emanation of the glory of the almighty," "a spotless mirror of the working of God, and an image of his goodness" (Wis 7:25–26), is a rhetorical precursor to the Christ-believing wives in Colossae. As in Colossians, the locus of wisdom is the household, the place where people live and where the wives have important leadership roles.

---

319. Typically translated to English as "submitting to one another" or as an imperative "be subject to one another."

320. Some manuscripts have the unlikely imperative ὑποτασσέσθωσαν or ὑποτάσσεσθε.

321. LSJ, s.v. διοικέω.

Husbands are called to love their wives. Believing husbands will see by this that they have their own marital obligations. No explicit argument is given with the statement, but to it is added the slightly cryptic "and do not be embittered toward them."[322] This *sensory texture* suggests that it was well-known that many husbands tended toward bitterness (πικραίνω, "to be bitter, resentful, exasperated") against wives. The directive to husbands, with its exhortation that they love their wives, reshapes the marriage relationship in deeply significant ways. Wives are to be treated with care. Unlike the Roman notion of marriage, where wives were for reproduction and mistresses, prostitutes, or slaves[323] were used to satisfy disordered, chaotic sexual appetites, the pattern of οἰκονομία in this directive brings in love and the implication that passions (e.g., bitterness) are to be controlled, in other words killed and put away as Col 3:5–7 demands.[324] The object of marriage is not only the production of children. Love is to function, that is, there should always be caring for the other, here wives specifically, even when domestic situations are strained or when bitterness and desire move men to look elsewhere. This was to call for a change of boundaries in the Roman-dominated culture. Males are regularly named first in household texts, not women, and consistent, never-ending ἀγάπη (as 1 Cor 13:4–8a) was not the expected basis of household hierarchy. Marriage and the household are being reconfigured into a reciprocal relationship in this exhortation. The authoritarian structures are not removed but are diminished. Men are implicitly directed to fit in. The usual expec-

---

322. The subject of the present passive imperative πικραίνεσθε is the husbands, not the wives.

323. See Maier, *New Testament Christianity*, 162; see also the description in Longenecker, *In Stone and Story*, 202–3. For overall view of Roman-Mediterranean marriage and family, see Carolyn Osiek and David L. Balch, eds., *Families in the New Testament World: Households and House Churches* (Louisville: Westminster John Knox, 1997); Bruce J. Malina, *The New Testament World: Insights from Cultural Anthropology*, 3rd ed. (Louisville: Westminster John Knox, 2001), 134–60. Colossians 3:5 has already directed believers to kill fornication and evil desire.

324. This is not to say that there was no affection among members of households, but the decision to love and care, not sensual emotion, is in mind. Talbert notes Stobaeus, *Flor*. 4.2.24 (fifth century CE), who refers to Pseudo-Charondas (sixth–fifth century BCE, who may be fictional) and also to Pseudo-Phocylides (100 BCE–100 CE?) as ancients who exhorted husbands to love their wives (Talbert, *Ephesians and Colossians*, 232).

SCENE THREE: DON'T BE DECEIVED. LIVE THE NEW REALITY   249

tations become entangled, interwoven, with new ones. One boundary is removed and replaced by another.³²⁵

Children are to obey the parents in all things, "for this is well-pleasing in (the) Lord."³²⁶ Children are directed to do as they are told. The direct argument is "this is well-pleasing in the Lord," the same words used in Col 3:18, which harks back to 3:1–4.

In a closely related wisdom imperative, fathers, who held complete authority over their children,³²⁷ are told they must not provoke their children so they do not become discouraged. This exhortation reveals some natural rhetorical assumptions. It assumes that children are present in the body-*ekklēsia*-household, that they are listening and are mature enough to get the idea of obedience. It assumes that parents, fathers in particular, are listening and attentive. Age levels of the children are not discriminated, though we can assume that infants are not in mind. Even older children, possibly adult children, were expected to respect the paterfamilias and could have household responsibilities to perform, for example, orderliness, various tasks, aspects of household and family business, and so on. The plural imperative ὑπακούετε, "obey," is, once again, stronger than ὑποτάσσεσθε, "fit in," applied to wives. But its occurrence assumes that believing parents, fathers in particular, will give good instruction to their children. They call their children to belief and good behaviors, not to disorder and self-interest. They teach children in the now-revealed mystery of Christ and ways of wisdom living. It is also assumes, probably from observation and experience, that fathers are sometimes unfairly or unnecessarily provocative in ways that discourage their children. Children are not distant, insignificant creatures: they are participants in the household and in the *ekklēsia* (see Mark 9:36). Fathers must not take a heavy-handed, tyrannical approach that could cause their children to lose heart.

Slaves, too, are assumed to be present in the body-*ekklēsia*-household, listening to the reading of the letter.³²⁸ The rhetorically dramatic exhortation to slaves (3:22–25) is woven into the **social and cultural texturing**

---

325. On this see especially Maier, "*Histoire Croisée*," 77–81, 89–90.
326. The phrase "in all things" "in every way," κατὰ πάντα, could mean "all the time." In Greek the locative "in the Lord" (γὰρ εὐάρεστόν ἐστιν ἐν κυρίῳ) is employed, not "to the Lord," as many English versions render it.
327. Maier, *New Testament Christianity*, 147.
328. The masculine plural δοῦλοι is generic and obviously includes δοῦλαι, female slaves (see LXX Exod 21:7, Nah 2:8).

of household management in ways that reconfigure thinking and behavior for Christ-believing slaves, who were human beings owned by other humans. The believing slaves are directed, like the children, to obey their masters according to the flesh "in all things" (ὑπακούετε κατὰ πάντα τοῖς κατὰ σάρκα κυρίοις). This rhetoric emphasizes obedience but also specifies their human masters (κύριοι and κυρίαι). Yet they are to do this "as to the Lord" (ὡς τῷ κυρίῳ, 3:23), that is, the Lord Jesus for, according to a unique clause, they "slave in the Lord Christ" (τῷ κυρίῳ Χριστῷ δουλεύετε, 3:24).[329] The most obvious **linguistic** and **social-cultural intertexture** is in the rhetoric of Gal 5:13, "but through love slave to each other" (ἀλλὰ διὰ τῆς ἀγάπης δουλεύετε ἀλλήλοις).[330] The obedience and slaving of slaves will be envisioned as their action of fitting into the body-*ekklēsia*-household.

Slaves as obedient human beings who are owned by others reflects, **intertexturally**, the sociocultural understanding of the ancient Mediterranean. There were clear lines of authority, famously stated by Aristotle (and believed by the dominating cultures):[331]

> The slave is not merely the slave of the master but wholly belongs to the master. These considerations therefore make clear the nature of the slave and his essential quality: one who is a human being belonging by nature not to himself but to another is by nature a slave, and a person is a human being belonging to another if being a man he is an article of property. (Aristotle, *Pol.* 1.4)[332]

> It is proper for the one party to be governed and for the other to govern by the form of government for which they are by nature fitted, and therefore by the exercise of mastership, while to govern badly is to govern disadvantageously for both parties (for the same thing is advantageous for a part and for the whole body or the whole soul, and the slave is part of the master—he is, as it were, a part of the body, alive yet separated from it; hence there is a certain community of interest and friendship between master and slave in cases when they have been qualified by

---

329. The dative phrase τῷ κυρίῳ Χριστῷ is understood as locative, "in the Lord Christ," matching the locative ἐν κυρίῳ in 3:18, 20.

330. Colossians 3:24 and Gal 5:13 are the only places in the New Testament where the second-person plural verb δουλεύετε occurs.

331. See Jeal, *Exploring Philemon*, 147–48.

332. Translations of this work follow Aristotle, *Politics*, trans. Harris Rackham, LCL (Cambridge: Harvard University Press, 1932).

nature for these positions, although when they do not hold them in that way but by law and constraint of force the opposite is true. (Aristotle, *Pol.* 1.6)

Slaves, it was imagined and believed, deserved to be slaves and should for that reason be obedient. Slaves were nonpersons. In the Roman Empire they were legal property of their owners and had no legal status as persons.[333] They were notoriously mistreated.[334] Marcel Mauss describes how "*persona* had become synonymous with the true nature of the individual.... Moreover, the right to the *persona* had been established. Only the slave is excluded from it. *Servus non habet personam*. He has no 'personality' (*personnalité*). He does not own his body, nor has he ancestors, name, *cognomen*, or personal belongings."[335] Certainly some enlightened people aimed to ameliorate how slaves were viewed and treated.[336] Still, they were viewed as inferior beings who, like children, were expected to obey. The sociocultural tradition of slavery extending back to Aristotle imagined slaves to be less intelligent than nonslaves: "For the slave has not got the deliberative part at all, and the female has it, but without full authority, while the child has it, but in an undeveloped form" (Aristotle, *Pol.* 1.13). The Christ-believing household slaves of the urban contexts of Colossae and other Lycus towns are directed not only to obey but not to engage in "eye slavery as people pleasers" (ὀφθαλμοδουλίαις ὡς ἀνθρωπάρεσκοι),[337] terminology indicating obsequious, ingratiating, and deceitful attempts to please in order to gain or maintain favor. By stark contrast, slaves are to behave in "singleness of heart, respecting the Lord" (ἐν ἁπλότητι καρδίας, φοβούμενοι τὸν κύριον). This invokes straightforward, honest, rather than self-serving behavior. All work they perform as slaves must be done devotedly, energetically, "out of soul" (ἐκ ψυχῆς

---

333. Jeal, *Exploring Philemon*, 147.

334. Sumney, *Colossians*, 233–34; Longenecker, *In Stone and Story*, 185–86.

335. Marcel Mauss, "A Category of the Human Mind: The Notion of Person; the Notion of Self," in *The Category of the Person: Anthropology, Philosophy, History*, ed. Michael Carruthers, Steven Collins, and Steven Lukes, trans. W. D. Halls (Cambridge: Cambridge University Press, 1985), 17. Slaves did sometimes possess property, but they did not own body and soul themselves.

336. See especially Seneca, *Ep.* 47, quoted in *Exploring Philemon*, 147–52. On the abusive treatment of slaves, see Longenecker, *In Stone and Story*, 184–85.

337. The word ὀφθαλμοδουλίαις obviously emphasizes the idea of slavery. It is employed in the New Testament only here and in Eph 6:6.

ἐργάζεσθε), that is, out of their human "livingness."[338] Everything is done "as to the Lord, not as to humans."[339]

Perhaps this makes an implicit **intertextural** connection with the description of the slave Onesimus, who is described as having been "useless" but is now "useful" (Phlm 11). Slaves are to keep in mind that the genuine reward comes not from their masters but from the Lord Jesus. This is, of course, a rhetorical allusion to the gospel itself, the mystery that has been brought to light, the hope stored in the heavens (1:5, 26–28). There is a warning in 3:24 that, while directly connected to the wisdom for slaves by the argumentative γάρ, should be understood as being true for all members of the household: "For the one who does wrong will receive what was done wrong, and there is no partiality." There is no special favor to be gained for believers who attempt to manipulate the οἰκονομία.

The rhetoricized message to slaves is the same one that has been in sight for all throughout the household wisdom, indeed from 3:5 onward: in the new reality disordered, chaotic, divisive living must not be practiced. The slaves in view are Christ believers, members of the body-ekklēsia-household, hence implicitly filiated. The wisdom calls for them to live faithfully, productively, and ethically in the environment they inhabit with all household members.

Masters, both men and women (κύριοι and κυρίαι) who own or manage slaves in a household, that is, the paterfamilias, a husband, a wife, or another person charged with the task, are themselves to "provide" (παρέχεσθε, "you yourselves provide," middle voice) "the just thing and the equal thing to the slaves" (τὸ δίκαιον καὶ τὴν ἰσότητα τοῖς δούλοις, 4:1). This rhetoric should make it clear to the Christ-believing masters that slaves are persons and that they should be respected and treated as equals. They are not to be treated as beings of lower intelligence who deserve and therefore must be ruled by people who have the power to dominate them. Justice and equality are what masters are to provide in the new reality of the body-ekklēsia-household. Masters must recognize what amounts to a warning about their own responsibilities to the Lord Jesus, who resides in the heavenly domain. They themselves "slave in the Lord Christ" (as 3:24). There is in this way an identification of masters and slaves: both groups work not for themselves but for Christ. While Paul is not called a slave in Colossians

---

338. Cf. Latin *anima*.

339. It is clear that the singular "lord" in 3:22–24 refers to the "Lord Christ" of 3:24, not to the plural "lords" (slave masters) of 3:22 and 4:1.

as he is in Rom 1:1, Gal 1:10, and Titus 1:1, both Epaphras (Col 1:7) and Tychicus (4:7) are envisioned as "fellow slaves" (σύνδουλοι) with Paul and Timothy. Epaphras is described as servant (διάκονος) and slave (δοῦλος) in 4:12. This quite dramatically shifts the dominating sociocultural views of the time. The master-slave class structure, though not at all fully resolved, much less abolished, is diminished. Masters-owners and slaves in the new reality of the *ekklēsia* are filiated persons and therefore must not discriminate between and among themselves. The overarching ethos is love, the connector of maturity, as 3:14 has already pointed out.

The overall *argumentative texturing* of the household wisdom functions to create an **ideological texture**. In other words, the wisdom, that is, the faithful, fruitful, and ethical living that the letter to the Colossians aims toward, reflects the new reality of life "in the light," in "the kingdom of the Son of his [Father God's] love," into which the Christ believers have been transferred (1:12–13). The new-reality ideology does retain the hierarchical system. Social layers continue with their inherent oppression.[340] Yet the rhetoric of the letter indicates that holy ones love each other (1:4, 8), they are encouraged to be "held together in love" (2:2), and they are "above all" to put on love (3:14). While in the household wisdom only husbands are explicitly directed to love (ἀγαπᾶτε τὰς γυναῖκας, 3:19), there is a contextual agapeic ideology or ethos being created where fellow believers, in whatever category they are classified, are directed to have genuine care and respect for one another. A power differential remains, but it has been dramatically reduced from how it functioned previously. The *argumentative texture* can be described in the following way:

> **Case:** Christ believers in the Colossian urban context live in recognizable households. Life in the households (οἰκονομία, "household management") is to be reshaped morally and behaviorally in developed, if imperfect, ways.
> **Rationale:** Typically disordered, unfair, hierarchical household management should become ordered in filiated ways appropriate to the new reality where love (ἀγάπη) dominates.
> **Result:** The believers will function well and faithfully in their body-*ekklēsia*-household contexts.

---

340. See *alternative culture*.

The **ideology** produced is of love, of modified household relationships in contrast to those typically observed in the ancient Mediterranean, of respect, and of controlled passions. It is about mutual care in the community where the holy ones fit in and thrive. It is an ideology of thoughtful, intentional orderliness. Together believers think of the above things in Christ, who is their life (3:2–4). This ideology of love binds them together in maturity (ὅ ἐστιν σύνδεσμος τῆς τελειότητος, 3:14). The ideology leads in turn to the creation of a culture, hence a **social and cultural texture** in Colossians. While the new culture is recognizably structured in the way of Greco-Roman households, the ideology and modifications produce a culture of caring, of patience, of getting along with people, of humility rather than pride, of unselfishness rather than competition, power, and control. Things are not the same in the new reality. Do not cause disorder and chaos in the family-household and by extension in the body-*ekklēsia*. The orderliness of households is **intertexturally** reminiscent of the Jewish wisdom of Sirach 7:19–29, where wives, slaves, children, daughters, parents, priests, the poor, mourners, indeed even cattle are to receive care and respect.

Still, many twenty-first-century readers and interpreters view the *Haustafel* in Colossians as imposing hierarchical and oppressive structures.[341] Many understand the verses to support and maintain male domination of women and households. Why does implied Paul not unambiguously and explicitly call for equality of wives and husbands and for slavery to be abolished, at least within believing households and for individual believers? Why are slave masters and owners not directed to manumit their slaves? Slaves are to be treated with justice and equality (4:1), so it can be asked why they are not here considered "no longer as slave(s), but more than slave(s), (as) beloved brother(s)," as Paul wanted for Onesimus according to Phlm 16? Things seem to many readers not to go far enough.

Examination of **intertextures** does not provide resolution to these concerns. While Gal 3:28 states that "there is no longer slave or free" and Rom 6:15–23 speaks of being freed from the slavery of sin (though with "obedience out of heart"), 1 Cor 7:20–24 tells slaves to be unconcerned about their slavery and to remain in the enslaved condition in which they were called. These verses encourage slaves to see themselves as free persons of

---

341. The language of the *Haustafel* is a leading reason why many scholars reject Pauline authorship of Colossians and propose dating well after Paul's death.

the Lord, as slaves of Christ.[342] But what morality allows for brothers to be owners-masters or persons owned by brothers? Logically, from a modern (and perhaps mostly Western) point of view, you cannot own your household members (or anyone) as commercial and servile commodities. You cannot righteously consider household members to be inferior. Nor may you imagine yourself to be inferior or disposable. Yet the household category of slave remains. The language remains difficult, and its implications are (and have been) far-reaching even if the wisdom ideas of life in the new reality to which people have been transferred are altered, reconfigured. Did it occur to the authors of Colossians that oppressive hierarchies and slavery do not fit in to the new reality? Probably not.

It is, of course, important to understand that corrupt hierarchies are oppressive because they are predicated on power. On the other hand, functional hierarchies are predicated on productive reciprocity. The hierarchy of Colossians 3:18–4:1 is a functional, productive, and reciprocal hierarchy. But it is still a hierarchy that retains divisions and oppressions. There is certainly much that we do not know about the early *ekklēsiai*. The reality is that life was difficult for most people in the Roman Mediterranean. Roman law did not do much to help ordinary people whether in Rome or the provinces. Government in the provinces was enforced by the army.[343] Social conventions were difficult to resist. For early Christ believers, the genuine interpersonal and moral support came from the new reality of body-*ekklēsia*-household. In the sociocultural conditions of the day, "Just as the ambition of Roman slaves was usually to gain freedom for themselves, not to abolish slavery as an institution, so the ambitions of the poor were not radically to reconfigure the social order but to find a place for themselves nearer the top of the hierarchy of wealth."[344] Colossians and early Christians similarly had no ambitions to overthrow the sociopolitical order. What they needed was wisdom instruction about how to get along with each other as productive and maturing believers. Calling for the ideology of love and modified household relationships indicated in the

---

342. See Jeal, *Exploring Philemon*, 204–6. See also Titus 2:9–10, 1 Pet 2:18–21, and 1 Tim 1:8–10, where slave traders (kidnappers?) are described extremely negatively.

343. See Beard, *SPQR*, 464, 490. "A reasonable estimate is that across the empire at any one time there were fewer than 200 elite Roman administrators, plus maybe a few thousand slaves of the emperor, who had been sent out from the imperial centre to govern an empire of more than 50 million people" (490).

344. Beard, *SPQR*, 472.

household wisdom was the level of development that authors of the letter were able to imagine at the time, or at least what they did imagine. It had orderly living in mind.

In a similar way, the household wisdom presents an internal hermeneutical issue. Colossians has from the outset placed Father God's Son, the Son's divine identity, the Son's kingdom, and the Son's authority over against the irrelevant imperial political domain of empire and the order of the elements of the world. The Lycus Christ believers have been encouraged to reject conformity to social and religious pressures. Yet they are, according to the household wisdom, called to acceptance and practice of adapted but recognizable Greco-Roman-Jewish traditions of households. Some social and political inequalities, certainly from a modern point of view, are not removed, not in an explicit way. How might this be understood? Perhaps an answer lies in the reality that humans have survived with the constant tradition of living in structured households and families where they work, play, eat, sleep, procreate, nurture children and the aged, and are productive in multiple ways.

Rhetorical Force as Emergent Discourse

Believers living in households in Colossae, Laodicea, and Hierapolis were intelligent, intentional persons who had made the decision to become followers of the Lord Jesus. They knew that in their urban sociocultural contexts many people ordinarily lived in households and that the households were structured and managed. They also knew, implicitly and experientially, that life in the traditional households of wives, husbands, parents, children, and slaves could be chaotic. Power and self-interest predominated. In these contexts the household wisdom of Col 3:18–4:1 emerges with a rhetorical force intended to move the body-*ekklēsia*-household toward an orderly, filiated, and loving οἰκονομία. The rhetoric aims to persuade people to get along with each other despite the pressures and urges they must regularly face. Typical family-households are envisioned even though not everyone lived or could live in them or wanted to live in them. The household wisdom retains features of the hierarchies of the time but also reconfigures, nuances, and limits authoritarian, domineering, oppressive behaviors particularly initiated by husbands, fathers, and slave masters that often occurred in them. Members of households continue in traditional roles but are urged to treat each other with love, nurture, honesty, justice, and equality.

The force of the household wisdom is not in the establishment and maintenance of a rigid, required system (recall that Paul, his coworkers, and many others did not fit the family-household description) but in a call for ordered and surprisingly reciprocal living in the Mediterranean context of the time.[345] The household wisdom accords with the maturity in mind from the beginning of the letter (1:9–12, 28). The force of the language encourages the holy ones to seek the above things, to look upward to Christ, not downward to the earth, to the realm of the στοιχεῖα. It directs behavior outward to the good of others rather than to self.

Step Ten: Walking Forward, Looking Outward (4:2–6)

Rhetography

This step continues and concludes the visual scene where the holy ones are urged to seek and think about the above things that properly reflect their way of life that has been hidden with Christ in God (3:1–3). The location shifts from observing them in functioning households of reciprocal love, justice, and equality to seeing them now, along with Paul and his coworkers, living responsibly relative to the proclamation of the gospel mystery and toward nonbelievers. The picture is inclusive in the ways that the grammatical forms draw attention to "you," "we," "I," and "outsiders." The focus is on the "holy ones" (see 1:2, 3:12), who continue to "walk" (περιπατεῖτε, 4:5; see 1:10, 2:6), that is, to live their lives, now within sight of and in conversation with "those outside" (τοὺς ἔξω, 4:5)[346] who are imagined in space external to the body-*ekklēsia* and to their households. This view looks toward ongoing life and faith and implicitly to completion of the rhetograph the letter presents. The audience members are presented as urban residents being directed to keep their eyes on where they are and on the people around them. There are always other people nearby in Colossae, Laodicea, and Hierapolis. The lives of the holy ones are lived in the presence of many others.

Virtual Paul is observed in his prophetic space, calling out and confronting people with encouragement to engage in priestly and wisdom behaviors. He addresses the entire community of believers, not the indi-

---

345. The household code is thus not, in my view, kyriarchal.
346. Where the accusative plural article τούς functions effectively as a relative pronoun, "those."

vidualized household categories of 3:18–4:1. The priestly space of all the believers praying, watching, offering thanks, and focusing on outsiders is portrayed as the larger scene of action. The rhetoric evokes blended images and sounds of the holy ones and Paul himself thinking and speaking in constant, watchful prayers of thanksgiving and intercession that bring the "mystery of Christ" back into mind (recall 1:26–27 and 2:2). Paul is heard directing the believers in their constant, persistent prayers. He has been praying all along (1:3, 9), and the believers are continuing determinedly in that blended priestly-wisdom mode themselves (present imperative προσκαρτερεῖτε). Paul calls them to be alert in their prayers, watchful in it in thanksgiving (γρηγοροῦντες ἐν αὐτῇ ἐν εὐχαριστίᾳ). The prayers of the holy ones (= "you"), perhaps regarding their own concerns, become simultaneously priestly intercession for "us" (ἅμα καὶ περὶ ἡμῶν), that is, for Paul, Timothy, and no doubt other coworkers (such as those mentioned in 4:7–14), so that God might open for them ("to us," ἡμῖν) a door for the word to speak the "mystery of Christ."[347] The unseen God opens a metaphorical door, a portal, and Paul and his fellow proclaimers pass through the apocalyptic entrance and speak the mystery. The proclaimed word has been a feature of the imagery from early in the letter ("the word of the truth of the gospel," 1:5), and the combined picture of "the word" and "the mystery of Christ" has been envisioned clearly (1:25–27, 2:2).[348] Now audience members see Paul and his coworkers again as prophetic-apocalyptic proclaimers of "the mystery of Christ" among the nations. Mental images become directly focused on Paul who, in a shift to first-person "I" language, calls himself an imprisoned proclaimer ("on account of which [the mystery] I have been imprisoned," δι' ὃ καὶ δέδεμαι, 4:3; see 1 Cor 9:16). Paul continues to speak, in a deeply personal way, about the necessity he experiences to make the mystery "visible" (ἵνα φανερώσω αὐτὸ ὡς δεῖ με).[349] Yet he appears bound literally and figuratively because of the gospel in a way reminiscent of his self-portrayal of suffering, proclamation, and labor described in Col 1:24–29.

The Colossian believers hear Paul telling them to continue walking (see περιπατεῖτε, 2:6), now explicitly in wisdom (ἐν σοφίᾳ). This brings into view again the prayer wishes voiced earlier for "spiritual wisdom and

---

347. While the grammar presents God as the subject of the clause, the pronoun ἡμῖν makes clear that Paul and coworkers are the speakers of the mystery of Christ.

348. I.e., "brought to light" (νῦν δὲ ἐφανερώθη, 1:26).

349. Note, again, the verb φανερόω, "make visible, bring to light."

understanding" (1:9) and wisdom in teaching (3:16). This time, however, the wise walking takes account of "those outside." The concerns and actions of the Christ followers may not be only about themselves. This presents a shift in the rhetography and the priestly rhetoric in a new direction and to a new space. Certainly outsiders have been seen before (2:8, 16–23), but the priestly behavior and rhetoric now has wisdom and priestly connotations: it envisions the same (kinds of) persons to whom Paul is moved to proclaim the gospel mystery. The believers must employ an efficient wisdom that "buys back the time" (τὸν καιρὸν ἐξαγοραζόμενοι). There is no time to waste. Speaking the word of the mystery of Christ is crucial.[350] The speech of the believers must "always be in grace" (ὁ λόγος ὑμῶν πάντοτε ἐν χάριτι).[351] Listeners see themselves speaking with gracious, carefully nuanced words toward the outsiders. Speech "prepared with salt" has flavor, power, and productivity to it that makes it palatable and moving. This is speech that is carefully nuanced. It is spoken by wise people who make the most of the time. It has effects on hearers (see Mark 9:50, Luke 14:34, Matt 5:13). The believers observed employing this seasoned speech are encouraged to recognize the necessity of answering each person and each question (εἰδέναι πῶς δεῖ ὑμᾶς ἑνὶ ἑκάστῳ κρίνεσθαι).

This step shifts the rhetographic vision back on to virtual Paul, his coproclaimers, and particularly on the body of assembled believers in Colossae, now in their blended priestly-prophetic-wisdom roles. These holy ones are praying, giving thanks, speaking the word, living (walking) wisely, seeking ways to speak and answer questions carefully with the required grace and nuancing. The power of this blended imaging is that it displays to the faithful believers in Colossae that they themselves are workers together with Paul and others in speaking about and living out the mystery of Christ. What they are prompted to visualize themselves doing is directed externally, toward outsiders, for the sake of the outsiders who, it is hoped, will come to know the mystery that has been brought to light.

Translation

> **4:2** Continue persistently in prayer, watching in it in thanksgiving, **4:3** praying at the same time also for us, so that God might

---

350. This fits with Paul's compulsion to preach the gospel, 1 Cor 9:16.
351. This verbless clause implies the imperative "Your word must always be…."

open to us a door for the word, to speak the mystery of Christ, on account of which I have been imprisoned, **4:4** so that I might make it visible as it is necessary for me to speak it. **4:5** Walk in wisdom toward those outside, redeeming the time. **4:6** Your word must always be in grace, having been prepared with salt, to know how it is necessary to answer each one.

Textural Commentary

These lines form a *progressive texture* that shifts the rhetorical direction toward the conclusion of the letter. They move away from the explicit household-management discourse of the preceding step while at the same time recalling terms and ideas employed near the beginning of the letter. Like all of Colossians, this step envisions the lives of believers going on into the future. There is no expectation of the parousia or of eschatological events, only of the continuation of life in Colossae and the Lycus and concern for careful living and speaking about the mystery of Christ.[352] The progression in this way reaffirms and reshapes the concerns of 3:1–4 about making Christ known, visible, shining, in believers' lives and now, by their prayers, in Paul's proclamation (ἵνα φανερώσω αὐτὸ ὡς δεῖ με λαλῆσαι, 4:4). There is explicit concern for living in wisdom relative to "those outside," that is, toward nonbelievers (v. 5). The progressive texturing is about faithful life going forward with a view to speaking the word of "the mystery of Christ." This progression demonstrates the developed understanding that life in the new reality into which believers have been transferred goes on even though there is opposition, suffering, perhaps imprisonment. So, whatever happens, pray, watch, give thanks, walk in wisdom, speak carefully.

While this step calls for specific behaviors by the audiences, the internal first-person *repetitive texture* in pronouns ("us," "me") and a verb (δέδεμαι,[353] "I have been imprisoned") draws attention to Paul and his coworkers and their work in word and speech. This reintroduces threads observed earlier in the letter, where Paul is portrayed as servant of the proclaimed gospel, as one who fulfills the word of God, who proclaims

---

352. The only reasonably clear allusions to the future are in the hope mentioned in 1:5, 23, 27, and these allusions are not clearly eschatological. See the commentary on Col 3:1–4.

353. This perfect passive form of δέω occurs only here in biblical literature.

and mediates the formerly hidden mystery of Christ the hope of glory (see 1:23, 24–28). The emphasis there and here is on the proclaimed gospel mystery and words spoken by Paul and others. Paul's practices of prayer and thanksgiving (1:9, 12) are now to be displayed by the holy ones (see 2:7, 3:17). They are to continue to walk (i.e., to conduct themselves, to live, 1:10, 2:6, 3:7, 4:5) appropriately relative to the gospel, with repetition of the emphasis on wisdom seen earlier (1:9, 28; 3:16; see 1 Cor 1:18, 2:4, 2 Cor 1:18, Phil 1:14). The necessity of the "word" (repeated in Col 1:5, 25; 3:16) and speech is driven home by the repeated δεῖ in 4:4, 6. The effect of the repetitive texture is to draw audiences back to crucial ideas and practices mentioned earlier, reinforcing the way of life focused on Christ and gospel. The gospel proclamation is a necessity, and the believers are persuaded to be participants.

Woven into the rhetoric of this step is a distinct *sensory-aesthetic texture* of word and speech.[354] This texturing is a necessary feature of the priestly-wisdom rhetorolect and spatiality[355] at work. The body zone of self-expressive speech is particularly notable.[356] It seems obvious that speech is connected directly with the body zone of "emotion-fused thought."[357] Believers pray, offer thanks, speak, redeem time, prepare their words fully and carefully, and provide answers for those outside. These are mediating actions of mind and mouth practiced for the benefit of believers (namely, Paul and his coworkers, vv. 3–4) and for outsiders (vv. 5–6). The rhetoric and bodily actions simultaneously evoke a **sacred texture** where Lycus believers intercede with God in prayer with the proclamation of the mystery of Christ in mind.

The image of a door for the word is the developed endpoint in the New Testament of an **intertextural** topos observed in the Pauline letters at 1 Cor 16:9 (similarly near the end of a letter) and 2 Cor 2:12 (see Matt 7:7–8, Acts 14:27, Rev 3:20). God opens the doorway as an apocalyptic action, and proclaimers walk through it to people who might listen. The necessary wise and graceful words and speech are to be "seasoned with salt" (lit. "having been prepared with salt," ἅλατι ἠρτυμένος).[358] The mean-

---

354. Robbins, *Exploring the Textures of Texts*, 29–36.
355. Of space and place.
356. Robbins, *Exploring the Textures of Texts*, 31.
357. Robbins, *Exploring the Textures of Texts*, 30–31.
358. This perfect passive participle of ἀρτύω, "to arrange, devise, prepare," occurs only here in the New Testament.

ing of this striking rhetoric has similarly striking **intertextures** that help to understand its force.[359] There are differing kinds of salts, including sodium salts (e.g., table salt) and potassium salts (e.g., potash, a fertilizer). Ancient agricultural culture knew this. Salt can be destructive. It can poison the soil, as Judg 9:45 envisions. On the other hand, it can be an ingredient in useful ritual preparations (i.e., mixed preparations). For the altar in the tabernacle, Moses was directed to "make incense blended as by the perfumer, seasoned [mixed] with salt, pure and holy" (Exod 30:35 NRSVue). Jerusalemites being confronted and castigated for evil are described as not having been "washed with water ... nor rubbed with salt" as newborns, apparently a usual birth ritual (Ezek 16:4). In the new temple described in Ezek 40–44, priests were to "throw salt on them [i.e., on sacrificial animal flesh] and offer them up as a burnt offering to the Lord" (Ezek 43:24 NRSVue). Salt, obviously, was regularly employed to make food palatable: "Can that which is tasteless be eaten without salt, or is there any flavor in the juice of mallows?" (Job 6:6 NRSVue). The obvious New Testament intertextures referring to salt are Matt 5:13, Mark 9:50, and Luke 14:34, where sayings that refer to salt and saltiness have to do with faithfulness and effectiveness. Salt in these intertextural contexts has to do with proper preparation and proper usage, with faithfulness, effective behavior, and tastefulness. Speech "prepared with salt," similarly, is well thought through, careful, accurate, graceful wording that presents the mystery of Christ with the goal that it be accepted.

Likely building on the philosophical, religious, and social tensions addressed in 2:8–9 and 2:16–23, there is a **social-cultural texture** in the concerns of 4:5–6. This is the challenge-response situation where wisdom toward persons outside (πρὸς τοὺς ἔξω) the community was advisable.[360] The gospel in word and speech often evoked objections and opposition when it entered spaces and places on the outside. Responses should be made "in wisdom" (ἐν σοφίᾳ) and in the consciousness that

---

359. Some commentators note Plutarch, *Garr.* 23 [514f], "they seek to ingratiate themselves with each other by seasoning with the salt of conversation" (e.g., Wilson, *Colossians and Philemon*, 294 with n. 11). Wilson points out that, according to C. F. D. Moule, the wording is in fact "about seasoning *life* with *words* as one seasons food with salt; it says nothing about seasoning *words* with *wit*."

360. On challenge-response see Robbins, *Exploring the Textures of Texts*, 80–82. The spatial description of "those outside" (τοὺς ἔξω) reminds of the spatial description of "the above things" (τὰ ἄνω, 3:1).

time is important and must be managed carefully ("redeeming the time"). Speech must be spoken "in grace, prepared with salt," the metaphor portraying careful words that strike hearers with kindness and generosity rather than combative argumentation. This is all about life in the city in the midst of an array of viewpoints and practices. It is about discipline in the places in which believers live.

Argumentative texture. These verses do not present a freestanding argument. The argument is the continuation and ending of the larger concern of Colossians regarding the maturity of doing good works and bearing fruit that began at 1:9–11, of addressing external pressures (2:8, 16–23), and the direct behavioral directives of 3:5–17.

> **Case:** The audience members are urban and household residents in Colossae and nearby Lycus Valley towns. They live among and interact with the population of nonbelievers in Jesus. They continue their good living in prayer and thanksgiving, concerned about proclamation of the word, and with wisdom and careful speech in their associations with outsiders.
> **Implicit Rationale:** These are the right priestly-wisdom things to do as Christ believers. They have been rescued out of the jurisdiction of darkness, and life is now lived in the new reality of the Son's kingdom. Life is not now the competitive, judgmental, despairing life they lived previously under the στοιχεῖα.
> **Anticipated Result:** The believers will behave in the ways encouraged. There may well be opposition or suffering, but they will have nevertheless done the right things.

The rhetoric of these verses interweaves an **ideological texture**. It creates priestly-wisdom, outward-looking ideology. This is the endpoint of the well-thought-through way of seeing and practicing life that Colossians encourages. Lycus Valley believers are urged to place themselves in blended priestly-wisdom space where they intercede in prayer for the sake of the proclamation of the mystery. They themselves speak to outsiders in careful, prepared ways. They inhabit a mediating space and role that aims to do good, to be productive, for those outside. The believers now inhabit the same ideological space and activity that virtual Paul and his coworkers inhabit. Their priestly-wisdom activity is a demonstration of Christ being made known/visible (3:4).

Rhetorical Force as Emergent Discourse

The power in this step is in how the shift to blended priestly-wisdom rhetorolect is designed to move the faithful to live ("walk") for the benefit of others: for proclaimers such as Paul and his coworkers and for outsiders with whom they come in contact. It will likely have elicited quick agreement. The believers, who have already been exhorted to ordered ways of living (3:1–4:2), are well aware that they face criticism and opposition (2:8, 16–23). Here they are encouraged to behave in ways that are for the good of people who are not members of the body-*ekklēsia*-household even though some of those persons are their critics. Prayer and wisdom are emphasized in the placement of nouns (τῇ προσευχῇ, ἐν σοφίᾳ) before imperative verbs (προσκαρτερεῖτε, περιπατεῖτε). Making the mystery visible (φανερώσω) recalls the rhetoric of making Christ visible in 3:4.[361] Making the mystery visible is to shine with the glory of Christ. Priestly and wisdom functions are clearly what believers should do. It is what they are in the new reality of the Son's kingdom. It is the prepared life where they carefully salt their speech so that it will be understood and effective.

This emergent rhetoric ties the concerns of the letter together with the encouragement to exercise honest and beneficial behavior for others. As people face life in the present realities of the city, with the pressures and opportunities it brings to behave in chaotic ways and where they are pressured to practice religion and politics in expected ways, they are given instruction on how to live. This for them is the necessary approach to life in the empire. They fit in while simultaneously they operate as believers for the good of nonbelievers. They are wise priests.

---

361. "To bring to light, to cause to shine." Both occurrences of φανερόω (3:4, 4:4) are aorist subjunctives.

The Closing (4:7–18)

Scene Four: Personalities Rhetoric (4:7–18)

The exhortations of 4:2–6 have provided the Colossians with subtle clues that the letter is heading toward a conclusion. The action of the final scene confirms this movement in three steps, verses 7–9, 10–17, and 18. Specified people come into view, all of them appearing as persons known to Paul and, with the possible exception of Tychicus, imagined to be known to the Christ followers in Colossae. Some are situated at the edges of the rhetograph as persons who have been listening in to what Paul has been saying. Some are visible in a house-*ekklēsia* located in Colossae. Others are located farther away in the *ekklēsiai* of Laodicea and Hierapolis (4:13, 15–16). A number of named persons, coworkers with Paul, send their own greetings. These are all meant to be viewed as real people and reflect important roles they played in the emerging filiated kingdom-body-*ekklēsia*-household into which they have been transferred (1:13). The first visual step is characterized by coworkers conveying information about Paul to the Lycus believers. The second and third steps are characterized by repetitive emphasis on greetings (4:10, 12, 14, 15, 18).

Step One: Tychicus and Onesimus Reporting (4:7–9)

Rhetography

Paul continues to speak to the holy ones in Colossae, but the visual focus is on imprisoned Paul and two named persons who work faithfully with him and are shortly to be sent by him to provide news and, presumably, the letter Paul is dictating. Paul speaks in a mediatorial role from priestly space, aiming to convey personal, pastorally comforting information about himself in his imprisoned circumstances along with others located around him (τὰ περὶ ἡμῶν, 4:8), which will be conveyed directly by Tychicus, who is visualized as "the beloved brother and faithful servant and fellow slave" (like Epaphras, 1:7), and the "faithful and beloved" Onesimus. Tychicus and Onesimus have been sent (ὃν ἔπεμψα, 4:8), and Paul, those with him, and now the Colossians anticipate their arrival. The visual implication is that holy ones in Colossae are concerned about Paul in his personal circumstances and are eager for information. They are watching for the arrival of Tychicus and Onesimus and expect the comfort of heart they will receive at that time (ἵνα ... παρακαλέσῃ τὰς καρδίας ὑμῶν). By bringing his beloved Tychicus and Onesimus into the Colossians' visual imagination, Paul evokes anticipation for a similar connection of love between the two brothers and themselves. Onesimus is evidently already known to them (v. 9). The expectation of the visit elicits a vision of a visible receptive, hospitable disposition among them for the men and for the messages they will bring. Tychicus and Onesimus are seen as brothers whose beneficial priestly discourse will be welcomed. Paul and his coworkers anticipate the holy ones' reception of information and encouragement.

Translation

> **4:7** Tychicus the beloved brother and faithful servant and fellow-slave in (the) Lord will make all things about me known to you, **4:8** whom I sent to you for this very thing, so that you might know the things concerning us[1] and he might comfort your hearts, **4:9** with Onesimus the faithful and beloved brother, who is from you; he will make known to you about everything here.

Textural Commentary

These verses portray a new scene in the *narrational* and *progressive textures* of the letter. The textural threads regarding personalities and actions now head toward a finished fabric. Two *repetitive textures* emphasize important ideas in this step: the employment of "knowledge" words (γνωρίζω [γνωρίσει, v. 7; γνωρίσουσιν, v. 9]; γινώσκω [γνῶτε, v. 8]) and five occurrences of second-person plural pronouns (ὑμεῖς). These repetitions make obvious that the holy ones in Colossae are to be informed and comforted about virtual Paul's circumstances from virtual persons whom he has sent

---

1. NA[28] and UBS[5] indicate the variant γνῷ τὰ περὶ ὑμῶν rather than γνῶτε τὰ περὶ ἡμῶν.

to them (ὃν ἔπεμψα πρὸς ὑμᾶς) for the purpose.² Knowledge provides comfort to worried hearts (Τυχικὸς ... παρακαλέσῃ τὰς καρδίας ὑμῶν). This texturing emphasizes the audience members and demonstrates Paul's priestly, mediating, outward-looking concern for them. He is committed, of course, to his own work of proclamation (v. 4) but also committed to good for the Lycus believers. It is virtual Paul's recognition of need that elicits the action to meet the need. The identity of the faithful and beloved brother Tychicus is indicated by **intertextures** in Acts 20:3–4 (as an Asian), Eph 6:21, 2 Tim 4:9–12, and Titus 3:12. The similarly faithful and beloved Onesimus might be—but is not necessarily—the same person of interest in the Letter to Philemon (named at Phlm 10).

Argumentative texture. The visual image implied by the rhetograph portrays the audience's faces of concern for Paul and his coworkers. With the arrival of the letter they will be watching for the arrival of Tychicus and Onesimus and will anticipate the comfort of hearts they will receive at that time. By bringing his beloved Tychicus and Onesimus into the collective visual imagination, Paul evokes anticipation for a similar connection of love between the two brothers and the Colossians. The argument is that Tychicus and Onesimus are on the way, that they will report when they arrive, and that the Colossians will be comforted. The implication is that stress the Colossians are experiencing concerning Paul and his coworkers will be alleviated.

This rhetoric begins to present an **ideological texture** of coworkers that continues through to Col 4:17. It is an ideology of knowledge and filiated care. Coworkers, in this case Tychicus and Onesimus, are persons who direct their efforts toward the knowledge and care of members of the *ekklēsia*. The ideology evokes a **social-cultural texture** in the rhetoric that is aimed at shaping people's lives toward the alternative culture centered on the mystery of Christ, where humans have been transferred to the new reality described early in the letter (1:12–14).³ The ideology is about care

---

2. The same aorist verb form, ἔπεμψα, occurs six times in the Pauline corpus (1 Cor 4:17, 2 Cor 9:3, Phil 2:28, 1 Thess 3:5, Col 4:8, Eph 6:22), each time referring to Paul sending someone to provide or receive information. See the aorist phrase ὃν ἀνέπεμψά σοι, "whom I send back to you," in Phlm 12. The phrasing is suggestive for the timing of Colossians being possibly not long after Philemon.

3. See *alternative culture* in the introduction. See also Robbins, *Exploring the Textures of Texts*, 87.

for people and how they are getting along in a difficult world. It flows from the concerns observed in 4:2–6.

Step Two: Greetings (4:10–17)

More people become visible around Paul as he voices their names and sends their greetings, indicating that they are recognizable, perhaps by sight but surely as persons known to be faithful, caring believers.[4] They are real humans, coworkers, envoys; perhaps some assist with preparing the letter. Most are imagined to be in a room with Paul, perhaps a place used for imprisonment, standing or sitting, perhaps waving a hand in greeting or saying, "Send a greeting from me!" as he speaks the letter into existence. They exhibit deep levels of maturity in the faith. Paul calls Aristarchus his "fellow captive" (συναιχμάλωτός),[5] perhaps thereby displaying him as physically imprisoned like Paul himself (see 4:3). Mark, who is here called cousin of Barnabas, voices a greeting.[6] There is an oblique reminder of a previously received (ἐλάβετε) directive[7] regarding Mark, that he be expected and received (δέξασθε αὐτόν) by the *ekklēsia* there. The content, circumstances, and reasons for the directive known by believers in Colossae are not revealed in the rhetograph. It does, however, portray Mark as already recognizable in Colossae. He can be imagined being received hospitably when he arrives at some future moment.[8] Greetings also come from Jesus called Justus and from some others who are Jewish (οἱ ὄντες ἐκ περιτομῆς, 4:11). All these persons are visible, supportive coworkers in the kingdom of God with Paul and are a great comfort to him. Epaphras, who has been in sight from the beginning of the letter (1:7) and, like Onesimus, is visually recognizable, sends his greeting. He is particularly noted, like Tychicus, as

---

4. We do not know in absolute terms whether the greetings are real or manufactured by virtual Paul in an attempt to sound authoritative to audiences after Paul had died.

5. Idiomatically a prisoner of war, a captive; lit. "taken with a spear" (see Rom 16:7; Phlm 23).

6. See the descriptions of John also called Mark in Acts 12:12, 25, and Paul's negative view of him, leading to a separation between Paul and Barnabas in Acts 15:36–39. See the more positive language about Mark, similar to what is observed here, in Phlm 24 and 2 Tim 4:11.

7. A strong term, ἐντολή, suggesting a divine command. Both Mark and Colossian believers seem subject to directives from Paul.

8. Literally "if he comes to you" (ἐὰν ἔλθῃ πρὸς ὑμᾶς). We do not know whether he arrived.

a slave of Christ with Paul. Epaphras is agonizing, struggling, facing anxiety for the holy ones all the time in his prayers. He envisions their future, seeing his friends in Colossae reaching maturity and being fully assured (πληροφορέω) in all the will of God. Placing this picture in their minds gives them the same vision of their future along with holy ones in Laodicea and Hierapolis (4:13).[9] Luke, like Epaphras, Tychicus, and Onesimus, is "beloved" and appears as a physician or healer (ἰατρός). Demas sends a greeting but is not otherwise portrayed (see Phlm 24; 2 Tim 4:10).

The visual angle shifts at verse 15 because Paul now calls on the listeners to convey greetings to filiated people outside the immediate scene. Greetings go to "the brothers in Laodicea" and to "Nympha and the *ekklēsia* in her house."[10] Nympha may well be resident in Laodicea. The hospitable Nympha has a leadership role as one to be greeted as a provider of meeting space. Paul directs that the letter be read in the *ekklēsia* of the Laodiceans, and one sent to Laodicea[11] to be read in Colossae. This language casts the imagery of readers holding the papyrus texts in their hands and addressing the *ekklēsiai* with voices heard attentively by all present, after which the letters are exchanged.[12]

In a last look at the holy ones in Colossae, they are observed hearing Paul directing them to speak to a man called Archippus. He is to "look at the ministry [he] received in (the) Lord, so that [he] might fulfill it." Presumably the holy ones know Archippus and are able to pass the slightly cryptic message along.[13] Paul presents as being confident that Archippus will receive the message.

Translation

4:10 Aristarchus my fellow captive greets you, also Mark the cousin of Barnabas (concerning whom you received a command:

---

9. Laodicea is mentioned in the New Testament only in Colossians and Rev 1:11, 3:14. Hierapolis is mentioned only here in the New Testament.

10. It is possible, if unlikely, that the named person could be Νυμφᾶς, a man, rather than a woman named Νύμφα.

11. A lost letter, presumably also written (i.e., spoken) or at least known by Paul.

12. The notion of speaking and listening is inherent to the meaning of the verb ἀναγινώσκω. See Rudolf Bultmann, "ἀναγινώσκω, ἀνάγνωσις," *TDNT* 1:343–44.

13. The name Archippus occurs in Phlm 2, one reason why many scholars connect Philemon with Colossae.

if he comes to you, receive him) **4:11** and Jesus called Justus, the ones being of the circumcision, only these coworkers in the kingdom of God became a comfort to me. **4:12** Epaphras who is from you greets you, a slave of Christ Jesus,[14] always agonizing for you in prayers, so that you might stand as mature[15] and fully assured in all (the) will of God. **4:13** For I testify about him that he has labored much for you and for those in Laodicea and Hierapolis. **4:14** Luke the beloved physician and Demas greet you. **4:15** Greet the brothers in Laodicea and Nympha and those in the *ekklēsia* in her[16] house. **4:16** And whenever this letter may be read to you, ensure that it also may be read in the *ekklēsia* of Laodiceans, and that you also may read the one from Laodicea. **4:17** And say to Archippus, "Look to the ministry which you received in (the) Lord, so that you may fulfill it."

Textural Commentary

The rhetoric of these verses continues the **ideological** and **social-cultural texturing** of filiated care. Named Christ believers who are with or closely associated with Paul have genuine care for believers in distant locations, so they send greetings. The leading **inner texture** that emphasizes this is in the *repetition* of "[he] greets you" (ἀσπάζεται ὑμᾶς, 4:10, 12, 14), followed by the imperative "greet" (ἀσπάσασθε, v. 15). It occurs again in nominal form in 4:18 with Paul's greeting. Epaphras, whose importance stands out as one who communicated "the word of the truth of the gospel" to the Colossians and had reported to Paul about their love in the Spirit (1:5–8), is here described with the emotionally charged language of agonizing for them in his prayers.[17] The *repetitive texturing* of the descriptor "beloved" (ἀγαπητός), employed five times in Colossians (1:7; 3:12; 4:7, 9, 14), here applied to Luke and just previously to Tychicus and Onesimus, points out virtual Paul's filiated care for his coworkers. The range of **intertextures** connecting the named persons range through Acts and the Pauline corpus. Aristarchus was dragged away with Paul and

---

14. Some manuscripts do not include Ἰησοῦ, "Jesus."
15. I.e., complete. The word τέλειοι may function as an adverb, "maturely," or idiomatically, "so that you might be mature."
16. NA[28] and UBS[5] indicate the variants αὐτῶν and αὐτοῦ.
17. On Epaphras, see Trainor, *Epaphras*.

Gaius by angered worshipers of Artemis during a riot in Ephesus (Acts 19:23–41). Aristarchus is identified as a Macedonian (19:29). Later, following three months in Greece (20:2–30), Aristarchus, now described as being from the Macedonian city of Thessalonica, traveled through Macedonia and, ahead of Paul, across the Aegean to Troas (20:5). According to Phlm 23–24, Aristarchus sent a greeting to Philemon and the *ekklēsia* in his house. Mark, cousin of Barnabas, noted as also bearing the name John, was from Jerusalem and seems to have joined Paul and Barnabas in Antioch and then traveled with them to Jerusalem (Acts 12:12, 25). Later, Mark seems to have deserted Paul and Barnabas at Pamphylia to return to Jerusalem (Acts 13:13). This led to Paul and Barnabas, with Mark, separating and traveling to different locations (15:36–41). Mark's name in Phlm 24 indicates that he and Paul became coworkers again later.[18] The name Epaphras also appears in Phlm 23, where he is similarly described as sending a greeting.[19] Both Luke and Demas are named as Paul's coworkers in Phlm 24. Both are mentioned again in 2 Tim 4:10–11, there noting that Demas, loving the present age, had abandoned his work with Paul. Luke is identified as "beloved physician," thus giving him status and possibly a specialized role among the coworkers.

These **intertextures** indicate a history of cooperative work and fellowship. The **ideology** of committed coworkers is prominent in these verses. They present a strong sense of solidarity with Paul. Their greetings demonstrate their own connections to the mystery of Christ and their intentions to do good, supportive things.[20] The texturing encourages a strong ideology of working together for the cause. Yet it is also clear that Paul and his traveling coworkers are not typical household members like the resident Colossian believers indicated in 3:18–4:1. There are no houses, no wives and husbands, no children, no slaves in sight among them. So the

---

18. See n. 6, above. See also 1 Tim 4:11, indicating Paul's assessment of Mark and wish for his assistance; also 1 Pet 5:13. Jesus called Justus, Col 4:11, is very unlikely to be the Joseph called both Barsabbas and Justus according to Acts 1:23.

19. The name Epaphras is a short form of "Epaphroditus … associated with the goddess Aphrodite" (Trainor, *Epaphras*, 7). Trainor suggests he might have been a "Hellenized Israelite." He is not the same person as Epaphroditus whose name appears in Phil 2:25, 4:18 (see Trainor, *Epaphras*, 7–10).

20. The authors of Colossians could, of course, have added in the names and greetings, derived from other letters or knowledge, in an attempt to give the letter Pauline authority.

precise household-management structure presented earlier is not the rule for everyone.

Repetitive texturing stands out in the rhetorical force of four imperative verbs (ἀσπάσασθε, ποιήσατε, εἴπατε, βλέπε, 4:15–17) that shift the action by calling the believers in Colossae to take specific actions. They are not only recipients of greetings and care from a distance, but they are to "greet" other believers, "make sure" that letters are shared and read, and "say" to Archippus that he must "look" to the ministry given to him. The *sensory texture* of the imperatives (i.e., the homoeoteleuton of the verbs) presses them toward transferring the care they receive from Paul and his coworkers to people they know live nearby. In these ways the priestly-wisdom discourse turns toward actions the recipients should practice for believers in Laodicea and adds a touch of prophetic, confrontational rhetoric in the directive to speak strongly to Archippus.[21] The name Archippus occurs in Phlm 2, where Paul calls him "fellow soldier." Another striking rhetorical feature occurs in 4:16, where the adverb of time ὅταν, "whenever," recurs a second time in the letter (see Col 3:4). With the *repeated* aorist subjunctive passive form ἀναγνωσθῇ ("may be read," twice in 4:16), repeated readings of Colossians and the letter to the Laodiceans are envisioned.[22] The *argumentative texture* in this step is in the subtle force of greetings, personalities, expressions of love, concern for groups and individuals, and imperatives. Explicit rationales are neither employed nor needed to make the case. The care of souls is understood and felt.

Step Three: Personal Greeting (4:18)

Paul has been speaking, but now, probably after the letter has been transcribed to papyrus, he takes up a stylus, the only mechanical writing he is envisioned doing himself in the letter, writes his own greeting, and signs his name (Παύλου, "of Paul"). He looks to the holy ones in the Lycus towns to think of him in a supportive and encouraging way: "Remember my chains." The picture is of Paul imprisoned, isolated from many fellow believers, contemplative, not doing more than communicating by letter.

---

21. We do not know any details about why the exhortation to Archippus was needed. Might he have been neglecting his ministry?

22. As noted in the comments on Col 3:4, the authors understood the difference between ὅταν (whenever) and ὅτε (when), which is employed in 3:7.

Audiences will discern implications of what they observe. Paul words a verbless postscript benediction: "Grace with you."

The rhetograph ends where it began, with a visualization of Paul, still standing as a prophetic-priestly apostle of Christ Jesus by the will of God (1:1). The closing portrayal leaves an embedded image of Paul in audiences' visual thinking. Receiving this intercession and benediction, people leave Paul and some of his coworkers on the virtual stage and go about their lives in Christ, in the believing body-*ekklēsia*-household, in the kingdom of the Son, having all of the imagery of the letter in their minds and memories, with God's grace sustaining them.

Translation

> **4:18** The greeting by my hand, Paul. Remember my chains. Grace with you.[23]

Textural Commentary

These words form the *closing texture* of the letter. The closing has been signaled from 4:2 onward, but this verse ends the letter in a straightforward way. The economy of words is striking. There are three sentences but only one verb, the imperative "Remember" (μνημονεύετέ). The verbless statements are nevertheless completely clear; the ideas and subtle emotions are unmistakable. Though Paul is described as chained, not able to come and go freely, he remains confident, concerned about others, encouraging. This is blended priestly-wisdom discourse: priestly because it is shaped by Paul's sacrificial living for the sake of the gospel and all the holy ones, wisdom because it continues to envision productive, blessed lives for the Lycus audiences. The verbless blessing "grace with you" closes the letter with allusions to its *sensory-aesthetic texturing* as it looks toward their lives continuing in the realities and behaviors the letter encourages:

> Christ in you, the hope of glory;
> watch out so you are not taken captive;
> you have been filled in him;
> don't let someone judge you;

---

23. Some manuscripts read ἡμῶν, "us." Some close the letter with Ἀμήν.

you were raised with Christ;
seek the above things;
you will shine with him in glory;
put on the new person;
let the peace of Christ umpire in your hearts;
be thankful;
sing;
fit in;
pray;
walk in wisdom.
Grace with you.

Rhetorical Force as Emergent Discourse

The writers and greeters of the letter recognized that the Christ communities of Colossae and the neighboring Lycus towns faced the pressures of living in the dominating Roman provincial context. The closing rhetoric demonstrates their strong support for the *ekklēsiai* with warm greetings, expressions of concern, genuine care, sincere prayers, all with a view to faithful wisdom living. The recipients are, as the letter has made clear, surrounded by people who believe in a range of deities including the imperial cult, and they face pressure to fit into the same uncertain, chaotic social and religious practices of their neighbors. The rhetoric of the letter has made clear that all they need, fullness, is what they already have in Christ, who is "all and in all" (3:11). The rhetorical force is pretty clear. The audiences are cared for, encouraged, loved by Paul and his various coworkers. There is an implicit encouragement that calls for them not to be daunted by the pressures they face where they live. They should also not be daunted by concerns about Paul's perceived circumstances. These closing verses have priestly-wisdom rhetorical force that offers encouragement from a distance out of recognition that the pressures of the cosmos, of empire, and of Lycus locations are not the locus of hope and security. This rhetoric of coworkers moves people through filiated, warm, interpersonal concern that is the true care of souls. It aims to create a mindset of trust in Christ. Such care of souls is what drives the entire letter.

Rhetorical Force as Emergent Discourse

Colossians is a profound document of creative, developed rhetorical discourse designed to drive home the knowledge that things are different now for humans, for the holy ones who have become believers in and followers of Christ Jesus, and for the entire created order of the heavens and the earth (τὰ πάντα, τὰ ἐπὶ τῆς γῆς, τὰ ἐν τοῖς οὐρανοῖς). The rhetoric of the letter enters the domain of the body-*ekklēsia* in Colossae and the Lycus. It simultaneously penetrates the sociocultural, political, religious, philosophical, and ideological domains of the ancient Mediterranean. The spaces have been altered. The holy ones have been transferred to the new reality of bright light in the kingdom of Father God's beloved Son. Despite how things may look and feel when facing pressures to conform to political, social, and religious expectations, they are encouraged to recognize that they no longer live in the dark jurisdiction of confused, chaotic, and uncertain existence of their local and Mediterranean environments. Their hope is stored up in the heavens. They need to be reminded and taught more about this new reality in clear, full ways that fill them with knowledge that moves them to secure, mature, and wise understandings of the glory of the mystery that has been brought to light in Christ. Colossians fills this need. The new reality extends from the precreational realm of Father God and his Son and has been brought about by God's apocalyptic actions that have made the letter recipients completely full in Christ, the one in whom all the fulness of deity houses (dwells).

This new reality in Christ makes all other supposed realities irrelevant. The perceived realities of rulers, powers, and authorities of hegemony, whether seen or unseen, of human traditions and the elements of the world, are still there, but they have been triumphed, led away in a procession as defeated captives. The holy ones can walk ahead securely and confidently toward deepened maturity and productive behavior, in the faith and love in which they have been rooted, founded, and securely established. The powers and elements of the world have been disgraced by

Christ Jesus, who ironically suffered disgrace in their presence. Christ's disgrace brought about their own disgrace in what they imagine to be their own realm of power. These things reflect the creativity of thinking and the development of ideas that led to understanding realities not grasped earlier.

Creativity initiates ideas and the development of ideas. Conversely, ideas and their development arouse creativity. Creativity and the development of ideas blend together and emerge in rhetorical discourse.[1] This is what occurred in the minds of the authors of Colossians and was communicated in words to the audiences. By the time the letter was written, likely significantly before that time, people such as Paul and others who were committed to the new faith had come to what was for them the natural creative development of their theological and practical knowledge. They engaged in reasoning about the nature and implications of their new reality in Christ. Their deep understanding of the gospel—including their intertextural, social, cultural, and ideological knowledge, along with their deep faith and sheer intellect—tied with their ability to use language and craft argumentation, moved them to speak and write the conceptual ideas and truths presented in the textures of the letter.[2] They considered central ideas of their faith: Who is Christ Jesus? What did God do in Christ? What makes us full, complete? Are Christ and the new reality adequate? Is anything more required? What are implications for living in the world? Virtual Paul and his fellow speakers-authors recognized that the hidden mystery now brought to light in Christ led them to a new storyline of existence that begins in the domain of Father God and his Son prior to the creation of the heavens and the earth. They understood that the new gospel reality is not provided by the seen and unseen thrones, rulers, powers, and authorities of the created order but by Father God in and through his Son.

The rhetorical force of the developed philosophical and theological discourse in Colossians produces ideologies in the minds and lives of Christ believers. Ideologies shape how people understand and function in the contexts they inhabit. This is to say that the rhetoric aims to persuade people to adhere to a particular set of values, to understandings of truth and how things should be done, and to the frame of mind conveyed in the

---

1. See the discussion of creativity in the introduction.
2. In SRI terms, they were able to blend knowledge and ideas from multiple places into complex third spaces.

gospel.³ This set of values and understandings is fully believed to be true and trustworthy, composed of realities from which the holy ones must not deviate or be persuaded to abandon in favor of deceptive and false thinking and practice.

Ideology of the Gospel

Recipients of the letter are reminded of the proclaimed truth and hope of the gospel they had heard (εὐαγγέλιον, 1:5, 23). They had become faithful and loving people in Christ who see the world through a gospel lens. In other words, they heard and believed the gospel as truth, and it affected their practice or walk of life. The believers are committed to the gospel, that is, the mystery now brought to light (1:25–27, 2:2–3), to the conviction that Jesus is Messiah, raised from the dead. Taking these things as truth means life must be viewed and practiced in new ways. The letter is designed to encourage continuation of the walk. The walk is headed toward knowledge and maturity in Christ (1:9–11, 28). The gospel is ideology that explains and gives order to life. Christ believers are persuaded to think and live in gospel ways.

Ideology of Hope

The rhetoric generates an ideology of hope. Hope is stored up in the heavens (1:5) as a reality of the present, not an expectation of the eschatological future. It is the true hope of the proclaimed gospel (1:23), the reality of "Christ in you, the hope of glory" (1:27). This hope is understood as secure in the heavens, something better than what is experienced in the uncertainty and disorder on the earth. It cannot be altered or removed by things on the earth. The stored hope, understood by faith, envisages the raised Christ Jesus, who is seated at the right of God (3:1). By contrast, a secure hope is not found on the earth, in the ways of the earth, of nations or powers, or in the elements of the earth. Life in the Roman and Mediterranean realms does not provide this stored hope. It offers unending pressure to conform to political, social, and religious ideologies and expectations and to the complaints of others who demand the conformity.

---

3. On ideological texture see Jeal, *Exploring Philemon*, 195–96. For full description see Robbins, *Exploring the Textures of Texts*, 95–115.

Humans cannot do enough to satisfy all the demands. Life in the Lycus was tenuous: suffering and death were always nearby. The hope stored in the heavens gives assurance that all is and will be well. The ideology of hope elicits a sense of security and fearlessness. The stored hope encourages the faith and love of Christ followers.

Ideology of the Son-Christ

The underlying philosophical and argumentative understanding of Colossians is that God's Son has existed and been active from before the beginning, from before the creation of the heavens and the earth. The Son is the image of God, creator of and preeminent over all things. This places him prior to and transcendent over the created order. The Son of God, Messiah Jesus, is the source of all good things. In him God has provided redemption, reconciliation, forgiveness, and peace. The authors of Colossians present this as the underlying reality of the gospel present in the domain of God before thrones, powers, authorities, and gods were imagined to exist. It is not a human construct nor composed of humanly produced political or religious entities. They came to this in their creative theological reasoning about who Christ Jesus must be. Their reasoning has drawn on what they know about the protological and personified existence of wisdom (σοφία), read or heard from texts such as Prov 3:19–20, 8:22–31, Wis 7:22–8:1, and Sir 1:4–10, 24:1–34.[4] The Son-image of God, the one in whom deity houses itself, who was present and active prior to creation in the domain (household) of God, now raised from the dead, is the one through whom God makes things right in the cosmos. Believers have died and been raised with him (Col 2:13, 20; 3:1). Good thinking, good behavior, and a sense of security in Christ are driven by this way of seeing reality. This philosophy-ideology is foundational for the argumentation of Colossians. It presents the alternative to the philosophical-ideological understanding of imperial Rome and the religious construct that humans must please and appease the gods in order to flourish.[5] The Christ ideology is about the formerly hidden mystery, the glory of which has been brought to light in Christ the hope of glory.

---

4. See the analysis of the **intertexture** of Col 1:15–20.

5. I.e., that benefactions and good things from deities depend on appropriate and correct human actions.

In Colossians this ideology is brought to its high point in the statement "Christ all and in all" (3:11).

Ideology of the New Reality in the Son's Kingdom

Christ followers have been transferred by the Father into the Son's kingdom (Col 1:13). This is an ideology of location. The rhetorical message is, "This is where you are, in the Son of Father God's kingdom." The transferral (or *metastasis*, 1:13) has moved humans from darkness into light and love. The ideology reshapes perspective, creating consciousness of the new reality in Christ and in the *ekklēsia*. This kingdom functions on the gospel and the precreational realities. To be in this kingdom is to be in the realm of light and love in contrast to the realm of darkness and shadow (1:3, 2:17, 3:4). The ideology conveys the understanding that believers are not to imagine themselves as dominated by other kingdoms, political entities, or ideologies. It recognizes that the things of the earth are transitory at best and dangerous at worst. Such kingdoms as those promote a deceptive sense of security built on the unstable foundation of human achievement. Christ alone is the hope of glory. The kingdom in which they now live, though to many seeming to be weak in the death of Christ, subverts the gospel of human empires by demonstrating that God provides what human effort cannot. This ideology moves people ahead fearlessly, unhesitatingly, even in the face of pressure to conform to the expectations and complaints of people around them.

Ideology of Fullness

The creative and developed theology-ideology of Christ recognizes that "in him houses all the fullness of deity bodily." From this it follows that "you have been made full in him who is head of every power and authority." The warning about a deceitful philosophy, human traditions, and elements of the world is against the claim that fullness of life is acquired by taking on and practicing disordered and frankly unhelpful humanly produced religious practices, some of them designed to satisfy the complaints of people who do not understand the gospel. The ideology conveyed in the rhetoric of Col 2:9–10 answers this by saying in effect, "No. We have been filled already." Do not try to fill what is already full. The way of the elements of the world is dangerous. It enslaves people to darkness and disorder and to failing attempts to acquire fullness of life.

Ideology of Circumcision

Colossians employs the imagery of the circumcision of Christ (2:11) as a way of describing the actions of God that make humans alive with Christ, providing forgiveness and freedom from the powers and authorities (2:12–15). Circumcision, of course, is about cutting and removing a piece of flesh. The metaphor represents the apocalyptic cutting and removal of the inhibiting existence in the disordered world (see 3:5–9). It calls the believers to recognize that the old life of conformity to the deceptive philosophy of human traditions and the elements of the world's expectations has been removed. Once removed, the "foreskin of your flesh" (2:13) is discarded. The new ideology of circumcision moves people ahead in their walk, not back to the pressure to do enough to acquire benefactions such as redemption, reconciliation, forgiveness, and peace by their own efforts and merits.

Ideology of Orderly Living

The letter evokes an ideology of orderly behavior in stark contrast to well-known disordered and chaotic practices. Recipients of the letter are imbued with an approach to living where they put to death disordered behaviors and clothe themselves with ordered and beneficial actions (3:5–17). Disordered actions are earthly, self-indulgent, divisive, and idolatrous. They set individual selfish urges and interests above behavior that reflects the above realm of God and the Son-Christ. The old person has been stripped off and the new person put on. These alterations of clothing promote an ideology of identity—people are identified by and behave in ways that mirror the clothing they wear. The orderly living is characterized above all by love. It is mature and peaceful. This is wisdom ideology. It is practiced not out of necessity or compulsion but because it is the right thing to do for people who are in Christ.

Ideology of Family and Household

From the outset Colossians portrays family (kinship) connections. God is "our Father God" (1:1) and the "Father God of our Lord Jesus Christ" (1:3). Recipients of the letter are brothers (and implicitly sisters) who together form the faithful and loving body-*ekklēsia*, people who are bearing fruit and growing in their lives as Christ followers. This rhetoric indicates the kinship ideology of the authors and simultaneously creates and reinforces an ideology of filiated relationships among the recipients. They live in the new reality of the Son's kingdom, where they are encouraged to envision themselves in a shared family-household relationship, an οἰκονομία to whom the mystery of God has been manifested, in whom God makes known the rich glory of the mystery: Christ in them (1:25–27). They are an urban, filiated body-*ekklēsia*-family, most of whom live in households. While not all Christ believers lived in traditional household circumstances—nor should they have been expected to do so—most did live in households where there were wives, husbands, parents, children, and slaves. Colossians admits the tradition but alters it by calling for higher and more pervasive provisions of care than were usual in Roman-dominated Mediterranean families. This is the development of family and household ideology observed in the letter. Household members are called to live together in safe, productive, caring relationships.

The true father is Father God, who has redeemed the members of the body-family in his Son-Christ. The genuine *pater* is not Caesar as *pater patriae*.[6] However imperfect the developed family-household ideology seems to be, it made for improved treatment of typical household members. It contrasts with the imperial ideology displayed on the Ara Pacis, the altar of peace in Rome. The Ara Pacis promoted political power, peace, priesthood (traditional Roman religion), and family. The family portrayed on the altar was the imperial family, visualized as a powerful Augustan imperial dynasty.[7] It was propaganda aimed at power and authority. Colossians presents and promotes the developed caring ideology of family in households in the kingdom of the Son of God, into which believers have been transferred. This is God's οἰκονομία. It is not concerned with status and power, only with Christ. It would speak loudly to Lycus Christ believers.

Ideology of the Care of Souls

From the outset, Colossians indicates that virtual Paul and his coworkers have had the growth and maturity of the holy ones in mind. Their prayers

---

6. Emperors from Augustus (2 BCE) to Caligula (37 CE), Claudius (42 CE), Nero (55 CE), Vespasian (70 CE), Titus (79 CE), Domitian (81 CE), Nerva (96 CE), Trajan (98 CE), and others subsequently were conferred with the title *pater patriae*, "father of the fatherland."

7. On the Ara Pacis see https://www.arapacis.it/en.

and thanksgivings testify to this (1:3–8, 9–12; 4:12). Paul is described as experiencing much anxiety for the believers in Colossae and Laodicea, concerned to encourage them, to emphasize the "mystery of God—of Christ—in whom are all the hidden treasures of wisdom and knowledge," so that they do not become deceived by persuasive arguments (2:1–4). Believers are encouraged to "seek the above things" (3:1) and to behave in ways that demonstrate care for others. The rhetoric of the letter looks toward the good of people, indicated in faith and love. This ideology of the care of souls is pervasive in the letter and extends to those outside in proclamation of the mystery of Christ and in careful interaction (4:2–6).

Ideologies create a culture. What emerges in Colossians is an alternative culture and rhetoric of wisdom that is dramatically different from what the Christ followers regularly encountered in their Lycus Valley environment.[8] The alternative culture of the new reality encourages the values of living that guide the walk through life. Living in the developed alternative culture did not mean that the dominant culture of empire, Phrygia, and the Lycus would not cause stressful opposition. The empty, deceitful philosophy continued to exist. The alternative culture of the Christ believers, however, informed them that they were secure in their faith. They should not allow themselves to be persuaded to give in to complaints and to pressures to conform to the dominant culture. They had died to the elements of the world and been raised with Christ. Sins were forgiven. Whatever stood against them was erased. They did not live in the shadow and should not revert to it. There is a new politic where individual good works, obedience, getting things right socially, culturally, and religiously, and pleasing complainants are not useful responses to life issues. There is only trust in God and what God has done in Christ. Do not be deceived. Keep on walking. Put on love (3:14). Anticipate glory. This is the rhetorical force of the Letter to the Colossians.

---

8. See *alternative culture texture* in the introduction.

Bibliography

"Ancient Writing Materials: Wax Tablets." University of Michigan Library. https://tinyurl.com/SBL7106b.
Anderson, Janice Capel. *Colossians: Authorship, Rhetoric, and Code.* TCSGNT. London: T&T Clark, 2019.
Aphrodisias homepage. https://tinyurl.com/SBL7106j.
"Aphrodisias Excavations." Aphrodisias Excavations Project. https://tinyurl.com/SBL7106i.
Aristotle. *Art of Rhetoric.* Translated by John H. Freese. LCL. Cambridge: Harvard University Press, 1926.
———. *Politics.* Translated by Harris Rackham. LCL. Cambridge: Harvard University Press, 1932.
Arnold, Clinton E. *The Colossian Syncretism: The Interface between Christianity and Folk Belief at Colossae.* Grand Rapids: Baker, 1996.
———. *Ephesians: Power and Magic; The Concept of Power in Ephesians in Light of Its Historical Setting.* SNTSMS 63. Cambridge: Cambridge University Press, 1989.
———. "Initiation, Vision, and Spiritual Power: The Hellenistic Dimension of the Problem at Colossae." Pages 173–86 in *The First Urban Churches 5: Colossae, Hierapolis, and Laodicea.* Edited by James R. Harrison and L. L. Welborn. WGRWSup 16. Atlanta: SBL Press, 2019.
———. *Powers of Darkness: Principalities and Powers in Paul's Letters.* Downers Grove, IL: InterVarsity Press, 1992.
Aune, David E. *The Westminster Dictionary of New Testament and Early Christian Literature and Rhetoric.* Louisville: Westminster John Knox, 2003.
Balch, David L. "Household Codes." Pages 25–50 in *Greco-Roman Literature and the New Testament.* Edited by David L. Balch. SBLSBS 21. Atlanta: Scholars Press, 1988.
Barclay, John M. G. *Colossians and Philemon.* NTG. Sheffield: Sheffield Academic, 1997.

Barth, Markus. *Ephesians: A New Translation with Introduction and Commentary*. AB 34, 34A. Garden City, NY: Doubleday, 1984.

Barth, Markus, and Helmut Blanke. *Colossians: A New Translation with Introduction and Commentary*. Translated by Astrid B. Beck. AB 34B. New York: Doubleday, 1994.

Beale, G. K. *Colossians and Philemon*. BECNT. Grand Rapids: Baker Academic, 2019.

Beard, Mary. *SPQR: A History of Ancient Rome*. New York: Liveright, 2015.

Becker, Eve-Marie. *Paul on Humility*. Translated by Wayne Coppins. BMSSEC. Waco, TX: Baylor University Press, 2020.

Bédoyère, Guy de la. *Domina: The Women Who Made Imperial Rome*. New Haven: Yale University Press, 2018.

Beetham, Christopher A. *Echoes of Scripture in the Letter of Paul to the Colossians*. Leiden: Brill, 2010.

Bernier, Jonathan. *Rethinking the Dates of the New Testament: The Evidence for Early Composition*. Grand Rapids: Baker Academic, 2022.

Betz, Hans Dieter, ed. *The Greek Magical Papyri in Translation*. Chicago: University of Chicago Press, 1986.

Bloomquist, L. Gregory. "Paul's Inclusive Language: The Ideological Texture of Romans 1." Pages 165–93 in *Fabrics of Discourse: Essays in Honor of Vernon K. Robbins*. Edited by David B. Gowler, L. Gregory Bloomquist, and Duane F. Watson. Harrisburg, PA: Trinity Press International, 2003.

———. "The Pesky Threads of Robbins's Rhetorical Tapestry." Pages 201–23 in *Genealogies of New Testament Rhetorical Criticism*. Edited by Troy W. Martin. Minneapolis: Fortress, 2014.

Brodd, Jeffrey, and Jonathan L. Reed, eds. *Rome and Religion: A Cross-Disciplinary Dialogue on the Imperial Cult*. WGRWSup 5. Atlanta: Society of Biblical Literature, 2011.

Brooks, David. "Bruce Springsteen and the Art of Aging Well." *Atlantic*, 23 October 2020. https://tinyurl.com/SBL7106a.

Bryan, Christopher. "A Digression: 'Great Literature?'" Pages 56–65 in *Listening to the Bible: The Art of Faithful Biblical Interpretation*. Oxford: Oxford University Press, 2014.

———. "The Drama of the Word." Pages 114–26 in *Listening to the Bible: The Art of Faithful Biblical Interpretation*. Oxford: Oxford University Press, 2014.

Bultmann, Rudolf. "ἀναγινώσκω, ἀνάγνωσις." *TDNT* 1:343–44.

———. "φανερόω." *TDNT* 9:1–10.

Burke, Kenneth A. *A Rhetoric of Motives*. Berkeley: University of California Press, 1969.
Cadwallader, Alan H. "Colossae." Bible Odyssey. https://tinyurl.com/SBL7106h.
———. *Fragments of Colossae: Sifting through the Traces*. Hindmarsh, Australia: ATF, 2015.
———. "The Gods in City and Country." Pages 45–73 in *Fragments of Colossae: Sifting Through the Traces*. Hindmarsh, Australia: ATF, 2015.
———. "Greeks in Colossae: Shifting Allegiances in the Letter to the Colossians and Its Context." Pages 224–41 in *Attitudes to Gentiles in Ancient Judaism and Early Christianity*. Edited by David C. Sim and James S. McLaren. LNTS. London: Bloomsbury T&T Clark, 2013.
———. "On the Question of Comparative Method in Historical Research: Colossae and Chonai in Larger Frame." Pages 105–51 in *The First Urban Churches 5: Colossae, Hierapolis, and Laodicea*. Edited by James R. Harrison and L. L. Welborn. WGRWSup 16. Atlanta: SBL Press, 2019.
———. "One Grave, Two Women, One Man: Complicating Family Life at Colossae." Pages 157–94 in *Stones, Bones, and the Sacred: Essays on Material Culture and Ancient Religion in Honor of Dennis E. Smith*. Edited by Alan H. Cadwallader. ECL 21. Atlanta: SBL Press, 2016.
Cadwallader, Alan H., and James R. Harrison. "Perspectives on the Lycus Valley: An Inscriptional, Archaeological, Numismatic, and Iconographic Approach." Pages 3–70 in *The First Urban Churches 5: Colossae, Hierapolis, and Laodicea*. Edited by James R. Harrison and L. L. Welborn. WGRWSup 16. Atlanta: SBL Press, 2019.
Cadwallader, Alan H., and Michael Trainor, eds., *Colossae in Space and Time: Linking to an Ancient City*. Göttingen: Vandenhoeck & Ruprecht, 2011.
Cahill, Thomas. *Sailing the Wine-Dark Sea: Why the Greeks Matter*. New York: Doubleday, 2003.
Campbell, Constantine R. *Colossians and Philemon: A Handbook on the Greek Text*. BHGNT. Waco, TX: Baylor University Press, 2013.
Campbell, Douglas A. *Framing Paul: An Epistolary Biography*. Grand Rapids: Eerdmans, 2014.
———. *Pauline Dogmatics: The Triumph of God's Love*. Grand Rapids: Eerdmans, 2020.
———. "Unravelling Colossians 3:11b." *NTS* 42 (1996): 120–32.

Canavan, Rosemary. "Unraveling the Threads of Identity: Cloth and Clothing in the Lycus Valley." Pages 81–104 in *The First Urban Churches 5: Colossae, Hierapolis, and Laodicea*. Edited by James R. Harrison and L. L. Welborn. WGRWSup 16. Atlanta: SBL Press, 2019.

Capon, Robert Farrar. *The Fingerprints of God: Tracking the Divine Suspect through a History of Images*. Grand Rapids: Eerdmans, 2000.

Carter, Warren. *The Roman Empire and the New Testament: An Essential Guide*. Nashville: Abingdon, 2006.

Charles, Robert H. *The Apocrypha and Pseudepigrapha of the Old Testament in English*. Vol. 2, *Pseudepigrapha*. Oxford: Clarendon, 1913.

Cid Zurita, Andrés. "Similar to Gods: Some Words in the Imperial Cult in the Roman Empire." *Gephyra* 20 (2020): 127–41.

Copenhaver, Adam. *Reconstructing the Historical Background of Paul's Rhetoric in the Letter to the Colossians*. LNTS 585. London: Bloomsbury T&T Clark, 2018.

"Creativity." *Psychology Today*. https://tinyurl.com/SBL7106l.

Crouch, James E. *The Origin and Intention of the Colossians Haustafel*. Göttingen: Vandenhoeck & Ruprecht, 1972.

"Cult in Lydia (Asia Minor)." Theoi Greek Mythology. https://tinyurl.com/SBL7106d.

"Cult in Phrygia (Asia Minor)." Theoi Greek Mythology. https://tinyurl.com/SBL7106c.

Culy, Martin M. "Series Introduction." Pages ix–xiii in *Colossians and Philemon: A Handbook on the Greek Text*, by Constantine R. Campbell. BHGNT. Waco, TX: Baylor University Press, 2013.

Delling, Gerhard. "στοιχεῖον." *TDNT* 7:670–87.

———. "ὑποτάσσω." *TDNT* 8:39–46.

DeMaris, Richard E. *The Colossian Controversy: Wisdom in Dispute at Colossae*. JSNTSup 96. Sheffield: Sheffield Academic, 1994.

Dowden, Ken. *Religion and the Romans*. London: Bristol Classical Press, 1992.

Dunn, James D. G. *The Epistles to the Colossians and to Philemon*. NIGTC. Grand Rapids: Eerdmans, 1996.

———. *The Theology of Paul the Apostle*. Grand Rapids: Eerdmans, 1998.

Elliott, Neil. *The Arrogance of Nations: Reading Romans in the Shadow of Empire*. Minneapolis: Fortress, 2010.

Fauconnier, Gilles, and Mark Turner. *The Way We Think: Conceptual Blending and the Mind's Hidden Complexities*. New York: Basic Books, 2002.

Fee, Gordon D. "Old Testament Intertextuality in Colossians: Reflections on Pauline Christology and Gentile Inclusion in God's Story." Pages 201–21 in *History and Exegesis: New Testament Essays in Honor of Dr. E. Earle Ellis*. Edited by Sang-Won Son. London: T&T Clark, 2006.

Fohrer, Georg. "υἱός." *TDNT* 8:340–53.

Foster, Paul. *Colossians*. BNTC. London: Bloomsbury T&T Clark, 2016.

Francis, Fred O. "Humility and Angelic Worship in Col. 2:18." *ST* 16 (1962): 109–34.

Francis, Fred O., and Wayne A. Meeks, eds. *Conflict at Colossae: A Problem in the Interpretation of Early Christianity Illustrated by Selected Modern Studies*. SBLSBS 4. Missoula, MT: Scholars Press, 1973.

Friesen, Stephen J. "Paul and Economics: The Jerusalem Collection as an Alternative to Patronage." Pages 41–78 in *Paul Unbound: Other Perspectives on the Apostle*. 2nd ed. Edited by Mark D. Given. ESEC 25. Atlanta: SBL Press, 2022.

Frye, Northrop. *Anatomy of Criticism*. Princeton: Princeton University Press, 1957.

"Gemma Augustea." Wikipedia. https://tinyurl.com/SBL7106e.

Gordley, Matthew E. *The Colossians Hymn in Context: An Exegesis in Light of Jewish and Greco-Roman Hymnic and Epistolary Conventions*. WUNT 2/228. Tübingen: Mohr Siebeck, 2007.

Grundmann, Walter. "ταπεινοφροσύνη." *TDNT* 8:1–26.

Harrison, James R., and L. L. Welborn, eds. *The First Urban Churches 5: Colossae, Hierapolis, and Laodicea*. WGRWSup 16. Atlanta: SBL Press, 2019.

Hart, David Bentley. *The New Testament: A Translation*. New Haven: Yale University Press, 2017.

Haught, John F. *God after Einstein: What's Really Going On in the Universe*. New Haven: Yale University Press, 2022.

———. *The New Cosmic Story: Inside Our Awakening Universe*. New Haven: Yale University Press, 2017.

Henten, Jan Willem van, and Friedrich Avemarie. *Martyrdom and Noble Death: Selected Texts from Graeco-Roman Jewish and Christian Antiquity*. London: Routledge, 2002.

Holloway, Paul A. *Philippians: A Commentary*. Hermeneia. Minneapolis: Fortress, 2017.

Hooker, Morna D. "Were There False Teachers in Colossae?" Pages 315–31 in *Christ and Spirit in the New Testament*. Edited by Barnabas Lindars and Stephen Smalley. Cambridge: Cambridge University Press, 1973.

Horace. *The Odes, Epodes, Satires, and Epistles*. London: Warne, 1889.
Horsley, Richard A. "The Gospel of the Savior's Birth." Pages 113–38 in *Christmas Unwrapped: Consumerism, Christ and Culture*. Edited by Richard A. Horsley and James Tracy. Harrisburg, PA: Trinity Press International, 2001.

———, ed. *In the Shadow of Empire: Reclaiming the Bible as a History of Faithful Resistance*. Louisville: Westminster John Knox, 2008.

———. *Paul and Empire: Religion and Power in Roman Imperial Society*. Harrisburg, PA: Trinity Press International, 1997.

Huttner, Ulrich. *Early Christianity in the Lycus Valley*. Translated by David Green. ECAM 1. Leiden: Brill, 2013.

"International Workshop on the Scientific Approach to the Acheiropoietos Images." ENEA. https://tinyurl.com/SBL7106f.

Jeal, Roy R. "Clothes Make the (Wo)Man." Pages 393–414 *Foundations for Sociorhetorical Exploration: A Rhetoric of Religious Antiquity Reader*. Edited by Vernon K. Robbins, Robert H. von Thaden Jr., and Bart B. Bruehler. RRA 4. Atlanta: SBL Press, 2016.

———. *Colossians-Philemon: A Beginning-Intermediate Greek Reader*. Wilmore, KY: GlossaHouse, 2015.

———. *Exploring Philemon: Freedom, Brotherhood, and Partnership in the New Society*. RRA 2. Atlanta: SBL Press, 2015.

———, ed. *Exploring Sublime Rhetoric in Biblical Literature*. ESEC 28. Atlanta: SBL Press, 2024.

———. *Integrating Theology and Ethics in Ephesians: The Ethos of Communication*. Lewiston, NY: Mellen, 2000.

———. "Melody, Imagery and Memory in the Moral Persuasion of Paul." Pages 160–78 in *Rhetoric, Ethic, and Moral Persuasion in Biblical Discourse*. Edited by Thomas H. Olbricht and Anders Eriksson. ESEC 11. New York T&T Clark, 2005.

———. "Sociorhetorical Intertexture." Pages 151–64 in *Exploring Intertextuality*. Edited by B. J. Oropeza and Steve Moyise. Eugene, OR: Cascade, 2016.

———. "Starting before the Beginning: Precreation Discourse in Colossians." *R&T* 18 (2011): 1–24.

———. "A Strange Style of Expression, Ephesians 1:23." *FN* 10 (1997): 129–38.

———. "Visual Interpretation: Blending Rhetorical Arts in Colossians 2:6–3:4." Pages 55–87 in *The Art of Visual Exegesis: Rhetoric, Texts, Images*.

Edited by Vernon K. Robbins, Walter S. Melion, and Roy R. Jeal. ESEC 19. Atlanta: SBL Press, 2017.

Jenni, Ernst. "Das Wort 'ōlām im Alten Testament." *ZAW* 64 (1952): 197–248; 65 (1953): 1–35.

Jervis, L. Ann. *At the Heart of the Gospel: Suffering in the Earliest Christian Message*. Grand Rapids: Eerdmans, 2007.

Johnson, Luke Timothy. *Constructing Paul*. Vol. 1. Grand Rapids: Eerdmans, 2020.

Juel, Donald H. *A Master of Surprise: Mark Interpreted*. Minneapolis: Fortress, 1994.

Kahl, Brigitte. *Galatians Re-imagined: Reading with the Eyes of the Vanquished*. Minneapolis: Fortress, 2010.

Kahnemann, Daniel. *Thinking Fast and Slow*. New York: Farrar, Strauss & Giroux, 2011.

Käsemann, Ernst. "A Primitive Christian Baptismal Liturgy." Pages 149–68 in *Essays on New Testament Themes*. London: SCM, 1964.

Kaufman, James C. *Creativity 101*. 2nd ed. New York: Springer, 2016.

Kaufman, James C., and Robert J. Sternberg, eds. *The Nature of Human Creativity*. Cambridge: Cambridge University Press, 2018.

Kearsley, Rosalinde A. "Epigraphic Evidence for the Social Impact of Roman Government in Laodicea and Hierapolis." Pages 130–50 in *Colossae in Space and Time: Linking to an Ancient City*. Edited by Alan H. Cadwallader and Michael Trainor. Göttingen: Vandenhoeck & Ruprecht, 2011.

Keizer, Heleen M. "Life Time Entirety: A Study of ΑΙΩΝ in Greek Literature and Philosophy in the Septuagint and Philo." Thesis, Universiteit van Amsterdam, 2010.

Kennedy, George A. *Comparative Rhetoric: An Historical and Cross-Cultural Introduction*. Oxford: Oxford University Press, 1998.

———. *Progymnasmata: Greek Textbooks of Prose Composition and Rhetoric*. WGRW 10. Atlanta: Society of Biblical Literature, 2003.

Kingsolver, Barbara. *The Poisonwood Bible*. New York: Harper Perennial, 1998.

Kittel, Gerhard. "δόξα." *TDNT* 2:233–37, 247–51.

Kloppenborg, John S. *Christ's Associations: Connecting and Belonging in the Ancient City*. New Haven: Yale University Press, 2019.

Kooten, George H. van. *Cosmic Christology in Paul and the Pauline School: Colossians and Ephesians in the Context of Graeco-Roman Cosmology,* with a New Synopsis of the Greek Texts. WUNT 171. Tübingen: Mohr Siebeck, 2003.

Korn, Marianne. *Ezra Pound: Purpose, Form, Meaning*. London: Faber & Faber, 1961.

Lapidge, Michael. "ἀρχαί and στοιχεῖα: A Problem in Stoic Cosmology." *Phronesis* 18 (1973): 240–78.

Lee, Margaret Ellen, and Bernard Brandon Scott. *Sound Mapping the New Testament*. Salem, OR: Polebridge, 2009.

Lightfoot, J. B. *Saint Paul's Epistles to the Colossians and Philemon*. London: Macmillan, 1879.

Lincoln, Andrew T. "Colossians." *NIB* 11:551–699.

———. "The Household Code and Wisdom Mode of Colossians." *JSNT* 74 (1999): 93–112.

———. "Liberation from the Powers: Supernatural Spirits or Societal Structures." Pages 333–54 in *The Bible in Human Society*. Edited by M. Daniel Carroll R., David J. A. Clines, and Philip R. Davies. Sheffield: Sheffield Academic, 1995.

Lohse, Eduard. "υἱός." *TDNT* 8:357–62.

Long, Fredrick J. "Ephesians: Paul's Political Theology in Greco-Roman Political Context." Pages 255–309 in *Christian Origins and Greco-Roman Culture: Social and Literary Contexts for the New Testament*. Edited by Stanley E. Porter and Andrew W. Pitts. TENTS 9. Leiden: Brill, 2012.

Longenecker, Bruce W. "Family and Solidarity." Pages 198–211 in *In Stone and Story: Early Christians in the Roman World*. Grand Rapids: Baker Academic, 2020.

———. *In Stone and Story: Early Christians in the Roman World*. Grand Rapids: Baker Academic, 2020.

MacDonald, Margaret Y. *Colossians and Ephesians*. SP 17. Collegeville, MN: Liturgical Press, 2000.

———. *The Power of Children: The Construction of Christian Families in the Greco-Roman World*. Waco, TX: Baylor University Press, 2014.

Mackay, Christopher S. *Ancient Rome: A Military and Political History*. Cambridge: Cambridge University Press, 2004.

Maier, Harry O. "Barbarians, Scythians and Imperial Iconography in the Epistle to the Colossians." Pages 385–406 in *Picturing the New Testament: Studies in Ancient Visual Images*. Edited by Annette Weisssenrieder, Friederike Wendt, and Petra von Gemünden. WUNT 2/193. Tübingen: Mohr Siebeck, 2005.

———. "Colossians, Ephesians, and Empire." Pages 185–202 in *An Introduction to Empire in the New Testament*. Edited by Adam Winn. RBS 84. Atlanta: SBL Press, 2016.

———. "*Histoire Croisée*, Entangled Bodies, Boundaries, and Socio-political Geography in the Letter to the Colossians." Pages 77–94 in *Borders: Terminologies, Ideologies, and Performance*. Edited by Annette Weissenrieder. WUNT. Tübingen: Mohr Siebeck, 2016.

———. "The Household and Its Members." Pages 134–73 in *New Testament Christianity in the Roman World*. ESB. New York: Oxford University Press, 2019.

———. *New Testament Christianity in the Roman World*. ESB. Oxford: Oxford University Press, 2019.

———. "Paul, Imperial Situation, and Visualization in the Epistle to the Colossians." Pages 171–94 in *The Art of Visual Exegesis: Rhetoric, Texts, Images*. Edited by Vernon K. Robbins, Walter S. Melion, and Roy R. Jeal. ESEC 19. Atlanta: SBL Press, 2017.

———. *Picturing Paul in Empire: Imperial Image, Text and Persuasion in Colossians, Ephesians and the Pastoral Epistles*. New York: T&T Clark, 2013.

———. "Reading Colossians in the Ruins: Roman Imperial Iconography, Moral Transformation, and the Construction of Christian Identity in the Lycus Valley." Pages 212–31 in *Colossae in Space and Time: Linking to an Ancient City*. Edited by Alan H. Cadwallader and Michael Trainor. Göttingen: Vandenhoeck & Ruprecht, 2011.

———. "Salience, Multiple Affiliation, and Christ Belief in the Lycus Valley: A Conversation with Ulrich Huttner's *Early Christianity in the Lycus Valley*." Pages 153–69 in *The First Urban Churches 5: Colossae, Hierapolis, and Laodicea*. Edited by James R. Harrison and L. L. Welborn. WGRWSup 16. Atlanta: SBL Press, 2019.

———. "A Sly Civility: Colossians and Empire." *JSNT* 27 (2005): 323–49.

Malherbe, Abraham J. *Moral Exhortation: A Greco-Roman Sourcebook*. LEC 4. Philadelphia: Westminster, 1986.

Malina, Bruce J. *The New Testament World: Insights from Cultural Anthropology*. 3rd ed. Louisville: Westminster John Knox, 2001.

Martin, Neil. "Returning to the *stoicheia tou kosmou*: Enslavement to the Physical Elements in Galatians 4.3 and 9?" *JSNT* 40 (2018): 434–52.

Martin, Troy W. *Apostolic Confirmation and Legitimation in an Early Christian Faith Document: A Commentary on the First Epistle of the Apostle Peter*. NIGTC. Grand Rapids: Eerdmans, forthcoming.

———. *By Philosophy and Empty Deceit: Colossians as Response to a Cynic Critique*. JSNTSup 118. Sheffield: Sheffield Academic, 1996.

———. "Translating ὑποτάσσεσθαι in First Peter as *Fitting in*, Not as *Submission*." *BR* 67 (2022): 59–80.

Mathieson, Ruth Christa. *Matthew's Parable of the Royal Wedding Feast: A Sociorhetorical Interpretation*. ESEC 26. Atlanta: SBL Press, 2023.

Mauss, Marcel. *The Category of the Person: Anthropology, Philosophy, History*. Translated by W. D. Halls. Cambridge: Cambridge University Press, 1985.

McKnight, Scot. *The Letter to the Colossians*. NICNT. Grand Rapids: Eerdmans, 2018.

Metzger, Bruce M., and Bart D. Ehrman. *The Text of the New Testament: Its Transmission, Corruption, and Restoration*. 4th ed. Oxford: Oxford University Press, 2005.

Moo, Douglas J. *The Letters to the Colossians and to Philemon*. PNTC. Grand Rapids: Eerdmans, 2008.

Moore, Michael Ryan. "What Is Economics? A Lesson on Choice and Scarcity." Wharton Global Youth Program, University of Pennsylvania. https://tinyurl.com/SBL7106k.

Mouat, L. H. "An Approach to Rhetorical Criticism." Pages 161–77 in *The Rhetorical Idiom*. Edited by Donald C. Bryant. New York: Russel & Russel, 1966.

Niebuhr, H. Richard. *Christ and Culture*. San Francisco: HarperSanFrancisco, 2001.

Norden, Eduard. *Agnostos Theos: Untersuchgungen zur Formgeschichte Religiöser Rede*. Darmstadt: Wissenschaftliche Buchgesellschaft, 1956.

Oakes, Peter. "God's Sovereignty over Roman Authorities: A Theme in Philippians." Pages 126–41 in *Rome in the Bible and the Early Church*. Edited by Peter Oakes. Grand Rapids: Baker Academic, 2002.

Oakley, Todd V. "The Human Rhetorical Potential." *WC* 16 (1999): 93–128.

Oepke, Albrecht. "ἀπεκδύω, ἀπέκδυσις." *TDNT* 2:318–21.

O'Gorman, Ned. "Aristotle's *Phantasia* in the *Rhetoric*: *Lexis*, Appearance, and the Epideictic Function of Discourse." *P&R* 38 (2005): 16–40.

Olbricht, Thomas H. "The Stoicheia and the Rhetoric of Colossians: Then and Now." Pages 109–29 in *Rhetoric and Scripture: Collected Essays of Thomas H. Olbricht*. Edited by Lauri Thurén. ESEC 23. Atlanta: SBL Press, 2021.

Oliver, Mary. "On Thy Wondrous Works I Will Meditate (Psalm 145)." Pages 134–38 in *Devotions: The Selected Poems of Mary Oliver*. New York: Penguin, 2017.
O'Neill, John C. "The Source of the Christology in Colossians." *NTS* 26 (1980): 87–100.
Oropeza, B. J. *Exploring Second Corinthians: Death and Life, Hardship and Rivalry*. RRA 3. Atlanta: SBL Press, 2016.
Osiek, Carolyn, and David L. Balch, eds. *Families in the New Testament World: Households and House Churches*. Louisville: Westminster John Knox, 1997.
Penner, Jeremy. *Patterns of Daily Prayer in Second Temple Period Judaism*. STJD 104. Leiden: Brill, 2012.
Philo. *Works of Philo Judaeus, the Contemporary of Josephus*. Translated by Charles D. Yonge. London: Bohn, 1854.
Pizzuto, Vincent A. *A Cosmic Leap of Faith: An Authorial, Structural, and Theological Investigation of the Cosmic Christology in Colossians 1:15–20*. CBET. Leuven: Peeters, 2006.
Plutarch. *Lives*. Vol. 6, *Dion and Brutus. Timoleon and Aemilius Paulus*. Translated by Bernadotte Perrin. LCL. Cambridge: Harvard University Press, 1918.
Pound, Ezra. *How to Read*. New York: Haskell House, 1971.
———. "In a Station of the Metro." Page 111 in *Personae: The Collected Poems of Ezra Pound*. New York: New Directions, 1926.
Price, Simon R. F. *Rituals and Power: The Roman Imperial Cult in Asia Minor*. Cambridge: Cambridge University Press, 1984.
Radner, Ephraim. *A Time to Keep: Theology, Mortality, and the Shape of Human Life*. Waco, TX: Baylor University Press, 2016.
Reicke, Bo, and Georg Bertram. "παριστήμι, παριστάνω." *TDNT* 5:837–41.
Richards, E. Randolph. *The Secretary in the Letters of Paul*. WUNT 2/42. Tübingen: Mohr Siebeck, 1991.
Rives, James B. *Religion in the Roman Empire*. Oxford: Blackwell, 2007.
Robbins, Vernon K. "Conceptual Blending and Early Christian Imagination." Pages 329–64 in *Foundations for Sociorhetorical Interpretation: A Rhetoric of Religious Antiquity Reader*. Edited by Vernon K. Robbins, Robert H. von Thaden Jr., and Bart B. Bruehler. RRA 4. Atlanta: SBL Press, 2016.
———. "The Dialectical Nature of Early Christian Discourse." *Scriptura* 59 (1996): 353–62.

———. *Exploring the Textures of Texts: A Guide to Socio-rhetorical Interpretation.* New York: Bloomsbury Academic, 2012.

———. *The Invention of Christian Discourse.* Vol. 1. Blandford Forum, UK: Deo, 2009.

———. "Rhetography: A New Way of Seeing the Familiar Text." Pages 367–92 in *Foundations for Sociorhetorical Interpretation: A Rhetoric of Religious Antiquity Reader.* Edited by Vernon K. Robbins, Robert H. von Thaden Jr., and Bart B. Bruehler. RRA 4. Atlanta: SBL Press, 2016.

———. *Sea Voyages and Beyond: Emerging Strategies in Socio-rhetorical Interpretation.* ESEC 14. Atlanta: SBL Press, 2014.

———. "Socio-rhetorical Interpretation." Pages 192–219 in *The Blackwell Companion to the New Testament.* Edited by David E. Aune. Oxford: Blackwell, 2010.

———. *The Tapestry of Early Christian Discourse: Rhetoric, Society and Ideology.* London: Routledge, 1996.

Robbins, Vernon K., Robert H. von Thaden Jr., and Bart B. Bruehler, eds. *Foundations for Sociorhetorical Interpretation: A Rhetoric of Religious Antiquity Reader.* RRA 4. Atlanta: SBL Press, 2016.

Robertson, Archibald T. *A Grammar of the Greek New Testament in the Light of Historical Research.* Nashville: Broadman, 1934.

Rogerson, John W. *Perspectives on the Passion.* Sheffield: Beauchief Abbey, 2014.

Sasse, Hermann. "αἰών." *TDNT* 1:197–209.

Scheidel, Walter, and Stephen J. Friesen. "The Size of the Economy and the Distribution of Wealth in the Roman Empire." *JRS* 99 (2009): 61–91.

Schniewind, Julius. "καταγγέλλω." *TDNT* 1:70–72.

Schweizer, Eduard. *The Letter to the Colossians.* Minneapolis: Augsburg, 1982.

Seitz, Christopher R. *Colossians.* BTCB. Grand Rapids: Brazos, 2014.

Seneca. *Epistles.* Vol. 1, *Epistles 1–65.* Translated by Richard M. Gummere. LCL. Cambridge: Harvard University Press, 1917.

———. *Moral Essays.* Vol. 1, *De Providentia; De Constantia; De Ira; De Clementia.* Translated by John W. Basore. LCL. Cambridge: Harvard University Press, 1928.

Stambaugh, John E., and David L. Balch. *The New Testament in Its Social Environment.* LEC. Philadelphia: Westminster, 1986.

Standhartinger, Angela. "A City with a Message: Colossae and Colossians." Pages 239–56 in *The First Urban Churches 5: Colossae, Hierapolis, and*

Laodicea. Edited by James R. Harrison and L. L. Welborn. WGRWSup 16. Atlanta: SBL Press, 2019.

Stegemann, Ekkehard W., and Wolfgang Stegemann. *The Jesus Movement: A Social History of Its First Century*. Minneapolis: Fortress, 1999.

Suetonius. *Lives of the Caesars*. Vol. 1, *Julius; Augustus; Tiberius; Gaius Caligula*. Translated by John C. Rolfe. LCL. Cambridge: Harvard University Press, 1914.

Sumney, Jerry L. *Colossians: A Commentary*. NTL. Louisville: Westminster John Knox, 2008.

———. "Excursus 3: Reading the Household Code." Pages 230–38 in *Colossians: A Commentary*. NTL. Louisville: Westminster John Knox, 2008.

———. "The Function of Ethos in Colossians." Pages 301–15 in *Rhetoric, Ethic, and Moral Persuasion: Essays from the 2002 Heidelberg Conference*. Edited by Thomas H. Olbricht and Anders Eriksson. ESEC 11. New York: T&T Clark, 2005.

———. "Paul and His Opponents: The Search." Pages 79–98 in *Paul Unbound: Other Perspectives on the Apostle*. Edited by Mark D. Given. ESEC 25. Atlanta: SBL Press, 2022.

———. "Writing in 'the Image' of Scripture: The Form and Function of References to Scripture in Colossians." Pages 185–229 in *Paul and Scripture: Extending the Conversation*. Edited by Christopher D. Stanley. Atlanta: Society of Biblical Literature, 2012.

Swart, Gerhard. "Eschatological Vision or Exhortation to Visible Christian Conduct? Notes on the Interpretation of Colossians 3:4." *Neot* 33 (1999): 169–77.

Tachau, Ernst. *"Einst" und "Jetzt" im Neuen Testament. Beobachtungen zu einem urchristlichen Predigt-Schema in der neutestamentlichen Briefliteratur und zu seiner Vorgeschichte*. FRLANT 105. Göttingen: Vandenhoeck & Ruprecht, 1972.

Talbert, Charles H. *Ephesians and Colossians*. Paideia. Grand Rapids: Baker Academic, 2007.

Taylor, Bernard A. "Deponency and Greek Lexicography." Pages 167–76 in *Biblical Greek Language and Lexicography: Essays in Honor of Frederick W. Danker*. Edited by Bernard A. Taylor, John A. Lee, Peter R. Burton, and Richard Whitaker. Grand Rapids: Eerdmans, 2004.

Taylor, Joan E. "Pontius Pilate and the Imperial Cult in Roman Judaea." *NTS* 52 (2006): 555–82.

Thaden, Robert H. von, Jr. *Sex, Christ, and Embodied Cognition*. ESEC 16. Atlanta: SBL Press, 2017.

Thiessen, Jonathan. "The Sublime and Subliminal in Romans 2–3." Pages 39–64 in *Exploring Sublime Rhetoric in Biblical Literature*. Edited by Roy R. Jeal. ESEC 28. Atlanta: SBL Press, 2024.

Trainor, Michael. *Epaphras: Paul's Educator at Colossae*. Collegeville, MN: Liturgical Press, 2008.

———. "Rome's Market Economy in the Lycus Valley: Soundings from Laodicea and Colossae." Pages 293–324 in *The First Urban Churches 5: Colossae, Hierapolis, and Laodicea*. Edited by James R. Harrison and L. L. Welborn. WGRWSup 16. Atlanta: SBL Press, 2019.

Treggiari, Susan. *Roman Marriage*. Oxford: Oxford University Press, 1991.

Visser, Margaret. *The Geometry of Love: Space, Time, Mystery, and Meaning in an Ordinary Church*. Toronto: Harper Perennial, 2000.

Wallace, Daniel B. *Greek Grammar beyond the Basics: An Exegetical Syntax of the New Testament*. Grand Rapids: Zondervan, 1996.

———. "Scribal Methods and Materials." Center for the Study of New Testament Manuscripts. https://itunes.apple.com/us/itunes-u/scribal-methods-materials/id446658178.

Wallas, Graham. *The Art of Thought*. Reprint, Tunbridge Wells, UK: Solis, 2014.

Walsh, Brian J., and Sylvia Keesmaat. *Colossians Remixed: Subverting the Empire*. Downers Grove, IL: InterVarsity Press, 2004.

Watson, Duane F. "Retrospect and Prospect of Sociorhetorical Interpretation." Pages 11–17 in *Welcoming the Nations: International Sociorhetorical Explorations*. Edited by Vernon K. Robbins and Roy R. Jeal. IVBS 13. Atlanta: SBL Press, 2020.

West, Thomas G. "Introduction." Pages 9–37 in *Four Texts on Socrates: Plato's "Euthryphro," "Apology," and "Crito" and Aristophanes' "Clouds."* Translated by Thomas G. West and Grace Starry West. Ithaca, NY: Cornell University Press, 1984.

White, John L. *The Apostle of God: Paul and the Promise of Abraham*. Peabody, MA: Hendrickson, 1999.

Wilson, Robert McL. *Colossians and Philemon*. ICC. London: Bloomsbury T&T Clark, 2005.

Wink, Walter. *Naming the Powers: The Language of Power in the New Testament*. Philadelphia: Fortress, 1984.

Winn, Adam, ed. *An Introduction to Empire in the New Testament*. RBS. Atlanta: SBL Press, 2016.

Winter, Bruce W. *Divine Honours for the Caesars: The First Christian Responses*. Grand Rapids: Eerdmans, 2015.

———. *Seek the Welfare of the City: Christians as Benefactors and Citizens.* Grand Rapids: Eerdmans, 1994.

Wright, N. T. *Colossians and Philemon.* TNTC. Grand Rapids: Eerdmans, 1986.

———. *Paul and the Faithfulness of God.* 2 vols. Minneapolis: Fortress, 2013.

———. "Poetry and Theology in Colossians 1.15–20." *NTS* 36 (1990): 444–68.

Yates, Roy. "Colossians 2:15: Christ Triumphant." *NTS* 37 (1991): 573–91.

Ancient Sources Index

Hebrew Bible/Septuagint		30:35	262
		31:3 LXX	78
Genesis	78, 98, 101	32:32–33	172
1	6, 98, 104	36:1 LXX	119
1:1	6		
1:2	102	Leviticus	
1:3–4	84	1:3 LXX	121
1:16	104	1:10 LXX	121
1:22	78	12:3	171, 172
1:26	216	16:5	46
1:26–27	88, 101	19:7 LXX	119
1:27	101	20:25–26	183
1:28	69, 78	26:1 LXX	172
3	202	26:30 LXX	172
3:4–5	160		
3:22–24	194, 202	Numbers	
5:1	101	6:14 LXX	121
9:6	101	10:10	182
11:4–9	194	16:9 LXX	121
12:3	132	28:11–15	182
16:4 LXX	245	29:6 LXX	181
17:1 LXX	172		
17:1–7	171	Deuteronomy	
17:14 LXX	172	4:6 LXX	78
17:23–25 LXX	172	4:19	181
19:31	103	10:8 LXX	121
19:33–34	103	10:9 LXX	79
27:32	103	10:16	172
34:24 LXX	172	17:3	181
		29:17	119
Exodus	79	30:6	172
4:22	103	32:6	46
20:17	222	32:9 LXX	79
21:7 LXX	249		
29:1 LXX	121		

Joshua		2:1 LXX	121
14:8 LXX	119	6:6	262
19:9 LXX	79	12:13 LXX	78
19:51 LXX	192	28:20 LXX	78
Judges		Psalms	144
9:45	262	14:2 LXX	121
		15:3 LXX	46
1 Samuel		22	46
13:17–18	104	24:7–10	144
		47:7–10 LXX	144
1 Kingdoms (LXX)		57:4 LXX	119
18:22	190	68:9 LXX	119
		69	46
2 Kingdoms (LXX)		81:3	182
15:26	190	89:27	103
		104:24	100
3 Kingdoms (LXX)		110:1	206
10:9	190	117:8–9 LXX	144
		119:43	69
2 Kings		119:160	69
2:3	222	145:3 LXX	159
2:5	222	145:3–4 LXX	144
2:7	222	145:12	222
2:15	222		
		Proverbs	
4 Kingdoms (LXX)		1:7 LXX	78
5:3	245	2:2–3 LXX	78
		2:6 LXX	78
1 Chronicles		2:12–20	78
22:12 LXX	78	3:19–20	99, 280
23:30–31 LXX	181	8:4	222
		8:22–31	99, 280
2 Chronicles		9:10 LXX	78
1:10–12 LXX	78	24:3 LXX	78
31:3 LXX	181		
		Ecclesiastes	
Ezra		2:3	222
3:4–5 LXX	181	2:8	222
		3:10	222
Esther			
3:9 LXX	198	Isaiah	
		1:13–14 LXX	181
Job		2:4 LXX	79
1:6 LXX	121	2:8 LXX	172

9:2	84	2:15 LXX	198
11:2 LXX	78	3	135
16:12 LXX	172	5:4 LXX	172
19:1 LXX	172	5:23 LXX	172
21:9 LXX	172	6	135
24:2 LXX	245	6:9 LXX	69
29:13 LXX	200	7:9	105
31:7 LXX	172	7:10 LXX	121
35:4	119	7:13 LXX	121
40:5	128, 144	7:18	46
42:16	84		
45:3	102	Hosea	
46:6 LXX	172	1:10	223
53	46	2:13 LXX	181
56:6	223	9:10 LXX	119
61:5	223		
63:16	46, 68	Amos	
64:7	68	7:14	222
Jeremiah		Micah	
3:4	68	2:3	223
3:19	68	4:2	223
4:4	172	4:5	223
8:1–2	181		
9:25–26	172	Nahum	
19:13	181	2:8 LXX	249
27:8 LXX	119		
31:9	68	Habakkuk	112, 131
31:34–34	85	2:4	112
		2:14	128, 144
Lamentations		3:17	69
3:1–3	84	3:18–19	112
Ezekiel		Zephaniah	
14:5 LXX	119	1:5	181
14:7 LXX	119		
16:4	262	Zechariah	
40–44	262	6:5 LXX	121
43:24	262		
44:6–7	172	Malachi	
46:1	181	2:10	68
46:6	181		
Daniel	135		
1:20 LXX	155		

Deuterocanonical Books

Tobit
5:3	172
9:5	172
12:7	136
12:11	136
12:15	121

Judith
2:2	137
2:4	137
14:10	172

Wisdom of Solomon
2:16	46
2:22	137
7:17	156
7:22–8:1	99, 100, 280
7:24	101
7:25	101
7:25–26	247
7:26	101
8	247
10:7	69
14:18	191
14:27	191
18:9	46
19:8	156

Sirach
	101
1:4–10	99, 280
3:10	46
7:19–29	254
11:34	119
24:1–34	99, 280
24:3–6	100
24:9	100–101

Bel and the Dragon
1:5	172

1 Maccabees
6:43–46	135
12:25	192

2 Maccabees
1:10–13	68
2:30	192
6:18–31	134
7:1–42	135
9:5	102
10:8	198
14:37–46	135
15:36	198

1 Esdras
5:52	181
9:17	181

3 Maccabees
1:3	172
4:11	198

2 Esdras
10:38	137

4 Maccabees
1:1–2	154
4:24	172
5:11–12	154
5:22	154
6	134
6:27–30	134
7:1–23	134
7:9	154
7:21–23	154
8:1	154
12:13	156
17:20–22	134

Old Testament Pseudepigrapha

Apocalypse of Zephaniah
7.1–8	172

1 Enoch
61.10	104
89.61–64	172
103.2	137

2 Enoch

20.1	104
24–25	99
24.3	137
53.2–3	172

Jubilees

1.23	172

Letter of Aristeas

256	154

Psalms of Solomon

17.13	119

Testament of Asher

6.5	119

Testament of Dan

6.8	119

Testament of Levi

3.8	104

Testament of Abraham

12.7–18	172

Testament of Job

11.11	172

Dead Sea Scrolls

Pesher Habakkuk

VII, 5	137

Psalm Scroll

XIX, 7	182

Rule of the Community

III, 17–26	78
III, 23	137
IV, 18	137
V, 5	172
V, 8–11	78

Temple Scroll

XLIII, 20	182

War Scroll

III, 5	46

Ancient Jewish Authors

Josephus, *Antiquitates judaicae*

3.238	182
4.113	120–21
12.241	172
18.11	154

Josephus, *Bellum judaicum*

2.119	154
7.389–406	135

Josephus, *Contra Apionem*

2.47	154
2.140–141	154

Philo, *De Abrahamo*

162	156

Philo, *De aeternitate mundi*

107–109	156

Philo, *De cherubim*

127	156

Philo, *De confusion linguarum*

138	103
146	103
147	102

Philo, *De decalogo*

53	156

Philo, *De fuga et inventione*

101	101

Philo, *De gigantibus*

8–16	104
52	172

Philo, *De mutatione nominum*
73–75   154

Philo, *De posteritate Caini*
15   103

Philo, *De sacrificiis Abelis et Caini*
118–119   103

Philo, *De somniis*
1.239   102

Philo, *De specialibus legibus*
1.305   172
1.316   46

Philo, *De vita contemplative*
3   156

Philo, *Legatio ad Gaium*
149–151   107
156   154
245   154

Philo, *Legum allegoriae*
1.55   172

Philo, *Quod deterius potiori insidari soleat*
54   100

Philo, *Quod omnis probus liber sit*
88–91   135

Philo, *Quis rerum divinarum heres sit*
133–134   156
140   156

New Testament

Matthew
4:16   184
5:13   259, 262
7:7–8   261
7:16–20   69
13:23   69
13:35   211
22:20   102
27:37   173

Mark
1:4   85
1:14–15   84
1:30   243
3:17   223
4:8   69
4:20   69
4:22   209
4:28   69
9:36   249
9:50   259, 262
10:44–45
12:16   102
14:58   172
14:64   209
15:26   173

Luke
1:79   184
8:15   69
10:21   211
12:11   103
14:34   259, 262
20:24   102
20:42   211
22:69   211
23:38   173

John
1:1–4   88
3:3   211
3:19–21   84
3:31   211
8:23   211
11:41   211
19:11   211
19:19–22   173

Acts
1:3   137, 272
1:23   121
     273

ANCIENT SOURCES INDEX 307

2:33–34	211	5:1–5	69
3:1	69	5:3–5	134
5:31	85, 211	5:10	120
7:55–56	211	5:10–11	120
9:13	46	6:4	162, 223
11:3	228	6:13	121
12:12	270, 273	6:15–23	254
12:25	270, 273	6:16	121
13:13	273	6:19	121
14:27	261	6:22	118
15:36–39	270	7:4–5	69
15:36–41	273	7:6	118
16:13–14	183	8:10	137
16:19–40	29	8:13	158, 221
18:7	183	8:15	68
19:23–41	273	8:29	102
19:29	273	8:34	211
20:2–30	273	8:35	134
20:3–4	269	8:38	103–4
20:5	273	10:12	229
20:19	191	11:15	120
21:1	107	11:30	118
23:33	121	12:1	120–121
		12:3	136
Romans		12:12	134
1:1	45, 70, 253	13:13	223
1:7	45–46	13:14	216, 225
1:8–10	68	14:7	84
1:9–10	78	14:10	208
1:10	68	14:13–23	182
1:17	112	15:6	68
1:19	209	15:15–16	136
1:20	102	16:7	270
1:23	102	16:22	27
1:24	221	16:25–26	17
1:26	221	16:25–27	136
1:29	222		
1:29–31	229	1 Corinthians	
2:7	210	1:1	45–46
2:10	210	1:1–2	45
2:28–29	172	1:2	45–46
3:21	118	1:3	46
3:23	210	1:4	46, 68, 78
3:24	85	1:8	69
4:20	210	1:18	261

Reference	Page	Reference	Page
1 Corinthians (cont.)		1:14	69
2:1	17	1:17	158
2:2	136	2:14	173
2:4	261	2:14–17	173
2:6–10	222	3:5–6	70
2:7	210, 211	3:18	102
2:14	174	4:4	102
3:5	69, 136	4:6	84
3:6–8	69	4:7–15	134
3:9–10	136	5:1	69, 172
3:12	229	5:14	162
4:14	243, 269	5:16	158
4:17	243	5:18–19	120
4:20	84	5:18–20	120
7:7	243	6:4	70, 136
7:8	243	6:4–10	134
7:11	120	6:14	84
7:20–24	254	7:4	134
7:26–35	243	8:2	134
7:27	229	9:10	69
9:5	243	10:2–3	158
9:16	258, 259	10:15	69
9:17	136	11:2	121
9:19–23	69	11:23	70, 136
11:7	102, 210	11:31	68
12:13	229	13:5	137
13:4–8a	248		
13:13	69	*Galatians*	
14:24	229	1:1	186
14:25	209	1:1–3	46
15:1–2	229	1:3	45
15:1–3	149	1:4	46
15:20	118	1:9	46
15:24	84	1:10	149
15:24–28	120	1:12	70, 253
15:40–43	210	3:8	149
15:49	102	3:11	131
15:50	84	3:27	112
16:9	261	3:28	216, 225
		4:3	25, 27, 229, 241, 254
2 Corinthians		4:6	155, 158
1:1	46	4:9	68
1:2	46	4:19	155, 158
1:3	68	4:26	137, 243
1:3–11	134	5:5–6	211
			69

5:13	70, 250	5:2	149, 247
5:16	223	5:3	222
5:16–26	226	5:3–5	222
5:19	221	5:6	223
5:19–21	222	5:6–16	212, 214, 222
6:17	134	5:8	149, 247
		5:8–11	84
Ephesians	119, 247	5:8–14	212
1:1	45	5:13	212
1:2	45–46	5:14	212
1:3	68	5:15	149, 247
1:7	82, 85	5:18–20	233
1:9	17, 136	5:19–20	247
1:10	136	5:21	23, 247
1:15	69	5:21–22	247
1:15–16	68, 78	5:21–30	242
1:17	68	5:22	247
1:20	211	5:27	121
1:20–21	211	6:6	251 n. 337
1:21	103, 105	6:12	84, 103–4, 150
2:1–10	119	6:19	136
2:2	119, 222, 223	6:21	269
2:3	172	6:22	269
2:4–6	203		
2:10	149	Philippians	
2:11	228	1:1	45, 70
2:11–22	119	1:1–2	45
2:12	119	1:2	46
2:12–22	118	1:3–4	68
2:13	118	1:4	68, 78
2:16	119	1:6	69, 208
2:17	118	1:11	210
3:1–10	17	1:12–18	134
3:2	136	1:14	261
3:2–20	136	1:19	69
3:9	136, 211	1:19–22	230
3:10	104	1:27	78
4:1	78, 149	2:3	191
4:3	191, 229	2:5–11	98, 164, 171
4:15–16	69	2:19	229
4:18	119	2:25	273
4:19	221–22	2:28	269
4:22–24	225	3:3	172
4:24	216	3:10	134
4:29–5:5	226	3:11	230

Philippians (cont.)
3:14	229
3:19	210
3:20	69
3:21	120
4:18	273

Colossians	143, 150, 153–55, 157–59, 168, 171–72, 174–75, 178, 182–87, 192, 194–95, 199–203, 208–13, 221, 229–30, 233–35, 242, 247, 252–56, 260, 263, 267–69, 271–72, 274, 277–78, 280–84
1	106
1:1–2	44
1:3	46, 101, 205
1:3–23	186
1:5	57, 69, 157, 205
1:5–6	69
1:6	19, 57
1:6–8	57
1:9	14, 160
1:10	70, 105
1:11	105, 210
1:12	79, 83–84
1:12–13	212
1:12–14	157
1:12–2:15	202
1:13	23, 83–84, 105–6, 227
1:14	83, 105
1:15	205, 220
1:15–18a	98
1:15–20	21, 23, 37, 83, 141, 160
1:16	6, 97, 221
1:17	97, 213, 218, 228
1:18	97, 183, 185, 205, 221, 226
1:18b–20	96–97
1:19	160, 185
1:19–22	230
1:20	97, 112, 202, 220–21
1:20–21	120
1:21	119
1:21–22	119
1:21–23	211
1:22	161, 172, 202, 226, 228
1:23	57, 69, 112
1:24	185
1:24–29	135, 139
1:25	83, 212, 227, 227
1:25–27	212
1:26	209, 211
1:26–27	14
1:27	137, 202, 210, 212
1:28	120, 137, 141, 212
2	144, 171
2–3	83
2:1	139, 141
2:1–3	112
2:2	141
2:2–3	201
2:3	228
2:4	79, 112, 141
2:4–5	141
2:4–23	112, 154, 214
2:6	160, 201
2:6–23	112
2:8	1, 106, 154, 156, 157
2:8–9	79
2:8–15	155, 160, 228
2:9	97, 171
2:9–10	201, 220, 228
2:9–15	23
2:10	1
2:11	1, 160, 161, 172, 173, 226
2:11–15	19, 160
2:12–13	203–5, 221
2:15	104, 120, 160 174, 226
2:15–20	112
2:16	183, 202
2:16–17	50
2:16–19	157
2:16–23	22, 23, 201–2, 205
2:17	185, 226
2:18	157, 202
2:19	70, 141, 226, 229
2:20	155, 157, 202–3
2:20–23	19, 157
2:21	202
2:22	208
2:23	157, 200, 208, 226

3:1	203, 205, 211	1:2	68, 78
3:1–2	220	1:2–3	68
3:1–4	127, 213	1:3	69
3:2	214, 221	1:4	232
3:3	211	1:6	134
3:3–4	210	1:10	69
3:3–9	211	2:5	222
3:4	202, 208–13	2:12	78, 84
3:5	214, 221, 226	2:20	210
3:5–7	224	3:5	269
3:5–10	226, 228	4:1	149
3:5–17	204, 214, 218–9, 221	4:3	221
3:6	120, 208, 223	4:5	221
3:7	208, 223, 224	4:7	221
3:8–9	224	5:2	208
3:9–10	225	5:4–10	84
3:10	102, 211, 213, 227	5:8	69
3:11	2, 14, 112, 160, 211, 213, 226–29, 230		
		2 Thessalonians	208
3:12	214, 226	1:1	45
3:12–17	213–14	1:2	46
3:14	213, 226, 229	1:3	68, 78
3:15	185, 213	1:4	68
3:15–16	220	1:6–10	69
3:16	219	2:2	208
3:17	218	2:13	232
3:18	229		
3:18–19	221	1 Timothy	26
3:18–4:1	23, 27	1:2	46
4:1	69	1:8–10	255
4:3	29	1:17	102
4:4	209	3:16	136
4:6	210	4:11	273
4:7	70		
4:7–17	27, 49	2 Timothy	
4:9	27	1:1	45
4:11	212	1:2	46
4:16	208	1:3	78
4:29–5:5	226	2:15	121
4:30	226	4:8	69
5:2	226	4:9–12	269
5:14	212	4:10	271
		4:10–11	273
1 Thessalonians		4:11	270
1:1	45	4:18	84

Titus		1:3	68
1:1	253	1:4	69
1:4	46	2:2	69
2:9–10	255	2:5	8
3:1	103–4	2:9	8
3:12	269	2:13–3:7	23, 236
		2:18–21	255
Philemon	27, 29, 183, 269, 271	3:22	211
1	45–46	5:5	191
1–3	45	5:13	273
2	271, 274		
3	46	2 Peter	
4	68	2:10	103, 155
4–5	68		
10	243, 269	1 John	
11	118, 252	1:5	84
12	269		
16	254	2 John	
23	70, 270	1	245
23–24	273	3	46
24	270, 271, 273	5	245
Hebrews		Jude	
1:3	101, 211	1–2	45
2:17–10:21	8	8	103
3:18	222		
5:12	155	Revelation	224
7:26	211	1:11	271
8:1	103	2:13	103
8:5	185	3:20	261
9:24	172	4:4	105
10:1	185	13:1	225
11:23	211	13:2	103
11:27	102	13:5–6	225
11:31	223	13:15	102
13:10–12	8	16:10	84, 103
		17:3	225
James		19:10	192
1:26	192	20:12	172
1:26–27	191	21:23–24	84
5:1–6	222	22:5	84
1 Peter			
1:1–2	45		
1:2	46		

ANCIENT SOURCES INDEX

Early Christian Writings

1 Clement
- 20.4 — 198
- 27.5 — 198

Didache — xi
- 8.3 — 69

Justin, *Dialogus cum Tryphone*
- 8.4 — 182

Greco-Roman Literature

Aristotle, *De anima*
- 428a–431b — 11

Aristotle, *Ethica nicomachea*
- 1.13 — 78

Aristotle, *Politica*
- 1.4 — 240, 250
- 1.6 — 240, 251
- 1.13 — 240, 251

Aristotle, *Rhetorica*
- 3.1.6 — 11
- 3.11.1 — 11
- 3.11.2 — 11
- 3.1.6 — 11

Cassius Dio, *istoria Romana*
- 59.26 — 138
- 59.28 — 138

Cicero, *Epistulae ad Atticum*
- 10.16.6 — 120

Demosthenes, *Epitaphius*
- 60 — 135

Diogenes Laertius, *Vitae philosophorum*
- 9.26–28 — 135
- 9.58–59 — 135

Epictetus, *Diatribi*
- 3.13.9–11 — 48
- 3.22.13 — 71

Herodotus, *Historiae*
- 2.104 — 171

Homer, *Ilias*
- 1.503 — 46
- 1.533 — 46

Horace, *Carmina*
- 2 — 109
- 12 — 108

Juvenal, *Satirae*
- 14.96–106 — 183

Longinus, *De sublimitate*
- 19–21 — 229

Lucian, *Nigrinus*
- 6–7 — 71

Pindar, *Olympionikai*
- 6.41f — 120

Plato, *Apologia*
- 28a–30b — 135

Plato, *Timaeus*
- 31–33 — 156

Plutarch, *De Alexandri magni fortuna aut virtute*
- 6 [329c] — 120

Plutarch, *De garrulitate*
- 23 [514f] — 262

Plutarch, *De Iside et Osiride*
- 67 [377f–378a] — 51

Plutarch, *Lysander*
- 18 — 52

Polybius, *Historiae*
    3.72.9   120
    16.25.7   120–21

Quintilian, *Institutio oratoria*
    6.2.24–36   11

Rhetorica ad Herennium
    4.15.21   228
    4.20.28   43
    4.28   92, 223
    4.28.38   39

Seneca, *Ad Lucilium*
    6.6   135

Seneca, *De beneficiis*
    4.7–8   52
    4.32.2   52

Seneca, *Epistulae morales*
    6.1   71
    11.8–10   71
    24   135
    47   251

Stobaeus, *Florilegium*
    4.2.24   248

Strabo, *Geographica*
    17.2.5   171

Suetonius, *Gaius Caligula*
    22   138

Virgil, *Aeneid*
    6.851–853   120
    12.171   120

Modern Authors Index

Anderson, Janice Capel 193
Arnold, Clinton E. 18, 103–5, 152, 156, 182–84,192
Aune, David E. xiii, 5, 229
Avemarie, Friedrich 135
Balch, David L. 184, 236, 243, 248
Barclay, John M. G. 152–54
Barth, Markus 25, 56, 61, 94, 106, 113, 119, 126, 147, 163–64, 205–6, 222, 228, 236
Beale, G. K. 79, 84, 93–94, 164, 183, 192, 237
Beard, Mary 23, 48–49, 104, 158, 237, 245, 255
Becker, Eve-Marie 232
Bédoyère, Guy de la 246
Beetham, Christopher A. 45, 69, 171
Bernier, Jonathan 29
Bertram, Georg 121
Bloomquist, L. Gregory 2, 53
Brodd, Jeffrey 50
Brooks, David 16
Bryan, Christopher 3, 27
Bultmann, Rudolf 209, 271
Burke, Kenneth A. 54
Cadwallader, Alan H. 20, 24, 47, 49–50, 104, 181–82, 184, 186, 192
Cahill, Thomas 5
Campbell, Constantine R. 25
Campbell, Douglas A. 24, 29, 164, 210, 213, 230, 234
Canavan, Rosemary 183
Capon, Robert Farrar 161
Carter, Warren 50, 105, 243

Cid Zurita, Andres 104, 106–7
Copenhaver, Adam 152–53, 184, 192–93
Crouch, James E. 243
Culy, Martin M. 164
Delling, Gerhard 155–56, 236, 244
DeMaris, Richard E. 184
Dowden, Ken 109–110
Dunn, James D. G. 46–47, 70, 77, 92, 105, 118, 161–62, 164, 216, 222, 236, 244
Ehrman, Bart D. 77
Elliott, Neil 4
Fauconnier, Gilles xiii, 16, 47
Fee, Gordon D. 171
Fohrer, Georg 223
Foster, Paul 17, 25, 28–29, 97, 113, 126, 182–83, 229, 237
Francis, Fred O. 191
Friesen, Stephen J. 243
Frye, Northrop 44
Gordley, Matthew E. 92, 171
Grundmann, Walter 232
Harrison, James R. 18, 21, 23, 50, 182–83, 193
Hart, David Bentley 126, 245
Haught, John F. 6–7, 213
Helmut, Blanke 25
Henten, Jan Willem van 135
Holloway, Paul A. 88, 99, 171
Hooker, Morna D. 152
Horsley, Richard A. 50, 106
Huttner, Ulrich 20–21, 23, 47–49, 50, 181, 193, 235

Jeal, Roy R.   xiii–xvi, 2–3, 9, 11–12, 24–25, 27, 29, 42–44, 48, 53–54, 64, 70, 87, 92, 119, 148, 151, 171, 207, 211, 213, 216–17, 223, 225, 229, 240, 250–51, 255, 279
Jenni, Ernst   7
Jervis, L. Ann   134
Johnson, Luke Timothy   186
Juel, Donald H.   15
Kahl, Brigitte   50, 156, 181
Kahnemann, Daniel   16
Käsemann, Ernst   102
Kaufman, James C.   14
Kearsley, Rosalinde A.   186
Keesmaat, Sylvia   50, 70, 106
Keizer, Heleen M.   7
Kennedy, George A.   15, 92
Kingsolver, Barbara   25
Kittel, Gerhard   210
Kloppenborg, John S.   235
Kooten, George H. van   182
Korn, Marianne   98
Lapidge, Michael   157
Lee, Margaret Ellen   26–27
Lightfoot, J. B.   62, 168
Lincoln, Andrew T.   45, 92, 106, 118–19, 162, 173, 192, 221–22, 244
Lohse, Eduard   223
Longenecker, Bruce W.   49, 50, 158, 190, 192, 215, 217, 222, 224, 234–35, 243, 245, 248, 251
MacDonald, Margaret Y.   47, 70, 96, 137, 209, 242
Mackay, Christopher S.   50–51, 110
Maier, Harry O.   20–24, 47, 50, 52–57, 105, 107, 164–65, 181–82, 193, 215, 227–29, 235, 240–42, 245–46, 248–49
Malherbe, Abraham J.   221, 236
Malina, Bruce J.   42, 248
Martin, Neil   157
Martin, Troy W.   23, 153, 184, 191, 199, 236
Mathieson, Ruth Christa   2, 5
Mauss, Marcel   251
McKnight, Scot   27–28, 153, 184, 237
Meeks, Wayne A.   191
Metzger, Bruce M.   77
Moo, Douglas J.   62, 64, 78, 92
Moore, Michael Ryan   243
Mouat, L. H.   54
Niebuhr, H. Richard   143
Norden, Eduard   92
Oakes, Peter   52
Oakley, Todd V.   57
Oepke, Albrecht   169
O'Gorman, Ned   11
Olbricht, Thomas H.   153
Oliver, Mary   213
O'Neill, John C.   73
Oropeza, B. J.   2, 45, 173, 231
Penner, Jeremy   181
Pizzuto, Vincent A.   93, 171
Pound, Ezra   43–44, 64, 98
Price, Simon R. F.   106–7
Radner, Ephraim   22
Reed, Jonathan L.   50
Reicke, Bo   121
Richards, E. Randolph   45
Rives, James B.   51–52, 109
Robbins, Vernon K.   xiii–xiv, 2–13, 19, 24, 29, 38, 40–45, 47–48, 53, 87, 91, 94, 98, 132, 142–43, 169–71, 174–75, 224, 226, 232, 261–62, 269, 279
Robertson, Archibald T.   199
Rogerson, John W.   54, 106
Sasse, Hermann   7
Scheidel, Walter   243
Schniewind, Julius   137
Schweizer, Eduard   184
Scott, Bernard Brandon   26–27
Seitz, Christopher R.   37
Stambaugh, John E.   184
Standhartinger, Angela   193
Stegemann, Ekkehard W.   21
Stegemann, Wolfgang   21
Sternberg, Robert J.   14
Sumney, Jerry L.   25, 61, 73, 92, 94, 126, 128, 131, 134–36, 153, 156, 159, 171, 182, 185, 191–92, 200–201, 221–22, 224, 232, 237, 245, 251

Swart, Gerhard 208, 212
Tachau, Ernst 119
Talbert, Charles H. 39, 71, 79, 95, 120, 126, 147, 153, 161, 191, 192, 221, 230, 248
Taylor, Bernard A. 164
Taylor, Joan E. 107
Thaden, Robert H. von, Jr. xiv, 10
Thiessen, Jonathan 229
Trainor, Michael 21, 58, 65, 272, 273
Treggiari, Susan 245
Turner, Mark xiii, 16, 47
Visser, Margaret 3
Wallace, Daniel B. 26, 191, 199–200, 208, 244
Wallas, Graham 15, 16
Walsh, Brian J. 50, 70, 106
Watson, Duane F. 3
West, Thomas G. 154
White, John L. 50
Wilson, Robert McL. 17, 25, 28, 36, 80, 88, 92, 126, 147, 150, 153, 164, 166, 183, 186, 191, 262
Wink, Walter 106
Winn, Adam 50
Winter, Bruce W. 50, 109, 156
Wright, N. T. 50, 92, 94
Yates, Roy 164

www.ingramcontent.com/pod-product-compliance
Lightning Source LLC
Chambersburg PA
CBHW050856300426
44111CB00010B/1272